James Aronson graduated from the Columbia School of Journalism and worked on the *New York Herald Tribune* and the *New York Times* before becoming editor of *Frontpage*, the publication of the New York Newspaper Guild. In 1948 he and Cedric Belfrage founded the *National Guardian*, which they jointly edited until 1967. He is the author of *Something to Guard: The Stormy History of the National Guardian, 1949–1967* (1978), as well as numerous articles in the *Nation, Monthly Review, Liberation,* and the *Antioch Review.*

Aronson taught journalism at New York University, the New School for Social Research, and Hunter College, where he was Thomas Hunter Professor of Communications. In 1979 he was the first American professor invited to teach journalism in the People's Republic of China. In 1988 he received a Special Olive Branch Lifetime Achievement Award in recognition of his work over half a century as a reporter, editor, author, and teacher.

Jim Aronson died in 1988 at the age of 73, just after completing the three additional chapters on the 1970s and 1980s that are included in this new edition of his book.

# The Press and the Cold War

by JAMES ARONSON

Monthly Review Press
New York

*Acknowledgment is hereby made to the following publishers for permission to quote from the following works:*

Cornell University Press, *The House Committee on Un-American Activities* by Robert K. Carr

Harcourt, Brace & World, Inc., *Senator Joe McCarthy* by Richard Rovere

Houghton Mifflin Company, *The Fourth Branch of Government* by Douglass Cater

International Publishers, *Again Korea* by Wilfred Burchett

*Journalism Quarterly* (Summer 1965), University of Minnesota School of Journalism, article by Neal D. Houghton

Random House, Inc., *The Making of a Quagmire* by David Halberstam

*Library of Congress Cataloguing in Publication Data*

Aronson, James.
    [New and expanded ed]
    The press and the cold war / by James Aronson. — New and expanded ed.
       p.    cm.
    Includes bibliographical references.
    ISBN 0-85345-805-7 : $33.00. — ISBN 0-85345-806-5 (pbk.) : $13.00
    1. Government and the press—United States.  2. Press and politics—United States.
3. United States—Politics and government—1945–  I. Title.
PN4738.A7  1990
071'.3—dc20

90-6020
CIP

Monthly Review Press
122 West 27th Street
New York, N.Y. 10001

Manufactured in the United States of America

*To Grambs*
*for time and confidence*

# Contents

*One Newspaperman's Life (A Preface)*     *vii*

**1**   From Zenger to Abdication     *10*

**2**   Counterpoint of Two Wars     *25*

**3**   Henry Wallace and Hysteria     *39*

**4**   The Frost on the Pumpkin     *51*

**5**   The Making of Joe McCarthy     *64*

**6**   A Tale of Two Editors     *87*

**7**   The News from Korea     *103*

**8**   The Prisoners of War     *117*

**9**   The Eastland Succession     *127*

**10**   The Target: The *Times*     *139*

**11**   The Bay of Pigs     *153*

**12**   The Missile Crisis     *170*

**13**   Vietnam: The Making of a Miracle     *180*

**14**   The Miracle Unmade     *192*

**15**   Patriotism and Policy     *206*

**16**    Free Rides to the Front    *218*

**17**    Journalism of the Absurd    *231*

**18**    Two Men of the Times    *246*

**19**    Freedom and Responsibility    *262*

**20**    The Alternative Press    *280*

**21**    The Roaring Seventies    *289*

**22**    The Constricting Eighties    *302*

**23**    Spooky Tales    *315*

     *Index*    *323*

# One Newspaperman's Life

## (A PREFACE)

My newspaper career began in my native Boston, on the *Evening Transcript,* a dying newspaper surviving on the glory of a past when T. S. Eliot described it as the little old lady in black bombazine; when its literary and dramatic criticism earned it a national reputation; and when a polite ripple of laughter could be drawn from the anecdote of the butler announcing to his dowager madam that there were several newspapermen at the door, "and the gentleman from the *Transcript.*"

When I arrived at the *Transcript* in 1937 with the traditional (for the *Transcript*) degree from Harvard and another from the Columbia Graduate School of Journalism, the paper was little more than a good workshop in journalism for a young newspaperman. It had a circulation of 30,000 in a city where no other newspaper had less than 100,000—and there were six other newspapers. A new man was called on to do just about everything, and he did it willingly—reporting, copy reading, feature writing, music and film criticism, and even editorial writing.

It was the time of the New Deal and of the Spanish civil war, and a curious young man, skeptical of organized education, religion, and politics, could learn much. It was a time also of a new kind of organizing—the Congress of Industrial Organizations (CIO)—and of the notion that journalists might have economic problems like those of clerks and maintenance men and advertising solicitors.

I did learn much on the *Transcript* about politics and Spain and labor. Not the least of my mentors was the *Transcript*'s music critic, Moses Smith, who had an able and unassuming knowledge of all three. I became an active member of the Newspaper Guild, which was then moving from the American Federation of Labor (A. F. of L.) into the CIO. (I recall collecting dues from the most proper Bostonian clerks who sat at rolltop desks and asked primly for my assurance that the A. F. of L. was not Communistic. Would a Harvard man lie?) The Guild was still so new that *Transcript* unit meetings were often held in private homes. When the business was done, many of us stayed to discuss Spain and politics and the newspaper. My skepticism of diplomacy and politics grew as the betrayal of Republican Spain became as clear as the concomitant rise of fascism in Europe. It was the beginning of my disenchantment with political liberalism.

Even more did I learn on the *Transcript* about newspapers. I learned, for one thing, how a reader could be influenced by careful choice of headline words and slogans. For example: Eleanor Roosevelt, as the wife of the President and the mother of a much-divorced brood, had expressed herself in favor of sensible divorce laws. On her arrival in Boston, where Cardinal O'Connell was dominant, reporters met her at the airport and questioned her on divorce. She reiterated her position, and the story was page one for every newspaper that day. I was on the copy desk and had to write an eight-column headline. I came up with various versions of: "MRS. ROOSEVELT REAFFIRMS DIVORCE STAND." None pleased the managing editor, John Gibbons, who had been brought in from New York (a sure sign of proprietary desperation) to save the paper. Finally, he called me over to his desk and said, "I think this will do it." I looked down and read: "FIRST LADY DEFENDS RENO."

I took the piece of copy paper with as much offended dignity as I could muster and said, "If that's the way you want it, sir . . ." I was worried that I might end up in the doghouse for my righteousness, but I did not. Gibbons told me later that he had been greatly amused by my struggle to keep my temper.

There was a similar experience with a story about a Massachusetts State Senate hearing on subversion. Afterward I got this penciled note from Gibbons: "I may be a Hicksite Quaker like Herbert Hoover, but no goddam Red is going to get a break in this paper as long as I am managing editor."

These incidents typified the strictures and the contradictions of Boston, and the seeming clash but actual collaboration of the rising Irish Catholic leadership and the established Protestant cultural and industrial hierarchy. Together they stifled any thought or hope of change and kept journalism in Boston at a level which mocked the reputation of the city as the Athens of America.

An offer of a job on the *New York Herald Tribune,* in December 1938, stirred excitement and relief. It was the opportunity to work in a great newspaper city and on the "newspaperman's newspaper." The *Tribune* had high standards. A young newspaperman working on it could learn enough to last a lifetime. There was a marginal pride in knowing that you helped put out a better newspaper than the fatter and richer *New York Times.* It was something like being the second son of the baron—you had more fun even if you knew you would never get the money.

But if the *Tribune* was marked by this admirable pride in craft, it harbored also a far less admirable hostility to industrial unionism. The craft unions were solidly entrenched, as they had been for years, but the younger Newspaper Guild had been unable to organize the shop. There was still no contract when I left in 1940 for the organized *New York Post,* liberal in politics, and experimenting, under a new ownership, in makeup and news presentation.

At the *Post* I learned at least three things: that I was working for a newspaper which, while seemingly closer to my developing political views, was less candid and forthright in its editorial views than either the Republican *Transcript* or *Herald Tribune;* that changes in type faces and a streamlined appearance can never camouflage a mediocre journalistic performance; that while there were class and professional distinctions on the conservative papers for which I had worked, on the liberal papers the distinctions were political. The surest way to isolation was the espousal of unpopular radical views.

Oddly enough, I had been preceded to the *Post* by the Hicksite managing editor of the *Transcript.* His contract in Boston had run out and the paper was beyond salvation. The death verdict had been decreed by the First National Bank of Boston and the United Shoe Machinery Corporation, which controlled the *Boston Herald.* The *Herald* coveted the *Transcript*'s prestige advertising. The *Transcript* finally died in 1943, after a last-minute offer by the employees to buy the paper had been turned down.

Gibbons was news editor at the *Post.* However he felt about "Reds," his contempt for liberals was monumental, and we were each maverick enough to find common ground in that sea of social democracy. We became good friends.

He often called me over to his desk, after a deadline, for a talk. Sometimes it began with his blocking out on a piece of copy paper his concept of the four cornerstones of world politics: Pope Pius XII, Franklin Roosevelt, Stalin, and Winston Churchill. On the border was Senator Robert A. Taft. One day he asked, while doodling, whether I was disappointed that I had not received an assistant editorship that ought to have gone to me. I was about to say, "Yes, but . . ." when he spoke in the

Victorian manner of his mellow mood, "You were not advanced, my young friend, because your political views are at variance with those held by the managers of this enterprise and therefore not acceptable to them."

He put his pencil down and looked at me over his glasses. He was telling me, of course, that there was still time to change my views if I had any thought about getting to the top. But I think we both knew what my answer had to be. The events in the world of the early forties, my work in the Newspaper Guild, and my reading had moved me into socialism.

As the father of a pre-Pearl Harbor child (as the draft boards unromantically termed them) and as a working newspaperman, I had not been called for Army service; but as the war continued I felt increasingly the need to be involved. Early in 1945 I took a leave of absence from the *Post* to go into training as a press control officer in Germany. The operation, ultimately under the Army's Information Control Division, was designed to set up a democratic press for postwar Germany. It was to be run and staffed by Germans, with no United States censorship except post-publication scrutiny.

We established some first-class newspapers. Unlike the prewar German press, they were supra-party papers and their editorial boards comprised persons from Catholic Centrist to Communist—the one essential qualification for membership being a record of at least some resistance to Nazism. The structure of the papers and the absence of editorial bias in news coverage were too much for the American Military Government: it launched a war against the Information Control Command, an autonomous setup outside the control of Military Government. Harry Truman was President; the Army officers at the clubs in Wiesbaden and Bad Homburg spoke increasingly of the "coming war" with the Soviet Union, and American fraternization with Germans, officially forbidden, was a booming affair. The nocturnal companions of the Military Government officers, mainly daughters of German industralists and imprisoned German army officers, became the diurnal guardians of these same Americans, screening out all undesirable elements—that is, the genuine anti-Nazi Germans. Our men on the editorial boards gradually were picked off and replaced by former Nazi publishers or their front men. It was time to go home. The future of Germany was being written.

The press venture had been for much of its time a combined Allied operation. I worked with an Englishman named Cedric Belfrage in setting up several papers. We had shared a sense of achievement in the quality of the papers as the end result of the *Zusammenarbeit* (we translated it as "together-work") of diverse elements and of their ability to publish papers less strident and partisan than most published in prewar Germany—or, we noted, in the United States. In the common effort, Belfrage and I became friends.

The excitement of Germany made for a dull return to the *New York Post* in 1946 and underscored the futility of writing such popular series as "What's Wrong with the Army?" (accompanied by a column in which ex-GIs were invited to "blow it out," as they once did in the Army *Stars and Stripes*). My season of discontent was growing longer. There was too little opportunity to make use of journalistic skills.

The *Post* had undergone a series of changes in management, and superficially its political position had become fairly progressive. But this did not mean much. There still could be no questioning of basic American policy. By the fall of 1946, I had the title of national news editor. This enabled me to develop prodigious arm muscles by discarding wire service news of considerable length (and some interest) which could not be squeezed into a tabloid newspaper already overstuffed with columnar advice to the psychologically stricken and the politically bemused. The *Post* was on its way to becoming the most active journalistic exponent of sex and social democracy, a formula which, when mixed with instant psychoanalysis, was remarkably therapeutic at the newsstands.

Then came an offer to work in the Sunday department of the *New York Times*. I accepted. At least there was some hope of becoming a newspaperman again rather than a compiler of news briefs. I was to be part of the anonymous team that put together the News of the Week in Review. It was an able crew and the research was extensive—but safe. All stories were "balanced," which meant that the interpretation was never favorable to a socialist country. When any action by the United States government was flagrantly out of order, the story would restore a semblance of order. Consummate skill in the balancing act was the mark of a good *Times* man, one whose membership on the team was never in doubt.

My first story was the Nuremberg executions, the carrying out of the sentence against the surviving Nazi leaders who had been found guilty of crimes against humanity. The story went easily because I was recently back from Germany and familiar with the research. My immediate superior took my copy and left the room. An hour later he came back and said, "He likes it." I said, "Who's he?" The room burst out in laughter. I had not noticed until then that all eyes had been focused on this little scene. It was the Moment of Truth, and the old hands had been through it often with the "new boy."

He, of course, was Lester Markel, the Sunday editor. After that episode, I learned that "he" was always spelled mentally with a capital "H." Markel was the perfect and permanent *Times* man, as his 45 years with the paper bear witness. He questioned neither the sanctity of the *Times* nor the superiority of the American way of life. He had developed a technical formula for the News of the Week—background, news, and interpretation—which, if it had been allowed the full scope of inquiring journalism, would have been a masterful approach. But it was not. The formula was hidebound by the editor's limitations which, in turn, were the limitations of the *Times* in general. Markel's style was apparent in the occasional long articles he wrote for the Sunday magazine after trips to Paris or London or Washington. Each was a masterpiece of banality.

This was the general standard set at the top. Dullness and pomposity would seem to render the product harmless, but they do not. The *Times* had acquired more prestige than any other paper in the United States. The balance of the news inevitably was weighted in favor of United States policy; the other side rarely received a full hearing. Washington and its officials were presented as patient, long-suffering, sometimes mistaken, and sometimes bewildered, but this bewilderment was mainly attributed to the other side's inability to understand the underlying nobility of United States motives.

By this time—1947—my political and social philosophy had made it increasingly difficult to write "objective" stories for a newspaper committed to United States policy, which was relentlessly developing the Cold War. A censorship so subtle that it was invisible affected everyone on the staff. The "approach" (it was never a vulgar "line") was made clear in casual conversations, in the editing of copy for "clarity," and in the deletion of any forthright interpretation as "emotionalism." Work became a conflict with conscience, although there was never an open challenge to conscience.

In this mood I took a leave of absence from the *Times* to become editor of *Frontpage,* the monthly publication of the Newspaper Guild of New York. There was of course an immediate sense of release in the new work, but it was also a revelation to see how the conflicts of the outside world of journalism entered into the smaller world of unionism. The leadership of the New York Guild was generally forward looking, but afflicted, I felt, with the parochialism of many older unions. For example, my efforts to make *Frontpage* more professional and to cover the problems of journalism nationally and even internationally were discouraged. Attempts to help members of the union understand, in a political and social sense, the nature of the newspapers for which they worked were also frowned upon. The union officers believed this material was "not what the people in the shops wanted."

If it was not what they wanted, it surely was what they needed. The Cold War had come into the union field, and the progressive leadership of the Guild was fighting for its life against those who sought to tie the union's interest to the "national interest"—that is, to prevailing United States policy. After an election in which the progressive leadership was defeated, I informed the Sunday editor that I would shortly return to my job at the *Times.*

A revealing and amusing incident occurred then. As I was planning my last issue of *Frontpage,* I noticed that *The Wayward Pressman,* the latest book by A. J. Liebling, the pungent critic of the press, was largely being ignored by the newspaper book reviewers. The *New York Times Book Review* had placed the review on page 42 of a 52-page section. I called Liebling and asked him if he would write for *Frontpage* an article on how the press reviews a book about the press. I told him there would be no payment.

"Fine," he said immediately. "How many words, and when?" His evil cheerfulness should have forewarned me—or maybe it did. The article appeared in the January 1948 issue of *Frontpage* under a headline that read: "The Wayward Bookman." Liebling in his article had fashioned a character named Alter Ego, and had engaged Mr. Ego in tart conversation about why the review of *The Wayward Pressman* had landed on page 42 of the *Times Book Review.* After all, an earlier review of a book by Liebling, *The Republic of Silence,* about the French Resistance in World War II, had got a full-page treatment on page 3, with an attractive layout. Mr. Ego, according to Liebling, was convinced that the relegation of the new book had been motivated by Liebling's sharp criticism in the book of the *New York Times.*

"If you persist in this notion, Alter," said Liebling, "I shall put you down as a malcontent—possibly as a *dangerous* malcontent." To which Mr. Ego replied: "Aw, go lean over backward in your ivory tower of Pisa. I still think they gave you the works." The day after the issue of *Frontpage* reached the newspaper shops, I received a letter on the imperial stationery:

Dear Mr. Aronson:

It is a little late now, but don't you think it would have been a good idea to get *our* side of the Liebling story before you ran that piece from him? It is, you know, quite a reflection on the *New York Times,* and, remember, you *are* coming back to work for us.

Yours sincerely,
Lester Markel

I *did* go back, and *He* never forgot. Three months later I submitted my resignation from the *Times.* The decision was not motivated by the

Liebling incident, but was cumulative. I had come to the conclusion that I could no longer work for a commercial daily newspaper, and an opportunity had come for a new kind of career. I joined Cedric Belfrage in planning the first issue of the *National Guardian*.

My decision actually had its roots in Germany. There were times when Belfrage and I were trapped by bad weather or lack of transportation, and those times were often passed in speculative talk about newspapers. For example, what it would be like to attempt a new kind of journalism in the United States, free of the restrictions and contradictions of the newspaper business as we had experienced it. (Belfrage was himself a skilled newspaperman who had worked in both England and the United States.)

With the help of an able and venturesome group of newspapermen and neophytes who rallied around in a borrowed upper Madison Avenue apartment, and with a generous offer of technical assistance from J. W. Gitt, publisher of the *Gazette & Daily* of York, Pennsylvania, we published in York, in August 1948, a preview issue called the *National Gazette*. It had articles by an illustrious roster of writers, some of whom became regular contributors: military commentator Max Werner, historian Frederick L. Schuman of Williams, British Labor MP Konni Zilliacus, author Louis Adamic, journalists James Dugan and John Lardner, British radio writer Arthur Calder-Marshall, and Anna Louise Strong. Joined in a managerial triumvirate by John T. McManus, film critic of the expiring experimental daily newspaper *PM,* we began publishing on a weekly basis as the *National Guardian* in New York on October 18, 1948.

From the beginning we knew we could not compete with the news-gathering resources of the commercial press. We concentrated rather on being a watchdog of the press—following, unscrambling, and analyzing the news and comment that appeared in the daily newspapers and the newsweeklies, and offering an antidote in the form of independently gathered news and comment that the general press would not print.

It is significant for the general thesis of this book that we were more successful in getting collaboration abroad than at home. Many newspapermen and women in foreign countries, including some of the first American political exiles, were eager to contribute for very little financial compensation to an American radical newspaper. Some had had their own experiences with the American press; others were excited by the prospect of a publication which would seek to restore the basic American democratic principles, so revered throughout the world, in the country of their origin. Except in the early days, the men and women of the working press in the United States shied away from the *National Guardian* as a source of discomfort and potential trouble, and refused even to write under pseudonyms.

There will be more, later in this book, about the trials and problems of a dissenting newspaper and my own experiences, as appropriate to the points I will seek to make. But at this juncture, I would like to express my deepest gratitude to four journalists of integrity who helped to guide my own life as a newspaperman, and who encouraged the writing of this book: Cedric Belfrage, for his inspiring friendship and comradeship-in-arms; the late John T. McManus and Leo Huberman, for the example of their own lives; and Alexander L. Crosby, for his generosity and skill as an editor.

# Postscript (1987)

I note that I titled this preface "One Newspaperman's Life." That was in 1969. Today I would call it "One Journalist's Life," even though I have not been chided by women colleagues or friends for the earlier gender exclusion. They were kind, but I have learned much in the intervening years about the struggle for equality in the newspaper industry.

What did one journalist do after experiencing his own "cultural revolution" at the *National Guardian* in 1967? Removed from a daily or weekly deadline for the first time in thirty years, I lay fallow (to give that time its gentlest description) for six months trying to chart my future. It was not easy. It took much sorting out to realize that the *Guardian* experience had not been personally directed, but that I had been in "the right place at the right time," as young people all over the world (China, France, Mexico) were rebelling against their elders, teachers, officials, and customs. There was no American exceptionalism. This bolstered my spirits somewhat and I came out of my cave to blink at the light and to talk to friends again.

What about teaching? one said. The light became brighter. I enlisted at the New School for Social Research in New York as a lecturer in journalism, then expanded to an adjunct professorship at New York University. It worked well. The students, in a more theoretical setting, became my young apprentices again, as had the young staff members on the *Guardian*. It was exhilarating to bring my thirty years of experience into the classroom, and I became aware that the three-decade review was as important for me as it was for the students who knew almost nothing of the major events of the recent past—let alone the role of journalism in these events. It was not their fault: it was a piercing comment on the teaching of history in the universities.

At the same time I became editor of the publications of the National Emergency Civil Liberties Committee, an organization that had come into being in 1951, at the height of the McCarthy hysteria, when the American Civil Liberties Union had decreed that persons accused of being Communists were beyond the patriotic pale and had even voted to dismiss Elizabeth Gurley Flynn, a legendary figure on the left and a genuine patriot, from its board because she was a Communist. Since I believed that the Bill of Rights was indivisible for all Americans, the new organization fitted in perfectly with my convictions. In between chores, I wrote three books (this one among them) on the problems of American journalism. I also contributed a regular column about the media to the *Antioch Review* and later to the weekly *In These Times*.

In 1974 I was offered an associate professorship to teach full time in the Communications Department at Hunter College of the City University of New York, and I accepted. I had no doctoral degree, but the university acknowledged the body of my writing in the field and dispensed with that requirement. Dr. Fulton Ross, then chairperson of the department, called to tell me I had been hired and what the salary was. After years of plantation wages on the *Guardian* and free-lance pittances from poor but noble periodicals, the salary at Hunter seemed like a fortune, and I accepted quickly. The next day Dr. Ross called back and said with what seemed to be an apologetic tone, "I was able to get you a thousand more." It was only much later that he told me he had been appalled at having had to offer me the original salary in light of my career.

The following year, on the thirty-eighth anniversary of my graduation from the Graduate School of Journalism at Columbia University, I was chosen to receive an award from the Columbia Journalism Alumni Association "for the advancement of journalism in all its forms during a lifetime of service." I have no doubt that the national soul-searching then under way after the American withdrawal from Vietnam played a part in the choice, but the recognition was warmly gratifying after all my years as a voice in the wilderness of dissenting journalism. The citation said in part:

Many of the views that James Aronson has expressed during his career in journalism seem quite routine these days. He has favored detente with the Soviet Union and recognition of the People's Republic of China. He has opposed a U.S. involvement in Southeast Asia. What sets him apart from other journalists is that he first expressed his view on the Soviet Union 30 years ago, on China 25 years ago, and on Southeast Asia 20 years ago. . . . He was always a journalist ahead of his times. He was a media critic before there were journalism reviews. He was a defender of the rights of newspaper people before there were reporters' committees. He was providing an alternative before there was an alternative press.

I recall the words that the late Wilfred Burchett, a journalist who is prominent in the pages that follow, had written to me from Paris, when I was leaving the *National Guardian* only seven years earlier: "Out of adversity there come new challenges and rewards." I am not sure I believed him at the time, but I most certainly did as my career at Hunter went forward. There are few things more rewarding than the opportunity to open young minds to the realities of the world around them, and observe the consequences of that opportunity. With the encouragement of two Hunter presidents, Jacqueline Wechsler and Donna Shalala, I taught my students not only journalism, but history, sociology, and political science—even if the lectures were not so labeled—because I felt they had to understand the nature of the media in relation to the other institutions of our society. Only then could they come to know the significance of the media.

In 1978 my colleague Cedric Belfrage and I wrote together a book titled *Something to Guard: The Stormy History of the National Guardian, 1949–1967*. It was as much a history of the times as it was of the newspaper, and our collaboration on the book was as comfortable and binding as had been our editorship of the *Guardian*. That, as co-authors know, is rare. At this writing, Belfrage at age 83, lives in Cuernavaca, Mexico, where he writes, translates books from Spanish into English, and remains as unyielding in spirit as ever. After an eighteen-year prohibition, under a "waiver of exclusion," he can visit quite freely the United States from which he was banished in 1955; which remains in force, he still cannot establish permanent residence here.

On invitation from the Academy of Social Sciences of the Peoples Republic of China, I went to Beijing in 1979 to set up a curriculum for teaching journalism in English to students who would one day be foreign correspondents for Xinhua (the New China News Agency) and China's big daily newspaper and magazines. The courses were given at a new Graduate Institute of Journalism attended by students with the equivalent of a bachelor's degree. In addition, I gave a series of ten lectures to an audience of five hundred working journalists from a score of publications in the capital area, in the auditorium of the news agency, on Western newspaper methods. I criticized quite sharply the quality of Chinese journalism, yet never once was there any attempt to persuade me to soften my criticism; quite the contrary, I was constantly encouraged to be tougher. With subsequent trips to China, I have spent almost a year there. The series of ten lectures have been published in Chinese as a book, *News-writing and Reporting*, which circulates among China's journalists. It is a continuing pleasure to have my students come through New York to visit their "old professor" en route to assignments in Washington, Ottawa, and Latin America. My Chinese mentor, Chen Lung, head of the overseas news department of Xinhua, reporting on the progress of my students abroad, once said to me, in a rendition of a Chinese saying: "You have many peaches and plums under heaven."

Promotion to a full professorship came early at Hunter, and in 1983 I was given the title of Thomas Hunter Professor of Communications, named for the founder of Hunter College who in 1870 had the uncommon foresight to found a woman's college in the City of New York. I became emeritus in 1985.

The inevitable question, on my fiftieth anniversary in journalism, is, would you do it all over again? The answer is, yes, I would; if not all, then most of it. I would surely like to wipe the slate clean of mistakes of judgment (and choice of words) that still cause me to wince; but then I know I would never be free of error in any new life permitted me. That, I believe, is a major lesson of life. I have experienced the best and the worst of journalism on the general press, the dissenting press, and in the teaching of communications. Earlier, when people asked me what I called myself, I answered: writer. Later I said: writer and teacher. There was an easy transition to the combined characterization.

When this book was first published in 1970, the major issues facing our nation involved, in the field of foreign affairs, the overriding fact of the Cold War with the Soviet Union, Latin America (Cuba particularly), Korea and Southeast Asia (the war in Vietnam). Domestically it was civil rights (the drive for equality by black Americans and the resistance to it) and civil liberties (the fight to maintain the Bill of Rights in the face of the McCarthy onslaught whose true name was Hooverism, for J. Edgar). These issues, as they were recorded and commented upon in the press of America, were the chief occupation of the book, as were the major newspapers of the nation and their treatment of these issues.

I take no pleasure in recording that these same issues are still among the chief concerns of America's policymakers today. It requires no special prescience to see that this would be the case if there were no major change in American policy. And still overriding these issues is the continuing adversarial relationship between the United States and the Soviet Union—a situation that has existed, with a break for collaboration against fascism in World War II, since the Bolshevik Revolution in 1917. This relationship affects every aspect of American life, the well-being of our people, their aspirations—and their survival under the menace of the Bomb. In the last analysis, it is the dominant issue in the survival of the world.

On the last page of the original edition of this book, I wrote: "Despite my grave doubts that the press of the country is willing to reform itself, I remain a realistic optimist about journalism. I believe that there is in the United States a company of honest journalists of all ages, conscious of the potential power of an informed people, who will never give up the effort to establish an honorable communications network." After an examination of the press in the intervening twenty years—tumultuous years during which the press more than ever has become news in itself—my doubts about the owners and managers of the media have been reinforced. My optimism about the people who work for them remains, but it is tempered by the belief that their best efforts require the support of the people who read the papers. This support will become effective only when the general public understands the role of the press in making and shaping governmental policies affecting the great events of our time.

This thesis, I believe, validates the concept of the continuity of history—that one must know the past to understand the present and to chart the future. In other words, to understand how the theology of anticommunism became institutionalized in the United States, it is necessary to understand the Palmer-Hoover raids of 1919–1920 as an unbroken line to the so-called McCarthy era of the 1950s, and the shaping of a foreign policy which made these domestic outrages necessary and continues to do so.

To understand Nicaragua requires a knowledge of United States-Cuban relations since 1959—and before. To understand the Iran/Contra affair requires an unvarnished history of the deceptions of Vietnam. To understand Korea today requires a clear view of Korea in the post-Word War II period and of course the United States military intervention in Korea itself.

The background is in this book. I believe it remains a solid foundation upon which to structure a valid interpretation of the great issues and events which have confronted us in the nearly two decades since the book was written—and always with the press as backdrop.

# The Press and the Cold War

# 1. From Zenger to Abdication

The men who drew up the Bill of Rights were not sentimentalists about the printed word. When they decreed that Congress shall make no law abridging the freedom of the press, they were not attempting to create a moat around a newspaper industry which, with their foresightedness, they might see expanding into a formidable force. They wanted to guarantee that the press would be free to criticize government without fear of reprisal, that it would persevere without interference as the tribune of a free people, speaking and crusading in their interest against an established authority which might seek to invade or corrode their rights. In essence, the First Amendment sought to guarantee that government could not censor the press, but that the press should forever have the right—and the duty—to censor government.

The opening gun in the battle for a free press in America was fired a half-century before the First Amendment was adopted, in the matter of John Peter Zenger vs. His Britannic Majesty's governor of the province of New York. Zenger, a German-born printer who founded the *New York Weekly Journal* in New York City in 1733, was in his own right neither a brilliant journalist nor a heroic figure. He was a competent printer with enough spirit and fortitude to cast his lot with a group of New York business and professional people vigorously opposed to the administration of the British governor, William Cosby, a high-handed, high-living, corrupt administrator who manipulated the courts and the judges to suit his prejudices and his pocketbook.

Zenger was arrested and charged with criminal libel for publishing a broadside attack on Cosby warning that the liberties and the properties of the people "are precarious, and that slavery is likely to be intailed on them and their posterity, if some past things are not amended." He spent nine months in jail, editing his paper from his cell with the help of his wife and friends, and came to trial on August 4, 1735. The impressive figure in the courtroom was not Zenger but an 82-year-old lawyer named Andrew G. Hamilton, of Philadelphia, who had come out of retirement to defend Zenger. The question before the court, Hamilton told a most attentive jury, "is not the cause of the poor printer, nor of New York alone. . . . It may in its consequence affect every freeman that lives under a British government on the main of America." With remarkable prescience, he told the jury:

> It is the best cause. It is the cause of liberty, and I make no doubt but your up-right conduct, this day, will not only entitle you to the love and esteem of your fellow-citizens; but every man who prefers freedom to a life of slavery will bless and honor you, as men who have baffled the attempt of tyranny; and by an impartial and uncorrupt verdict, have laid a noble foundation for securing to ourselves, our posterity and our neighbors, that, to which nature and the laws of our country have given us a right—the liberty—both of exposing and opposing arbitrary power (in these parts of the world, at least) by speaking and writing Truth.

The jury ignored the directives of the judge and returned a verdict of not guilty, thereby establishing truth as the most effective defense against libel, and stripping from the judges their power to determine alone what was libelous. More important, the verdict nourished the root principle which was to inspire the First Amendment: If a jury in colonial America could determine that a newspaper had a right and duty to criticize a royal government, then surely newspapers in a free America ought to have that right underwritten and protected as a foundation of freedom.

This principle was carried forward even more vigorously by the press in the years between the Zenger trial and the rise of the revolutionary movement. The newspapers of this time were a powerful force in uniting the colonists and exhorting them to self-determination. Their contribution to the success of the Revolution cannot be underestimated. The tenacity and commitment of their editors persisted into the post-Revolutionary era which saw the first clashes between press and government, as well as the first charges of government management of the news. President Washington, smarting under unaccustomed attacks by the press, denounced the offending newspapers as scurrilous and irresponsible, establishing a precedent which has been repeated by almost every succeeding President. To counter the sharp criticism in the press, the early Presidents —including Thomas Jefferson—set up and quietly supported newspapers in Washington, Philadelphia and New York which became poorly disguised organs of the administration in power. They merely whetted the pens of the independent editors who went after them and their hidden sponsors with renewed scorn.

Freedom was embraced with a kind of wild abandon in the first decades of the nineteenth century. Newspapers were almost always individually owned, and the personal mark of the editor-publisher was ever-present— often with responsibility the casualty of a brilliant but erratic and violently partisan mind. Considerable journalistic license accompanied the jockeying for political power, and some of the staunchest defenders of freedom of the press fell victim to unprincipled editors who were doing a job for the political opposition. But the remarkable increase in the number of newspapers allowed for great diversity of opinion. In 1830 there were more newspapers with a greater readership in the United States than anywhere in the world. It was a time when almost anyone who wanted to have his say could afford to have it. The quality of the papers varied enormously, but it was in essence a healthy time.

There followed the rise of the big-city newspapers, particularly in New York, and the great egocentric publishers who have become newspaper legends: James Gordon Bennett of the *Herald;* Horace Greeley of the *Tribune;* William Cullen Bryant of the *Post;* and Charles Anderson Dana of the *Sun.* Circulation wars coincided with the Civil War, during which many newspapers descended to new lows of irresponsibility in their attacks on President Lincoln and in their efforts to build circulation. But except for a period during the Civil War, when the military expressed alarm at the coverage of the war ("giving aid and comfort to the enemy"), the concept of freedom of the press remained strongly imbedded in the public consciousness.

Technological improvements in printing and press work and the beginning of telegraphic communication forced the papers, because of pressing competition, to improve their content and, in many cases, their standards. With greater travel and interchange, people in cities on the Eastern seaboard could compare their own newspapers with those of the Midwest and the South where a new breed of crusading editors was exposing civic corruption and seeking to raise social standards.

In the post-Civil War era, and especially the last two decades of the nineteenth century, the American press changed from old to new, from a parochial, individualistic approach to a more sophisticated corporate approach, as the country grew in fantastic fashion and the nation became preoccupied with this growth. The cities were expanding at a phenomenal rate, and population was growing with industry. People had money and wanted goods, and the factories were pouring out their products. Advertising became a prime method of buying and selling, and the newspapers the medium. As competition among newspapers increased, publishers began paying more attention to efficient management and production practices to improve their position in the race for profits. The scramble for money is demonstrated by these figures: In 1880, there were 850 daily newspapers in the English language; in 1890, there were 1,967. The newcomers were almost entirely evening newspapers, reflecting a concentration on the home audience, the women who did most of the shopping for consumer goods and of course read the advertisements beforehand.

The newspaper publishers began to identify their own enterprises more closely with the business community, and as costs rose and the craft unions began making their demands, the class instinct became dominant. There was a greater stress on responsibility in journalism, but responsibility was subject to varied and often subjective interpretation. Newspapers printed more news, with a major assist from the wire services which had recently been organized, and they paid considerably more attention to public service on the community level. But editorial pages gradually shifted their emphasis away from criticism of government and government practices and adopted a more protective tone. Appeals for national unity in a burgeoning nation were common. A permanent Stars and Stripes was unfurled in the masthead of many newspapers, and its appearance often was accompanied on the editorial page by a flagrant distortion of patriotism.

A classic example of hysteria-driven journalism was provided just before the turn of the twentieth century, when William Randolph Hearst, Sr. and Joseph Pulitzer, Sr. declared war on Spain after the battleship *Maine* had been sunk at Havana and prodded President McKinley and the Congress to make the war official. This marked the dawn of American imperialism. Sixty years later, Cuba figured prominently in American journalism again. The distortions were more sophisticated, but the lack of responsibility was just as gross, and the dangers for the nation and the world in the nuclear age far greater.

Journalism was a giant industry as the twentieth century opened. In 1904, commentator Arthur Brisbane said: "Journalistic success brings money. The editor has become a money man. 'Where your treasure is, there your heart will also be.' " In his telescopic fashion, he was right. Occasionally an irate advertiser did storm into the office of a crusading editor and threaten to remove his advertising, but the necessity arose more frequently in the movies than in real life. In real life the heart of the publisher was secure in the treasured highlands which were the source of his revenue.

In the first decades of the twentieth century, newspapers were bought
and sold with the frenzy of stock market speculators, and the newspaper
chains began their spectacular rise. Hearst bought 16 newspapers between
1919 and 1934. Individual newspapers merged to counter the competition of the chains and their massive appeal to advertisers. In the course of
his swashbuckling career, Hearst established or purchased 42 daily newspapers. Scripps-Howard at its peak controlled 19.

After the wholesale manipulation, swapping, and merging came the
consolidation process, during which staffs were pared down, features
shifted from paper to paper, and new mergers instituted to cut costs and
increase profits. In 1940, there were 17 daily newspapers in the Hearst
chain; in 1969, 18 years after Hearst's death, his sons and heirs were
managing seven papers (in addition to 12 magazines, four radio-TV
stations, a feature syndicate and a paperback book company).

Personal journalism by the end of World War II was almost entirely out
of fashion, although it reappeared in sporadic form in the Hearst chain
when the old man commanded space for his banal one-sentence-para-
graph front-page editorials denouncing bolshevik Russia; or in the
Scripps-Howard press with Roy W. Howard's interviews with famous
world figures. Corporate journalism does not lend itself to individual flair,
and almost the last flicker of flamboyance was extinguished with the
emergence of a new kind of bloodless newspaper chain after World War
II—the conglomerates assembled by men like S. I. Newhouse, Britain's
Roy Thomson, James S. Copley and John H. Perry. Even the word
"chain" fell into disrepute. "Chain sounds like a bunch of hardware
stores," John S. Knight, who owns six dailies, told the *Wall Street Journal*
in 1965. "We operate as a group." For many people "chain" and "group"
were interchangeable. In fact, Newhouse was described by an official of a
Springfield, Massachusetts newspaper which Newhouse had acquired
after a bitter battle in 1960 as "a graveyard superintendent [who] goes
around picking up bones, preying on widows and split families."

The new group publishers were prominent in the business pages of
newspapers and the journals of journalism ("It is the business of newspapers," Lord Thomson was fond of saying, "to make money"), but they
were almost faceless in the newspapers they owned (Knight was an exception). When they bought into a town, they generally left the managerial setup intact (at least until they determined who was culpable for
losing money under the old management). They permitted the paper to
declare its own political policy (a safe measure in a time when the services
of an oracle are required to distinguish between the two major political
parties). And then they diligently applied themselves to the pursuit of

profit, according to the gospel as enunciated by Thomson. There were vestigial aberrations from the declared policy of autonomy for individual newspapers, such as the comment by William Randolph Hearst, Jr. that he did not want someone sounding off with his own national or international policy: "Then it would be his newspaper and not ours." The publisher explained further: "Our editorial policy hasn't changed much. It's still basically our country's interest way above anyone else's. I don't fall into that one-world, do-gooder class." In a monotonous sea of group hypocrisy, this chip-off-the-old-block candor was almost refreshing.

There were, however, few newspapers in his chain or out, 180 years after the adoption of the First Amendment, whose editorial content would cause Hearst Junior any concern about do-gooders or one-worlders taking over. Conservative conformity had become the byword as the press had been shrunk to manageable size for modern living. From a peak of 2,200 daily newspapers in 1900, there were 1,753 in 1969. But in only 45 of 1,500 cities were there competing daily newspapers under separate ownership. The total number of newspapers has remained relatively unchanged since the end of World War II, despite the death of several dozen well-known big-city newspapers. The seeming stability is accounted for by the increase in the number of suburban dailies, some today with circulations as high as 400,000. More significant than the overall figures is the mortality among newspapers in the nation's largest cities. Where once there were 14 dailies in New York and eight in Boston, each city now has three. The most striking figure of all is that there are 1,455 cities with only a single newspaper publisher.

Despite the consolidation of newspapers, circulation has risen (although not in proportion to the increase in population). At the end of 1968, daily newspapers were selling at the rate of 62,535,394 a day—an increase of almost a million over 1967, and of 10 million over 1948, when there were 30 more papers.

The merging of newspapers and the formation of conglomerates have paid off handsomely. Despite a popular impression to the contrary, television has not cut into newspaper profits—there's plenty for everybody in the communications field. The Bureau of Advertising of the American Newspaper Publishers Association reported at the beginning of 1969 that advertising revenues (the main source of newspaper profit) in 1968 amounted to $5.4 billion, or 22 per cent more than the total for television and radio combined. Advertisers spent $295 million more in newspaper advertising in 1968 than in 1967. The total advertising volume for all the media was $18.3 billion, an increase of 5.6 per cent over 1967. The *Los Angeles Times* in January 1969 alone sold 5,460,290 lines of advertising to lead the nation's papers. This was almost 2 million lines more than the *New York Times,* which ranked fourth. Regularly listed among the ten leaders are such cities as Santa Ana, San Jose, Phoenix, and Miami, indicating that the affluent society follows the sun, both for vacations and for permanent living, and advertisers follow the society. The figures also testify to the lure of the advertising dollar away from some of the Northern big cities to suburbia and the suburban dailies.

These statistics do not offer the image of an economically ailing industry. The April 1969 meeting of the American Newspaper Publishers Association heard with jubilation a United States Department of Commerce report that "unprecedented growth by every measurement has characterized the newspaper industry during the past ten years." Newspapers have indeed vanished, but those that remain have become fatter and richer. Gardner Cowles, chairman of Cowles Communications Inc., which owns several monopoly-market newspapers, said in 1965: "If you own a newspaper in a one-newspaper market, and if you give it competent management, little misfortune can befall you. You can sleep well." For the proprietors of the chains—in 1965 they controlled 750 dailies, more than double the number in 1945—the key to the tranquillity of record-setting profits, as Cowles noted, is the monopoly market. "We like an isolated market," said Paul Belknap, executive director of the Thomson Newspapers Inc. Few chains seek a place in the metropolitan market, and Vincent J. Manno, a newspaper broker, supplied the reason: "Whenever two newspaper ownerships compete, on a fairly equal basis, they neutralize one another financially."

The antidote for neutralization was outlined for practical-minded publishers by *Forbes* magazine on December 1, 1967. The next time someone in your neighborhood makes a crack about the fate of newspapers in New York City, said Forbes (the individually owned *Herald Tribune* and the Hearst *Journal-American* had just been merged with the Scripps-Howard *World-Telegram & Sun* into an indigestible *World Journal Tribune*), give them something to think about with this set of figures:

> The rule of thumb evaluation of the worth of metropolitan city newspapers is to take the circulation and—if the paper has no competition—to multiply the figure by $100. If there is competition, multiply by $30. That is why the finances of newspaper mergers are basically so simple and mergers so attractive. If a city has two morning newspapers, each with 200,000 circulation, each is theoretically worth $6 million. Merge them, and you eliminate duplicate subscriptions, and have one morning newspaper with a circulation of, say, 300,000 worth $30 million.

It's that simple—pure economics. When a newspaper dies, other newspapers print nostalgic stories about "a death in the family," how a newspaper has a soul and a character, and it is like losing a part of yourself, but that's the way life is—the Lord giveth and the Lord taketh away. What also has been taken away, but is not discussed, is a competing point of view, however minimal, and the right of people to read opposition comment. Replicas of old front pages flourished in the columns of other newspapers and magazines when the *World Journal Tribune* expired in 1967, but the snarl of the jackals fighting over the carcass was shut out. Throughout 1968 there were reports that the *New York Times,* the *Daily News* and *Time* magazine were considering new publications in the New York evening field, where the once ailing *Post* now had a monopoly. The *Times* and the *News* actually produced trial issues privately, but all plans were abandoned. The *Forbes* philosophy prevailed.

From the profit point of view, the reasoning was sound. Both the *News* and the *Times,* morning newspapers in a "morning newspaper town," were flourishing. Although the lack of competition had produced some slackness in reportorial zeal (or a slackening of managerial encouragement of such zeal), there was no evidence of this in the promotional material and slogans of the two newspapers. The *News* was customarily shrill and accusing: "If you don't read the *News,* you don't read New York." The *Times* was its accustomed smug self: "You don't have to read it all, but it's nice to know it's all there."

In each case, although neither paper had a monopoly in New York, there was success because each paper was unique in its own way. The *News* had become a habit, particularly among the older population, which found reassurance in its concise news presentation, cleverly insolent headlines, sports coverage, and comfortably familiar features. Also reassuring to lower middle-class prejudices were its phony folksy editorials about law and order, the threat of communism, and skillful manipulation of the race issue which left white attitudes unshaken while avoiding offense to many black readers.

The *Times* had over the years assiduously applied itself to achieving the reputation as the most prestigious newspaper in America, and perhaps the most influential. Its slogan was almost accurate: It was *almost* all there, and in some cases there was even a surfeit of detail. But at times the omissions were glaring, the positioning calculated, and the abundance of material confusing. Yet it was must reading in every newspaper office in the country because of the wealth of material produced by its enormous staff and facilities, and it was not uncommon (particularly before the development of the New York Times Service) for the contents of the *Times* to reappear rewritten as original material in afternoon newspapers in the city and in the metropolitan area.

There was another secret to the *Times*'s success: ownership of vast holdings of paper mills and forests on the North American continent. This enabled the *Times* to sell newsprint to itself at a cost far below that of other papers—or to sell it at the going rate and realize a profit that was poured back into the enterprise. One result was the ability to produce fat newspapers without hardship, whereas for other newspapers the practice was prohibitive because of the high cost of newsprint.

On February 7, 1969, the *Times* took a full-page advertisement in the *Times* to sum up its most important achievements for 1968. It was uncommonly modest in its headline: "Nothing but a lot of words." But the body type was less modest. Among the achievements listed were majority control of a book company, video educational films, the third largest news service in the country, a radio station, the *Times* on microfilm and the Times Index for sale to schools and libraries.

But the bedrock of the enterprise was the daily news report: a total of 74,000,000 words in 1968. Supplementing this was the New York Times Service, which supplied the basic news report to 300 newspapers in the United States and 30 countries abroad—with a combined readership of more than 40,000,000.

The daily circulation of the *Times* averaged just over 1,000,000 (an estimated 2,690,000 readers), and 1,540,000 on Sunday (4,450,000 readers). About 36 per cent of all corporation executives in the United States read it, as did every fifth American vacationing abroad. Half the readers had family incomes exceeding $14,500 a year. The *Times* had published a record 86,419,738 lines of advertising in 1968, an increase of 3,305,060 over 1967, and comprising well over half of all advertising in New York City newspapers.

The annual payroll was $72 million, distributed among 6,022 employees, half in production and distribution, and about 900 in the news and editorial departments. Four hundred reporters and editors were based in the home office (82 additional on the Sunday staff), 32 in Washington and 40 abroad. These staff members produced 12,972 pages of news from 3,600 different datelines. The average size of the weekday paper in 1968 was 84 pages, and 577 on Sunday. The average weight of the Sunday paper was over 5.1 pounds. The monster birth was on Sunday, October 17, 1965, when the scale registered 7.8 pounds.

Weight, bulk, and standardization characterize the modern American newspaper. The technological revolution since 1960 has increased efficiency and reduced costs. The one remaining problem for the publishers is the unions, which have understandably resisted the introduction of methods sharply decreasing the number of jobs. Yet the publishers have the stronger position, for the unions have been forced by the technological

advances to make concessions, and strike insurance protects the publishers. During the long strikes in New York, Detroit, and Cleveland in
the 1960s there were no serious losses for the publishers.

The final newspaper product, the result of new web offset presses,
computer systems, and modernized letterpress equipment, is an outstanding achievement. But what of the content of the newspapers? Before
World War II the ratio of editorial matter to advertising was 60 per
cent to 40 per cent. Today the ratio has been more than reversed. Yet
despite the preponderance of advertising content, the newspapers print
more news than ever before. In addition to the Associated Press and the
United Press International, news services are available from the *New
York Times,* the *Los Angeles Times-Washington Post,* and others.
Reuters, Agence France Presse, and the *London Observer* provide daily
and weekly news files from abroad.

Despite these services—or, perhaps, because of them—the press of
America is marked by a prefabricated standardization of news which is
constricting and frightening. Newspapers seem to come from a colossal
sausage machine which grinds out words in digestible packages to suit
each region of the nation. The same commentators appear in the papers
coast to coast the same day—James Reston and Joseph Alsop, Max
Lerner and William F. Buckley, cheek by jowl with the comic strips and
the service columns, and often substituting for the newspaper's default-
ing editorial comment. A large number of daily newspapers in the smaller
cities still publish "canned" editorials and political cartoons supplied by
the syndicated word factories whose products generally are so bland that
they may be used in papers of varying political views without offense. The
blandness disappears when law and order, the Communist threat, and
campus disorders are discussed, but the serviceability of the editorials
remains unimpaired. Pouring into the editorial offices every day from the
syndicates are pictures, news features, women's features, drawings, maps,
cartoons, sports columns, political commentary, advice to the lovelorn
(modernized for a swinging generation), horoscopes, farm advice, stamp
and coin columns, dressmaking guides, household hints, book reviews,
and film and theater criticism.

There has thus come into being an unofficial and loosely associated
national news network that in one way or another affects every newspaper in the country. Such a service has its positive aspects in bringing
into some areas a broadened news diet that nourishes the parochial waste-
lands, but it also tends to ensure that all persons will be similarly influenced by the news and commentary they absorb daily. It follows that they
will tend to think alike, and their thinking will be encouraged to support

the "national interest." The national interest is interpreted for them by the managers of the syndicates and the owners of the newspapers, businessmen who identify themselves, because of their conglomerate financial concerns, with national policies that protect these financial concerns—including investment in the huge war plants sweetly described as defense industries. For these proprietors, newspapers are no longer entities in themselves, with individual character, courage, and a dedication to public service, but simply properties to be listed among their holdings along with real estate, fertilizer, electronics, and aerospace rocketry. Unlike fertilizers, however, newspapers deal with information, ideas, and opinions that ought to help people understand and shape national policies. The economic centralization of newspapers, along with the rest of industry, is a disastrous detour for what used to be known in town hall forums as the free exchange of ideas in the marketplace of public opinion.

This is not what the framers of the Bill of Rights had in mind when they established protections for newspapers unique in written constitutional law. They may have anticipated that newspapers would become great commercial entities in a free enterprise system, but they did not envision a situation in which newspapers would become almost exclusively profit-making enterprises, using the First Amendment as a wall against criticism and "interference" in their efforts to concentrate ownership in fewer and fewer hands for the acquisition of ever greater profits. The evil of bigness in itself may be debatable, but the dangers of monopoly news and monopoly opinion-making are not.

Before civic groups and university convocations, newspaper publishers who are strangers to their own newsrooms present themselves as custodians of freedom of the press. At the annual meetings of the American Society of Newspaper Editors and the American Newspaper Publishers Association, editors and publishers congratulate themselves for producing what they describe as the freest press in the world. They cite by rote the code of ethics which the editors' society adopted in 1923 as written proof of their virtue, and then proceed to the main business at hand—the discussion of profits and merger possibilities.

What has this to do with freedom of the press under the First Amendment in the declining decades of the twentieth century? In a positive way, very little; in a negative way, ominously much. The American press is committed to the American way of life under capitalism. Any other way —particularly the socialist way—is equated with sin and deviltry. Within this concept, publishers, editors, reporters, and commentators enjoy complete freedom of the press and may say what they will. This includes criticism of governmental methods and practices, legislation before Congress or local legislatures, investigation of corruption in high places (rare, but still undertaken), generalized reporting about pollution and destruction of natural resources, concern over fluctuating social and moral values in the nation—but never basic criticism of national policies. Two striking examples underscore this point:

At the beginning of 1968, the *Boston Globe* undertook a survey of editorial opinion among 39 major United States newspapers, with a total circulation of 22 million, to determine their position on the war in Vietnam. The results showed that several newspapers had in the previous months become critical of the escalation of the war in Vietnam, some had become "more hawkish," *but not one newspaper advocated withdrawal of American troops from Vietnam, although millions of Americans had expressed themselves in favor of withdrawal.* It is more than likely that the result would have been the same if the survey had been extended to cover all 1,753 daily newspapers in the country.

Before Senator Joe McCarthy was put out of commission in 1954, 20 authorities on China in the United States foreign service had resigned, retired, or been reassigned to non-Chinese activities. In each case, the action had been well publicized in the press. But what McCarthy accomplished within the newspaper industry itself was less well publicized because the publishers preferred it so. Between 1945 and 1950, distinguished specialists connected with the Institute of Pacific Relations (a prime McCarthy target) had reviewed 22 of 30 books on China for the *New York Times.* In the same period these experts had reviewed 30 of 35 books on China for the *New York Herald Tribune.* The book review sections (daily and Sunday) of these two newspapers were the most prestigious in the country. *From 1952 to 1955, years of McCarthyite prevalence, not one of these authorities was engaged to review a single book by either the* Times *or the* Herald Tribune. During those four years, editorials denouncing McCarthy's methods rang out with increasing frequency in both papers. But in the back rooms, the Senator's methods were being copied.

Hypocrisy is commonplace in an industry where the least vicious and most respected publications are perhaps the most efficient adjuncts of established power because they disarm and mislead their readership with greater sophistication. This practice is hardly exclusive to the United States, but it is more striking here because the press of other nations does not hold aloft the standard of the First Amendment nor does it operate under its provisions. For all its surface brilliance and technical achievements, the American press lacks candor and curiosity—let alone courage—in its news coverage, interpretation, and editorial positions. Hardly a day goes by when an event does not occur—say, the shooting down of an American intelligence plane by the North Korean air force—which begs for questions to be asked of the United States government, and answers demanded. Yet the questions are rarely asked by the newspapers, and the answers of course are not volunteered. Presidential press conferences have become routine exercises in which the highest-paid members of the working press and the national television networks ask routine questions—often cleared beforehand with the White House—and the prevailing sentiment is not to embarrass either the President or the national policy. Those who break the rules (or seek to break them) in this gentlemen's club find themselves quickly frozen out.

The highly paid columnists and commentators, with private access to governmental news sources which they are determined not to endanger, cater to the national interest by underscoring the findings of the working press. In the early days of the Republic, Presidents privately financed newspapers and editors who would do their bidding. Today the press serves the government without pay.

Beyond the question of what newspapers do and do not print, and how they present what they do print, is the increasing realization that the public does not have access to its press. Newspapers have become so costly to establish, and the monopoly situation has become so prevalent throughout the country, that even millionaires hesitate to undertake new ventures—not that their point of view would differ from the already established press. For any group in basic political opposition, particularly a radical one, the only resort is to bootstrap, subsidized operations which are self-limiting in circulation, distribution, advertising, and income, if any.

A classic example of the difficulties facing a maverick newspaper in modern competition was provided by the experience of the experimental New York newspaper *PM,* launched in June 1940 by Ralph Ingersoll, who resigned as publisher of *Life* to undertake the venture, on a stock issue of $1,500,000. *PM* was not radical; it was more nearly left-liberal. It stated in its credo that it was "against fraud and deceit and greed and cruelty," and it proposed "to crusade for those who seek to improve constructively the way men live together." It was "against people who push other people around." It took no advertising. A measure of its appeal to working newspapermen is the fact that there were 11,000 applications for the 150 jobs.

*PM* failed. Marshall Field III, the Chicago millionaire who was eccentric enough to believe a newspaper's function was not "viewing with equal impartiality both sides of the struggle between the strong and the weak, the big and the small, the monopolists and the independents," poured $5 million into the paper, but *PM* never achieved the 225,000 daily circulation it needed to break even (it averaged about 165,000). Although in 1946 it began to take advertising, the big advertisers looked the other way. In 1948 it was sold and became the *Star,* but the mark of death was on the enterprise and it expired in 1949.

*PM* was an erratic paper, and its quality was uneven. But it sought valiantly to maintain its founding principles and it fought many noble campaigns in the genuine public interest. Although there were many internal reasons for its failure, the major reasons were external: the hostility of other newspapers and the inability of a public to change long established habits of newspaper reading and buying. The trade journals (especially *Editor & Publisher*) treated *PM* and its ideals savagely. The press in general subjected it to a vicious smear campaign because of its liberal and iconoclastic presentation of the news. Sophisticated publications like the *New Yorker* sneered at it with barbed humor. Newsdealers were persuaded by the big newspapers not to display it, or to keep it off the stands altogether. In the face of this hostility and slander, it is remarkable that *PM* survived for as long as it did.

The great majority of American newspapers exclude from their pages any extensive expression of opposition to present national policies. Among the silenced are antiwar groups, political and radical minorities, civil liberties organizations, and the large amorphous entity known as the New Left. Of course the newspapers cover college demonstrations, peace marches, and ghetto protests—with emphasis on the violent aspects—but the underlying motivation and philosophy of the opposition groups have rarely been presented in depth.

This policy of exclusion has stirred considerable public comment and has forced a debate in the professional journals and elsewhere about the pretensions of freedom of the press in America and its denial in fact. The debate has brought into sharper focus the intent of the First Amendment and has to an extent put the newspaper industry in a defensive posture at a time when opinion surveys have indicated a general public skepticism about the credibility of the press.

The American Civil Liberties Union, a staunch defender of the First Amendment, early in 1969 was considering a court action—on the basis of the First Amendment—to require newspapers to grant access in print to persons with unpopular ideas. The "right of access" proposition was based on a constitutional expert's interpretation of the First Amendment that "restraining the hand of government is quite useless in assuring free speech if a restraint on access is effectively secured by private groups"—

that is, by the publishers of newspapers. The intent of the suit was to force newspapers to open their pages to radical and unpopular ideas. The action proposed also a legally enforced "right of reply" to persons attacked in newspapers. Right-of-reply laws are already on the books in Nevada and Florida, although they are not well known and have rarely been invoked.

The implications of the ACLU suit were far-reaching in light of the First Amendment provision that Congress shall make no law abridging the freedom of the press. But since the press has effectively abridged the right of the public to free and full expression, the suit could be salutary in bringing the whole controversy about freedom of the press out in public where it belongs—a debate addressed directly to the question whether the American press is free and responsible according to the purposes and the principles of the First Amendment as it was drawn in 1789.

It is relevant to raise the question of freedom of the press in socialist countries, and to come to the conclusion that government control produces woeful results whether the government is capitalist or socialist. But here too a distinction must be drawn: The press of the socialist countries is openly under the control of the governments of those countries, and there is no pretense about individual control; the press of the United States insists that it is privately owned and controlled and free of government stricture.

It is the contention of this book that the press of the United States has to a large degree become a voluntary arm of established power. In the pages that follow, this thesis will be argued in an examination of the conduct of the press in time of crisis during the Cold War years, particularly as the crises concerned foreign policy. In essence, the book is a study of the degree to which the newspaper industry has abdicated its role of public service.

# 2. Counterpoint of Two Wars

The date of the opening of the Cold War is most commonly set in 1946, early in the post-World War II Truman Administration, when the wartime alliance between the United States and the Soviet Union was being dismantled. But an excellent case can be made for fixing the date as March 3, 1918, the signing of the Brest-Litovsk Treaty, when the Soviets effected a peace with Germany and refused to continue in a war— World War I—which the people of Russia had rejected.

The 1918 date, in any case, marked the origin of the journalistic Cold War against Communism. Incontrovertible documentation for this claim was presented in a 42-page supplement to the *New Republic* of August 4, 1920, entitled "A Test of the News," by Walter Lippmann and Charles Merz. Lippmann, who was soon to become editor of the *New York World,* had been for several years an editor of the *New Republic;* Merz, an Army lieutenant in 1918, wrote for *Harper's* and the *New Republic,* and was to join Lippmann on the *World.* The authors examined news stories and editorials in the *New York Times* from March 1917 to March 1920 (ironically, Merz became editor of the *Times* in 1938) and compiled what Harrison Salisbury of the *Times* has termed "the first, and still in many ways the classic analysis of American press coverage of Soviet events" (*Columbia Journalism Review,* Fall 1963).

Up to the time of the Brest-Litovsk Treaty, the Lippmann-Merz report said, news of the Bolshevik Revolution had been handled in a misleadingly optimistic manner, then in a "rather uncritically pro-Bolshevik fashion," in the belief that the Soviets would continue to fight the Germans. After March 1918, "organized propaganda for intervention" colored the news until President Wilson announced a month later that there would be no United States intervention in Russia. Following a brief pause for refueling, the newspaper crusade for action by Washington picked up again. On July 12, 1918, Wilson approved intervention. After the Armistice in November, the Red Menace returned to dominate the news in the United States and, Lippmann and Merz said, became "one of the most significant things" contributing to continued intervention. On December 13, 1918, a *Times* editorial said: "Having entered Russia for a purpose, why not carry out that purpose?" The purpose, the editorial said, was to "drive the Bolsheviki out of Petrograd and Moscow."

In the first two years of the Soviet Union, Merz and Lippmann found, the *Times* had reported the government collapsing 91 times; Petrograd toppled six times; on the verge of capture three times more; burned to the ground twice; in a state of absolute panic twice; in revolt against the Bolsheviki six times; and in a state of starvation constantly. The victories of the White armies were enormous ("Mr. Harold Williams's reports from Denikin's army were obviously queer at the time and are ridiculous in the light of events") and the casualty figures and captured weapons totals were many times larger than the armies and materiel in all of Russia. The compilators simply added up the *Times* figures to reach that conclusion. Lippmann and Merz demonstrated how Americans were misinformed on every important question involving Russia. From January 1919 through the first half of 1920, Soviet Russia was pictured as an aggressor against Poland and a "Red invasion of Europe" declared to be imminent. In fact, during most of this period, Polish troops were deep in Russian territory. Soviet offers to negotiate settlements with the Allied powers were invariably distorted. The *Times* said on March 14, 1920:

There has been no doubt at any time in Washington official circles that the Soviet "peace" drive represented nothing more than a scrap of paper policy of the Soviet leaders, a mere tactical move, and that what they really sought was a breathing spell in which to concentrate their energies for a renewed drive toward world-wide revolution.

For the last fifty years the word peace has been incarcerated between quotation marks by the *Times* and most other newspapers whenever it is used by a socialist country. It has been liberated from the quotation marks only when its employer can produce pure capitalist credentials—neutral nations could not be entrusted with the word, John Foster Dulles determined. Thus "peace" became a fellow traveler of the Red Peril, two words which are never caught with their upper cases down. The Red Peril, Lippmann and Merz wrote, "has appeared at every turn to obstruct the restoration of peace in Eastern Europe and Asia and to frustrate the resumption of economic life." In the name of liberation, the people of these areas were to be prevented from exploiting their own resources for the benefit of themselves. Lippmann and Merz summarized their findings thus:

> From the point of view of professional journalism the reporting of the Russian Revolution is nothing short of a disaster. On the essential questions the net effect was almost always misleading, and misleading news is worse than none at all. . . . The Russian policy of the editors of the *Times* profoundly and crassly influenced their news columns. For subjective reasons [the *Times* staff] accepted and believed most of what they were told by the State Department, the so-called Russian Embassy in Washington, the Russian Information Bureau in New York, the Russian Committee in Paris, and the agents and adherents of the old regime all over Europe. . . .
> The office handling of the news, both as to emphasis and captions, was unmistakably controlled by other than a professional standard. So obvious is this fact, so blatant is the intrusion of an editorial bias, that it will require serious reform before the code which has been violated can be restored.

The news as a whole, said Lippmann and Merz, was "dominated by the hopes of the men who composed the news organization. . . . In the large, the news about Russia is a case of seeing not what was, but what men wished to see. This deduction is more important, in the opinion of the authors, than any other. The chief censor and the chief propagandist were hope and fear in the minds of reporters and editors." The effect of this censorship and propaganda was to counteract the increasing popular demand in the United States that "the Allied statesmen must reevaluate their policy of indecision, intervention, and blockade."

In an addendum to their report, Lippmann and Merz wrote in the *New Republic* of August 11, 1920, that in June and July 1920 there had been many predictions of Soviet collapse, and commented:

> Not the least interesting thing about these reports . . . is that they often contrast with warnings of a world-wide menace. . . . Presumably no human institution can simultaneously be both cadaver and world-wide menace. But that is not to reckon with the practice of playing the news both ways. The *Times* has recently published many warnings of the Red Peril. One of them (July 28) necessitated the devotion of 1,000 words to the utterances of General Erich Ludendorff, "the famous German war leader." A curious spectacle—the German Junker invoked to show the world the way to peace.

Although "the reliability of the news is the premise on which democracy proceeds," Lippmann and Merz found that on "the supremely important event of the Russian Revolution," the American people "could not secure the minimum necessary information." Despite this, the report could find "no reason to charge a conspiracy by Americans. They could be fairly charged with boundless credulity and an untiring readiness to be gulled, and on many occasions with downright lack of common sense."

By "Americans," the authors obviously meant the men who controlled the news media. There was, of course, no need for conspiracy. These men had few differences with the government, if any. As to credulity and gulling, Lippmann and Merz themselves had determined that the news as a whole was "dominated by the hopes of men who composed the news organizations," and that they saw "not what was, but what men wished to see." The credulity and gulling, therefore, were self-induced; and if there was no conspiracy, there certainly was an unspoken agreement on the need to institutionalize the Red Peril and the concomitant distortion of the news about the theory and practice of socialism in the first socialist state. The policy continued when other socialist states came into being.

In the first volume of *The Cold War and Its Origins* (Doubleday, 1961) D. F. Fleming summed up (significantly for the course of East-West relations) the Lippmann-Merz revelations of the journalism of that period:

This exposé does not leave much on the credit side of the ledger in the books of the Allied intervention in Russia. Aside from very limited indirect military benefit in North Russia there is little to record except the negative virtue of keeping communism on the defensive. All of the five major campaigns of intervention failed disastrously, leaving Russia exhausted and embittered, but with a greatly strengthened Soviet regime firmly committed to totalitarian methods of survival and of ruling. Instead of exorcizing the great Red nightmare the interventions of 1918-20 fixed it in the uneasy slumbers of the West.

For this troubled sleep the press of the United States merits a special insomnious award, both for its coverage of foreign affairs and for its role in the domestic counterpart to the intervention in the Soviet Union—the invasion of the civil rights and liberties of the American people. The Armistice of 1918 brought an end to the wartime truce between industry and labor. In January 1919 the shipyard workers of Seattle walked out in protest against a reduction in wages. Within three weeks a general strike had paralyzed the city. That was the beginning. In succeeding months strikes swept the major industries: printing, construction, telephone, railroads, shipping, transportation, and textiles. In September and October, 500,000 coal miners and 350,000 steel workers went out, bringing the national strike total to 2 million. Alarming as this upheaval was to industry and government, it was not unexpected. Through the spring and summer months, elaborate plans had been made by the Department of Justice to counter the worker unrest and link it to the Bolshevik menace abroad. The target was the "radical movement" and its alleged threat to the nation. Attorney General A. Mitchell Palmer, in an article in the *Forum* magazine of February 1920 entitled "The Case Against the Reds," said:

> Like a prairie fire the blaze of revolution was sweeping over every American institution of law and order. . . . It was eating its way into the homes of the American workman, its sharp tongues of revolutionary heat were licking the altars of the churches, leaping into the belfry of the school bell, crawling into the sacred corners of American homes seeking to replace marriage vows with libertine laws, burning up the foundations of society.

Under Palmer's guidance and the direct supervision of J. Edgar Hoover, General Intelligence Director of the Bureau of Investigation, spies, paid informers, and special operatives were sent into unions, organizations of the foreign born, and left-wing groups. A special Justice Department publicity bureau was set up to spread stories through the country about a Moscow-directed plot to overthrow the government in Washington. Press releases were issued daily with such headings as these: "U.S. Attorney General Warns Nation Against Bolshevik Menace," "U.S. Department of Justice Urges Americans to Guard Against Bolshevik Menace," "Press, Church, Schools, Labor Unions, and Civic Bodies Called Upon to Teach True Purpose of Communist Propaganda."

On November 7, 1919, the second anniversary of the Bolshevik Revolution, Palmer moved into action. Hundreds of foreign-born citizens were arrested throughout the country, many of them at meetings marking the anniversary of the Revolution. On January 2, 1920, raids were conducted in 20 cities with the assistance of state and city police. More than 1,000 were arrested in New York, and 400 in Boston, where the prisoners were marched in chains through the streets. On January 3, the *New York World* reported the roundup of "2,000 Reds" involved in a "vast working plot to overthrow the government." The *New York Times* headline read: "REDS PLOTTED COUNTRY-WIDE STRIKE—ARRESTS EXCEED 5,000—2,635 HELD." An editorial in *Editor & Publisher,* the trade journal of the newspaper industry, said later: "When Attorney General Palmer started his so-called 'radical raids,' so many newspapers entered into the spirit of that infamous piece of witch-hunting that the reputation of the American press suffered heavily." That spirit was exemplified in a *New York Times* editorial of January 5, 1920:

> If some or any of us, impatient for the swift confusion of the Reds, have ever questioned the alacrity, resolute will and fruitful, intelligent vigor of the Depart-

ment of Justice in hunting down these enemies of the United States, the questioners
have now cause to approve and applaud. . . . This raid is only the beginning . . .
[The Department's] further activities should be far-reaching and beneficial.

The link between the Palmer raids and the intervention in Russia was
spelled out by the *Times* that same day. It was unpatriotic enough to
demand higher wages and a shorter work day and to insist on the right of
protest, but, the *Times* noted, "these Communists are a pernicious gang.
In many languages they are denouncing the blockade of Russia." The
panic spread to the legislative halls. In Washington, the House of Representatives refused to seat Victor Berger, a Socialist elected from Milwaukee. In Albany, the New York State Assembly expelled five duly
elected Socialist members on the ground that they were affiliated with
"a disloyal organization composed exclusively of traitors." Of this action
the *Times* said editorially on January 7, 1920: "It was an American vote
altogether, a patriotic and conservative vote. [The expulsion] was as
clearly and demonstrably a measure of national defense as the declaration
of war against Germany."

Oswald Garrison Villard, as editor of the *Nation,* protested against the
"authenticated cases of torture, sadism, and crime committed by agents
of the Department of Justice" and the entire insanity of the Palmer
method. In its issue of June 12, 1920, the *Nation* urged the impeachment
of Palmer. Villard recalled in his biography, *Fighting Years:*

> We had little aid from the press in this fight. . . . The Associated Press frequently
> refused to carry the news of what took place and to accept protests against lawless
> officials. The independent weeklies were as outspoken as we and, of course, the
> *Baltimore Suns,* the *New York World,* and the *St. Louis Post-Dispatch.* The most
> powerful newspapers like the *New York Times, Tribune,* and the *Chicago Tribune*
> either kept silence or approved.

In the end, the great majority of persons arrested were freed by the
Department of Labor, which then had the power to do so, and by the
courts. The action of the New York Legislature, despite the *Times*'s blessing, got hoots of derision from citizens who doubted that the Empire
State could be toppled by five socialists. "The nation was saved," Zechariah Chafee, Jr. wrote in *Free Speech in the United States.* "The American
people, long bedrugged by propaganda, were shaken out of their nightmare of revolution." But dawn showed that the nightmare was not revolution but reaction, and it was real: the job had been done. Under the pressure of the combined forces of industry, government, and press, the major
strikes had been broken, wages driven down, the open shop restored, and
the ranks of the unions decimated.

It is commonly said that history repeats itself. It would be more accurate to say that the forces which seek to maintain the status quo, in each succeeding generation, employ the same philosophy and tactics to prevent change—refining the methods used to persuade the public that change is somehow evil. The Soviet Union emerged from World War II as an ally of the Western powers. During the war, Western statesmen acknowledged that the policy of "containing" the Soviet Union had been the motivating force in the revival of German militarism under Hitler, had wrecked the League of Nations, and had led to the war. The Teheran and Yalta agreements were championed by President Franklin D. Roosevelt on the basis that enduring peace—and the survival of capitalism—turned on the abandonment of the containment policy. The agreements acknowledged the great-power status of the Soviet Union and restored to it territory that had been taken from it after World War I.

But even before the end of World War II, plans were being made to reverse the Yalta spirit and to restore the policy of containment—to revert to the post-World War I policy of quarantining the "contagion of Russia" behind Clemenceau's "barbed wire entanglements from the Arctic Ocean to the Black Sea." One month after Roosevelt's death in April 1945, Winston Churchill called for "Anglo-American armies" to police the world. He denounced the Soviet Union for implementing armistices with Eastern European nations—actions that had been taken under the terms of the Yalta agreements.

In August 1945, Churchill, whose Conservative government had been voted out of office in the Labor landslide a few weeks earlier, brought back into usage the phrase "iron curtain." According to the *London Times,* the phrase had been used first by Hitler's Finance Minister von Krosigk and employed frequently by Hitler's Propaganda Minister Goebbels. Churchill's invocation of the iron curtain came in a declaration of anguish over alleged mistreatment of Germans in Soviet-occupied territory. In this same speech, he advocated the use of atomic weapons to deal with "passionate ideologies."

Historians of the Cold War say that Churchill brought profound influence to bear on President Truman. If so, the influence was borne on a receptive mind since the new President was as avidly anti-Communist as the former Prime Minister. Drew Pearson wrote on June 22, 1955, about an incident that took place when Truman had been in office only 11 days, in April 1945. He served notice on Soviet Foreign Minister Molotov in a White House discussion that the United States would seek to exert its will even in the areas of the most vital concern to the Soviet Union. Charles Bohlen, who served as interpreter, said he "had never heard a top official get such a tongue-lashing." Truman's truculence at the session with Premier Stalin at Potsdam and the hostile attitude of the United States government toward the Soviet Union at the founding sessions of the United Nations at San Francisco, in June 1945, further attested to the launching of the Cold War. Arthur Krock in the *New York Times,* March 23-24, 1946, reported that Truman had begun to draft what was to become known as the Truman Doctrine in September 1945, only days after the surrender of Japan.

Most Americans believed, after the founding of the United Nations, that an era of international good will and peace had been introduced, and that this would be reflected in a more relaxed atmosphere on the home front. Texas Democrat Martin Dies, chairman of the House Committee on Un-American Activities, had declined to run for reelection in November 1944, and three committee members had been defeated in that election. It was expected that the committee, which had been getting outsize headlines for its mischief since 1938, would be retired. But when the new Congress met in January 1945 the committee was made permanent, and John E. Rankin, Democrat of Mississippi, moved forward. Rankin marked time until after the surrender of Japan in August and then began issuing press releases and making public statements sounding the alarm over the efforts of "Soviet imperialism" to dominate the world. Networks of "saboteurs" and "espionage agents" were being tracked down. Communist renegades and "students" of Soviet affairs—all of them with honorary degrees in Kremlinology—testified in committee and in the newspaper columns. Following is a typical exchange, reported solemnly in the press, between Rankin and William C. Bullitt, former Ambassador to the Soviet Union:

> *Rankin:* Is it true that they eat human bodies there in Russia?
> *Bullitt:* I did see a picture of a skeleton of a child eaten by its parents.
> *Rankin:* Then they're just human slaves in Russia?
> *Bullitt:* There are more human slaves in Russia than ever existed anywhere in the world.
> *Rankin:* You said before that sixty per cent of the Communist Party here are aliens. Now what percentage of these aliens are Jews? . . .

The domestic offensive of the Cold War had begun. On February 9, 1946, in Moscow, Stalin, in an obvious bid to reduce tensions, said in a review of the wartime alliance that World War II had been converted into a genuine anti-fascist people's war, and that the goal of the Soviet Union, in a world free of tension, was "a mighty upsurge of the national economy" to rebuild a devastated land. Winston Churchill, vacationing in

Florida, flew to Washington the next day, reportedly to confer with Truman about a speech he was to give at Westminster College in Fulton, Missouri, on March 5. Westminster was the alma mater of one of Truman's White House cronies, military attache Colonel Harry Vaughan. Truman accompanied Churchill to Fulton, where the "iron curtain" Churchillian rhetoric crashed down like the blade of a guillotine severing Europe into two halves. In *The Cold War and Its Origins,* Fleming wrote:

If there is a Third World War, Churchill's Missouri speech will be the primary document in explaining its origins. His was the full-length picture of a Red Russia out to conquer the world. Backed by the immense authority of his war record, and by the charm of his great personality, it preconditioned many millions of its listeners for a giant *cordon sanitaire* around Russia, for a developing world crusade to smash world communism in the name of Anglo-Saxon democracy. In print Churchill's battle cry became the bible of every warmonger in the world. It said all they had wanted to say and with his great name behind it, it could be used endlessly with great effect.

It was so used in the press of the United States. In a poll taken immediately after the Fulton speech, only 18 per cent of the public was recorded as approving of it. A survey a month later showed 85 per cent approval. A crisis atmosphere had to be created to make Washington's foreign policy credible. It was a calculated strategy. For example, on March 21, 1946, C. L. Sulzberger wrote in his column in the *New York Times* that the crisis over Iran had been whipped up to reverse "the momentum of pro-Soviet feeling worked up during the war." In November the Republicans won a substantial victory in the Congressional elections. Columnist Marquis Childs in the *New York Post,* November 30, 1946, said that the "cry of communism, which was raised by the Republicans from one side of the country to the other," was a major contributor to the victory. He recalled that on September 30, FBI Director Hoover had "let loose a resounding blast against Communists in the U.S., saying more or less that they were at work at every level and in every organization. . . . This could be the prelude for the kind of Red hunt that took place after World War I."

Throughout the winter Washington concentrated on the Soviet "threat": Truman made several bristling speeches; John Foster Dulles, Republican adviser to the State Department, warned against "appeasement"; Under Secretary of State Dean Acheson met with influential leaders of both political parties and influential newspapermen (Secretary of State George C. Marshall was preparing to go to Moscow for talks on Germany) to lay before them what he described as the Soviet plan to encircle Turkey to gain control of three continents. These briefing sessions were to prepare the way for public support for the Truman Doctrine. The President had long been fashioning the text, but had been waiting for the appropriate moment to make it public. The occasion was the announcement of the British withdrawal from Greece, carefully planned with the State Department. The chief architect of the Doctrine's language, according to Leigh White in an article in the October 4, 1947, *Saturday Evening Post* entitled "Truman's One-Man Brain Trust," was Clark Clifford, who would later succeed Robert McNamara as Secretary of Defense in the Johnson cabinet. Clifford wrote seven drafts. The key sentence, edited for emphasis by Truman himself, was: "I believe that it must be the policy of the United States to support free peoples who are resisting attempted subjugation by armed minorities or by outside pressure."

Several newspapers which at first had been uneasy about Churchill's speech at Fulton ("a blockbuster [flung] into the disordered and tottering streets of man," said the *New York Herald Tribune*) shed their misgivings about the Fulton policy as extended and implemented by Truman; but their attitude was defensive. On March 14, a *Herald Tribune* editorial insisted that the Doctrine was not a proclamation of American imperialism: it was "emphatically not a declaration of war upon Russia." The *New York Times* on March 13, sounding like the *Times* of 1919, described it as "nothing less than a warning to Russia to desist from the physical aggression and diplomatic attrition that have characterized her policy since the war." By May 11, the *Times* had joined the *Herald Tribune* in telling the country what the Doctrine was not: "No one in his senses and not deliberately misrepresenting the situation," it said, characterizing critics as criminally insane, "would treat the Truman Doctrine as a military adventure." After all, only $400 million was being requested for economic aid and military assistance for Greece and Turkey. The *Chicago Tribune,* however, refused to dissemble. On March 13 it said:

Mr. Truman made as cold a war speech yesterday against Russia as any President has ever made on the occasion of going before Congress to ask for a declaration of war. He gave notice that Russian communism is regarded as an enemy force which will be resisted wherever it is encountered, and that, if he has his way, the United States will go out of its way to seek encounters.

A few newspapers expressed concern. The *Chicago Daily News* (March 15) said the United States was "asking for a war with Russia." But the vast majority of the press went along with Truman. The *St. Louis Post-Dispatch* said Truman had committed the honor and prestige of the United States: there was now "no turning back."

Truman was making other commitments, as the business and financial writers made clear. The headlines and captions in *Business Week* (March 22) read: "New Democracy, New Business. U.S. Drive to Stop Communism Abroad Means Heavy Financial Outlays for Bases, Relief and Reconstruction. But in Return American Business Is Bound to Get New Markets Abroad." In the *New York World-Telegram,* the financial editor wrote: "All of this is a much safer and profitable state of affairs for investors. It is good news of a fundamental character." Fundamentalist *Time* magazine agreed. In a safer climate for candor, it wrote a year later, March 24, 1947:

> The loud talk was all of Greece and Turkey, but the whispers behind the talk were of the oceans of oil to the south. As the U.S. prepared to make its historic move, a potent group of U.S. oil companies also came to an historic decision. With the tacit approval of the U.S. and British governments, the companies concluded a series of deals—biggest ever made in the blue-chip game—to develop and put to full use this ocean of oil. . . . Jersey Standard and its partners were going to spend upwards of $300 million in the stormy Middle East to bring out this oil.

There is little doubt that fear of depression and the need for economic expansion were the other side of the coin of the policy of containment. Truman was candid about these matters in speeches prior to issuing the Doctrine. At Waco, Texas, March 6, 1946, he said that the United States was "the giant of the economic world" and would therefore "determine the future pattern of economic relations." The pattern was "free private enterprise" which, the President suggested, was the precondition for freedom of speech and worship. Six days later came the Doctrine. It was, in effect, a declaration of war, not only against the socialist world which offered no military threat, but also against the people of non-Communist Europe who were demanding liberation from their own politically and economically repressive governments, and who were increasingly looking eastward, to socialism, for alternatives. Thus "free private enterprise" was seen threatened by people who had already seized control of the means of production (in Eastern Europe), and by people who were angry at being exploited by economic overlords (in Western Europe and increasingly in Asia). To maintain and broaden markets for United States industry, it was necessary to "halt the spread of revolutionary radicalism," William Appleman Williams wrote in *The Tragedy of American Diplomacy* (World, 1959). Of the Truman Doctrine, he said:

> It was the ideological manifesto of American strategy, described by the head of *Time*'s Washington bureau as a program to promote "trouble on the other side of the Iron Curtain." As Acheson remarked, the American government entered upon "no consultation and no inquiry" about the possibility of achieving the stated

objectives either through negotiations with the Russians or within the framework of the United Nations. . . . Some of its crusading fervor seems clearly to have been the result of a conviction, most candidly expressed by Senator Arthur Vandenberg, that it would be necessary to "scare hell out of the American people."

The scare technique soon became apparent: Eleven days after the Doctrine was enunciated, Truman issued Executive Order 9835, the Loyalty Order, placing under the scrutiny of the federal investigatory and police agencies 2.2 million federal employes, from topflight executives to janitors in small-town post offices. "That," said Truman, as quoted by Marquis Childs in his column of April 20, 1947, "should take the Communist smear off the Democratic Party." If the smear came off the politicians, the brush was applied liberally to the general population. In June the Congress enacted the Taft-Hartley Act which, the American Civil Liberties Union said, "put many of [labor's] hard-won rights of more than a decade in a legal strait-jacket." Arrest and persecution of the foreign-born, far more refined and selective than in the Palmer raids 25 years earlier, became common. Investigations of "Communism" sprouted like stinkweed all over the country. Blacklists of persons in the arts and professions were compiled. In his newsletter *In Fact,* George Seldes wrote at the time:

> There is fear in Washington, not only among government employes, but among the few remaining liberals and Democrats who have hoped to salvage something of the New Deal. . . . There is fear in Hollywood. . . . There is fear in the book publishing houses. There is fear among writers, scientists, school teachers, liberals; among all who are not now part of the reactionary movement. . . .

In the December 1947 issue of the *Protestant* magazine, Abraham L. Pomerantz, deputy chief counsel to the U.S. prosecution staff at the Nuremberg trials, warned:

> The approach, copied from the Nazis, works this way: The press and radio first lay down a terrific barrage against the Red Menace. Headlines without a shred of substance shriek of atom bomb spies, or plots to overthrow our government, of espionage, of high treason, and of other blood-curdling crimes. We are now ready for the second stage: the pinning of the label "Red" indiscriminately on all *opposition.*

As though to vouch for the accuracy of Pomerantz's script, the Attorney General's first list of "subversive organizations" was published that month, and, playing its role in Tom Clark's production, the press became increasingly paranoid and parochial. Mayor Moore, a member of the United Nations radio and television section, wrote of his depression over the coverage of United Nations news in an article in the Montreal weekly *Saturday Night*. In their editorial policies, he said, most American newspapers seemed to believe that "the more we find out about countries we don't like, the more we will be convinced of their perfidy; while the more other countries get to know us, the more they will appreciate our shining righteousness. Frequently, this pernicious piece of illogic is, of course, purposeful." He cited the conforming nature of the Pulitzer Prizes: The reporting award in 1947 went to Frederick Woltman of the *New York World-Telegram* for his articles during 1946 on "the infiltration of communism in the United States."

A sentence in a letter to the *Nashville Tennessean* of March 24, 1948, succinctly summed up the cumulative effect of the press support of Truman's policy: "Anyone who reads the newspapers and listens to the radio is aware of the necessity of being ready to defend our country." The National Opinion Research Center, in response to the question whether the American public expected a new world war within 25 years, reported the following results: At the end of 1945, the affirmative answer was 32 per cent; end of 1946, 41 per cent; end of 1947, 63 per cent. By March 1948, the Gallup Poll reported, 73 per cent believed a third world war was inevitable. Fleming concluded in *The Cold War and Its Origins:* "The conversion to a war mentality was already well along. . . . Throughout this period most of the press continued to fan the war fever." Joseph and Stewart Alsop wrote in the *New York Herald Tribune* March 17, 1948: "The atmosphere in Washington today is no longer a post-war atmosphere. It is, to put it bluntly, a pre-war atmosphere." The majority of American newspapers, said Professor Curtis MacDougall of Northwestern University's school of journalism, was convincing most Americans that war was the only solution to current national problems. MacDougall, who has written several books on the policies and practices of American journalism, in a speech in Colorado at the time, gave an example of the method used to whip up war sentiment:

> Eddy Gilmore of the Associated Press wrote from Moscow a fortnight ago that there was no comparable war fever there at all. But his dispatch was printed on inside pages, if it was used at all. If Gilmore's objective report had been the opposite, it would have been streamer-headline news in every paper subscribing to the AP report.

To MacDougall, the attacks on civil liberties in the United States were the most disturbing of all. Instead of opposing these "anti-democratic trends," he said, a large section of the press was "aiding and abetting the hysteria."

The Cold War drums roused into action an organized opposition to the hard-line foreign policy. The opposition centered mainly in the National Citizens Political Action Committee (NC-PAC). This organization, which appealed largely to middle-class and professional persons, had done a remarkable job of campaigning for Franklin D. Roosevelt in the 1944 elections. After Roosevelt's death, NC-PAC worked to keep the New Deal spirit alive and to persuade Truman to hold to Roosevelt's policies. The latter effort soon proved hopeless.

NC-PAC was an outgrowth of the Congress of Industrial Organizations Political Action Committee (CIO-PAC) and the precursor of the Progressive Citizens of America (PCA). The PCA, in turn, gave way to the Progressive Party, which was formed in 1948, with Henry Wallace opposing Truman and Thomas E. Dewey in the Presidential election. The role of the press in relation to Wallace and the founding of the Progressive Party is a classic case in the history of news perversion.

# 3. Henry Wallace and Hysteria

As the "visionary dreamer" of the New Deal, who wanted to give a "quart of milk to every Hottentot," Vice-President Henry Wallace was a favorite target of conservative columnists and a considerable number of Congressmen. To appease the conservative elements in the Democratic Party, a physically and politically weary Roosevelt had agreed to dump Wallace for Senator Truman of Missouri as his running mate in the 1944 election. Thus another accidental President would serve during a critical time in American history.

Appointed Secretary of Commerce in the Truman cabinet, Wallace became increasingly uncomfortable about the postwar direction of foreign policy. After a series of speeches critical of Administration policy—particularly one at Madison Square Garden on September 12, 1946, under the sponsorship of NC-PAC—Wallace was forced out of the cabinet on September 20. The event received enormous press coverage, largely because of Truman's ineptness (he approved the speech beforehand and disowned it afterward) and because of speculation over Wallace's future and the possibility of a third party.

Wallace became editor of the *New Republic* on December 16, 1946, and continued his criticism of the Administration. The Truman Doctrine was promulgated ten weeks later, followed by the Loyalty Order, and Wallace went on a speaking tour of England and four other European countries denouncing both the doctrine and the order. This produced angry press comment at home and an uproar in the Senate, where Wallace's remarks were regarded as a treasonable offense against his native land. The *Saturday Evening Post,* May 1, 1947, said editorially after Wallace's tour:

Now that the show is over, it looks as if Anglo-Saxon solidarity may have been cemented on at least one thing: heartfelt gratitude to the late FDR for giving Henry the business in the Democratic Convention of 1944.

Wallace followed his European trip with a national tour in May 1947 under the sponsorship of the Progressive Citizens of America—and the press opened up. The *Cleveland News* published an open letter on May 2.

This is no welcoming greeting, on the occasion of your speech in Cleveland tonight. . . . With (we believe) the majority of clear-thinking Clevelanders, we felt shocked that you would take your disagreement with our national foreign policy to the platforms of foreign countries at a dangerous time like the present. We estimate you as irresponsible for having done so.

The press clearly did not approve of Wallace, but many citizens did: by the end of June 1947 the PCA claimed 25,000 members in 19 states. Wallace continued his barnstorming, and press disapproval grew with the size of the crowds he attracted. On November 12, the *Pittsburgh Sun-Telegraph* commented:

It does not follow that because a man may occasionally agree with a Communist he is a Communist. . . . But when a man, or any group, consistently follows all of the party line, it is reasonable to suspect that there is more in it than mere coincidence.

The same day, the *Pittsburgh Post-Gazette* editorial, under the heading "Doc Wallace's Elixir," said:

Unquestionably there are in Mr. Wallace's audiences many sincere liberal and progressive citizens, along with a lot of Pinks and chronic malcontents. It remains to be seen if the Wallace elixir is potent enough to blend dissenting groups into a cohesive third party. Meanwhile we must look upon the effort with concern. There is in it the seeds of a dangerous class conflict we would like to see this country spared.

Class conflict was far from Wallace's liberal politics, but he met conflict head-on in other areas, particularly on the question of race. When he went South to speak, he insisted that the audiences not be segregated. Ralph McGill, editor of the *Atlanta Constitution* and often cited as a Southern moderate, wrote on November 15, 1947, that Wallace's trip had made many people "angry to the point of being violent."

In Atlanta, one of the cities where Mr. Wallace will speak, his sponsors, the Communist-infiltrated Southern Conference for Human Welfare (with its officials apparently getting most of the "welfare") will be grievously disappointed if someone does not create a disorder so as to give them the publicity they seek. Since there is a great deal of similarity between the mental mechanism of the Ku Kluxers and the officers of the SCHW, we are likely to see a Klan picket line or some other form of protest. Indeed, if there is one I trust someone will look under the robes to see if they be the hired pickets of the SCHW or the real McCoy of the Klaverns.

Threatened with a libel suit, McGill made a partial retraction two months later, denying that he was impugning the politics or the honesty of the SCHW officials. But of course he had firmly tied the Red flag on both Wallace and the Southern Conference.

The debate within the PCA over a third-party ticket headed by Wallace became brisk. When Wallace announced his candidacy late in December, there were defections by many prominent liberals from the PCA, and with their departure came a new press barrage. Stewart Alsop wrote in his syndicated column on December 21:

The Wallace third-party movement has been indecently exposed for what it is: an instrument of Soviet foreign policy. Since the PCA invited him to head a third party, the whole movement has been stripped bare. The bones revealed are communistic bones.

Columnist Dorothy Thompson said that the Communists had picked Wallace to run. In the *Detroit News,* Blair Moody (later a U.S. Senator from Michigan) wrote:

Extreme leftists, meaning Moscow's American agents and those who follow their line, are doing their best to split the liberal movement and elect a reactionary President next November. That, according to the strategy the Communists think is canny, would be the surest way to wreck the country and bring on a violent overturn via depression. . . . Step No. 1 in this campaign is to get Henry A. Wallace to run at the head of a third-party ticket.

Many observers accepted this line of speculation, as Curtis MacDougall made clear in *Gideon's Army,* a three-volume history of the Progressive Party. He cited an article by James Thrasher headed "What Makes Henry Run?" and distributed by the Newspaper Enterprise Association (Scripps-Howard) which recalled Wallace's remark that he would prefer conservative Republican Senator Robert A. Taft of Ohio to Truman. It was a "good guess," said Thrasher, that the Progressives hoped to swing three or four pivotal states to the Republicans, with Taft as the candidate. MacDougall reported:

I have found this piece, signed by Thrasher, in the *Gloversville* (N.Y.) *Herald* for January 5 and in the *Ogdensburg* (N.Y.) *Advance-News* for January 11. I have also found it, without Thrasher's signature, in 37 other newspapers as a local editorial on various days in late December 1947 and the first three weeks of January 1948. It may have been used in others, but even if not, the strong nature of the journalistic opposition to the Progressives is indicated.

The opposition was indeed strong. But even more strongly apparent was the attempt by the press to fix in the public mind the image of a third-party movement as Communist-inspired and therefore an agency of the Soviet state.

The early months of 1948 witnessed a further increase in tensions between the United States and the Soviet Union. A West German government was formed in January and precipitated a Soviet move to get the Western powers out of Berlin. In February, the Communist Party took over full control of the Czechoslovak government. In June, the Berlin blockade was set up.

In this atmosphere the Presidential campaign of 1948 was launched. The Republicans sought to brand the Democratic Administration as "soft on Communism," a phrase which was to become a classic cliché, and the Administration outdid the Republicans to prove its hardness. In consonance with both parties, the press hammered away at the theme that rapprochement with the Soviet Union was hopeless. Early in May 1948 United States Ambassador Walter Bedell Smith called on Foreign Minister Molotov in Moscow to emphasize that the policies being proposed by Wallace (they were warmly received by the press in the Soviet Union) would never be adopted by the United States. Toward the end of his bristling statement was a platitudinous sentence to the effect that the door was always open to discuss a reduction of tensions between the two countries. To the embarrassment of Washington, Molotov took this point up and offered immediate talks. In Los Angeles the day the story broke, the evening *News* headline read: "U.S. Note, Russian Reply Raise Hopes for Peace." The next morning the *Los Angeles Times* headline was: "Russian Note Arouses Suspicions of Truman." That evening the Los Angeles *Examiner* proclaimed: "U.S. Won't Bow to Russ." In 24 hours the press had recovered its unequilibrium.

On occasion the press moved from comment on policy to direct action, as in the case of the *Columbus Citizen*. A house was rented in the late winter of 1948 in Columbus by Frank Hashmall, an organizer for the Communist Party, from a stepson of Dr. Richard C. Morgan, curator of archeology at the Ohio State Museum in Columbus. The *Citizen* published photographs of the house, listing the address and phone number, accompanied by cautions against violence in dealing with Communists "who thrive on martyrdom." Some citizens of Columbus got the inverted message and made sporadic attacks on the house. This, along with violence against distributors of Wallace campaign literature, brought protests from other citizens, and moved the newspaper to say editorially March 26, 1948: "Evidently when you pinch a Communist a Wallacite howls. The Commies and the Wallace crowd seem to have a connecting nervous system, like a two-headed calf." On March 30, as 400 persons looked on, a gang of 30 men invaded the Hashmall house (the family was away) and smashed almost everything it contained. The next day the *Citizen* published a photograph of a moving van being loaded with those few family possessions which had not been destroyed. Dr. Morgan was fired by the State of Ohio for the "indiscretion" of his stepson.

This was the mood during the months the Progressive Party sought to get on the ballot in several states. In April the *Pittsburgh Press* began publishing the names of all signers of petitions for the new party in western Pennsylvania. On the third day of the list, April 13, this editorial appeared in the *Press:*

Gideon's Army, as Henry Wallace calls his followers, doesn't seem to like daylight. We are amazed at the sharp reaction of the Henry Wallace forces against publication of the names. . . . The strange thing is that those who yell so loud about the legal right of signing petitions should complain against the exercise of the legal right to publish them.

The *Press* published 222 names on the first day and suggested that the FBI might check on them. The next day the paper announced that several petition signers had declared themselves duped and wanted their names withdrawn. Actually, according to MacDougall, only 20 retracted and 20 more were known to have been called in by their employers and told to withdraw their names or be fired. All told, about 1,000 names were published from April 11 through April 30. Among the papers in other states which published names of petition signers were the *Nashville Tennessean, Birmingham Post, York* (Pa.) *Dispatch, Xenia* (O.) *Gazette, Zanesville* (O.) *Signal, Concord* (N.H.) *Monitor & Patriot* and *Boston Herald.*

The founding convention of the Progressive Party was held in Philadelphia in the last week of July 1948. Peter Edson in his syndicated *Scripps-Howard* column of July 27 described it as "the darndest thing that ever happened," a characterization that was also earned by the press coverage. There were more than 3,000 delegates from every state and station in life, and they provided a large canvas for color which the press was ready to apply with a ruby-colored brush. Throughout the week many of the delegates were housed in tents and trailers in a lot across from the convention hall. They truly presented a cross section of America, but to Anne O'Hare McCormick of the *New York Times* they were "politically displaced persons." She was close to the mark, without meaning to be. Columnist Thomas L. Stokes found at the convention "the tone of tragedy, like the throbbing minor theme of a great orchestra, despite the excited gaiety and enthusiasm generated by its preponderantly youthful chorus. These people . . . were suffering from a persecution complex that provoked them to strike out bitterly in all directions."

Columnist Hal Boyle spotted the inevitable mother who "pulled out a plump breast" to feed her child "in a crowded corridor," but nobody paused to stare except, presumably, Boyle. Peter Edson, recovering from his initial stupefaction, discovered that the delegates were being subverted:

> There never was a political convention in which the program was so stage-managed, the candidates so handpicked, the platform so dictated by special interests. . . . It may be that [the delegates] are merely being used to promote what the American Communists are most interested in—the Russian foreign policy line.

Joseph and Stewart Alsop also judged the convention to be "stage-managed," and Miss McCormick found the atmosphere "too reminiscent for the comfort of observers who have witnessed similar scenes for a potential 'savior' in Rome in the Twenties and in Berlin in the early Thirties. . . . In a way the genuine emotion behind it makes the fanfare more disturbing."

Milburn P. Akers of the Associated Press described the platform as "one on which William Z. Foster, head of the Communist Party in the United States, can stand as well as Henry Wallace." The *Philadelphia Inquirer* in a preview editorial July 23 determined that between the "mongrel" party and "the Reds it has been a case of love at first sight." The next day the *Inquirer* published a picture of a cluster of delegates under the banner of the Progressive Party of Alabama. The caption read: "Members of the Alabama delegation raising their clenched fists in the traditional salute of Left-Wingers." One of the delegates wrote to a friend:

> A photographer from the *Inquirer* had a bunch of young Alabamians pose under a banner we had. In asking us to show some of the "old college spirit" he shook a clenched fist and everybody duly imitated him. Next day—"Ala. delegation gives traditional left-wing salute." Old as the hills, but it worked. And one of many.

Most of the reporters in attendance wrote collections of clichés which might well have been assembled in advance. In the *Des Moines Register* of July 27, Jack Wilson began: "The Communist manipulators of the Progressive Party went back to New York Monday with the party controls locked in their satchels." W. H. Lawrence, in the *New York Times* of July 26, agreed: "With Communists and Fellow Travelers in complete control, the Progressive Party approved its 'peace, freedom, and abundance' program." *Time* magazine on August 2 termed Henry Wallace "the centerpiece of U.S. communism's most authentic looking facade."

The *New York Herald Tribune,* ever mindful of good breeding and good tweed, imported English writer Rebecca West to describe the proceedings. Miss West found the young people "horrible indeed, . . . embryo Babbitts . . . too stupid to understand how the world is run." The girls "had that restless look that comes of profound insecurity." The boys had "sullen eyes and the dropped chins" which, the clinical Miss West explained, "mean a brain just good enough to grasp the complexities of life and to realize that it would never be able to master them."

In an interview during the convention, Representative Vito Marcantonio, a leader of New York's American Labor Party, commented:

> I've been in politics 24 years and never have I seen a worse distortion by the press than its coverage of this convention. And get this, it's been a race between the so-called respectable *New York Times* and Westbrook Pegler to see who can hit the lowest blow.

The effect of this kind of press coverage on the public mind was predictable. In his campaign meetings Wallace and his running mates were subjected to constant abuse, egg-throwing, provocative actions which broke up meetings, and physical violence. Many newspapers published righteous editorials on freedom of speech and assembly—the same newspapers which had printed inflammatory editorials and articles on the new third party. The nonconformist *Cass Lake* (Minn.) *Times* summed up:

> The newspapers of the country are holding up their hands in holy horror at the egg-throwing. . . . These primitive acts of primitive men have been condemned as cowardly, unfair, intolerant, and un-American. We cannot see much difference between the throwing of eggs and tomatoes at Wallace and the hurling of epithets that have branded him as a Communist. We do not know which is worse—throwing eggs and tomatoes or cartooning Wallace as a slave of Stalin. The mob has taken seriously the newspapers' attacks on Wallace.

The campaign of 1948 was conducted against an obbligato of witchhunting and spy scares. The first Smith Act indictments of the Communist Party leadership came on the eve of the Progressive Party convention, and the House Committee on Un-American Activities had undertaken a publicized investigation of "spies in government." President Truman, sensing in the large turnouts for Wallace a ballot boomerang of his own Red scare, began to backtrack. He denounced the Congressional investigations as a "red herring," and compared the 1948 witch-hunts with the Alien and Sedition Act prosecutions of 1798. There were threats to subpoena Wallace, but he was never called. Many Progressive Party activists, however, who had been in government service during the New Deal era were subpoenaed by the Un-American Activities Committee. On August 13, 1948, Harry Dexter White, former Assistant Secretary of the Treasury, was called. Three days later, after a severe ordeal before the committee and in the press, he died of a heart attack.

On August 12, Wallace charged the Un-American Activities Committee with "political gangsterism and tyranny." Behind its patriotic smokescreen, he said, were "the international capitalists and the munitions makers whose profits go up and down precisely with the degree of international crisis that can be whipped up—with the amount of Red scare which can be engendered for the purpose of addling the brains of the American public." It was his most cogent statement on the connection between foreign policy and the witch-hunts.

A massive addling job was done by *Look* magazine in its August 3 issue. Bold headlines asked: "Could the Reds Seize Detroit?" Below were posed photographs of masked gunmen with knives. *Look* never quite answered its question, but in the course of its inquiry it assumed that it was only a matter of time before the Soviet Union would attack the United States. "A sickle," it said, "is being sharpened to plunge into the . . . industrial heart of America"—Detroit, with its "vulnerable factories," its lake frontage, and its proximity to Canada. Pictures and captions told the grim story of men with machine guns taking over the communications centers first . . . dead telephone girls on the floor . . . engineers and radio announcers shot to death through glass windows . . . a Communist terrorist stabbing a radio operator in the back . . . criminals released from prisons . . . children blown up on bridges . . . cars wrecked in the ensuing labor chaos. One reassuring note was permitted: "The Reds will find the Detroit police department tough foes."

In September, Attorney General Clark added several groups to his subversive list, and in October the Department of Justice instituted Smith Act proceedings against persons in Colorado, California, and Ohio. These were states where the Progressive Party was showing considerable strength. (Two months earlier, the *New York Sun* said the Smith Act indictments "are timed by accident or design to embarrass acutely Communist backers of Henry A. Wallace.") The press noted consistently through the campaign that the Progressive Party leadership was the "same kind" of persons who were the targets of the Un-American Activities Committee and the Attorney General. S. Burton Heath, syndicated columnist of the Newspaper Enterprise Association, said in an article in the *New Philadelphia* (Ohio) *Times* (the article was used as an editorial in at least six other Ohio papers): "At last the American people are waking up to the grave danger created by the Communist fifth column that masquerades as a political party in our midst." Curtis MacDougall observed in the third volume of *Gideon's Army:*

> Most editorial comment was of the same sort. Of rational analysis of the Progressive viewpoint there was little or none, except very early in the year, immediately following Wallace's announcement of his intention to run. After . . . Harry Truman's violent outbursts in March, Wallace's successful transcontinental speaking trips during the spring and, especially, the enthusiastic founding convention in July, the tone changed. The press as a whole even stopped admitting that personally Henry Wallace was a nice fellow, albeit naive, impractical, too idealistic, and a dupe. . . . After the spy hearings got under way, some editorial comment came close to charging outright and deliberate collaboration, between the Progressive Party and the Kremlin, against the best interests of the United States.

On November 4, 1948, two days after the election, Walter Lippmann wrote:

> It can be said with much justice that of all Roosevelt's electoral triumphs, this one in 1948 is the most impressive. For it was the Democratic Party as Roosevelt transformed it and developed it which won this surprising victory.

"This surprising victory" was the election of Harry Truman over Governor Thomas E. Dewey of New York, who had been declared a sure winner by the Gallup, Roper and Crossley polls and who had had the support of 78.8 per cent of the press. (Wallace was endorsed by one-tenth of one per cent of the press.) In the last weeks of the campaign, Truman had out-Wallaced Wallace to the extent that thousands who might have voted for Wallace, at the last moment in the privacy of the polling booth pulled the Democratic lever in the hope that Harry Truman meant what he had been saying. What he had been saying was that "the government of the United States firmly rejects the concept of war as a means of solving international differences." He had proposed sending Chief Justice Fred Vinson to Moscow to talk reconciliation with Stalin. He did not send Vinson and may never have intended to, but the effect was electric: he had presented himself to the public as a man in search of peace and reason. He had said, "We must continue to fight to assure full human rights and equal opportunity for all mankind. For my part I intend to keep moving toward this goal with every ounce of strength and determination I have." He had said, "I completely reject the idea that we should eliminate the New Deal. Instead, we should build upon it a better way of life." In a post-election analysis in the *National Guardian* newsweekly, November 8, 1948, Wallace wrote:

> We brought the issues of peace and the New Deal into the campaign. Without us, the American people in 1948, as in 1946, might have had to choose only between two brands of reaction. We forced these issues, hammered at them, mobilized behind them until at last—point by point—the backsliding party of Harry Truman was forced to return to the principles of Roosevelt in a belated attempt to regain the confidence of progressive America.

During the campaign, virtually none of the press had noted the similarity between the Wallace program and the publicly stated Truman program, nor the extent to which the backsliding Democratic Administration had already abandoned the New Deal. But after the election, the press was generous. The *Wall Street Journal* stated on November 8:

> It is said by political commentators that Mr. Wallace made a bad showing because he got few votes [slightly over 1 million, and half of those in New York State]. What they neglect is that Mr. Wallace succeeded in having his ideas adopted, except in the field of foreign affairs. . . . Mr. Truman began to suck the wind from the Wallace sails by coming out for more and more of the Wallace domestic program. Now these promises are in Mr. Truman's platform and the men who see eye to eye with Mr. Wallace on domestic, economic, and social questions are among those who can rightfully claim a share of the credit for Mr. Truman's victory. We have not before us any modified New Deal. What we have is the New Deal in its extreme form. . . .

The falseness of the *Journal's* New Deal alarm soon became apparent, but the description of the Truman strategy was accurate.

The inaccuracy of the newspaper predictions about the election generally resulted in some hilarious and some costly episodes afterwards. A Dewey victory had seemed assured by the time many persons (including editors, publishers, and commentators) had gone to bed. A big election night party had been planned at the home of Mrs. Ogden Reid, publisher of the *New York Herald Tribune,* to celebrate Dewey's election. *Life* magazine was going to press with a cover picture of Dewey. *Kiplinger's Weekly* had 32 pages on what business might expect from President Dewey (the prospect was bountiful). The brothers Alsop were busily advising President-elect Dewey on the reorganization of his State Department. (The Alsops later wrote testily, in *The Reporter's Trade:*

"We have learned by harsh experience that the behavior of the American voters at any given moment in history is a great deal harder to predict than the behavior of the tides of history. We have made many mistakes—all newspapermen do. . . .") Rube Goldberg had drawn an inspiring cartoon for the *New York Sun* celebrating the Republican victory. The Cleveland edition of the *Chicago Tribune* was on the baggage cars announcing a Dewey victory. Drew Pearson was printing the list of guests for the Dewey Inaugural. The *Journal of Commerce* Washington edition (it was published in New York) was on the trucks with this headline: DEWEY VICTORY SEEN AS MANDATE OF A NEW ERA.

Mrs. Reid's party was a dismal affair. It cost Henry Luce $500,000 to scrap the cover of *Life*. The Alsops, breathing hard on a fast track, had no emergency column to substitute for their advice to the never-never President. *Kiplinger,* the *Chicago Tribune* front page and the *Journal of Commerce* for November 3, 1948, became collector's items. The *Sun*'s cartoon appeared as a large white space except for three words in 14-point capital letters: RUBE GOLDBERG REGRETS.

Don Hollenbeck, in his radio program "CBS Views the Press," took as his post-election text to describe the press performance a quotation from the Book of Job: "Is there iniquity in my tongue? Cannot my taste discern perverse things? . . . Teach me and I will hold my tongue; and cause me to understand wherein I have erred. . . ."

But the weeks after the election made it clear that it would take more than a heavenly discourse to bring discernment to the editorial sanctuaries. *Editor & Publisher* explained it this way: Since the United States does not have a national press, the newspapers wield their influence locally. Since Presidents are elected by the total vote of the states instead of by a national vote, the newspapers, after all, were accurate locally. "From these comparisons," said *Editor & Publisher,* "it may seem that any criticism of the daily newspapers on a national basis because of the elections is unfounded." Hollenbeck replied:

This would seem to establish a new high in casuistry, and it might seem comic except that it reflects all too clearly the fact that while newspapers in the country may individually confess themselves to having been made monkeys of by the voters, the basic thinking of American journalism hasn't changed much.

In the *New York Times,* James Reston wrote a letter to his editor:

The great intangible of this election was the political thinking of the Roosevelt era on the nation . . . and we did not give enough weight to it. Consequently, we were wrong, not only about the election, but, what's worse, on the whole political direction of our time.

The political direction was an increasing unrest among the electorate over the prospect of economic distress and the possibility of a new war so soon after the end of World War II. Harry Truman knew this and deliberately altered his campaign to manipulate and mislead public opinion. The press either did not know the extent of the unrest, or did not want to report it. In my opinion, the newspapers did know—and misrepresented the facts. The press was no longer in the business of reporting or reflecting public opinion. It was seeking to *become* public opinion by means of the self-fulfilling prophecy: If you said something often enough, people would come to accept it and it would happen. When this practice is followed by adversaries, we call it brainwashing.

# 4. The Frost on the Pumpkin

Having established its claim to the Roosevelt mantle, the Truman Administration settled down in earnest to tear it apart. With the Republicans it launched a bipartisan campaign to identify dissent from the Cold War with treason. The spy scares with their interminable headlines whistled down the winter winds. The Pumpkin Papers, unearthed on the farm of Whittaker Chambers in Westminster, Maryland, had all the earmarks of a Halloween prank, but the motives were sinister, as the Alger Hiss case would show.

A few days before Christmas 1948, Lawrence Duggan, director of the Institute of International Education and former chief of the Division of Latin American Republics of the State Department, died in a fall from the sixteenth floor of a New York office building. He had been questioned a few days earlier by the FBI in the Hiss-Chambers case. Immediately after his death, Representative Karl E. Mundt of South Dakota, whose name later became part of the hyphened Mundt-Nixon bill, called in reporters to tell them that Duggan had been named by Isaac Don Levine, a professional anti-Communist journalist, as a transmitter to Chambers of secret official documents for the Soviet Union. When a reporter asked whether there were other names on the transmission-belt list, Mundt replied, "We'll give them out as they jump out of windows."

Apparently chagrined that his temporarily separated Siamese twin had captured a headline on his own, Representative Richard M. Nixon, Republican of California, a few days later called in the press himself. The *New York Times* printed this headline on the story of the news conference: "DUGGAN IS CLEARED BY NIXON OF SPYING." Duggan had never been charged with espionage by the House Committee on Un-American

Activities, of which both Mundt and Nixon were members. He had never appeared before a jury or before the Committee. Yet he was "cleared" in a newspaper headline of an act of which he had never been accused. The accusation had been made, however, by inference, in newspaper headlines and stories; and his suicide—as his death was decreed—in a climate of hysteria may well have fixed his "guilt" forever in the public mind. It took incredible perseverance for a person like Alger Hiss to maintain his balance and at least outer calm as newspaper editors sent photographers into the subways to photograph him and reporters to park outside his door to record the comings and goings of his family.

Despite the hysteria, there were many concerned Americans who persisted in opposing the Truman Doctrine and the Atlantic Pact as a threat to world peace and sought to maintain a line of communication with their professional colleagues in the Soviet Union and Eastern Europe. Their goal was to influence public opinion away from Washington's Cold War policy by demonstrating that there was no threat from the socialist world. Toward this end the National Council of the Arts, Sciences, and Professions, a nationwide organization of progressive-minded intellectuals and artists, issued a call for a Cultural and Scientific Conference for World Peace in New York, March 25-27, 1949. In its call to American intellectuals, the Council, under the chairmanship of Professor Harlow Shapley, the Harvard astronomer, said:

> Your work of the past, present, and future is not going to be worth anything at all if the present ominous trends here and abroad lead us into a third world war. The scale of preparation for war (commonly called defense) is tremendous. The next world conflict . . . would end our way of life, whether we seem to win, lose or draw. . . . We do not think the question worthy of debate as to whether or not capitalism and socialism CAN exist together. Both DO exist. The only question worth discussing is how to restore the mutual acceptance of that fact, which brought victory in World War II, and which alone can avert World War III.

The call was issued February 21. Shapley announced at the same time that the Soviet government had agreed to the attendance of Dmitri Shostakovitch, the composer, and several leading Soviet artists and scientists. That was news, and for one day—and one day alone—the press and the wire services generally treated the story respectfully, speculating with appropriate curiosity on what the State Department would do about visas. From that point on, the press generously cooperated on three levels—governmental, intellectual, and hysterical—to fasten the Red label on the conference and picture it as a foreign plot to subvert the American way of life. As the State Department formulated its visa approach, inspired stories from Washington gave the journalistic signals. By March 10, subscribers to the service of the Newspaper Enterprise Association were presented with a feature story which began: "The most ambitious intellectual front in the history of Communist promotion is scheduled this month for the symbol of American wealth and luxury, the Waldorf-Astoria." Scores of papers headlined that story: "U.S. 'PINK COMINFORM' WILL HUDDLE IN LUXURY." A few days later, Lyle C. Wilson, Washington bureau chief of the United Press, characterized the meeting—two weeks in advance—as "the let's-all-love-Russia clambake."

The State Department finally approved the entry of 22 delegates from Communist countries and refused admittance to several distinguished non-Communist Western European guests simply by calling them Communists. This tactic was employed to ensure that the conference in the public mind would be "Communist-inspired," since almost all the foreign guests would be from Communist countries. The hysteria-wing of the three-pronged attack then came in on cue. The House Un-American Activities Committee announced that the conference would be under "constant surveillance," and Representative Donald L. Jackson, a California Republican, told the House that "Shostakovich has the same right to attend a cultural conference as a rattlesnake has to be at the altar of a church."

Hearst's *New York Journal-American* reported that 100,000 "loyal Americans" would picket the conference; a maximum of 2,000 showed up, some of them inviting Shostakovich to "jump out the window." A counter-conference of Americans for Intellectual Freedom was organized by the State Department, and its publicity office issued a stream of press releases reporting that sponsors of the ASP conference were withdrawing in droves; that at least two Soviet delegates were "secret police agents"; that conference expenses were being paid by the Cominform; that American music and literary agents had set up "a reign of terror" among writers and musicians forcing them to support the conference. All the unsubstantiated charges in the releases were amply reproduced in the newspapers. Where the reports were susceptible of refutation, the news was ignored or buried. Actually, only 12 of the 550 sponsors withdrew.

Despite the counter-pressures, 2,800 persons registered as delegates from 21 states and 83 universities and technical institutes; 8,000 persons attended the various panels, and 20,000 persons came to the final rally at Madison Square Garden. It was clear that many participants did not espouse the single-guilt theory that any one nation was wholly responsible for the threat to world peace. Dr. Shapley declared in his opening statement that the Soviet Union and the United States were "so obsessed by pointing out each other's shortcomings that they ignore their own." This did not fit in with the prevailing press theme that the conference would be "Moscow-dominated," so a temporary shift in line was instituted and the *New York Sun* headlined the report on the Shapley speech: "SHAPLEY ARRAIGNS RUSSIA." At Madison Square Garden, a Hearst cameraman kept his camera aimed at the audience (it was common practice for the FBI to photograph individuals and crowds at such meetings) and one incensed spectator tried to grab the camera. The *Journal-American* story on the incident began: "Inflamed by anti-American speeches made by Soviet delegates and other foreign Reds . . . about 30 yelling men leaped upon photographers . . ." The *Daily Mirror* (also Hearst) said editorially of the foreign guests: "Throw the bums out." The *World-Telegram* said "Phooey" on culture. The *Herald Tribune* gave first place in its Sunday edition to the rival conference, sparsely attended, at which former Communists vied with former residents of Communist countries in consigning the Soviet Union to the outer reaches of hell.

The National Council of the ASP, after examining the press coverage of the event, decided to publish in book form a report of the conference entitled *Speaking of Peace.* It asked a "well-known New York newspaper reporter" to review the thousands of newspaper clippings on the conference in order to write a prologue to the book describing the atmosphere in which the conference was held. In an italicized precede to the newspaperman's prologue, the editor of the book said: "A sad but apt commentary on the temper of the times is [the reporter's] prudent request for anonymity as a means of avoiding friction with his employer." These were the reporter's conclusions:

The gathering . . . in all probability received more newspaper space than any recent meeting held in the United States, save for the national political conventions. This does not mean, however, that the American people were thoroughly and precisely informed of what was said. . . . On the contrary, they were misinformed—partly by chance, but mostly by cool editorial calculation—with an expansiveness and unrestraint surprising to even the most sophisticated students of the fine art of influencing the public. Save for a very few newspapers—notably the *New York Times* and the *Chicago Daily News*—the American press either actively participated in, or passively cooperated with, the campaign to discredit and harass the conference, to smear the delegates and guests. Thousands attended, and more thousands were turned away for lack of space. . . . Yet what happened *at* the conference is an untold story, for, unfortunately, that was not considered news. Except for the *Times* and the *News,* no newspaper even attempted to report fairly what the peace conferees had to say, much of it critical of communism and of Soviet policies, much more of it in a search for a path to peace and in an attempt to give the world a nudge along it.

This was the fate of the first convocation to advance the cause of peace since the end of World War II. Here was an opportunity for the press of America to extend the dialogue for sanity throughout the country. Instead it chose to strangle the exchange. Recalling Cyrus Sulzberger's comment in 1946 in the *New York Times* that the first postwar crises had been whipped up to reverse "the momentum of pro-Soviet feelings worked up during the war," it was evident in 1949 that the whippers were crowding one another in the newsrooms of America.

On April 11, two weeks after the Waldorf conference, Drew Pearson in his weekly radio broadcast disclosed an event which had taken place in Hobe Sound, Florida, at the end of March and had gone unreported, although it was known to many in Washington. In the middle of the night, after a fire siren had sounded, a man was apprehended running through the streets screaming: "The Red Army has landed!" It was Secretary of Defense James V. Forrestal. He was flown to the Naval Hospital in Bethesda, Maryland. On May 22, he eluded attendants and jumped through a screened window to his death. In his book *High Treason,* published in 1950, Albert E. Kahn wrote:

> The suicide of Forrestal epitomized the anti-Red hysteria which gripped the land like some contagious psychosis at the time of his death. . . . effected by a prodigious *tour de force* of propaganda. Every conceivable promotional device and propaganda technique [was] galvanized into an intense and incessant anti-Communist campaign which permeate every phase of the nation's life.

Sometimes the galvanizing was accomplished by negation or omission, as was the case involving the *New York Times* correspondent in Turkey, Aslan K. Humbaraci. On May 2, 1949, he resigned in a letter to his editor. In seeking to report factual news about United States military aid to Turkey under the Truman Doctrine, he wrote, he had "met with systematic hostility and discrimination by the ruling circles in my country, by officials of the United States Embassy and especially of the United States Military Mission." Difficult as that was to circumvent, his reporting in the *Times* itself, "when it was not completely suppressed, was cut, rewritten, buried somewhere in the back pages or distorted, if it did not happen to fit in with State Department policy." In his letter to managing editor Edwin L. James, Humbaraci said:

The suppression of civil liberties, the brutal treatment of peasants by a ruthless gendarmerie, the police terror in the towns, the revolt of the peasants in remote Anatolian villages, the arrest and imprisonment and torturing of political prisoners, the persecution of intellectuals, the scandalous abuse by officials, and the official support extended to the extreme right wing have found no place in the columns of the *New York Times*. Further, I cannot remember any anti-Russian news from any sources in Turkey that has not been published in the *Times*—especially news depicting Russia as Turkey's enemy and the menace to Turkey's existence.

By midsummer 1949, the nation's newspapers, magazines and military journals had taken on the appearance of Pentagon map rooms with their graphic descriptions and forecasts of the strategy and tactics of atomic warfare against the Soviet Union. On July 25, the North Atlantic Treaty Organization documents were signed and the *New York Daily News* commented: "Let's stow the baloney and double-talk and admit there is a treaty creating a military alliance which contemplates war on Soviet Russia." Most American newspapers had already passed the contemplative stage and had declared war on the Soviet Union, as their handling of sensitive domestic news demonstrated. The outcome of the first trial of Alger Hiss and its aftermath were indicative of their treatment of spy scare stories.

On July 18, a jury had failed to reach a verdict in the first Hiss trial on perjury charges and was dismissed. Several newspapers expressed their indignation over the failure of the jury to convict, and most of the newspapers in New York went after the Federal District trial judge, Samuel H. Kaufman. They reported that some bar associations had been opposed to his appointment to the Federal bench in the first place, and that his conduct of the trial had proved the validity of the misgivings. They seized on a report that the jury foreman had expressed a pretrial opinion of Hiss's innocence. In fact the judge had offered to dismiss the foreman (an Army reserve officer and an executive of the General Motors Acceptance Corporation) on a motion from the government, but the government had refused to make the request. The foreman denied he had ever discussed the case outside the jury room. Representative Nixon charged that Kaufman's "prejudice . . . against the prosecution" had been "obvious and apparent," and the charge was page one news for several days. Demands for Congressional investigations of Kaufman served to prolong the publicity.

The *Herald Tribune* was zealous in tracking down jurors to buttress the attacks on the judge. Interestingly, hardly any newspapers raised the possibility of perjury charges against Whittaker Chambers, chief witness for the prosecution, although seven instances of his perjury had been established at the trial.

The press barrage after the first trial was calculated to prevent an acquittal or a hung jury at the second trial. It would take a brave juror to withstand the public abuse and the private pressure (by crank mail and telephoned threats, for example) to which jurors at the first trial had been subjected. Their names and addresses had been supplied by the *New York Journal-American*.

In motions preceding the second trial in October, the defense presented 40 newspaper articles which it said tended to create bias among readers and asked that the trial be shifted to Vermont. The Circuit Court of Appeals denied the petition, saying that the people of Vermont "get all the news they get in any part of the United States." While this was a reasonably accurate estimate of the quality of news presentation in the American press, it was pertinent that there were fewer papers in Vermont than in New York to contribute to the quantity of prejudice against Hiss. Further, jurors in Vermont might be less likely to be intimidated by mailed threats and telephoned abuse.

The defense found it difficult, in preparing for the second trial in January 1950, to persuade crucial witnesses to appear. The press campaign after the first trial and the assiduous FBI with its visits to prospective witnesses had intervened.

Something else had intervened to add to the hysteria of the times. It was President Truman's dramatic announcement in September 1949 that the Soviet Union had detonated an atomic device. Moving events a step further, *Life* magazine on October 10 published an article on atomic warfare and introduced it with the question: "Can Russia Deliver the Bomb?" Accompanying the article was a photograph of the damage caused by the explosion of a bomb in Wall Street on September 16, 1920, opposite the building housing J. P. Morgan & Co., which had killed 30 persons and injured hundreds more. No one had ever been arrested for the crime, and no motivation had been discovered—although radicals were blamed by guesswork. But the *Life* caption on October 10, 1949, attributed the guilt. It read: "In 1920 Reds Exploded Bomb in Wall Street, Killed 30, Wounded Hundreds."

Few readers would recall the incident, and fewer still would check the accuracy of the caption. But the editors knew the caption was false and chose to print it to bridge the 29-year gap from dynamite bomb to atomic bomb. The purpose was served, as it had been at the time of the Palmer raids: Reds—domestic or foreign—always use bombs against unoffending Americans. If an ordinary Red bomb in 1920 could kill 30, a refined Red atomic bomb in 1949 could kill 3,000,000.

In the public mind, thanks to the efforts of the press, Alger Hiss was marked as a man who had passed State Department documents to Whittaker Chambers for transmission to the Soviet Union. He was convicted in January 1950 and sentenced to five years in prison—five years in which the political life of the United States was shaped as much by his conviction as by any other event except one. For also rooted in the public mind, thanks once again to the press, was a firm conviction that the Russians could not master the technique of atomic fission without assistance from spies in the United States. Six months after Hiss's conviction, Julius and Ethel Rosenberg were arrested on a charge of conspiracy to commit espionage—that is, of having conspired with others in 1944 to transmit to the Soviet Union secret information concerning atomic fission.

Though there was no link between the Hiss case and the Rosenberg case, the press of the United States did its utmost to further the great mid-century myth of the international Communist conspiracy and to create in the public mind the impression that all who sought to counter this myth were guilty of treason, or at least potential treason.

From the day Julius Rosenberg was arrested, three weeks after the outbreak of the Korean war, through the trial in March 1951 of the Rosenbergs and Morton Sobell (who served 19 years of a 30-year sentence as a co-conspirator) and the death sentence on April 5, 1951, through the execution of the Rosenbergs on June 19, 1953—the cry was treason. Yet not one of the three had been indicted, tried, or convicted for treason, for which an overt act must be charged and proved. This false impression was fostered in inflamed headlines, news stories, columns, and editorials.

"Judge Kaufman . . . apparently hopes to shock other would-be traitors," said a *Christian Science Monitor* editorial on April 7, 1951. "This punishment, the severest ever applied for treason by a civil court in America, may act to deter imitators." A Gallup poll in January 1953 found a majority in favor of death for traitors: "The issue of the death penalty for treasonable offenses has stirred up considerable interest throughout the country because of the conviction of Ethel and Julius Rosenberg as wartime spies." In the *New York World-Telegram* of June 17, 1953, syndicated Scripps-Howard columnist Robert C. Ruark wrote: "I have no way of knowing, as I write this, whether they'll pull the switch on the Rosenbergs on June 18, but in the interest of deterring further experiments in treason, I certainly hope so."

The *Columbia Law Review* described the trial as "the outstanding 'political' trial of this generation," although it did not explain the doubt indicated by quotation marks for the word "political." To the Hearst press, the politics were clear. An editorial in the chain's newspapers maintained:

The importance of the trial cannot be minimized. Its findings disclosed in shuddering detail the Red cancer in the American body politic—a cancer which the government is now forced to obliterate in self-defense. The sentences indicate the scalpel which prosecutors can be expected to use in that operation.

The incredibility of these charges was easily evident to anyone who read the massive record of the trial. But the Rosenbergs' attorney, Emanuel Bloch, sought vainly to persuade a single editor of a daily newspaper that the effort should be undertaken—or that there was any question whether justice had been served. The search led finally to the *National Guardian*. Cedric Belfrage was editor at the time, I was executive editor, and John T. McManus general manager. We worked in harmony as a managerial team, and it was a rare policy decision that was not unanimous.

I received a call one day in the early summer of 1951 from a friend on the staff of the Hearst *New York Mirror*. He wanted me to meet someone involved in an important political trial. The someone turned out to be Bloch, prowling the city like the Ancient Mariner, and he stopped me entirely as he related his efforts to prepare the defense for his clients and his experiences with the communications media.

When Bloch finished, the *Mirror* man proposed that I help him in an organized effort to persuade various colleagues on the New York daily press that the Rosenbergs did not have a fair trial and that the case had ominous political significance. The effort would be wasted, I said. While I was sure we could bring the point home to some, the atmosphere of fear and intimidation was so prevalent that they would not dare to take the initiative, and if they did, they would meet an editorial stone wall. The only hope was in a publication which was neither bending to, nor manufacturing, hysteria.

I returned to my office and asked Belfrage and McManus to hear the story. There was silence until Belfrage said: "How do we start?" Without hesitation, we had determined to try to set out the facts in a case which we saw as a frame-up of three innocent persons—a case which could stifle dissent in our country for years to come. We sensed—if we did not know—that we would be exposing ourselves and the *National Guardian* to reprisals which could land us in jail and kill our publication. But both as journalists and as political radicals, we believed it had to be done. The first assignment was given to a special reporter, William A. Reuben, with several weeks' time to read and analyze the trial record and interview as many persons involved in the case as possible.

In August 1951, the first article in a series by Reuben appeared under the headline: "Is This the Dreyfus Case of Cold War America?" That was the opening gun in a two-year campaign which reverberated around the world. Out of it emerged a Committee to Secure Justice in the Rosenberg Case which came to include scores of distinguished persons in the sciences, the arts, and religion. Yet despite constant pressure from the committee and from individual petitioners, the press, holding firm with the Executive and Judicial branches of the government, remained unbreachable.

The role of the New York press deserves special condemnation. The editor of the *Herald Tribune* refused to see a delegation from the Rosenberg Committee. The paper had adequate information on the case, he said. The *Herald Tribune,* along with every other newspaper in New York, consistently ignored committee press releases reporting pleas for clemency from notable figures in every part of the world. There was for weeks an almost complete blackout on the news that Pope Pius XII had made three intercessions in the case. Even the Catholic press proscribed the Pope.

The *New York Times* refused all advertising on the case. Its radio station WQXR rejected a committee request for paid spot announcements. The *Times*'s advertising censors met with a delegation of prominent persons from the committee, but the censors did not budge. Charles Merz, editor of the editorial page, refused even to meet with the delegation.

When there seemed a faint hope for clemency or judicial review, a new burst of hysterical articles appeared in the *New York Post* and the *World-Telegram.* On June 19, 1952, one year to the day before the execution of the Rosenbergs, Max Lerner reported in his *Post* column about a clemency meeting in the Flatbush section of Brooklyn:

> I looked around the room, and what I saw were vultures and victims. The vultures were the half-pint commissars, exploiting the emotions of unsuspecting Jews. The victims were the group of lower middle-class men and women, huddled together in their anxiety. The climax of the evening was a speech by a little orthodox rabbi, Mayer Sharff of Williamsburg. He wore a skull cap and a long black coat with a prayer shawl under it and a magnificent growth of beard. He was the prize catch of the cynical men who ran the meeting. . . . Why did he let himself be used by them?

Rabbi Sharff was available for a reply to the question, but Lerner never put it to him. It served better as a prize piece of rhetoric by a cynical columnist for an unsuspecting readership. A year later, on June

21, 1953, with the Rosenbergs comfortably dead for 48 hours, Lerner wondered "whether the death sentence was either necessary or wise." The chief beneficiaries, he said, were "the men in the Kremlin who must be breathing more freely today because Julius and Ethel Rosenberg will be forever silent."

In his gossip column in the *Post* and several score papers around the country, Leonard Lyons published inspired warnings to Rosenberg sympathizers that their contributions to the defense were being noted and their activities scrutinized. He implied that the deeply moving Death House Letters which the Rosenbergs had written almost daily to each other had been ghost-written. (In fact, the *National Guardian* had photostats of the original letters.) And no ghost was necessary to demonstrate the role of the press to the Rosenbergs. On December 7, 1952, Julius wrote to Ethel: "I am amazed at the fabulous newspaper campaign organized against us." And five days later: "It is indeed a tragedy how the lords of the press can mold public opinion by printing . . . blatant falsehoods. The pressure campaign is in high gear and many weak people will be scared off. . . . There is a new whipping boy in our land, 'the Rosenbergs,' and all 'respectable people' will have to cleanse themselves by throwing stones at us."

In the last weeks of the Rosenbergs' lives, the worldwide clamor against the death sentence became so fervent (in France virtually every newspaper editorially was urging clemency) that the news could no longer be suppressed in the press of the United States. Thus the news of Pope Pius's intervention became public, even though the *Times* did a little turkey trot on two succeeding days with the following headlines:

POPE MADE APPEAL TO AID ROSENBERGS
POPE MADE NO PLEA TO AID ROSENBERGS

In the final days before the execution, news flooded into the newspapers. Top-name reporters were assigned to the story, and there were press vigils at Sing Sing and in Washington when it became known that an open telephone line from Sing Sing had been installed in the White House for a last-minute "confession" by the Rosenbergs—in return for which their sentence would be commuted to life imprisonment.

The quality of the coverage changed in the stories by the working press, though not in the columns and editorial pages, where the vindictiveness continued and threats and snarls greeted any move toward clemency or judicial review. (Contrary to the belief that has persisted to this day, the case was never reviewed by the Supreme Court.) But in

Union Square, reporters wept as Mrs. Sophie Rosenberg pleaded for the life of her son and daughter-in-law.

Shortly after 8 P.M. on Friday, June 19, 1953, Ethel and Julius Rosenberg were put to death in the electric chair. A thoughtful government had hurried to complete its business before sundown that Friday so as not to desecrate the Jewish sabbath. Outside the White House, when the news came, the pickets seeking clemency lowered their signs. Cheers arose from hecklers across the street, and cars sounded their horns in approval of the government's action. The pickets raised their heads and once more held aloft the signs reading "Mercy."

The details of the execution filled columns in the newspapers of June 20. Nothing was spared, but between the lines there was a note of indecision, as though the reporters who had written the stories and the men who had edited them were experiencing their first qualms. The qualms, however, were not present in the editorial sanctum of the *New York Herald Tribune* that Friday night. The lead editorial in the newspaper on June 20 said:

> Last evening Julius and Ethel Rosenberg died in the electric chair. . . . They were tried in open court by a jury of their peers and found guilty. . . . Meanwhile every facility for petitioning for clemency was granted to the supporters of the defendants. They had access to the press . . .

It would take years for the truth of Dr. W.E.B. Du Bois's brief and profound elegy to become apparent. As the bodies of Ethel and Julius Rosenberg were being lowered into their graves, he said, "These people were killed because they would not lie." That was all he said.

Emanuel Bloch, the Rosenbergs' attorney, added some bitter truths in an article in the *National Guardian* of June 29, 1953:

> I remember very well those first grim days of March 1951, following the trial and sentence, when every avenue of information and publicity suddenly closed. With the slamming of the door of the Death House on the Rosenbergs, a conspiracy of silence settled on the press. Our great newspapers which, during the trial, had seized eagerly upon every propaganda release of the prosecution, closed their pages to all news about the victims. From the government's point of view, and from the point of view of its ally, the press, the Rosenbergs were as good as dead. The next news item would be the announcement of their execution.
>
> To us of the defense this was a desperate situation indeed. The Rosenbergs and their family had no money—no money at all—to pay even the out-of-pocket expenses of the appeal. If the press was closed to us, what chance did we have of raising through public subscription the thousands of dollars needed?
>
> The deadly conspiracy to forget the Rosenbergs was shattered by the *National Guardian*. [Its editors] saw the meaning of this attack upon an obscure engineer

and his wife. The Rosenberg Case, which had died in all the great papers, came alive in the *National Guardian*. To the *Guardian* is due the credit of first showing to the world what the world now recognizes as a barefaced, political frame-up.

If the world recognized it, Bloch's own country was not a part of that world—as he was to find out in the months after the execution. Continuing his efforts to seek vindication for the Rosenbergs and a new trial for Morton Sobell, his fatigue increased. In January 1954 the Bar Association of the City of New York petitioned the Appellate Division of the New York State Court to take action against Bloch for his characterization, at the funeral of the Rosenbergs, of the trial and execution as an "act of cold, deliberate murder." On January 30, 1954, Bloch was found dead in his apartment in Manhattan. The death was attributed to a heart attack. He was 52.

Messages of condolence came to New York from all parts of the world. In Paris hundreds of lawyers gathered in their robes to lay a wreath in Bloch's memory at the memorial to the dead in the Palais de Justice. Editorials of tribute appeared in the press of Western Europe. In the press of the United States there was silence—as eloquent as had been the silence on the open line from the Death House to the White House.

The death of Emanuel Bloch came four years after the arrest of the Rosenbergs in 1950—a year which was a signal one in many ways. That year Alger Hiss went to prison, and Richard Nixon went to the Senate. Whittaker Chambers was enshrined as a saint who by his "confession" had ennobled the profession of lying in the national interest. The press vigilantly sought out new threats to the American way of life—in addition to Hiss and the Rosenbergs—and it found them in profusion.

It found also a splendid new champion in the struggle against the "international Communist conspiracy." He was Senator Joseph R. McCarthy of Wisconsin.

# 5. The Making of Joe McCarthy

The conviction of Alger Hiss was the touchstone for the meteoric career of Senator Joe McCarthy as the scourge of Communism. In the political maneuvering of a midterm election year—1950—the Truman Democrats, the Dixiecrats, and the Republicans vied with one another to parade before a bewitched electorate the most accomplished record of anti-Communism. Haunting the capital was the specter of the Soviet bomb; but if the bomb had a sobering effect on the trigger-happy executives, there was no public evidence of this state. Rather, since it was accepted as gospel that the primitive Russians could not have developed the bomb by themselves, the major question in Washington was "Who gave the bomb to Russia?"

Into the spotlight stepped Joe McCarthy, holding in his hand "a list of 205 . . . a list of names that were made known to the Secretary of State as being members of the Communist Party and who nevertheless are still working and shaping policy in the State Department." This was February 9, 1950, in Wheeling, West Virginia. The next day, in Denver, the 205 had been converted from Communists to bad security risks. A day later, in Salt Lake City, McCarthy had reconverted the risks to card-carrying Communists but had reduced the number to 57. McCarthy made banner headlines that second week of February 1950, and he remained on page one almost without fail for more than four years.

The major concern with the discussion of McCarthy here is not to determine what made Joe run, but how Joe was able to run. How was he able to act and accuse with such license and publicity?

McCarthyism was neither a new nor an unusual phenomenon. It was an extension and public exaggeration of the prevailing policy of anti-

Communism which did not warrant a new name. The ground had been thoroughly prepared for McCarthy since the end of World War II and the emergence of the Soviet Union as a great power which offered an alternative to capitalism. Communism had been firmly established in the American mind as a dirty word describing an evil way of life. The propagation of this premise had ebbed and flowed and been increased to flood tide whenever established power wished to stifle domestic opposition. The year 1950 was a time for flood. In their book *The Reporter's Trade* (Reynal and Co., 1958), columnists Joseph and Stewart Alsop wrote:

> No purely political issue seemed to us bigger or more burning in the whole period of our work together [than McCarthyism]. But to call it a domestic issue is to misconstrue the real nature of McCarthyism. Like almost all the other great excitements of the postwar years—the Alger Hiss trials, the flaming B-36 row, the brief but savage rumpus over the firing of General MacArthur—McCarthyism was a by-product of the Cold War. More specifically, McCarthy was a by-product of the time when the Cold War became hot—the time of the fighting in Korea. Before the summer of 1950, McCarthy was essentially a fringe politician. McCarthyism was an ugly phenomenon of which the political reporter had to take account, but no more than that. It was only after the Korean war began that McCarthy became the decisive, dominating political force which he remained for four sordid, shameful years.

McCarthyism was not a by-product of the Cold War: it was an instrument of the Cold War. It is more than a misconception to group McCarthyism with the Hiss trials and the MacArthur incident. Hiss was not a by-product of the Cold War: he was a victim who became a slogan. Nor was MacArthur a by-product: he was a military arm of the Cold War which reached out too recklessly for power and got lopped off. In the last analysis, this was McCarthy's fate also. He served at the pleasure of the master—the established power—and when he overstepped his mark and sought to become a determinant in the master class, he was destroyed. McCarthy was as necessary to the advancement of the Cold War as Attorney General Palmer and his crusaders were to the anti-Bolshevik campaign after World War I. His witch-hunt facilitated the dismantling of the wartime alliance with the Soviet Union, and the advancement of the Truman Doctrine.

McCarthy was not groomed by the masters of power for his role as was, say, General Eisenhower. Eisenhower arrived at the White House by way of the presidency of Columbia University which had civilianized him. But McCarthy was spotted as a useful instrument of the Cold War by a dependable scout, Monsignor Edmund Walsh, dean of the Georgetown University Foreign Service School—a training ground and virtually an adjunct of the State Department. Jack Anderson and Ronald W. May, in their book *McCarthy, the Man, the Senator, the "Ism"* (Beacon, 1952), described a meeting on January 7, 1950, a month before Wheeling, and six months before the Korean war began, during which McCarthy expressed to Walsh his concern over his flagging political fortunes and his need for an issue in the 1952 campaign, when he would come up for re-election. "How about Communism as an issue?" Walsh is quoted as saying. There was no question of Walsh's devotion to the State Department's Cold War policy, and there was little doubt of his perspicacity in selecting so cynical an agent of virtue and godliness as McCarthy. If Walsh was unable to foresee the extent to which McCarthy would go to remain in the headlines and that he would ultimately prove a hindrance to the Cold War, others were not so shortsighted. Among those others were the editors of newspapers which came under McCarthy's fire as unlikely transmission belts for "the international Communist conspiracy." On May 22, 1950, following McCarthy's assaults on Owen Lattimore and John Paton Davies for their role in shaping American policy in the Far East, the *Washington Post* said in an editorial:

For weeks the capital has been seized and convulsed by a terror . . . a roaring bitterness, the ranging of Americans against Americans, the assault on freedom of inquiry, the intolerance of opposition.

The editorial did not underestimate "the cancerous evil of totalitarianism" which directed the Soviet Union and confronted the United States with "a secret conspiratorial force in our midst." But, it said, if the burden of proof were placed on the accused, it would be "burning down the house of the American way of life in order to get the rats in it." It feared that McCarthy and the lesser witch-hunters were draining the strength of the winter soldiers of the Cold War. It was as "foolish to reckon the witch-hunters the true foes of Communism as to reckon lynch mobs as the true foes of the sex maniacs." The effect would be to "drive out of government the very brains which alone can give us victory in the Cold War." The pairing of Communists and sex maniacs was enlightening of the editorial mind but not of the objective situation. The witch-hunters were no more after Communists than the lynch mobs were after sex maniacs. The real goal was to preserve the status quo against demands for political and economic change by persons who were beginning to insist on social justice.

The *Washington Post* recorded, but did not view with alarm, more dignified but equally terrifying performances a month earlier. At the annual meeting of the American Society of Newspaper Editors in Washington April 23, Secretary of State Acheson described Russian Communism as a threat to the existence of our government. Only a strong United States, he said, stood "between the Kremlin and dominion over the entire world." Five days later, former President Herbert Hoover made a rare descent from his suite in the Waldorf Towers in New York to the ballroom below. There, before the convention of the American Newspaper Publishers Association, he asked for the expulsion of the Communist nations from the United Nations and the formation of "a new united front of those who disavow Communism." The *Herald Tribune* April 29 said the speech was greeted with a "thunderous, almost impassioned ovation."

It is clear that McCarthy's foreign policy—his entire career from 1950 on was based on foreign policy and its making—differed hardly at all from Acheson's or Hoover's. McCarthy's record showed remarkable agreement with the three most powerful lobbies in Washington, all of which had easy access to the State Department: (1) the German lobby, which sought a strong industrialized and militarized Western Germany; (2) the China lobby, one of whose dominant figures was Alfred M. Kohlberg, a wealthy dealer in Chinese curios, among which the prize piece was Chiang Kai-shek; (3) the Catholic Church lobby, for which Communism was the secular devil who threatened its worldwide human and material holdings. What, then, accounted for McCarthy's remarkable rise in an area in which there was so little disagreement among so many practitioners? In their book on McCarthy, Anderson and May wrote:

> You can discount [McCarthy's] personal ambition: that may have started the McCarthy flywheel, but it was the press that kept the wheel turning. You can discount his native cunning; had it not been for the Fourth Estate he'd have used this talent in a vacuum. Any way you slice it, it adds up to the same thing: If Joe McCarthy is a political monster, then the press has been his Dr. Frankenstein.

The buildup, said Anderson and May, began in Wisconsin's north country, where the "hustling young circuit judge" got a favorable press. As a Marine, he circulated his own version of the Rodgers-Hammerstein *South Pacific,* with himself as the male lead, and "watched it pop out like the measles in one back-country paper after another." This was the myth of "Tail-Gunner Joe," the valiant fighter of the South Pacific theater in World War II, and the wounds that allegedly forced him out of the service. Actually, McCarthy quit the Pacific area in 1944 to enter the far more profitable political wars of Wisconsin. His "wounded leg," which appeared in most stories as a combat wound, was the result of a non-

combat piece of horseplay, magnified out of all proportion. When Mc-
Carthy transferred his operation to Washington as a Senator, Anderson
and May wrote:

> Capitol Hill reporters learned to like the smiling, accommodating Senator from
> Wisconsin, who always had something to say. Even if his pronouncements were
> far-fetched, they were always good for a Night Final line. . . . But the headline
> that capped all other McCarthy headlines exploded on the morning of February
> 10, 1950, across the nation's front pages—after his Wheeling, West Virginia,
> speech . . . and [the press] gave it full play. . . . For the rest of the year, the magic
> name "McCarthy" appeared more often in the teletyped stories that moved out of
> Washington than the name of any other Senator. How did Joe do it?
> Part of the answer lies in the newspaper fraternity's devotion to the prin-
> ciple of objectivity. It is a violation of the unwritten creed for newsmen to mix
> opinion with fact; and so they gave Joe's wild accusations complete and factual
> coverage: They were telling the truth when they wrote: MC CARTHY CHARGES 205
> REDS IN STATE DEPARTMENT. Joe indeed had made that charge. As to the truth or
> falsehood of his statement, the reporters felt that was out of their line; appraisals
> of Joe's accuracy were left for the columnists and editorial writers.

In *The Fourth Branch of Government* (Houghton Mifflin, 1959)
Douglass Cater, for many years a Washington correspondent for the
*Reporter* magazine and later a White House assistant in the Johnson
Administration, pursued the "McCarthy miracle."

> McCarthy's skill . . . lay primarily in his capacity to stage a single issue so as to
> dominate the channels of communication and to distract a national audience. . . .
> He knew how to rule the headlines. . . .
> He had not even shown an awareness of the publicity potential of the Red Hunt
> until after the two-year period during which Alger Hiss was being exposed, tried,
> retried, and finally convicted. Then, in February 1950, only one month after Hiss
> received his sentence, McCarthy was off. Brandishing stage prop documents, which
> he never let anyone examine, he ingeniously mixed the proper proportions of the
> misplaced concrete and the farfetched abstraction to meet the requirements of
> newsmen. . . . It was as if the press yearned for the really big lie. . . . Nothing in
> the procedures of Congress or the press compelled him to reveal what he had [in
> the Wheeling speech]. His feat lay in transferring this myth of spy-infested
> America to more responsible newspapers.

Like many other analysts, Cater dwelt on the McCarthy method. He
would call a press conference in the morning to announce a sensational
afternoon press conference. That was enough for a big headline in the
afternoon newspapers. In the afternoon the press conference might or
might not be held. If it was held, it might produce new charges contained in documents waved by McCarthy before the newspapermen but
never turned over to them. If it was not held, the reason would be an

eleventh-hour hunt for a "mystery witness" whose information was so vital to the national security that he had already possibly fallen victim to the "international Communist conspiracy." "McCarthy held the headlines day after day," said Cater, "several times a day for the A.M.'s, the P.M.'s, the Seven o'Clock, and the late evening news . . . He knew the ingredients for the 'lead,' the 'overnight,' the 'sidebar.' Of many things McCarthy was contemptuous, but he never neglected his press relations."

McCarthy had a talent for publicity "unmatched by any other politician of this century," said Richard H. Rovere, Washington correspondent of the *New Yorker* magazine, in his book, *Senator Joe McCarthy* (World, 1960). "The reporters . . . were beginning to respond to his summonses like Pavlov's dogs to the clang of a bell." Rovere recorded the story of two reporters lolling around the Senate Office Building when along came McCarthy. "You two looking for a story?" he asked. McCarthy then asked them to join him on the subway car into the Senate where, patting his breast pocket, he said that he was going to subpoena President Truman. "You're not serious, Joe," said the reporters. "What are you going to subpoena him for?" "To testify about Harry Dexter White," said Joe. (White had been dead three years by that time.) Rovere wrote:

Of course it never happened—that is to say, Truman never testified, but the story got into print, even though the reporters to whom it was given were angry about the system that required them to publish "news" they knew to be fraudulent but prohibited them from reporting their knowledge of its fraudulence.

Among the newspaper critics of McCarthy who wrote about his relations with the press there is a common theme: It was the very "objectivity" of the free American press that prevented it from exposing McCarthy's lies in its news columns. This is how Rovere put it:

In time, what appeared to be the susceptibility of the press to McCarthy was held to be the cause of his lamentable successes. Why did the press publish this liar's lies? McCarthy knew the answer: it was not because publishers in general wished to circulate his mendacities or even because he had achieved a glamor that made him irresistible to the readers. It was because he had achieved a high elective office, because what he said counted for something (in fact, a great deal, as time went by) in the affairs of this nation, and because there was always the possibility that there *was* a mystery witness or that he *would* force Harry Truman to testify.

Rovere cited Walter Lippmann's comment: "McCarthy's charges of treason, espionage, corruption, perversion are news which cannot be suppressed or ignored. They come from a United States Senator and a politician . . . in good standing at the headquarters of the Republican party. When he makes such attacks against the State Department and the Defense Department, it is news which has to be published." Then Rovere continued on his own:

It was also, of course, news that a United States Senator was lying and defrauding the people and their government, but—in large part because McCarthy was a true innovator, because he lied with an unprecedented boldness, because he invented new kinds of lies—even those newspapers that were willing to expose him found that they lacked the technical resources. If he was to be called a liar, someone had to call him a liar. The American press was simply not set up so that it could feature a "MC CARTHY LIES" feature alongside a "MC CARTHY SAYS—" story. If his fellow Senators had been ready to challenge each mendacity, or if either of the two Presidents of his day had been willing and able to denounce him regularly, it would have worked. But that was not to be.

In *The Fourth Branch of Government,* Cater extends the theme of the mystique of objective reporting:

The extent of the communications failure McCarthyism presented can be measured by the fact that few of the reporters who regularly covered McCarthy believed him. Most came to hate and fear him as a cynical liar, who was willing to wreak untold havoc to satisfy his own power drive. But though they feared him, it was not intimidation that caused the press to serve as the instrument for McCarthy's rise. Rather, it was the inherent vulnerabilities—the frozen patterns of the press—which McCarthy discovered and played upon with unerring skill. "Straight" news, the absolute commandment of most mass media journalism, had become a straitjacket to crush the initiative and the independence of the reporter.

An ethical rule of the American Society of Newspaper Editors, entitled Fair Play, reads: "A newspaper should not publish unofficial charges affecting reputation or moral character without opportunity given to the accused to be heard." Responsible newspapers, Cater said, tried hard to live up to this rule and they failed "only when the accused, like Owen Lattimore, turned out to be in the wilds of Afghanistan." In practice, Cater said, it worked out like this:

Late one afternoon, Senator McCarthy might name a person, more likely a series of them. All through the evening the accused's telephone kept ringing. He was told briefly the nature of the charge against him—let us say, "top Soviet agent" —and asked for a brief reply.

But the dilemma for the reporter and the headline writer remained. McCarthy's charge was controversial and unexpected—a news count of two. The denial was controversial and completely expected—a news count of one. Both were equally lacking in proof. Nobody carried credentials on his person to prove that he is *not* the "top Soviet agent."

Rovere and Cater and most of the journalistic critics of McCarthy thus have presented the press as an honorable, lumbering giant shackled and muzzled by the inexorable laws of a free press, unable to tell the truth about McCarthy. But the Anderson-May image persists of a journalistic Dr. Frankenstein, pecking away at his typewriter in an office in the National Press Building in Washington to create an ink-stained monster. The portrait of the press of the United States as an objective entity is a myth. There is nothing in the Canons of Journalism that compelled reporters to accept and editors to publish information allegedly contained in uninspected documents waved at them by a Senator. Such reports, if their content proved to be false, might have been excused once or twice on the ground of deadline or overzealous reporting. But when this happened day in, day out for four years, when every reputable Washington correspondent knew that the disseminator of this information was a proved liar, there was no shred of an excuse. Objectivity was mocked when almost every story was weighted in favor of McCarthy's fraud.

No other Senator was allowed by the press to make such undocumented and unsubstantiated charges without challenge. The case of McCarthy was particularly unusual because he had been selected by the vote of the same Washington correspondents as the worst member of the United States Senate. (The day this poll was announced, William T. Evjue of the *Madison* [Wis.] *Capital Times* recalled, the story was topped by a story about McCarthy frying chicken for some friends, and a picture of McCarthy with a new broom [sweeping clean] on the Capitol steps in Washington.)

There was a basic reason, however, for the so-called objectivity of the reporters and their editors. This was the acceptance of McCarthy's stated aim, however much the reporters and editors may have deplored his methods (not all of them did). The aim was to rid the country of the American branch of the "international Communist conspiracy" which threatened the American way of life. If a few innocents got hurt along the way, it was too bad, but that was the way it had to be. Innocents get hurt in all wars, and America was at war with the most insidious enemy ever encountered. The President had said so, Secretary Acheson had said so, the publishers of the American press had said so. This acceptance is made apparent in Cater's overgenerous description of the reporters' efforts to balance McCarthy's charges with responses from those who were accused by him.

But a victim of McCarthy was not "charged," as Cater put it: he was named. Why then should a person who is not charged in a court of law or accused in a grand jury indictment be placed in the position of having to deny something he almost certainly never was—for example, "top Soviet agent"? Why should newspapermen assume the role of out-of-court prosecuting attorneys and demand to know by telephone whether a man is willing to admit or deny that he is a "top Soviet agent"—the penalty for admission being a prison sentence for sedition or treason, and for denial, the possibility of a trial for perjury. McCarthy's charge, said Cater in a most unobjective opinion, was more newsworthy since it was unexpected; the denial would be expected and therefore not so newsworthy. Cater's comment about a person not carrying credentials to prove that he was not the "top Soviet agent," even if it was meant jokingly, is a theme for Kafka.

McCarthy knew—and the newspapermen knew—that a person named by McCarthy was branded with a virtually ineradicable stigma. The truth never caught up with McCarthy's lie as circulated by the press. In his book *The Loyalty of Free Men* (Viking, 1950), Alan Barth, editor of the editorial page of the *Washington Post,* demonstrated how the Mc-Carthy-press process worked:

By the simple stratagem of charging a man with disloyalty, instead of with treason or espionage or sabotage, it is possible to evade the constitutional requirements that he be indicted by a grand jury, that he enjoy a speedy and public trial by an impartial petit jury, that he be informed of the nature and cause of the accusation and confronted with witnesses against him, that he be accorded the benefit of compulsory process to obtain witnesses in his favor. He is indicted and tried and sentenced by Congressional committee or administrative tribunal, with the same men acting as prosecutors, judges, and jury. The presumption of innocence supposed to surround him is ignored. The mere charge of disloyalty is treated as evidence of guilt . . .

It is the press which executes, so to speak, the sentences passed by congressional committees or by mere individuals speaking under the immunity from suits for slander or libel afforded by Congress. Newspapers especially tend to make headlines out of accusations and to treat denials less prominently. This stems in large measure from the concept of news as sensation and is scarcely less true of those newspapers that strive for objectivity than of those that deliberately use their news pages to serve editorial biases.

The concept of news as sensation was demonstrated admirably from the outset in the reports of McCarthy's speech to the Senate on February 20, 1950, following the uproar over the Wheeling charges of Communists in the State Department. By this time McCarthy had settled on the figure 81, among whom, he said, were three very special cases who held the key to the "international conspiracy" in the State Department. Rovere's retrospective view of this performance is pertinent. In *Senator Joe Mc-Carthy* he wrote:

> Few newspapers could print—because few readers would read—reports of a length sufficient to give the true gamey flavor of the performance. Even if they had wished to do so, it would have been difficult to get the reports, for McCarthy's presentation had been so disorderly, so jumbled and cluttered and loose-ended, that it was beyond the power of most reporters to organize the mess into a story that would convey to the reader anything beyond the suspicion that the reporter was drunk. There was a bedlam quality to McCarthy's speeches that seldom got through to those who never read them.
>
> What did filter through, then, to a moderately conscientious reader of a moderately conscientious newspaper was the news that a United States Senator had delivered a long and angry speech giving what he claimed were details on 81 persons who he insisted were Communists in the State Department. . . . But no newspaper could print the truth—because no newspaper could be sure it *was* the truth—that he had failed to identify even one Communist in the State Department. The reader might be advised by a favorite columnist or a radio commentator that McCarthy's past record did not inspire much confidence; at the same time, if he sought further enlightenment, he would be reminded that it had been far from impossible for Communists to get into the State Department. Alger Hiss had been convicted just one month earlier, and the Hiss trial had produced the name of at least one other Communist, Julian Wadleigh, who had betrayed Department secrets.

Rovere, the upholder of the canon of objectivity, in this apologia presented himself as a subjective purveyor of obfuscation, and as a first-rate example of Barth's thesis of the newspaperman-as-executioner. A study of the newspapers of the time has failed to turn up a story in which McCarthy's speech to the Senate was described as disorderly, cluttered, jumbled, or loose-ended. If this was the case—and there is no reason to dispute Rovere on this point—it would have been simple objective reporting to say so. Further, if the story of the speech was important enough for almost every newspaper in the nation to put it on page one, it is reasonable to ask why so few newspapers printed the text of the speech to allow their readers to judge it precisely on its contents. This would have eliminated the need for reporters to battle the bedlam in their news stories and to risk the reader's charge of "drunk."

Rovere might have noted, but did not, that McCarthy used the Hiss case to launch his new career. Rather, he accepted the unproven McCarthy charge of Communists in the State Department and went beyond the convicting jury in the second Hess trial: he marked Hiss as a Communist and a traitor by describing Wadleigh as *"at least one other Communist who had betrayed Department secrets."* Hiss had been convicted on a charge of perjury—denying that he had delivered State Department papers to Chambers and that he had known Chambers after 1936. Wadleigh testified that he himself had taken State Department documents, but said he had no knowledge that Hiss had done so. The retrospective Rovere thus compounded his absolution of the press in the making of McCarthy with some nimble McCarthyism of his own.

Writing two years after McCarthy's death in 1957, Cater noted that McCarthy "did not turn up evidence to warrant conviction of any one of the countless numbers he put the finger on. . . . He did not succeed in setting up a single contempt citation that could be sustained in the courts." It was not necessary to wait until 1959 to come to this conclusion: it was apparent to any newspaperman willing to dig for the facts. But few did, even though, as Rovere wrote, McCarthy had proved to be "an outrageous four-flusher" who could easily have been exposed if the will had been there.

McCarthyism, said Cater, was an "unparalleled demonstration of the publicity system gone wild, feeding on the body politic like a cancerous growth. It showed that publicity could be used as a crude instrument to bludgeon hapless officials" who were unable "to find an effective defense against its bludgeoning." Nor could either of the two Presidents who had to reckon with McCarthyism find "a satisfactory counter-publicity weapon."

The reason for the failure would seem to be obvious: McCarthy's theme was anti-Communism. This was the avowed policy of the two Presidents and their Administrations. The most effective counter-weapon to McCarthy would have been a denunciation and abandonment of the policy, or of the most vocal exponent of that policy—Senator McCarthy himself. Since neither of the Presidents nor their advisers were willing to adopt the first course, abandoning the policy, they had to adopt the second course, abandoning McCarthy. When the time was appropriate, when McCarthy had become an embarrassment to the President in office, to the armed forces, and to the image of the United States abroad, they implemented their decision.

The newspaper industry resents studies of the performance of the press by persons or groups outside the industry as infringement by amateurs. But in most areas of its performance, and particularly in relation to investigatory committees of Congress, it has forced others to take a closer look because the industry itself has undertaken so little inquiry of its own and offered almost no self-criticism. In 1952 Cornell University Press published a work entitled *The House Committee on Un-American Activities, 1945-1950,* by Robert K. Carr, professor of law and political science at Dartmouth College. While the book concerned itself mainly with the House committee, it went thoroughly into the whole question of Congressional investigation of "subversive activity," and its conclusions apply to McCarthy and the press.

Publicity, said Carr, in agreement with Rovere, Cater, Anderson, May, and most other journalistic analysts of McCarthy's career, has been essential to all Congressional investigations; it is a rare committee that has not depended heavily, since Martin Dies in 1938, "upon front-page press coverage of its activities as a means of effecting its purposes." The continuation of "screaming headlines" for thirty years Carr attributed to the committee's awareness of the news value of its activities and "the press's own enthusiasm to tell the committee's story." Carr wrote:

In the end, it is fair to say that the process by which the committee's labors and findings have been reported to the American people by the press, magazine, radio, and motion picture has become an integral and essential part of the investigation itself. This fact has clearly been recognized by members of the committee and its staff, and they have planned and executed the committee's program accordingly.

Committee members and staff set about to establish close relations with certain newspapers and newspapermen, and confidential information began to leak in both directions; anonymous and unofficial statements were planted in the press, virtually giving the statements official imprint, and a steady flow of sensational material was provided by the committee and "enthusiastically utilized by many papers." As a result, "a good deal of the news about the committee printed by the press has no basis in official action and has gone well beyond the mere reporting of events as they have taken place." Carr continued:

This ease with which any member of the committee has found it possible to obtain almost unlimited attention in the press for his remarks, whether casual or calculated, has been . . . helped by the irresponsibility of an important part of the American press, which, either because it could not resist the opportunity to use a cheap, sensational story, or because it was thereby furthering its own prejudices, was unable to distinguish between an authoritative statement of an official spokesman and the mere babblings of a single member.

In the House Committee on Un-American Activities rivalries were intense, in contrast to the Senate Permanent Subcommittee on Investigations, where McCarthy was the undisputed leader. In the House committee, members developed their favorite newspaper leaks and information-swapping agencies. Committee counsel Robert E. Stripling acknowledged that the committee's pamphlet *100 Things You Should*

*Know About Communism* was "prepared with the considerable aid" of Frank C. Waldrop, editor of the *Washington Times-Herald* (since absorbed by the *Washington Post*). He said that "newspaper friends of the Committee" had made inquiries for him at the Justice Department about the Department's reported plan to drop the Hiss case before it came to trial. The inquiry of course renewed the Department's flagging interest. Richard Nixon often referred to his close relations with Bert Andrews of the *New York Herald Tribune*. Whittaker Chambers, in his book, *Witness*, said it was Andrews who suggested to the committee the use of the lie detector in the Hiss-Chambers hearings.

It was Edward Nellor of the *New York Sun* (he also doubled for the *Washington Times-Herald*) who put the committee in touch with Chambers. Stripling again is the source of this information. The *Sun*, on August 12, 1948, took credit for initiating the Elizabeth Bentley-Whittaker Chambers espionage circus in Congress. If the *Sun*'s claims were valid, Carr pointed out, "it is obvious that Nellor enjoyed the benefit of leaks from the federal grand jury in New York" before which Miss Bentley and Chambers testified and whose proceedings, of course, are supposed to be secret. It is possible that the Hiss-Chambers hearings "would never have been held had not newspapermen supplied the committee with leaks concerning the proceedings of the federal grand jury in New York." Carr, in his general conclusions on the press, said:

While the larger responsibility for the inadequacies of the story [about Congressional investigations] that has reached the American people certainly rests with the committee itself, the press has not distinguished itself in its reporting of the story. . . . Newspapermen do have a great deal of discretion in selecting the stories that they think are worth telling and also in deciding how vigorously and persistently they will dig for the many details of such stories which are by no means on the surface merely waiting to be published. By and large, even the more respected and responsible papers have not been able to resist the temptation to emphasize the lurid aspects of the story, or to stress the testimony that suggested wrongdoing, while playing down the testimony that suggested the absence of wrongdoing. Nor have they taken the initiative in pointing out the obvious biases and errors in the testimony of irresponsible witnesses or even been able to avoid the introduction of new errors in their own reporting. . . . Even the best papers have all too frequently played up sensational witnesses, however irresponsible their testimony, have failed to report adequately the testimony of calmer witnesses or the replies of those who have been attacked, and have opened their columns too readily to the most trivial, ridiculous, or incredible musings, speculations, and predictions of committee members.

In his book *The Un-Americans* (Ballantine Books, 1961) Frank Donner, an attorney who has served as counsel for many uncooperative witnesses at Congressional investigatory hearings, supported Carr's conclusion:

> If newspapers have a duty to report what takes place in a hearing, they should also report what has not taken place. It is impossible to discover from accounts of Committee hearings what the purpose of the hearing is supposed to be and whether hearings conform to the purpose. Beginning with the Hollywood hearings in 1947, the press—even when critical of the Committee—has rarely bothered to explore the gap between the Committee's exposure activities and legitimate functions as an agency of Congress. Few newspapers have asked: Is exposure a function of a Committee of Congress? Even moderate newspapers have acted as glorified press agents for the Committee's informers. An informer may fall on his face in public, but the press is either indifferent or silent.

Donner described a practice which was common knowledge to working newspapermen and Congressional committees—the operation by some newspapers, particularly in the late 1940s and early 1950s, of their own exposure mills. They trained reporters who specialized in "inside dope on the local Reds." In some cases, they latched on to an informer who had already testified before anti-subversive committees, or bought his "I-was-a-Communist-dupe" confessions before he launched his career as a witness. The practice was almost entirely abandoned after 1958 for various reasons: many Hearst and Scripps-Howard newspapers —the chief practitioners—closed down; the public evidenced a great boredom with the repetitious accounts; and by-lines themselves had died or disappeared as a result of drink, dope, general deterioration, or suicide. In one case, that of Howard Rushmore, an investigator for McCarthy, it was murder (of his wife) *and* suicide. But before the decline, exposure was a flourishing business and many newspapers took great pride in their accomplishments. After the House Un-American Activities Committee, then headed by Harold Velde, came to Seattle in 1954, the *Seattle Post-Intelligencer* congratulated itself in an editorial.

> The names exposed by *Post-Intelligencer* reporters from the 40s on were the same as those exposed in the House hearings. So thoroughly had reporters for this newspaper done their work that hardly a new name came out of the exhaustive Seattle hearings—merely confirmation of the painstaking evidence that had been gathered and published over the last ten years.

The editorial was especially appreciative of its reporter, Traynor Hansen, who had sought out Mrs. Barbara Hartle, a Communist leader, after her Smith Act conviction and "encouraged her to break with the Communist Party." "Her decision," said the editorial, "might have been indefinitely delayed except for this reporter's initiative."

Although he ably documented the role of the press in building up the witch-hunting committees and therefore the atmosphere of hysteria in the country, Professor Carr allowed his own firm conclusion to drift off into a kind of societal dilemma. Here he found accord with Rovere, who wrote that "one of the many secrets McCarthy seemed to know (without, probably, knowing that he knew) was that the American press reflects the American mind." Carr's formulation went like this:

The press is what it is, and when a society insists on hunting witches and doubting its own integrity, it is only wise to assume that its press will play along with such insistence and doubts and give the people what they seemingly want to read, and give it to them in colorful style and generous quantity.

Both the Carr and Rovere positions seem to me to be alarmingly misleading. The American press does not reflect the American mind—it reflects the views of established power which in turn seeks to mold the American mind to accept its prejudices. The American press seeks to shape public opinion, or even to replace public opinion, by fostering and presenting a unanimity of view which it then offers *as* public opinion. It was not "society" that insisted on hunting witches: it was governmental and industrial power assisted by what Carr himself termed an "enthusiastic" press. American society was not the instigator of the witch-hunts. There was, in fact, continuing outspoken opposition to the House Committee on Un-American Activities and an early revulsion to the McCarthy method which was silenced in part by the weight of the enormous uncritical publicity given by the press to the Senator's activities. In almost every instance where public opinion has grasped the role of domestic repression in halting opposition to foreign policy, the press has proceeded, as a voluntary arm of government, to spread fear and hatred. The McCarthy era was indeed a prime example, in Cater's words, of. a "demonstration of the publicity system gone wild, feeding on the body politic like a cancerous growth." But McCarthyism was a misnomer for what was happening. McCarthyism was in a sense the prevailing law of the land, but it was not McCarthy who made the law. His path had been cleared by the Smith Act, the Walter-McCarran Immigration Act, and the Internal Security Act of 1950, all passed by overwhelming votes in the Congress. The atmosphere in the early 1950s was one of loyalty oaths and tapped telephones, suspicion and timidity engendered by inquisitors, and images of Bolshevik hordes fanning out from Europe to Asia. The United States, under the mantle of the United Nations, was engaged in a hopeless war in Korea, and France was heaving its next-to-last gasp of colonial asthma in Indo-China. "Society" in America did not inaugurate the era of American Imperialism; it was made an instrument of this policy by the shapers of the American destiny. The purpose of McCarthy and the witch-hunters in general was not to thwart the "Communist menace," but to stifle independent thought which could lead to organized opposition to American policy.

As an honest and fair-minded political scientist, Carr would have been wiser to rest on his own documented findings rather than to place on "society" the onus for the transgressions of the press. Rovere, as a practicing journalist, knew the press from the inside and therefore knew better. Yet while there can be no excuse for the role of the press in the McCarthy Era, there ought to be no surprise. The newspaper industry, as part of the establishment complex, simply played its accustomed role even as, in accustomed fashion, it wrapped itself in the protective parchment of the First Amendment to ward off the slings and arrows of at least a small, outraged part of society.

The policy of anti-Communism remained intact before, during, and after the heyday of McCarthy. McCarthy himself phrased it with earthy accuracy in a story he liked to tell about Senator John W. Bricker, Republican of Ohio, who said to him: "Joe, you're a real son of a bitch. But sometimes it's useful to have sons of bitches around to do the dirty work." Stated less crudely, the same forces that sponsored the political career of the indisputably legitimate President Eisenhower were responsible for the rise of McCarthy. Both men were necessary for the aims of American policy in the decade of the 1950s, though the roles they played in performing their task differed. McCarthy led the advance detachment preparing the ground which the Administration then occupied. Thus, yesterday's extremism became today's respectability. But the program and the goal remained the same and had the leadership and support of both Eisenhower and McCarthy.

In the campaign of 1952, Eisenhower was reported to be furious with McCarthy for imputing treason to General of the Army George C. Marshall. He said he did not approve of "character assassination" and was not going to campaign for, or give blanket endorsement to, anyone who proceeded in a manner that was not "decent, right, or fair." But when McCarthy won his primary and the Presidential campaign train rolled through Wisconsin, Eisenhower was side by side on the rear platform with McCarthy, saying: "The purposes that [McCarthy] and I have of ridding the government of the incompetents, the dishonest and, above all, the subversive are one and the same. Our differences, therefore, have nothing to do with the end result we are seeking. The differences apply to the method."

Even the method itself was adopted as official policy when McCarthy got too close to the White House. In December 1953 Attorney General Herbert Brownell, in a speech delivered with White House approval, criticized Harry Truman for his "blindness" about Harry Dexter White and the alleged spies in government. There had been talk that McCarthy was thinking of the Presidency in 1956, and the White House was said to be somewhat uneasy. But the uneasiness more likely was produced by McCarthy's investigation of the Army Signal Corps at Fort Monmouth, New Jersey, an investigation which McCarthy himself later conceded was groundless. The *Wall Street Journal* on December 3, 1953, came close to the mark on White House strategy: "It was for the precise purpose of stealing Mr. McCarthy's thunder that the President is said to have given advance blessing to Attorney General Brownell's criticism . . ."

The press played its normal role throughout this period. The *New York Times* ran headlines reading: "ROSENBERG CALLED RADAR SPY LEADER"; "RADAR WITNESS BREAKS DOWN: WILL TELL ALL"; "MONMOUTH FIGURE LINKED TO HISS RING." Later the *Times* acknowledged that it had done its readers a "great disservice, though an unavoidable one," in its coverage of the Signal Corps investigation. The *Times* conceded there was no truth in any of the Fort Monmouth spy stories, but said it had had no alternative to printing them. "It is difficult, if not impossible," said the *Times,* "to ignore charges by Senator McCarthy just because they are usually proved false. The remedy lies with the reader." Richard Rovere commented on this statement in *Senator Joe McCarthy:*

> To many people, this was rather like saying that if a restaurant serves poisoned food, it is up to the diner to refuse it. Yet the *Times* was, I believe, essentially right, for I suspect there is no surer way to a corrupt and worthless press than to authorize reporters to tell the readers which "facts" really are "facts" and which are not. Certainly in those countries where this is the practice, the press serves the public less well than ours.

It would hardly seem to be "serving the public" to print without challenge "facts" which reporters and editors should have regarded as highly questionable because they came from a source—McCarthy—whom they had come to know as highly suspect. It was not so difficult as Rovere suggested for reporters to get to the facts, nor for a newspaper editorially to question the character and motives of an investigation like Fort Monmouth. The reader depends on his daily newspaper for facts; he has no choice but to accept them or reject them. If he rejects them out of instinct, he is left with what he believes to be a false set of facts, but no truth. If the facts eventually come out—as they usually do—it is long after the event. The reader may then upbraid his newspaper and insist that the next time it seek out the truth. But by this time the newspaper has forgotten Fort Monmouth and may be busy with another case of tainted news.

"Objectivity," which would seem to be at the core of the Roverian dilemma, depends on many factors which often are entirely nonobjective. Melvin Mencher of the *Albuquerque Journal* (he later became a professor at the Columbia Graduate School of Journalism) demonstrated this in a review of the handling of a story on McCarthy and Adlai Stevenson, the Democratic candidate for President in 1952, in the *Nieman Reports* (Winter 1962). During the 1952 campaign, McCarthy issued a statement about a speech he was to give, and the Associated Press in its lead on the story said McCarthy asserted he would "show connections between [Stevenson] and known Communists and Communist causes." In his actual speech, which the AP also reported, McCarthy named neither a single Communist nor Communist cause associated with Stevenson. The AP story did not record this fact. If someone had taken the time to compare the two McCarthy statements, Mencher said, and then called Mc-Carthy a liar, undoubtedly AP would have carried the criticism as "objective journalism."

Some papers played the Stevenson story down on the ground that McCarthy had made similar charges before and it was not news, in the strict sense. The second paragraph of the *New York Times* story said, "Senator McCarthy did not present any new material in his speech." The *Milwaukee Journal* employed a device (Rovere would have disapproved) which it had been using for some time in dealing with McCarthy: its story had a parenthetical refutation of one of McCarthy's points. Some newspapers buried the story; others listed all the accusations; still others eliminated most of the detailed allegations. In some stories McCarthy "blasted," "charged," and "accused." In others he "tried to give his listeners the impression" or "sought to impress" or "reviewed virtually all of his previous charges." This would indicate, said Mencher, "that objectivity is actually relative to the reporter, the desk, the makeup man and to less tangible forces." Less tangible, perhaps, but more influential forces, such as sympathy or hostility toward Stevenson on the part of editor or publisher. It would also indicate that the *Milwaukee Journal* practice, if employed by other newspapers in the interest of immediate correction of false statements or distortions of fact, could have served the principle of objectivity far more effectively than the publication of one-sided material emanating from the Senator.

In the last weeks of 1953, neither the *Times* nor any other New York newspaper seemed interested in "new material" about McCarthy, particularly if it was being offered by persons who had suffered at McCarthy's hand. In November a group calling itself the Trade Union Veterans Committee announced plans in New York for a "public trial" of McCarthy, with witnesses drawn from among those "who were attacked and maligned, or who are under attack now by McCarthy." The charges against McCarthy were three counts of violation of the Criminal Code of the United States: acceptance of bribes while in office; violation of the Corrupt Practices Act; and conspiracy to subvert the Constitution. The trial date was set for January 6, 1954. Numerous halls refused to house the meeting, and radio and television stations expressed no interest in covering. Every New York metropolitan newspaper refused advertisements for the meeting. In only one instance was an explanation offered: the *New York Post,* which had accepted a check in payment for an advertisement, then returned it with a note reading, "Because of censorship the advertisement was omitted." News of the trial spread rapidly, however, and the newspapers which had refused the advertisements embarked on a campaign in editorials, columns, and nonobjective news stories to mark the event as a "Moscow trial" organized by "Reds." Five thousand persons filled the St. Nicholas Arena in Manhattan for the trial, and 2,000 more listened in a smaller hall in the same building. McCarthy was found guilty as charged, but on Capitol Hill he was still free and in favor, as President Eisenhower's State of the Union message that same week demonstrated. The *Washington Post* said:

> When President Eisenhower socked the Reds it was like Old Glory being unfurled in the breeze, or the United States Cavalry arriving on the scene just in time to save the settlers from an Indian massacre. . . . Nothing else in the 55-minute speech evoked anywhere near such applause.

A few weeks later, Attorney General Brownell was proudly listing the record of the Eisenhower Administration: legal action against 54 Communist Party leaders, 12 "front" groups, and 714 "subversive" aliens; 12 unionists indicted on charges of falsely signing Taft-Hartley affidavits; and a proposal under study to outlaw the Communist Party. McCarthy was on a nationwide tour sponsored by the Republican National Committee, and it must have been a heady experience—so heady that it led McCarthy to make the move which eventually would destroy him. He denounced a respected Army officer, Brigadier General Ralph W. Zwicker of the Army Signal Corps at Fort Monmouth, as "not fit to wear the uniform" and undertook an investigation of the Army loyalty-security program. Speculation about McCarthy's ambitions for the White House in 1956 grew again, but Walter Lippmann disagreed. McCarthy's immediate objective, he said in his column of March 8, was to show that even in the Army he is a bigger man than they are, and thus to expand his power by making himself feared. [McCarthy is] a candidate for supreme boss—for dictatorship—of the Republican Party. . . . His unconcealed purpose is to break and subdue the President and the Executive branch of the government, the Republican Party in Congress, the national organization of the party. If any Republican still thinks that McCarthy's prime target is Communism and not the capture of the Republican Party, he will live and learn differently.

The forces that had set McCarthy in motion back in 1950 now moved in unison to stop him. The White House took up the challenge and defended the Army; the Senate ordered an investigation of McCarthy; and the press cried "Enough!" On February 26, 1954, the *New York Times* said editorially:

This question [the Army's handling of the security investigation] sinks into unimportance compared to the question of a Senator pillorying a distinguished Army officer because the orders under which the officer acted are displeasing to the Senator. This fight ought to have been fought on the basic issue of whether or not the Executive branch of this government, including the Army, is being run by President Eisenhower or Senator McCarthy. The Administration has attempted to appease a man who cannot be appeased. We do not believe that the American people are so blind that they will fail to see what happened here. What happened here is a domestic Munich, and all the pious platitudes in the world will not hide that fact.

The *Washington Post* editorial on that same day also had a German analogy.

Who now dares, without threat of smear, proclaim the traditional doctrine that a man is innocent until proved guilty? The inquisitor is now the prosecutor, judge and jury. The confusion and distortion over the security risks in government are the direct result of this corrosion. The Foreign Service has been sacrificed on the altar of the false god, McCarthy. Now it is the military service. McCarthyism has succeeded in deflecting our attention from the real enemy in Communist imperialism to the suspicion of our neighbors. That is the way Germany, and particularly the German army, went under Hitler.

The editorial outrage was still confined to McCarthy's methods (the Communist imperialist enemy remained the universal anathema), but now these methods were threatening to discredit an institution vital to the fight against Communism—the United States Army—and, through it, the Presidency.

What the press would not discuss—and what was at the core of the matter—was discussed by two legal experts who served in the office of the Army General Counsel during the Army-McCarthy hearings in the spring of 1954. They were Norman Dorsen, professor of law at New York University, and John G. Simon, professor of law at Yale. In an analysis entitled "A Fight on the Wrong Front" in the *Columbia University Forum,* Fall 1964, they wrote that the Army loyalty-security program was fully enforced by the Army, and there was no dispute between the Army and McCarthy on this score. In fact, McCarthy's efforts caused the Army to apply its program even more vigorously and the civilian employes at Fort Monmouth suffered far more at the hands of the Army than they did at McCarthy's hand. The article concluded:

> It was not Senator McCarthy who damaged Monmouth employees and Army draftees as much as their Pentagon superiors. McCarthyism could injure individuals only to the extent that those in power cooperated with it. Thus, destroying Senator McCarthy was not alone what the country needed. It also needed public officials who had the instinct, intelligence, and courage to do the right thing at the time when the issues arose—not two or three years later, when shelving McCarthyism would no longer create a storm. Senator McCarthy did present the ultimate test of the Administration's mettle, and the Administration, by eliminating him, eliminated the challenge. But that should never have been necessary.

Certainly, Dorsen and Simon agreed, the Senator's decline and fall dated from the hearings: "Prolonged exposure to the public weakened his position as the man on horseback and sent him a horseless rider down the road to Senate censure and lonely obscurity."

The obscurity came swiftly, but the censure was delayed and, finally, mitigated. The original censure resolution was introduced on July 30, 1954, by Senator Ralph Flanders, Republican of Vermont, but was postponed after Senator William Knowland, Republican of California, raised strenuous objections. The resolution read: "Resolved, That the conduct of the Senator from Wisconsin is contrary to Senatorial traditions, and tends to bring the Senate in disrepute, and such conduct is hereby condemned." The Knowland move to postpone was supported by 75 Senators. The actual censure motion came December 2, and the vote was 67 to 22. The main basis for the censure had been changed, however, from the long-standing charges against McCarthy for general misconduct to a list of specific statements he had made about the select committee of the Senate that had been named to judge him.

And suddenly McCarthy was not news. The reporters who had been assigned to cover him for five years (they were known as the Goon Squad) were reassigned. When McCarthy spoke on the Senate floor, or when a speech was scheduled, the reporters in the press gallery found they had pressing business elsewhere. Pavlovian journalists who once responded salivating to his ringing calls for press conferences responded to other bells and turned to avoid him when they saw him coming down a corridor. Stories about his activities (he still sought to recapture the old magic with an occasional thrust) were buried inside the papers. Why did it happen? In *The Fourth Branch of Government,* Douglass Cater expressed bewilderment: "McCarthyism was killed as surely as it had been bred by the power of publicity. Nobody, not even the editors, could tell you why."

If the editors could not tell why, it was because they would not tell why. McCarthy had been assigned to oblivion by the established power. No decree was needed; it was understood. As a creature of the same established power, McCarthy had no personal army to overturn the sentence. He was finished. The time had come to rule out the McCarthy method. It was no longer needed—the job had been done and McCarthyism-without-fanfare had become prevailing policy. The task now was to get rid of the embarrassing instrument through which the policy had been institutionalized. Somehow, the question of journalistic objectivity in the coverage of McCarthy was no longer a problem. He was still a Senator, still the chairman of an important committee, but he was no longer news. If he was not news, there was no problem about the "mechanics" of the free press which had prevented reporters from detecting and communicating the basic fact of McCarthy's lies, as Cater phrased it, when he was destroying people daily on page one of the nation's press.

The altered attitude toward McCarthy as news was underscored by Edwin R. Bayley, a political reporter from the *Milwaukee Journal* throughout McCarthy's rise to power, who later became dean of the Graduate School of Journalism at the University of California at Berkeley. McCarthy never communicated directly with Bayley because the *Journal* had been a severe critic of the Senator. But he sent messages, usually complaints about the handling of stories, through Dion Henderson, an Associated Press staff writer in Milwaukee. Henderson's office adjoined the *Journal* city room. He was then writing a novel about a politician, and the figure of McCarthy fascinated him. Whenever the Senator came to Milwaukee during the last two years of his life, he would visit with Henderson. In an article in the *New Republic* of May 16, 1960, Bayley wrote:

What they talked about, most of all, was newspapers. McCarthy was obsessed with the subject. He was bitter when, after his attacks inevitably turned against the Eisenhower Administration, he found himself relegated to the back pages. Why, he asked over and over, was the same kind of attack big news in '50 and nothing much in '55?

One Saturday afternoon Henderson came into the *Journal* city room with a statement that McCarthy had given to Henderson with a bet that the *Journal* would not print it. He had been reading Jefferson, McCarthy told Henderson, and the statement had been influenced by his reading. In it, he upheld the right to dissent, to hold unpopular, even subversive opinions; that was our most important right, he said, and no man should be persecuted for his beliefs. The statement was entirely out of character, and both newspapermen wondered whether it might not be a McCarthy trick to test the *Journal*. In any case, Bayley decided, it was something that could not be handled in a routine fashion, and his story sought "to put it in perspective, to indicate that I did not know whether it meant anything, but that this was what McCarthy had said. I tried to show how it conflicted with McCarthy's previous statements and actions, without being too editorial about it, and left it to the reader to make the judgment."

He turned the story in. It did not appear in the Sunday paper. On Monday he inquired and couldn't find anyone who knew of a decision not to use the story. Henderson had written a story also which had gone out over the AP state wire. His recollection was that two or three state papers had used 50 to 100 words on Monday in a routine rewrite of the original Saturday story. Bayley concluded about the *Journal* blackout:

> I think the *Journal*'s decision probably was right. It might have been a hoax, a last attempt to exploit the press. McCarthy might have repudiated it. Henderson, however, thinks that McCarthy might have changed the whole direction of his career if the story had been run. If the story had been printed and noticed, it might have had the effect of showing up McCarthy as what he is now quite generally believed to have been—a reckless cynic who loved excitement and the feel of power, but who stood for nothing in particular. I think it was a last foolish gamble with what was left of his political capital to prove a minor point to himself about the newspapers he hated. It was a gamble that he thought he had won.

Gamble or not, it proved conclusively a major point: McCarthy was no longer news. The sacred canon of objectivity no longer applied. He was still a Senator, still the man who had commanded more headlines than any other figure in America for five years, but the signal had been given and, without need for meetings or conferences, the world of journalism had decreed him to be less than routine.

# 6. A Tale of Two Editors

At the peak of his power, when his encounters with the press were never regarded as routine, Joe McCarthy attempted a different kind of gamble. He sought to make headlines about the press itself. The first major confrontation came on April 24, 1953, when the Senator subpoenaed James Wechsler, editor of the *New York Post,* to a closed hearing in Washington; a second session with Wechsler was held May 5. The *Post,* an anti-Communist newspaper, had long been a critic of McCarthy, and in 1951 had published a 17-part series about him entitled "Smear Inc.—A One-Man Job." At that time McCarthy had responded with an "exposé" of Wechsler's record as a member from 1934 to 1937 of the Young Communist League. Wechsler's record, however, was hardly a private affair. He had made almost a ritual of public confession of his association with the Communist Party and his break with it in 1937. In 1946 he resigned from the New York experimental newspaper *PM* on the ground that it was "Communist dominated." In 1948 he was a founder of Americans for Democratic Action. He had by 1953 established himself as an eminently respectable anti-Communist liberal and was frequently called in this role to appear on radio and television discussion programs.

The April 24 hearing ostensibly was held to discuss books by Wechsler which McCarthy had determined were on the shelves of State Department libraries overseas. It soon became clear, however, that the subjects on McCarthy's mind were Wechsler's views, the policies of the *New York Post,* and criticism of McCarthy. About five minutes were spent on the books and five hours on Wechsler and the *Post.* During these five hours, Wechsler sought vigorously to assert his anti-Communist credentials and noted that he had become aware of and fought against the Red Peril long before McCarthy. He had, said Wechsler, given perhaps the first editorial support to Whittaker Chambers's charge against Alger Hiss. He presented a letter he had received from Representative Richard M. Nixon (he was Vice President at the time of the hearing) commending him for an editorial on the Hiss case. He cited his attacks on "the [Henry] Wallace movement which was, in my judgment, the most serious threat in recent years of Communist strength in America." He offered as evidence a collection of editorials in the *Daily Worker* denouncing him for his anti-Communism. At that point, in his inimitable fashion, McCarthy asked Wechsler whether he had had a hand in causing the *Daily Worker* editorials to be written.

Wechsler insisted that McCarthy's methods were hindering the fight against Communism, and he protested what he regarded as an invasion by McCarthy of the freedom of the press. "I believe," said Wechsler on April 24, "the object of this proceeding is . . . a reprisal against the *Post* for its fight against the chairman of this committee. I believe I would not be here if I were not the editor of the *Post* and I did not engage in such a fight."

"Did you feel," Senator McCarthy asked, "that it is your status as a newspaperman that gives you some special immunity, or do you feel that we have the same right to call newspapermen as we have to call lawyers and doctors?"

"I ask no special immunity," Wechsler replied. "I say only that I believe I am here because I am a newspaperman and because of what I have done as a newspaperman."

Wechsler asked that the testimony be made public so that he could submit it to the American Society of Newspaper Editors for an inquiry into a violation of the freedom of the press. But there was a price. The testimony could not be made public, McCarthy said, until it was complete, and the transcript lacked a response to a request by McCarthy that Wechsler submit to him a list of persons whom he had known to be Communists between 1934 and 1937—his Young Communist years. Wechsler agreed. Among the sixty names he supplied were those of colleagues on the *New York Post*. "A grave issue of conscience was involved in my decision to make this list available," Wechsler explained. "I am doing so because I believe that the paramount issue is the attack which Senator McCarthy is waging on the freedom of the press." Wechsler made it plain that he wished to disassociate himself from those who had invoked the First and Fifth Amendment, before Congressional committees. In his book, *The Age of Suspicion* (Random House, 1953), he elaborated on his decision:

Ours is an age of suspicion—suspicion rooted partly in our legitimate anxiety about the Soviet threat to free society and heightened by the awesome dread of atomic annihilation. In such an age silence is no answer. Its misuse by the Communists has deprived it of any eloquence it ever had. Indeed it might be said that our republic is haunted by two kinds of silence—the calculated reticence of those who have something to hide and the deepening timidity of others who have nervously concluded that it is safer to have nothing to say. . . . Moreover, there is in the American tradition a very real belief that the man who has nothing to conceal will speak up when spoken to; muteness has not often been equated with valor.

There *have* been figures in American history, beginning with Salem, who remained mute under questioning and are universally regarded as valorous. (Perhaps some of them might not maintain their silence over Wechsler's interpretation of the American tradition.) But if Wechsler had any qualms, they were not evident in his comment that "Joe McCarthy wanted silence, not submission, and I was determined not to walk into his trap." So he turned in the names and asked that they not be made public with the transcript of the testimony because so many on the list "were fooled as I was" and some had "repudiated Communism as decisively as I have." Publicity "could do them irreparable harm and serve no conceivable national purpose. . . . If not only I but others who have long ago broken with Communism can be subjected at this late date to this kind of attack for the political errors of youth, young people who are now similarly realizing that they have been misled by the Communists may bitterly decide there is no way they can honorably regain their status in society . . . Surely the proper disposal of the list would be its transmission to the Federal Bureau of Investigation."

McCarthy agreed to submit the list to the FBI "for its information," but said it first would have to be checked by his own staff. The ultimate disposition of the list is not known; it may be surmised that its backlash has been felt by many on the list who would be reluctant to make such matters public. They were, after all, according to Wechsler, persons who had honorably regained their place in society after youthful indiscretions.

Whatever may be said of Wechsler's posture at the hearings, McCarthy's attack against him and the *Post* jolted several newspapers into editorial expression. In almost every instance, the editorials noted that Wechsler had cleansed his soul of Communism and was therefore untainted and defensible. The *New York Times* wrote on May 9, 1953:

We believe it is the citizen's duty to respond fully and frankly to Congressional investigators (as Mr. Wechsler did), just as it is the duty of the investigators scrupulously to observe the citizen's constitutional rights. We think that newspapermen are no more immune from investigation in respect to allegedly subversive or seditious activity than anyone else. The mere fact that a man works on or writes for a publication does not give him any special privilege if, as and when his loyalty comes under scrutiny.

But there is another basic American principle involved here, too, and that is the principle of freedom of the press. The real question is whether or not Mr. McCarthy was using his undoubted right of investigation as a cover for an attempt to harass and intimidate Mr. Wechsler as an editor who has bitterly and uncompromisingly opposed Mr. McCarthy. It is our opinion after reading the transcript that this is just exactly what Mr. McCarthy was doing.

The repeated references to the editorial policy of the *New York Post* revealed clearly what was in Mr. McCarthy's mind. The Senator has every right to attack the *Post* or any other newspaper if he wants to, but we think it gets very close to an infringement on one of America's basic freedoms if he uses his vast powers as chairman of an investigating committee of the United States Senate to accuse an editor of continued subservience to "the Communist ideal" because that editor's writings are not to his liking.

As the Wechsler hearings ended, McCarthy announced that he was extending his investigation of the news media and hired Harvey Matusow, a former Communist, to look into the newspaper, radio and television industries in New York City. Matusow, in speeches in Montana during the election campaign of 1952, had insisted that there were 126 dues-paying Communists on the Sunday staff of the *New York Times* (there were only 93 employes altogether on the Sunday staff). There were 76 hard-core Reds on the editorial and research staffs of *Time* and *Life* magazines, Matusow reported, and 25 more in the New York bureau of the Associated Press. Henry Luce's hard-core brigade was revealed after *Time* magazine, which had reported McCarthy's activities with sober respect for at least two years, had become somewhat critical of the Senator's methods. McCarthy had remarkable sensitivity to such developments and responded immediately. He said he felt it was his duty to inform *Time* advertisers that "*Time* publishes falsehoods for a purpose. These advertisers are entitled to have it called to their attention if unknowingly they are flooding American homes with CP-line material . . . If they continue to advertise in *Time* magazine after they know what *Time* is doing, in my opinion no one who is for America and against Communism should buy their product." Neither *Time* nor the advertisers were unduly shaken by this warning, but *Editor & Publisher* finally was moved as much by the economics of the situation as by the ethics to deplore McCarthy's attempts to "intimidate or silence critics." Columnist Marquis Childs suggested in his column May 9, 1953:

It happens that a much wider segment of the press has criticized McCarthy during the past three months. This may explain the new campaign he is launching. . . . The meaning of all this is clear enough for anyone to read. Critics of McCarthy will be investigated by Matusow and hauled before the Senator. This is intimidation in a crude form. You be a good boy, and play with us, or at least you keep quiet and you will be left alone.

Wechsler sent the transcript of his hearing to the American Society of Newspaper Editors, and a special committee was appointed by President Basil Walters to study and comment on all relevant material in the case. On August 12, the special committee made its report. It noted carefully that it had not considered its function as committing individual members or the board of directors or the ASNE itself to "any uniform opinion or to any course of action," or to "pronounce any judgment on the public service of anyone in politics or in journalism." With these all-encompassing disclaimers, it announced that its eleven members had been unable to agree whether freedom of the press had been infringed in the questioning of Wechsler. The committee reported

disagreement [that] ranges from the opinion that Senator McCarthy, as committee chairman, infringed freedom of the press . . . to the contrary viewpoint that the Senator's inquiries did no damage to this freedom. In between are committee members who were disturbed by the tenor of the investigation, but do not feel that this single interchange constituted a clear and present danger to freedom of the press justifying a special challenge.

The report found that McCarthy had "probed into the [*New York Post*'s] editorial policies" and "into the political affiliations of members of the staff, with particular emphasis on editorials and columns critical of Senator McCarthy and other Congressional investigators," as well as the FBI. In this area, said the report, the question of infringement arises. Then, having gone through the transcript without coming to a judgment, the committee offered this advice to its fellow editors: "We urge that every member of this Society read the transcript of the testimony. We believe that only in this way can all the complex factors affecting the issues be judged." The report went on:

If, as some members believe, Senator McCarthy was using the power of government to probe into a newspaper's editorial conscience and challenge its right to criticize government; and if (in the language of a concurring opinion by two justices of the Supreme Court in a case in this field) he held a club over speech and over the press "through the harassment of hearings, investigations, reports, and subpoenas" —then the conclusion of these editors is understandable.

If, on the other hand, the questions were designed only to establish Mr. Wechsler's personal opinions as expressed in print and attempt to relate them to his disputed attitude toward communism, without any intention to punish or to challenge his right to these opinions, the opposite conclusion is equally understandable.

Having made this tortured charge to a jury of its peers, the special committee helpfully suggested that any editor who might be subpoenaed consult his lawyer as to whether he should answer questions relating to his editorial or news judgment. Since they were not constitutional lawyers, the editors on the committee said, they could offer only opinions, and not a final answer, but "if there is a genuine constitutional question here, then it should be raised and settled." The report ended with this resounding platitude:

This committee feels that the issue raised by this hearing serves a useful purpose. It focuses upon an essential and constitutionally guaranteed freedom a fresh vigilance and enforces a salutary re-examination in each editorial mind of the editor's ideas and responsibilities.

Four committee members, however, felt it necessary to go beyond this platitude. They called the report's conclusions inadequate and submitted statements clarifying their own views. These views received three inches in a 30-inch story filed from Washington by its own correspondent to the *New York Times* August 13, 1953. Two of the inches were consumed by the names and identification of the dissenters who, according to the *Times* story, felt that McCarthy's methods were "not only a threat to freedom of the press but also 'a peril to American freedom.' " The dissenters were J. R. Wiggins, committee chairman, managing editor of the *Washington Post;* Herbert Brucker, editor of the *Hartford Courant;* William M. Tugman, editor of the *Eugene* (Ore.) *Register-Guard;* Eugene C. Pulliam, Jr., managing editor of the *Indianapolis News*. Wiggins, in addition, provided a historical summary of conflicts between the press and the legislative branches of government which helped enormously to clarify the issues in the Wechsler case.

As though responding to a comment six weeks earlier by Louis M. Lyons, curator of the Nieman Foundation at Harvard, that American editors generally were explaining away in "equivocal rationalization" the McCarthy-Wechsler controversy, the four dissenters noted that the First Amendment speaks in "unequivocal language." They said, quoting an opinion in *Bridges v. California* in the Supreme Court in 1941, that "the unqualified prohibitions laid down by the framers were intended to give to liberty of the press, as to other liberties, the broadest scope that could be countenanced in an orderly society."

Neither the fact nor the extent of the abridgment is to be tested by the fortitude against intimidation of the particular editor or other person subjected to summons and inquiry. The test is not the capacity of resistance against the "finger of government leveled against the press," enjoyed by editors as a class of daily metropolitan newspapers or other newspapers. The protection of the First Amendment is not solely for the very courageous or the very orthodox or the very secure. The "preferred position granted speech and press by the First Amendment" attaches to all who may wish to . . . hear or read, however timid or unorthodox or insecure they may be or feel. Freedom of the press is not for the newspaper press alone. What journalism defends against all pressures of government is the right of all men, readers and hearers as well as utterers, to share information and opinion. [The quotations are from the concurring opinions by Justices Douglas and Black in *U.S. v. Rumely.*]

The dissenters concluded that (1) freedom of the press could not long survive "the repeated exercise by Congress of unlimited inquiry into the conduct of newspapers"; (2) questioning such as that to which Wechsler was subjected, if frequently repeated, "would extinguish, without passage of a single law, that free and unfettered reporting of events and comment thereon, upon which the preservation of our liberties depends"; (3) newspapers required to account to government agencies for their news and editorial policies "would exist in such permanent jeopardy that their freedom to report fully and comment freely inevitably would be impaired"; (4) the right of the people to know and to criticize their government suffers "whenever a single newspaper, however worthy or unworthy, is subjected by one Senator, however worthy or unworthy, to inconvenience, expense, humiliation, ridicule, abuse, condemnation and reproach, under the auspices of government power"; (5) if a proceeding involves the extension of legislative power beyond its decreed constitutional limits, then the principles involved cannot be altered by the motives of legislators or newspapermen. In a boldface final paragraph, the dissenters were entirely unequivocal:

Newspapermen, by the very choice of their profession, avail themselves of the privileges and immunities of a free press, guaranteed in the Constitution, and they assume at the same time certain obligations and duties, not the least among which is to defend the freedom of the press against all attack. Where such an invasion of freedom occurs, other citizens may speak or remain silent without being identified with trespass; but the silence of the press is invariably construed, and properly construed, as an indication that no trespass has occurred and its silences inevitably will be summoned to the support of like trespasses in the future. In our opinion, therefore, whatever inconvenience results, whatever controversy ensues, we are compelled by every command of duty to brand this and every threat to freedom of the press, from whatever source, as a peril to American freedom.

McCarthy's response was typical. In a letter written August 14, 1953, to the seven other members of the special ASNE committee, he asked for an investigation of Wiggins, the committee chairman, and "the extent to which through his paper, the *Washington Post,* [he] has prostituted and endangered freedom of the press by constant, false, vicious, intemperate attacks upon anyone who dares expose any of the undercover Communists." He offered his "full cooperation" in any such investigation. Of course, nothing came of this. It was McCarthy's blunderbuss technique of seeking to smother criticism. The press also responded in typical fashion: it gave more space to McCarthy's attack on Wiggins and the *Washington Post* than it had given to the findings of the ASNE committee.

The principles set forth by the dissenting editors of the ASNE were soon put to the test. They were not upheld. I had personal experience of the failure, along with Cedric Belfrage, with whom I was a co-founder of the *National Guardian.* Belfrage's experiences were more painful than mine.

After his April 24 hearing, James Wechsler said he believed he would be "the first of a long line of editors who are going to be called down here because they refuse to equate McCarthy with patriotism." It is hard to estimate how long the line would have been if McCarthy had not sought to take over the United States Army, in addition to the State Department, but in any case Belfrage and I were second in line, only three weeks later. At the time he was editor of the *National Guardian,* and I was executive editor.

Late in April, on his Sunday night radio program ("Calling Mr. and Mrs. America, and all the ships at sea . . .") columnist Walter Winchell directed the attention of "interested persons" to statements made about Belfrage by Elizabeth Bentley, one of the most publicized of government informers. Winchell described the *National Guardian* as a "pro-Commie rag" for its defense of Alger Hiss, its opposition to United States intervention in Korea, and its insistence that the conviction of Ethel and Julius Rosenberg was a gross miscarriage of justice. (The campaign to prevent the execution of the couple was then at its peak.) Two days after the Winchell broadcast, Belfrage received a subpoena to appear on May 4 in New York before the House Committee on Un-American Activities (then headed by Harold H. Velde, a Republican of Illinois). The subpoena followed closely the publication of articles in the *National Guardian* presenting new information in the Rosenberg case and charging perjury in prosecution testimony. Velde said in an opening statement at the hearing:

I have asked that Cedric Belfrage be subpoenaed to appear before the [committee] and I guarantee we will try to find out just what goes with the *National*

*Guardian* . . . I cannot overemphasize the sinister effect on Americanism that Belfrage and his Communist-inspired propaganda machine promotes.

With the aims of the hearing clearly outlined, and the *National Guardian* thus characterized by the committee chairman at the outset of the hearing, the *National Guardian* issued this statement:

The summoning of the *National Guardian*'s editor is . . . a move to persecute and if possible intimidate the editor of an independent news-weekly which consistently has opposed the policies of war, repression and plunder of the Eisenhower Administration and the previous bi-partisan administration of President Truman. Failing —as the committee knows it must—to intimidate the *National Guardian*'s editor, it is the committee chairman's declared intent to use these hearings to calumniate and if possible destroy the publication in the eyes of its readers and of the public generally.

The statement was given to all newspapers in New York and to the wire services. No major daily used any part of it. Before Belfrage's appearance, the *National Guardian* had announced a "fight-back rally" for May 3, the eve of the hearing; the press ignored this release, and there was no coverage of the overflow rally. The *New York Post,* whose editor had just described his own subpoena to the McCarthy committee as "a flagrant attempt to intimidate editors who are fighting McCarthy," ignored Belfrage's appearance before the Velde committee. This was doubly ironic in light of a *Post* editorial published in September 1951 which had said:

If American newspaperdom has any fighting faith in its own purpose and traditions, if it has any real dignity and pride, the next time McCarthy hits a newspaperman from behind . . . every paper from New York to San Francisco will let him have it with such a deafening blast, he won't know what hit him.

The *Post* may not have equated McCarthy with Velde, but the link was clear to the *Nation* magazine. It coupled Wechsler's appearance before McCarthy with Belfrage's before Velde, called both "disturbing omens," and concluded that "the American press is now confronted by a danger without parallel in its history." In the press of Western Europe there was little doubt that Belfrage's subpoena was an attack on freedom of the press. In Paris the weekly *L'Observateur* commented: "The progressive journalist [Belfrage] is in danger of paying dearly for a curiosity capable of saving the lives of the Rosenbergs." Belfrage's curiosity was great and he did pay dearly; but the Rosenbergs paid most dearly of all as a sacrifice to the Cold War. They were executed at Sing Sing six weeks later, on June 19, 1953.

On May 12, a United States marshal appeared at the *National Guardian* office in New York with a "command" for Belfrage and me to appear before the McCarthy committee the following day in Washington. Not until we entered the hearing room for an executive session did we learn that the reason for our summons was "government operations in Germany." Belfrage and I had been in occupied Germany at the end of World War II as press control officers of a combined Allied operation under the supervision of Supreme Headquarters Allied Expeditionary Forces (SHAEF). Belfrage was a British citizen who lived in the United States but served in British uniform. Our job, in collaboration with U.S. Army Intelligence, had been to survey the field for potential licensees for the new German press (the Nazi press had been entirely shut down) we were helping to establish in the United States Occupation Zone; to make recommendations to higher headquarters; and to help the papers get started.

The directives under which we operated, signed by General Dwight D. Eisenhower, were clear: No newspaperman who had had any involvement with the Nazi press was eligible as a licensee. The Information Control Command, to which we were assigned, was directed by Brigadier General Robert A. McClure, and all our recommendations ultimately had to be approved by him. Our work and our reports became part of the official Army record, as did the letters of commendation we had both received. What interest then would the McCarthy committee have in our work in Germany?

Quite a bit, as it turned out. McCarthy's chief counsel, Roy Cohn, and his assistant counsel, G. David Schine, had just returned from a McCarthy mission in Western Europe to "investigate State Department personnel." In a nine-day tour in which they said they had interviewed 147 persons and collected three briefcases of documents, they had visited Paris, Berlin, Bonn, London, Munich, Vienna, and Frankfurt. In Frankfurt they had discovered, in conversation with Nazi-tainted newspaper editors whom Belfrage and I had rejected, that Communists had been named to boards of licensees on newspapers which we had helped bring to life. The fact that these Communists had long since been replaced by Cold War-minded guardians of Germany's future did not matter. Nor did it matter that these Communists had originally been approved, as Communists, by General McClure to be licensees. The "junketeering gumshoers," as Cohn and Schine came to be called, had struck red gold. They had found the trail of two subversive Army personnel who had labored in Germany to create a Red press and then gone back to the United States to found a Red newspaper—the *National Guardian*—which was currently leading the fight to prevent the execution of Ethel and Julius Rosenberg, at whose trial Cohn had been an assistant prosecutor. What better weapon with which to club President-General Eisenhower, who had sanctioned our activities in Germany, and who was showing signs of discomfort over the McCarthy crusade at home? Hence the order for a command performance before the McCarthy committee May 13.

Belfrage and I appeared separately in executive session. My hearing opened on a gracious note. McCarthy apologized for the lack of a private room in which I might consult counsel. There were no hot lights—just McCarthy and Cohn, counsel and I, and a silent stenographer. There were questions on Germany and my newspaper career which were answered fully, except for questions on politics and associations, which I refused to answer. Occasionally a wandering committee member dropped in—Senator Henry M. Jackson, Democrat of Washington, who wanted to know if the statute of limitations had run out on the job questionnaire I had signed for the German operation so that I might be open to a possible perjury charge; Senator Stuart Symington, Democrat of Missouri, who wanted to know whether I considered myself a good American. McCarthy offered me the opportunity to go to the FBI and tell them all, with a guarantee of strictest confidence regarding the information I might give. I could think about it over night.

Belfrage's private session was more abrupt. After a preliminary skirmish, McCarthy said he would order to be present at the public hearing the next day a representative of the Immigration and Naturalization Service to determine why Belfrage was still in the United States. Belfrage had applied for citizenship in 1937 and had had one year remaining of his five-year waiting period when he took a war job with British Intelligence in 1941. He was not credited with the four years of his waiting period, on the ground that he had left the country (on war service). Before he was permitted to return to the United States, where he had lived most of the years since 1926 and where his two children were born, he was forced to produce an affidavit from his wife guaranteeing that he would not become a public charge.

The next day, May 13, a flawless spring day in Washington, the spectator seats in the Senate Caucus Room in the Capitol were filled with Americans from hundreds and thousands of miles away, come to the nation's capital to see democratic government in operation. The doors swung open and Senator McCarthy swept in. He gave a pat on the back to the Capitol policeman at the door, a familiar wave to the crowded press tables. The Senator's own table was well attended. At his left the glowering Cohn, at his right Senator Symington, the senior Democrat on the committee; in the background, the apprentices—among them young Robert F. Kennedy—and an assortment of hacks and hangers-on. Strung out to the right and left were the lesser Senators of the committee, leaning in toward the kleig light center.

As McCarthy opened the session, his smile vanished. The face became the stern visage of the Defender of the Faith and Public Morals. The witness was in the dock. The graces of yesterday were gone—the press was present now. What followed is a recurring nightmare: insults and abuse, threats and humiliation and, under the rules of the inquisition, the frustration of the gang-up. Refusal to respond to questions about politics and associations brought threats of citation for contempt and indictment for perjury. References to my work on the *New York Post* and the *New York Times* brought snide comments from McCarthy, with leers at the *Post* and *Times* reporters at the press tables.

In the press rows at the hearing were men and women with whom I had worked on other newspapers. All were civil, some cordial, but none had any questions that went deeper than the mischief of the day. We had asked several of them to meet with us outside the Caucus Room after the hearing to answer for them questions we would refuse to answer for McCarthy. We informed those who came that we were not Communists, but that we felt it was our right—our duty—to remain silent before a committee of Congress which we felt had no authority to inquire into our beliefs and associations.

We explained why we had invoked the Fifth Amendment rather than the First. Our lawyer had reasoned in a four-hour argument that if we invoked the First we would almost surely be cited for contempt, be convicted, and, in the existing climate, go to prison. He said the *National Guardian* would suffer and perhaps even be forced to suspend publication if its two chief editors were jailed. In effect he put the issue as one of survival of the paper as against the issue of personal principle, however valid that principle might be.

We also explained to the reporters why we had refused to answer questions about the *National Guardian* and our association with it. If we had conceded association with our newspaper, the next questions probably would have been (and we would have been required under threat of contempt citation to answer): Who are the other staff members? Who contributes financially to the paper? Will you produce your subscription files? We felt that such questions went beyond the jurisdiction of the inquiry; that they would seek to intimidate us and, through us, our readers; that we had a moral obligation—as did any newspaper editor—to keep the trust of privacy with our readers, among whom were Communists, Republicans, vegetarians, agnostics, Jehovah's Witnesses, and agrarian socialists. We had never asked them questions about themselves and insisted that no committee of Congress had the authority to ask us about them. Only the *New York Times* printed even the barest bones of these comments, adding the dates of my employment on the Sunday *Times,* with the exact date of my resignation in 1948.

The attitude of fear and conformity that manifested itself in the Washington press corps was depressingly apparent. For example, Jack Olsen, a Washington correspondent of the American Broadcasting System, in 1951 polled the Washington press corps with questionnaires on McCarthy. He received 211 replies, many of them with thoughtful evaluations of the Senator. For every friendly evaluation, eight were hostile. One reporter characterized McCarthy as "a disgrace to the nation," and then added in a postscript: "The fact that I prefer not to sign my name to this is one evidence of the harm that McCarthy has done to the country." Only a few of the 211 signed their names.

The day after the hearings, May 15, Belfrage and I were in the office we shared in the *National Guardian,* with the staff gathered around to hear our Washington story. Two large representatives of the Immigration Service appeared as we were talking, placed Belfrage under arrest on a deportation warrant, and took him to Ellis Island for custody as a "dangerous alien." No charge had been made against him and no deportation proceeding had been instituted. On June 10 he was ordered released on $5,000 bond by Federal District Judge Edward Weinfeld in a habeas corpus proceeding, and his movements were restricted to the New York area. Government efforts to put him back in jail failed, and a deportation hearing was ordered in August 1954. The hearings continued for weeks on charges relating to Belfrage's alleged membership in the Communist Party in 1937-38. On December 9, 1954, his deportation was ordered, under the provisions of the Walter-McCarran Immigration Act. A Board of Immigration Appeals affirmed the deportation order, and on May 13, 1955, exactly two years after his appearance before the McCarthy committee, Belfrage again was arrested and imprisoned. Since Ellis Island had been closed, he was sent to the Federal Detention Center on West Street in New York. Efforts to obtain his release again on bond proved fruitless. After Belfrage's third month in prison, my colleague John T. McManus and I made a decision for him. Believing that an appeal to the "Cold War Supreme Court" headed by Chief Justice Fred M. Vinson was hopeless, we counseled him to accept deportation to England where he would function as correspondent-at-large with the title of "Editor in Exile." It took considerable persuasion, since he was willing to remain in jail "till hell froze over," but he finally agreed, with reluctance, and left the United States in August 1955.

This skeletal rendition of the Belfrage story does no justice to the vigorous two-year fight that was conducted to permit him to remain in the United States and to continue as editor of the *National Guardian*. But that part of the story as it relates to the press is pertinent. In a statement issued immediately after the hearings in May 1953, the *National Guardian* said:

> Clearly it is the spearhead of an attempt to suppress all remaining opposition voices in the press. It is more than time that the editors and the publishers of the press throughout the country recognized the storm warnings. They will be next. If they refuse to defend editors of small publications, whatever their point of view, they are aiding and abetting the destruction of the First Amendment which guarantees freedom of the press.

This statement, as was the case with other efforts on behalf of Belfrage, was met with silence by the vast majority of the newspapers. For them, freedom of the press was for the respectable many, but not for the few who ventured into unrespectable opposition. I. F. Stone commented in the May 30, 1953, issue of his *Weekly:*

> The *National Guardian* is one of the few voices left which disagrees with the official Cold War line. . . . There are few Americans left who dare speak up openly for peace. The attack on Belfrage and the *National Guardian* is an attempt to intimidate and silence these few . . . The respectables look the other way. The *New York Times* spoke up for Wechsler of the *Post,* but the *Post* did not speak up for the *National Guardian*. True, Belfrage's case is more difficult: He neither confessed, recanted nor informed. But the difference clarifies the real issue which must be faced if freedom of the press is to be preserved.

Repeated efforts to involve the press in the protest were futile. Not only was there no interest, there often was open hostility.

When Belfrage was arrested for the second time and jailed in May 1955, I undertook a campaign of letter-writing to several newspapers, among them two for which I had worked and whose editorial page editors I knew personally, the *New York Post* and the *New York Times*. I wrote also to the *Washington Post,* the *St. Louis Post-Dispatch,* the *York* (Pa.) *Gazette & Daily,* among others. In a letter to the editor of the *Times,* for publication, I commented on the fact that Belfrage was being held in jail without grand jury charge and on the freedom of the press issue involved in the Belfrage case. I urged the *Times* to comment editorially on the matter. A few days later a call came from a member of the editorial board of the *Times* saying that the letter was being accepted for publication, but it was too long, and would I agree to certain deletions. The deletions all dealt with the free press issue. Feeling that the first order of business was to achieve Belfrage's freedom (an editorial was promised), I agreed to the deletions rather than have the letter discarded altogether. The letter did appear, and with it an editorial denouncing the government's action in holding Belfrage without charge. There was no comment on the free press issue. A similar but stronger editorial appeared in the *St. Louis Post-Dispatch*. The *York Gazette & Daily* discussed both the question of bail and press freedom. From James Wechsler of the *New York Post,* the first prominent press victim of McCarthy, and from J. R. Wiggins of the *Washington Post,* the chairman of the special ASNE committee and one of the four dissenters in its report on the Wechsler-McCarthy hearings, there was no acknowledgment of my letter and accompanying material. And, needless to say, there was no editorial comment in either paper.

Let us here recall the conclusion of the ASNE dissenters in the Wechsler case: "In our opinion, therefore, whatever inconvenience results, whatever controversy ensues, we are compelled by every command of duty to brand this and every threat to freedom of the press, from whatever source, as a peril to American freedom." Obviously there were exceptions—those who fought not only against McCarthy's methods but against his basic premise that there was an international Communist conspiracy (with an American branch) which endangered the American way of life. If a person espoused the view that both McCarthy's methods and his basic premise were the genuine threats to the nation, he was apparently indefensible. This position was delineated in an editorial in the *New York Times* May 9, 1953, after the Wechsler hearing. Listing with approval Wechsler's record of anti-Communist activity, it said: "All of this carried no weight with Mr. McCarthy. Mr. Wechsler's crime seems clearly to be that he has also fought Mr. McCarthy's methods." The editorial went on:

> The rising threat of Communist aggression is and has been for years a matter of the gravest concern to all of us in the free world. It is not only right but necessary that we take every possible defensive step to meet this real and growing danger. We have to build up our armaments, we have to support our allies in Europe and in Asia, we have to use force to resist aggression whether in Korea or Greece, we have to develop our own political, social and economic strength as well as military. But in the process of alerting ourselves and our friends to the Russian imperialist-Communist menace—which "peace offensives" do not dissipate—some

Americans have become frightened. Fear leads to panic, and panic can lead to the subversion of our most precious institutions. Americans have to be alert, strong and steady. But they do not have to be scared. It is contrary to the best interests of our country to capitalize on fear.

Senator McCarthy himself would have been hard-pressed to criticize this summary of United States foreign policy, except for the *Times*'s remarks about fear and panic. Wechsler, a year later, made it plain that he saw no diminution of the Red Peril as he spoke from the barricades of the Maryland chapter of the Americans for Democratic Action in January 1954. He said:

We are an embattled democracy. The threat of Soviet imperialism is real. So is the challenge of Soviet espionage and sabotage. The way to meet the challenge, I suggest, is through calm, effective counter-intelligence . . . If I were operating by the McCarthy method, I would be tempted to ask: Which side are you on?

In an inverse way, both the *Times* and Wechsler were saying that McCarthy was or ought to be on their side, and if he would only reform his method, there would be no problem at all. Thus, the counterpoint cases of Wechsler and Belfrage demonstrated two things: (1) It was impossible to halt McCarthy if his critics agreed with his basic premise of the Red Peril; (2) there was patent hypocrisy in the newspapers' assertions on the universality of the First Amendment.

For the newspaper industry, the First Amendment was divisible. It was an umbrella for the many who went along with the Cold War policies of the government. But those who found these policies contrary to the Constitution had to walk in the rain. And if their heresy was compounded by alien status, there was exile.

# 7. The News from Korea

The war in Korea was the deadly parallel to McCarthy. One bolstered the other, and the press bolstered both. The argument over who had launched the aggression on June 25, 1950, became useless as events rapidly overcame debate, and within a matter of days the United States had pressured the United Nations into declaring an official collective "police action" in Korea. Washington also ordered the Seventh Fleet into the Taiwan Straits (where it has remained ever since as a counterforce to China), vastly strengthened its military position in the Philippines, and became the banker and arsenal for the French colonial wars in Indo-China.

There was no logical reason for the North Koreans to have instigated a war which would be certain to draw in the United States. The government in Pyongyang was making great strides in industrializing the north, with both Soviet and Chinese assistance. Syngman Rhee, the United States-installed president of South Korea, had suffered a devastating defeat in an election on May 30, 1950, at the hands of a political combination which favored the unification of Korea. In the absence of a new crisis, Rhee's days were numbered. Rhee did his utmost to engender a crisis. He intensified his repressive actions (112 political figures, including 30 candidates, had been arrested during the election campaign) and ordered the army to make provocative forays across the 38th Parallel demarcation line. American generals began arriving in Seoul in early June and all South Korean army leaves were canceled. In Washington the South Korean ambassador told the State Department that his country was on the verge of collapse and asked for armed intervention. The Democratic Front of Korea—an organization dedicated to the unification of North and

South Korea—sent emissaries south, under the aegis of the United Nations Commission in Korea, to propose talks on reunifying the country. The emissaries were arrested and jailed. John Foster Dulles flew into Seoul, and on June 19 promised the National Assembly that the "Communist grip on the North" would soon be loosened. The United States Joint Chiefs of Staff in Tokyo ordered a detail of the largest and newest bombers to the Far East. The next day Dulles, in homburg hat and looking for all the world like the chairman of the board of an international undertakers' cartel, posed for the now-famous picture in the trenches of the South Korean army just below the 38th Parallel.

The war broke at dawn on June 25. If the Soviet Union had prior knowledge that the North Koreans were planning an attack, or if, as the United States charged, the Soviet Union had masterminded the attack, Moscow staged an impeccable dissembling act. The Soviet delegation had been boycotting the United Nations Security Council because of the refusal to seat the People's Republic of China in Taiwan's place. Moscow for months had been engaged in a peace offensive which was demolished by the outbreak of war in Korea. There was, contrary to the United States contention about the inspiration of the fighting, considerable evidence that the Soviet Union was caught off balance by the war's outbreak. It failed to order its delegation back into the Security Council in time to prevent the United States from raising the United Nations flag over United States expeditionary forces. Moscow has never acknowledged its colossal blunder in missing the chance to label the war in Korea as a United States war.

The chief beneficiaries of the war were not the Russians or the North Koreans, but Syngman Rhee and the United States Joint Chiefs of Staff, and the hard-liners in the State Department who were seeking ways to contain the successful Chinese revolution. Beyond this, the economic indicators in the United States were pointing down, and Korea offered a splendid opportunity for retooling for war production and profits, and for testing refined methods of mass annihilation on a people of color, as had been done at Hiroshima and Nagasaki. The State Department's propaganda chief, Assistant Secretary of State Edward W. Barrett, said in San Francisco after the news of the June 25 clash that the Soviet peace offensive had been bothering the State Department. "We can really go to town on this now," he said. "The one and only benefit from the whole occurrence is that it shows up to intelligent people on both sides of the Iron Curtain the rank hypocrisy of the Kremlin's so-called peace offensive."

The whole thrust of Washington's propaganda was that the Soviet Union had instigated the Korean war. Later, when the Chinese came in, the line shifted (not without some creaking) to point the finger at Peking as the instigator. By then Barrett had left the State Department to found his own publicity firm which, in 1954, became a division of the public relations firm of Hill & Knowlton. He went from there to become dean of the Graduate School of Journalism of Columbia University, where he continued his public relations activities in behalf of the school with considerable success until his resignation in August 1968.

As to the actual origin of the aggression on June 25, 1950, there is some fascinating confusion which appears to have been manufactured after the fact. In its first edition of June 26, the *New York Times* said in its Korean story lead, "This morning, according to the South Korean Office of Public Information, South Korean troops pushing northward captured Kaeju [also spelled Haeju], capital of Wranghoe province, which is a mile north of the border." It was later verified that Kaeju was six miles north of the 38th Parallel. This same statement appeared in a story in a later edition of the *Times,* but with a new lead attributing the start of aggression to the North Koreans.

On June 25 the United States Armed Forces Radio Service, Voice of Information and Education, reported from Seoul:

> The origin of the fighting appears confused—at some points South Korean troops are operating north of the 38th Parallel. One South Korean unit advanced and found themselves in possession of the town of Haeju.

The formulation is one of boyish surprise, almost as though the Dreadnaught Boys had come out of the woods, peered about, and said, "Hello, here we are in Haeju." An even more astonished interpretation was given by Associated Press correspondent Oliver H. P. King. His version appeared in a letter to Fyke Farmer, a Nashville attorney, who had sued to test the constitutionality of President Truman's order committing the United States to war without a declaration by the Congress. In his letter dated March 4, 1954, from Korea, King wrote:

> To my knowledge the Korean Office of Public Information released no information on June 25, 1950, June 26 or June 27: the sudden attack by the North Koreans caught officials off guard. . . . The information I received came from KMAG (U.S. Korea Military Advisory Group) and this is how the "capture" of Haeju came about: South Korean forces below the 38th Parallel in the West were put to flight by the invading northerners. Those who could fled in boats. But there weren't enough boats. Those unable to escape marched east by north to attempt to make it by land. They were obliged to enter Haeju and to their delight discovered the city deserted of North Korean forces, who had pushed south against them. In other words, by their circuitous route they had dodged the enemy. They then

proceeded southward with their flight and most of them made it to the quickly withdrawing friendly lines.

Thus correspondent King circuitously maneuvered the delighted South Korean forces north, then south, apparently hopscotching over the North Korean army (which was advancing south) to the safety of the "quickly withdrawing friendly lines" (which seemed in the first instance to have been withdrawing north). With this explanation, King assumed the role of Pentagon spokesman. He wrote to Farmer:

The basis of the first reports that the south had attacked the north was the Communist propaganda radio at Pyongyang. After the surprise attack had been launched, the radio spread propaganda reports that the south had started the war, but believe me, that's the baldest of Red lies. The U.S. advisory group had been reduced to 500 men, its commanding general was en route by ship home from Japan and the senior officer was in Japan bidding him goodbye. By U.S. policy the South Koreans had practically no reserve ammunition, no tanks, no military combat planes, big bazookas or artillery. The Communists were the ones with all these. In my opinion and that of others who were here at the time, the United States had no intention of defending South Korea, much less aiding in an attack on the north. President Truman's declaration was a big surprise—and might even have surprised some officials in his State Department.

This does not accord with Dulles' pledge to the South Korean Assembly June 18, nor with the top-level military sessions in Tokyo all through June, nor with Walter Sullivan's June 25 report to the *New York Times* from Hong Kong that "the warlike talk strangely has almost all come from Southern Korean leaders. . . . On a number of occasions Dr. Rhee has indicated that his army would have taken the offensive if Washington had given its consent." Most pointedly it does not accord with a letter to Farmer from the *New York Times* foreign news editor Emanuel R. Freedman written on March 5, 1954, one day after King's letter. Freedman said:

The third paragraph of the *Times* report of June 26, 1950, on the outbreak of hostilities in Korea stated specifically that the report of the capture of Haeju had come from the South Korean Office of Public Information. Our correspondents were gathering information from a number of sources at the time. You must appreciate that in so fluid and confused a situation they were not yet in a position to evaluate and verify each such report. In an effort to present as complete a story as was possible, they reported as much as they could learn, giving the attribution where they were unable to verify it with their own eyes. That was the case in the report of the capture of Haeju, as made public by South Korean officials.

Despite Freedman's attribution of zeal to *Times* correspondents, no further attempt was made (at least nothing was published) to determine exactly who gave the order to launch the aggression; nor did any other major newspaper or wire service pursue the inquiry. To this day, it is universally accepted in the United States that the North Koreans launched the war, despite the fact that they had everything to lose and little to gain, and that all circumstances point to the war as being in the interest of Syngman Rhee's short-range survival and the United States's long-range policy of containment of Communism in Asia. The wisdom of this course seemed to go unchallenged by the AP's Oliver King and every other correspondent and commentator outside the radical press.

At home, in accordance with the established Cold War foreign policy pattern, the FBI swung into action according to prearranged plans, as the *New York Post* put it. In the *New York Daily News* columnist Ed Sullivan applauded the jailing of "dangerous jerks." Westbrook Pegler called for the execution of all Communists. Walter Winchell noted with approval the increased blacklisting of actors, writers, and technicians in radio and television, and his parent newspaper, the *New York Daily Mirror,* asked, "Isn't it time to do something about our native Communists . . . shall we let these thugs go free?" In the second volume of *The Cold War and Its Origins,* D. F. Fleming wrote:

> The interminable Korean war fed the fires of McCarthyism until most of the year 1954 was given over to vast national circuses, inquisitions and judgments centering around the man whose skyrocketing power over us shook the confidence of all the allies in our sanity as a nation. His investigating committee and others led the nation in an orgy of Red-hunting, witch-hunting and scapegoat killing. . . . The achievement of this sad state of mind and reputation in the world was of course due to the excess whipping up of the Cold War itself, but the three-year extension of the Korean war which followed our attempt to take over North Korea was the inflamed center of the Cold War during all this time.

The inflammation was deep-seated. Not one major daily newspaper opposed the intervention in Korea or disputed the official version that the North Koreans had instigated the fighting. Almost alone, even among the left-wing journals, the *National Guardian* opposed the intervention from the outset and questioned the origin of the war. I was executive editor at the time, and it was my function to deal with mail from subscribers who were canceling their subscriptions for reasons of editorial policy or content. In the early months of the Korean war the job got out of hand. At the outset of the war the circulation of the *National Guardian* was 54,000. Within two years it had dropped to 22,000. The reason was fear. Most of the cancellations were from government employes, teachers, and employed professional persons. Cash contributions were often enclosed with a request for anonymity. Many letters were deeply moving in their apology; a few were threatening, but the threats were generally born of fear. We learned that the FBI had been visiting subscribers asking them if they were aware of the true nature of the *National Guardian*. Local post offices apparently were cooperating with the FBI and, in violation of the law, permitting examination of mail bundles of the paper.

One area where circulation actually increased was among the investigatory and intelligence agencies of the government. The Internal Revenue Service sent inspectors to the office to determine whether our tax records and payments were in order. They were. We were constantly aware of the possibility of such visits and maintained our records with scrupulous care. Staff members whose names were listed in the paper were subjected to threatening and obscene telephone calls for weeks, or to calls made by organized brigades of night workers at regular intervals after midnight. In my case this harassment lasted four months, and it took considerable ingenuity to defeat the sleep-wrecking operations of the phantom callers. A sympathetic telephone company employe informed us that all our office phones were being tapped. We assumed this was true also of our home phones.

When the casualty lists mounted and the prospect of "victory" became dimmer, some newspapers began to express misgivings about the military aspects of the war; but still none questioned basic United States policy or investigated the war's origins in a fashion that might bring this policy into serious question. The experience of one reporter who did is instructive. He was I. F. Stone, the publisher of *I. F. Stone's Weekly*, then a columnist for the *New York Daily Compass*, which had succeeded the newspaper *PM* and the *New York Star*. Like the overwhelming majority of Americans, Stone at first had accepted the official version of events—a clear case of unprovoked aggression by the North Koreans with the complicity of the Soviet Union. In August 1950 he went on roving foreign assignment with a base in Paris. He read the press of Paris and London and compared the stories of experienced correspondents published in those papers with stories in the United States press based on official communiqués from General Douglas MacArthur's headquarters in Tokyo. The discrepancies were glaring. Even the severe censorship in Tokyo could not conceal them. He began an investigation which resulted in a full-scale reassessment of his view of the Korean war.

His first articles were published in the *Compass* and in the Paris *L'Observateur*, a liberal weekly edited by Claude Bourdet, a Resistance hero. The articles caused a great stir in Paris diplomatic circles, but in the United States the press ignored them. In the February 15, 1951, issue of *L'Observateur*, Bourdet wrote:

If Stone's thesis corresponds to reality, we are in the presence of the greatest swindle in the whole of military history; I use the term advisedly, for it is not a question of a harmless fraud [*galejade*] but of a terrible maneuver in which deception is being consciously utilized to block peace at a time when it is possible.

Stone sought unsuccessfully to get his second article, "The Origins of the Korean War," published in England, and then wrote a book describing his investigation and his conclusions. Again he looked to England, but he was told that the British atmosphere was rapidly being "coordinated" by Washington, and that he ought to seek a publisher in the United States —his material was too critical of United States policy to see the light of print in England. Although Stone used as his source material for the most part United Nations documents and official United States government statements to dispute the accepted version of the war, 28 American publishers turned his book down. The quality of the work was exemplary, most of them said, and it was of great importance, but it was—and this was said only off the record—too hot to handle.

In the fall of 1951, the editors of the *Monthly Review,* an independent socialist publication, learned from Stone about his manuscript and determined immediately to publish it. It appeared in the spring of 1952 as *The Hidden History of the Korean War.**

In a foreword the editors of *Monthly Review,* Leo Huberman and Paul M. Sweezy, said they had regarded the Korean war at the outset as a civil war but, like Stone, had accepted the version of the North Koreans as aggressors. By the fall of 1951, they had become convinced that the war "was the outcome of deliberate and sinister maneuvering by those with an interest in war in the Far East," and that the subsequent course of the war, the failure of the United States to stop it when it was evident that it could be stopped, the prolongation of the truce talks—"that all of these things would be found on careful examination to have the closest possible relation to the origins of the war." Despite Stone's reputation as a journalist of the utmost integrity and thoroughness, the book was almost entirely ignored in the book review sections and the news columns of the general press.

If the press had given Stone's book the attention it deserved, and if the editorial page editors had, on the basis of its unchallengeable documentation, called for a full-scale congressional investigation of the origins of the war and United States policy, there almost certainly would have been a national outcry for an end to the war and the war-breeding policy. But the press instead acted in the "national interest" to suppress facts which

---

* The book was reissued by Monthly Review Press in 1969.

would embarrass the bipartisan leadership. In harmony with Senator McCarthy, John Foster Dulles (who at the time was Republican adviser to Truman's Secretary of State Acheson) was warning against the menace of the "international Communist conspiracy." Korea was the main exhibit in the showcase window of the menace-makers, and nothing would be permitted to crack the glass. Instead of receiving the gratitude of a grateful nation, Huberman and Sweezy were summoned before witch-hunting committees—Huberman before the McCarthy committee in 1953 and Sweezy before a New Hampshire inquisition. Sweezy was indicted for contempt and convicted, but his conviction was set aside by the United States Supreme Court.

Not only radical critics were suppressed and ignored. Reginald Thompson, a well-known British war correspondent who was sympathetic with United States policy, published in England a book entitled *Cry Korea* in 1952. He was critical of the conduct of the war and its effect on soldiers on both sides, and of the senseless destruction of Korea. Thompson's book could not find a publisher in the United States, and even the British edition could not be obtained at book stores or in libraries in this country.

The international conspiracy theme took hold editorially and graphically in the press early in the war, as was demonstrated by a book published by American correspondent Harrison Forman in 1945 titled *Report from Red China* (Henry Holt). Among its many pictures of the Chinese Red Army was one showing three smiling soldiers exhibiting machine guns captured from the Japanese in 1945. The caption read: "Tsu Chi (on the left), Chen Wai-on, and Liu Chuan-lieu, three heroes of the 77th Regiment. Tsu Chi lost his right arm in the engagement in which the Japanese machine guns were captured." On October 28, 1950, five years later, the *Los Angeles Mirror* published the same picture on page 2, crediting AP Wirephoto. The caption read: "THEY MAY BE FIGHTING IN KOREA TODAY. Grinning Chinese Communists display late model heavy machine guns of Russian design. Many reports of Chinese intervention in Korea battle are pouring in." Not only had the smiles turned into grins (always a sinister shift) but there was a precise bit of editorial amputation in the photograph and caption as they appeared in the *Mirror*: The names of the soldiers had vanished, along with any indication that Tsu Chi had only one arm. The original photograph showed Tsu's entire body; the *Mirror* picture was cropped at his right shoulder. Surrounding the *Mirror* picture were stories with such headlines as: "China Reds Aid Commies; Stem Big Advance" and "Christ Lives on 'Mid Red Terror."

On November 4, the *Mirror* published a letter from a United States

Marine noting that the guns were "not Russian-designed, as you said, but leftovers from the Japs. So please call a spade a spade. It will help us get out of this mess if we are honest." An editor's note appended to the letter read: "You and others who called us on this one are right. It was an unintentional error, not an effort to twist facts."

A query to the Associated Press disclosed that it was not an AP picture as labeled. The *Mirror* said it had learned subsequently that the photo had in fact come from Acme. The picture, dated October 27, 1950, was located at Acme. It had been sent from New York with this caption: "Kunuri, North Korea: Grinning Chinese troops wave as they practice with machine-guns. Maj. Gen. Yu Hae Hueng, commander of the 2d South Korean Corps, announced October 27 that 40,000 Chinese Communist troops have entered Korea. Armed with heavy weapons, some of them are already fighting as part of a North Korean division." There was no mention of the machine guns being Russian, as the *Mirror* caption stated. An Acme staff member said, "Of course, all the Chinese photos we have moved recently are old stuff, taken in the last war." There was no explanation for the fictitious Kunuri dateline, which gave the impression that the grinning Chinese were in Korea in 1950 for the Korean war.

A journalistic atrocity on a much greater scale was perpetrated in October 1951 when a 130-page special issue of *Collier's* magazine "previewed" World War III—"the war we do not want"—with text and pictures describing the atomization of Moscow and the occupation by "UN" Americans of a Soviet Union reduced to chaos. Playwright Robert E. Sherwood and author J. B. Priestley were engaged, at considerable price, along with *New York Times* military expert Hanson Baldwin, Senator Margaret Chase Smith, Republican of Maine, and *Christian Science Monitor* editor Erwin D. Canham to compile a fantasy about life under socialism.

The war was described as starting with an attempt on the life of Yugoslavia's President Tito in May 1952 by Russian agents who dressed as peasants and chewed explosive-filled cigars which they hurled at Tito—obviously with imprecise aim, since he survived. It ended with the United States bringing the gift of civilization to surviving Soviet citizens by means of a Walter Winchell column addressed to "Mr. and Mrs. Russia"; Russian editions of *Time, Life, Collier's,* and *Reader's Digest;* a stage production of *Guys and Dolls;* the loan of Walter Reuther to restore democracy to Soviet labor unions; and a display of Hattie Carnegie hats in Moscow's Dynamo Stadium (seating capacity 100,000).

There were some rumblings of discontent at the United Nations about the depiction of a United Nations flag planted in "Moscow Occupation

Headquarters." But there was no immediate reaction from the American press, except for news summaries of the *Collier's* articles. No one noted a parallel between the *Collier's* "international Communist conspiracy" and the "international Jewish banking conspiracy" fostered by the spurious *Protocols of the Elders of Zion,* used by Hitler to stir warmindedness among the German people. The *Collier's* presentation, in like manner, seemed designed to scare the American public into supporting ever-greater military appropriations.

The *Collier's* fantasy did succeed in frightening Washington's allies—not because of the Red Menace but because of the paranoid mentality it revealed. At the Chaillot Palace in Paris, where the 1951 United Nations Assembly was meeting, the *Collier's* special was prominently displayed on the newsstands. The cover showed a GI standing with a drawn bayonet against a map of an occupied Soviet Union, with the United Nations flag over "occupation headquarters." In a takeoff, the weekly *L'Observateur* had on its front page the drawing of a Soviet soldier looking as starry-eyed and as noble as the GI, poising his bayonet before a map of an occupied United States. The title read: "A psychoanalysis of *Collier's*—23 Americans dream out loud." The 23 were described not as "madmen or practical jokers, but respected writers." Similar ridicule and alarm were expressed in newspapers in London, Canada, Germany, and Mexico. The developing expression of horror eventually stirred an uneasiness in the United States and produced a rebound condemnation of the *Collier's* tour de force in several newspapers. In the *Nation,* D. F. Fleming wondered "how each author came to take part in the enterprise, and whether any of them really understood what the impact of the whole would be. If many of them did, then it is much later than we thought."

Late or not, the planners of the *Collier's* article were acutely aware of a time factor which coincided with the needs of the United States government at a critical juncture in international diplomacy. The United Nations Assembly was about to meet in Paris. The Korean truce talks, which had begun on July 10, 1951, had been interrupted since August 23, when a series of incidents caused a North Korean-Chinese protest and a one-day cancellation of the negotiations by the North Korean-Chinese side. The United Nations Commander, General Matthew Ridgway, seized on the cancellation and, despite the expressed wishes of the North Korean-Chinese side to resume negotiations, announced to the world that the talks were finished.

In Washington pressure mounted for getting the Korean war back in full swing, and a major offensive was launched at the end of August which soon enveloped a third of the battle zone. The renewal of fighting served as a backdrop for the United States to push through a Japanese peace treaty in San Francisco early in September which ignored the Chinese altogether and gave the Soviet Union virtually no voice in its provisions. If harmonious truce negotiations had been in progress in Korea, this maneuver would have been far more difficult, if not impossible. This strategy was made public, in reverse fashion, early in October by Ernest A. Gross, deputy United States delegate to the United Nations, when he said in a talk before the United Nations Correspondents Association in New York that a cease-fire in Korea would permit the Soviet Union to launch a "phony" peace offensive at the General Assembly in Paris.

It was in the interest of United States policy to maintain the fiction of North Korean-Chinese intransigency at the truce talks and of the persistence of the Red Menace generally. What better method to further both ends and raise the slogan of "peace through strength" than an article such as the one in *Collier's*? Was there collusion between government and the magazine? There did not need to be any. The magazine simply assumed, like the rest of the press, that United States policy is pure, and that information from the United States is honest. The *New York Times* demonstrated this faith in an editorial on October 11, 1951, in discussing the state of the Korean truce talks. "After suspending truce operations for seven weeks on trumped up grounds," it said, "the Communists have now agreed to resume talks at a new site and under new neutrality controls." The facts were, as Stone sets forth in *The Hidden History of the Korean War,* that the grounds were not "trumped up" but were clear provocations by the United States command; that the Chinese and North Koreans had been ready throughout the seven weeks to resume talks, and the willingness of the United States to renew talks was motivated by the collapse of the United Nations offensive which, at a cost of thousands of lives, had bogged down in a hopeless stalemate.

Incredibly, on October 12, a United States plane strafed the neutral zone at Panmunjom, the new truce-talk site, killing a boy who had been walking home on a dirt road from a fishing trip, and wounding another. With appropriate compassion, the *Times* said, "It is expected that the Communists will use the incident—true or not"—to insist on stricter guarantees of the neutral zone. When correspondent David McConnell of the *New York Herald Tribune* asked Brigadier General Frank A. Allen about an earlier B-26 strafing of the truce-talk zone at Kaesong and what precautions were being taken to prevent a recurrence, the chief army public relations officer admonished him, "Don't forget which side you're on." The truce talks were resumed on October 25. There was a lull in the battle zones, but another war broke out—this time between the United States correspondents and the United Nations High Command in Korea.

Censorship throughout the Korean war had been severe, but at the truce talks at Kaesong and at Panmunjom it became almost total. Correspondents assigned to the United Nations Command were not permitted to speak with United Nations negotiators; they were briefed, several hours after each session, by a United States Army officer who had not even been at the talks. They were refused permission to inspect documents presented at the discussions and were dependent entirely on United States armed forces public relations officers in Korea and at supreme headquarters in Tokyo, where the imperial hand of General MacArthur was evident in every communiqué.

When the truce talks first opened in July, the chief North Korean negotiator, General Nam Il, proposed a cease-fire at the 38th Parallel. The UN chief, United States Admiral Turner Joy, sought to have the line fixed at 32 miles north of the parallel, which would have meant a surrender by the North Koreans and Chinese of the impregnably fortified mountains under their control. Admiral Joy informed the Western press that the North Koreans had refused to discuss a cease-fire at the 38th Parallel, and this version—completely untrue—was conveyed in thousands of headlines in the United States for weeks before the fact emerged that it was the United States which was refusing to discuss the 38th Parallel. Then the United Nations public pronouncement was modified, again falsely, to make it appear that Nam Il was unwilling to discuss a cease-fire along the existing battle line.

The duplicity of the official United States releases to the Western press was exposed in large measure by two correspondents assigned to the North Korean-Chinese command—Alan Winnington of the *London Daily Worker,* and Wilfred G. Burchett, an Australian who had covered the war in the Pacific for the *London Daily Express* and who had sent out the first eyewitness report of the atomic devastation of Hiroshima. Burchett had been in China writing a series of articles for the Paris daily *Ce Soir* and had asked to be assigned to the truce talks. When he and Winnington arrived at Kaesong, there was some consternation in the Western press corps at the sight of white faces among the darker Korean and Chinese press corps. One American photographer, Burchett noted in his book *Again Korea* (International, 1968), jotted down on his caption sheet, "Two white Commies." Burchett was soon recognized by correspondents who had served with him in the South Pacific and the reunion was cordial. The cordiality changed from social to business when it became evident that Burchett and Winnington had access to all the documents and the exchanges of the truce negotiations denied to the Western correspondents. The two became a regular source of information for their fact-starved and misinformed American and British colleagues.

An even more stringent censorship policy became effective soon after the talks were resumed in October. Newsmen who for months had had normal working relations with Burchett and Winnington were recalled to Tokyo. Some of them, Burchett said, later gave him the reason: The bits of truth they had been able to get past the censors had caused havoc in the public relations setup of General Matthew Ridgway. Washington pressure had been exerted on the publishers and editors, demanding more loyal behavior from their representatives in Korea. "Fraternization" was frowned upon. Burchett and Winnington were given the coloration of the enemy, and correspondents who previously had joined in the sessions between journalists of both sides were warned not to talk to the "Red" correspondents.

Brigadier General William P. Nuckols, United States Army public relations chief in Korea, turned up at the resumed talks with Howard Handelman, International News Service bureau chief in Tokyo, at his side. It was Nuckols who had told the Western correspondents that the United Nations was seeking a cease-fire along the actual battle line when actually it was asking for Kaesong and the surrender of 625 miles of territory, facts kept from the Western newsmen. When Burchett and Winnington disclosed them to their Western counterparts, there was a confrontation with Nuckols, who denied their accuracy. Handelman, who, according to Burchett, was Nuckols's confidant at Panmunjom, filed a story that evening reporting that Nuckols "had warned against accepting the Red newsmen's versions" of the issues. Thoroughly confused, the next day the American newsmen asked Burchett and Winnington into their press tent for a demonstration on the United Nations map of the precise truce-line positions Burchett said the United Nations was demanding. One correspondent gave Burchett a tracing of the United Nations map and asked him to take it back to the Chinese-North Korean headquarters to pinpoint the exact lines. Nuckols was outraged, and the correspondent who had made the request was not seen at Panmunjom for weeks. In his own story of the occurrence, Handelman said Burchett and Winnington had "asked to come" to the United Nations press tent and had demanded a map because the "Communist delegates had refused to pinpoint their version of it." This, of course, was a cover for a most uncomfortable situation. In *Again Korea,* Burchett picked up the thread of the story:

When we took the tracing back to Kaesong, we discovered that the map displayed in the Allied press tent was one especially faked for correspondents. We returned it with the precise lines pinpointed and the correspondents saw they had been tricked. They had a stormy session with Nuckols, but the story was out. The next day the American delegates dropped the demand for Kaesong.

On November 4, the North Korean-Chinese delegates proposed a demarcation line along the exact existing battle line. The United Nations delegation had been maintaining that this was the line it had been proposing all along (actually it had never proposed it). When the North Koreans and Chinese called their bluff, they were confronted by a dilemma of their own making: Although the United Nations side had never proposed the battle-line settlement, world opinion, having accepted the United Nations propaganda position, was quite prepared for this settlement. There was little the United Nations side could do about it, but they managed to confuse even that little. The next morning Burchett and Winnington learned that correspondents assigned to the UN had not even been informed of the North Korean-Chinese battle-line proposal of the day before—so once again they told their Western colleagues. Burchett wrote in *Again Korea*:

> After we told them, they rushed to Nuckols and accused him of withholding vital information. They then returned to us and said Nuckols denied that any new proposals had been made. We gave them a copy of the English text as it had been read in the conference tent the previous day. Back they went to Nuckols again, several of them livid with anger this time because, among the newsmen covering the talks, a hard core of journalists was used to digging for facts. Nuckols read through the document as though he were seeing it for the first time and tried to retreat by describing it as "a suggestion rather than a proposal." But it made the headlines in the western press the next day, and from then on even Handelman was less eager to be seen at Nuckols' side.

In Tokyo the voluntary civilian press agents were still operating intact for the United Nations command. The United Press, in a dispatch from there November 14, charged the enemy with deviousness in wanting to stop the killing. It reported that the North Koreans had "openly repudiated their long-standing agreement that hostilities would go on until a full armistice was signed." But British newspapers were becoming outspokenly critical of the stalling, and in the United States press there began to appear worried comments. On November 18 the *New York Times* said that the United States tactics were allowing the enemy to charge that "the Allies did not really want a truce." More importantly United States troops were becoming restless and bitter because men were being killed and wounded for no apparent reason. Something had to be done—and something was.

# 8. The Prisoners of War

In Pusan, a most unlikely outpost for an important announcement, Lieutenant Colonel James M. Hanley, judge advocate general of the Eighth Army, on November 14, 1951, called in South Korean "stringers" (part-time reporters who help cover less important events and places) to give them a dramatic piece of news. The enemy, he said, had killed 5,500 UN prisoners of war. The total was increased the next day to 6,270. Topping an Associated Press compilation, the *New York World-Telegram & Sun* printed this headline: "REDS BUTCHERED MORE AMERICANS THAN FELL IN '76." The Associated Press quoted Hanley as saying he had made public his charge because he thought "the American soldiers at the front ought to know what they are up against." What they were up against was a lying government—their own.

The Pusan announcement obviously was made to counter troop dissatisfaction with the progress of the truce talks, as subsequent events were to prove. In the days that followed, suspicion was expressed, particularly in Europe, that the Pusan sensation was clumsy propaganda. Gradually the figures were reduced to a few hundred, and in the discussion of prisoner exchanges that soon followed at Panmunjom, the Pusan charge never even came up. There were no second thoughts on the Hanley statement in the American press, which had pushed the atrocity charges for all they were worth. A *New York Herald Tribune* editorial was headed: "The Communist Brutes." The *Times* editorially said the Communists had "butchered prisoners in cold blood," and the *New York Post,* while critical of Hanley's method of presenting his charges, said: "The Communists are ruthless enemies whose disregard for human life is notorious." The *Post*'s comment was particularly mindless in light of the 10,000

Americans killed in battle since the truce negotiations had opened July 10. The monthly American average of dead and wounded since July had been 4,400. The MacArthur command in Tokyo put the enemy losses at 54,000 a month during the same period. But the taste for the war in the United States had grown so sour that even the Hearst press began to doubt the figures. United Press correspondent Robert C. Miller said in a talk before a Nevada editors' conference in the spring of 1952 that General James A. Van Fleet, the United States commander in Korea, had told his corps commanders that if he believed their figures of enemy casualties, "there wouldn't be a live Chinese or North Korean opposing us."

The Hanley report could have been immediately proved a fraud on the basis of material that had been published at least six months earlier. But the material had appeared in a left-wing newspaper, and it was—and remains—a policy of the press to ignore or minimize material from such a source. The source was the *National Guardian,* which had based its stories on material published in the *China Monthly Review,* an English-language magazine founded as a weekly in Shanghai in 1917 by John W. Powell. Powell had been a prisoner of the Japanese in World War II and was so poorly cared for that both his feet had to be amputated after his release. Publication of the magazine continued until 1953 under the editorship of Powell's son, John W. Powell Jr.—four years under the Chiang administration, and four years under the revolutionary government.

In its March 7, 1951 issue, the *National Guardian* published excerpts of articles from the *China Monthly Review* about United States prisoners in Korean camps, photographs of camp life, and excerpts of letters written by the prisoners to their families. In an introductory note the *National Guardian* said:

Families all over the United States today have relatives in camps in North Korea for duration of the "police action" in which Korea is being laid waste by forces under the UN flag. Fed the same propaganda as the GIs themselves about the North Korean and Chinese "hordes," the relatives of these POWs are desperately anxious for their captured sons, husbands and brothers. As a public service the *National Guardian* this week publishes material which by every test we are able to make we believe to be authentic.

The names of POWs were published in three consecutive issues. The *National Guardian* was deluged with letters requesting information about sons and husbands who had been reported as missing in action. The names were available to all publications in the United States—and to the armed forces which, it was known, were monitoring the North Korean shortwave radio. It would have been a simple matter for the United States government to verify the broadcast names and serial numbers. Many prisoners had sent messages to their families by way of the China Peace Committee in Peking and had signed petitions in camp calling for an end to the war. But the United States armed forces refused even to confirm the prisoner status of men whose pictures had appeared in the *National Guardian*. The reasons offered were that the Chinese-North Korean lists were "unreliable" and might be "propaganda." The real reason was that the government was appalled by the number of GIs who had signed peace petitions, and sought to keep the matter quiet.

Early in May the Hearst and Scripps-Howard press took cognizance of the *National Guardian*'s lists and, in articles overlaid with the "international Communist conspiracy" theme, denounced the *National Guardian* for a piece of "dirty work." The weekly was belabored for printing the name and address of the China Peace Committee, which had offered to send to any prisoner a monthly letter from his next of kin. Instead of arousing public indignation against the *National Guardian,* the Hearst and Scripps-Howard articles brought a flood of new requests to the *National Guardian* and a barrage of angry questions from worried parents and wives to the Defense Department.

The outcry became so intense that the government finally announced it had prepared a form "for the use of families seeking to communicate with relatives who are prisoners of war." Amusingly, the Defense Department listed as the forwarding agency the "Chinese Committee for Peace" in Peking. I knew the department had taken the name from the *National Guardian*'s pages because we had initially abbreviated the committee's name (the full title was the Chinese Committee for Peace and Against American Aggression) on the assumption that this bellicose mouthful might inhibit some families from writing. Thus the Defense Department became a collaborator, according to the Hearst-Scripps-Howard bill of particulars, in the "world Communist conspiracy."

There was no reason to doubt the authenticity of the names which, by this time, were being published also by Hsinhua, the official Chinese news agency. The *National Guardian* was scrupulously careful not to exploit the lists in any way. It did not circularize the families but urged readers to notify families where possible and to use the utmost discretion with respect to their privacy and anxiety. We offered to send to any family a copy of the issue in which the name of a relative appeared. The sole aim of the campaign was to relieve suspense. Hundreds upon hundreds of letters were received, some containing requests and some expressing gratitude for a found relative. Yet not one newspaper of general circulation showed enough courage to print the names of prisoners during this entire period.

On December 18, 1951, in an almost wordless exchange at Panmunjom, the North Korean negotiators handed over to the Americans a list of 3,198 American prisoners of war, confirming more than 1,000 names which had been published in the *National Guardian*.

As 1951 drew to an end, and the truce talks still appeared endless, the Ridgway press policies caused despair to the correspondents assigned to the United Nations command. Sydney Brooks of Reuters wrote from Tokyo headquarters, "There are many here who believe that the methods adopted at Kaesong and Panmunjom have reduced the prestige and integrity of the United Nations." He was referring to the news of the negotiations given out by the United Nations command. But the command had no alternative: it had come to the truce negotiations blind to the realities of the battlefield. No victory was near, none was in sight. To maintain the fiction of United States superiority, the command had to maintain an attitude of superiority at the conference table—in effect, to demand surrender—and give out false and misleading information to the press. Since the North Koreans and Chinese genuinely wanted to end the war, it was in their interest to issue the facts accurately and promptly. This set of circumstances is what placed Burchett and Winnington in their unique position as briefers to the Western correspondents, who, as events confirmed the briefers' reports, came to trust the "Red correspondents" in direct ratio to their mistrust of the United Nations briefing officers.

In the wrangle that accompanied the discussion on the exchange of prisoners in the winter of 1951-52, there were frequent stories renewing the Hanley charges of mistreatment and murder of United States prisoners. At one point Burchett informed some American correspondents that he had visited several POW camps and had found the prisoners in good condition. Soon thereafter he was visited by an Associated Press executive who made him an extraordinary proposal. The AP man said, according to Burchett:

> If you say our prisoners are alive and well, then I believe you. But we have a veteran photographer, "Pappy" Noel, who was taken prisoner. If what you say is true, why not let us send a camera and film up the road to "Pappy." Let him take pictures of the prisoners. We'll publish them in the hometown papers and people will start screaming to get them home again.

Somewhat doubtful of the reply, Burchett put the request to the North Koreans, who responded immediately: "Why not? Let them send a camera up to him." A few days later scores of American newspapers were displaying pictures of GIs in North Korean prison camps in obvious good health, playing basketball, volleyball, and football. Noel was given permission to go from camp to camp, and he sent back a flood of pictures with names and addresses of prisoners which were given great prominence in the hometown newspapers. Many similar photographs, with names, had been published almost a year earlier in the *National Guardian,* and offered to the general press. But it was not until the AP gave the photographs its blessing that member newspapers felt they could use them.

The United Press, smarting over the AP scoop, approached Burchett in turn with an ingenious proposal: Would the North Koreans permit them to parachute a photographer behind the enemy lines, let himself be captured, and then work the camps like "Pappy" Noel? The idea did not go down well with the North Koreans, who suggested that the photographer could get killed before he hit ground. UP made an alternate proposal: General William F. Dean, commander of the United States 24th Division, had been reported captured, but Ridgway's staff had reported "absolute proof" that Dean was dead. If Dean was alive, could a picture of him be obtained for exclusive distribution by UP? Burchett went to Pyongyang for approval, took pictures of Dean, and gave the negatives to UP. With the cooperation of the enemy, Burchett thus assured equal treatment of the United States wire services. He also sparked a major earthquake in Tokyo. In *Again Korea,* he wrote:

General Ridgway exploded when the U.S. Army paper *Stars and Stripes* carried a double-page spread on General Dean, sleek and trim in a double-breasted suit, playing chess with his Korean guards, doing physical exercises, shadow boxing and walking in the forest. Not only was a whole propaganda myth blown to smithereens but U.S. troops began to wonder why they should be freezing and dying at the front when General Dean and the other POWs were leading a good life in safety behind the lines. The editor of *Stars and Stripes* was sacked and sent home. The first issue under the new editor published a scathing attack on AP and others who fell for "red propaganda."

Immediately thereafter, in February 1952, Ridgway issued an official memorandum prohibiting contacts between the "United Nations" and "Communist" correspondents. It said:

The UN Command viewed with growing apprehension the practice of some reporters of excessive social consorting, including the drinking of alcoholic beverages, with Communist journalists. [Certain Allied correspondents] were abusing their news coverage facilities for the purpose of fraternization and were consorting and trafficking with the enemy.

The United Nations journalists ignored the ban. The day after it was issued even those who had avoided Burchett and Winnington in the past went out of their way to greet them and, under the furious gaze of General Nuckols, shared with them a bottle of "anti-freeze." Editors who a few months earlier had been cabling their men in Korea for atrocity stories now wired them to ignore the Ridgway order. A delegation of correspondents went to Japan and, with the support of the home offices, forced Ridgway to rescind his order. "It is impossible," said Burchett in his book, "here to recount the whole fantastic history of the talks, but a certain basic understanding of the frame of mind of the U.S. military who ran the talks and finally signed the agreement is a key to understanding the development of events in today's Korea and, more particularly, tomorrow's Korea."

This judgment was supported by the UP's Robert C. Miller in a talk to the Nevada Editors Conference in the spring of 1952. He said the American public had frequently charged its newspapers with not printing the truth—charges which had been met "with loud denials usually accompanied by violent gestures." But, he said, the critics were right: "We are not giving them the true facts about Korea, we haven't been for the past sixteen months and there will be little improvement in the war coverage unless radical changes are made in the military censorship policy." He said it was Ridgway's own edicts and the silence imposed on United States briefing officers that forced the American correspondents to seek out Winnington and Burchett. "Unfortunately," he said, "the Reds, using their old trick of mixing truth with propaganda, were more accurate and better sources of information. United Nations sources either denied or withheld comment on Communist-supplied information, then belatedly acknowledged its truth weeks afterward."

Miller could not concede that the Communists might regard truth as the best kind of propaganda. But his own comments on truth in the news revealed him in hopeless battle with the military, although he seemed unaware of it, because he accepted the basic premises of the Cold War. His talk continued:

If any section of our government, civilian or military, finds it can operate without fear of public scrutiny, it may be tempted to take measures which would not be in the best interests of the people and the nation . . . We are fighting a desperate, costly battle against Communism which we call the Cold War. Our most devastating weapon in this fight is truth . . . We, the press, are the big guns in this fight, and when censorship prevents us from obtaining and broadcasting the truth, we are being denied our most explosive ammunition.

There are certain facts and stories from Korea that editors and publishers have printed which were pure fabrication. You didn't know that when you printed them. Many of us who sent the stories knew they were false, but we had to write them because they were official releases from responsible military headquarters, and were released for publication even though the people responsible knew they were untrue.

What a devastating admission! Miller's second paragraph completely demolishes his high-minded, if misguided, first paragraph. Having glorified the press as watchdog of the public interest, he then allowed the government to call the watchdog to heel in the Cold War. To describe as "responsible headquarters" a source which deliberately deceives the American public is self-delusion. For a correspondent to send information which he knows to be false seems inexcusable. But given Miller's logic, it was inevitable. For if a correspondent believes that he and his newspaper or wire service are big guns in the Cold War, then he must man those guns and use whatever information is handed to him. That is precisely what Miller did. He was a good Cold War soldier.

Along with many other correspondents, Miller was trapped. Telling the truth about the hot war in Korea, or about almost any battlefront in the Cold War, would riddle United States policy. The North Koreans and Chinese knew this and skillfully used accurate information to the utmost. Hence the UN Command sought, with the help of the Western press, to suppress or distort the facts. When this was no longer possible, the Command was forced to concede that it could not win the war.

Thus the truce came, on July 27, 1953, three years after the police action had begun, and two years after the truce talks had got under way. The truce was forced by three factors: (1) the revulsion of the American public against the war as the truth seeped out; (2) the determination of the North Koreans, with first-rate assistance from the Chinese, to resist the invader; (3) the collapse of French colonialism in Indo-China, which impelled the United States to divert its attention from Korea to greener fields of exploitation and a seemingly more viable strategy to contain China.

It was impossible, Burchett said, to tell the Korean story without a fuller understanding of the American military mind. An incident in January 1952 supplied some understanding. A Filipino delegation, visiting the Eighth Army headquarters of General Van Fleet in Korea, found the general in a reflective mood. "Korea," he said, "has been a blessing. There had to be a Korea either here or some place in the world." Since the military is the police force of the government's foreign policy, this kind of rocking-chair reflection by a general need occasion no surprise. But what does one say about the journalistic mind which knew it had been given lies by its own side and the truth by the enemy, and yet persisted in furthering the lies? The results, which included 54,000 dead Americans, served only to exacerbate international tensions. That, obviously, was the intent of those who gave out the misinformation.

In September 1953, I made a study of press treatment of news about the exchange of prisoners in Korea which had been completed that month. During the weeks of the exchange, the press in the United States carried lurid headlines and stories about alleged "death marches," atrocities, and brutalities inflicted on the GIs by the North Koreans and the Chinese.

The United States Army was worried about "Operation Big Switch," as the exchange was called. The Army disclosed that captive Americans had written 29,000 letters home and "virtually all of these letters contained Communist propaganda to some degree." One degree may have been the assurances that the POWs were getting enough to eat, adequate medical care, and decent treatment. The United Press reported August 1 that military censors would forbid returning prisoners from "revealing all their experiences in the Red prison camps. [They will be required to] sign statements that they understand the censorship rules. The statements will bind prisoners even after they return home and talk with newsmen operating outside the military censorship." The returnees were watched and lectured to by specially trained counterintelligence personnel at rest camps in Korea, on troopships on the way home, and at hospitals after they arrived. Keyes Beach wrote in the *San Francisco Chronicle,* August 11:

> This is a fear-ridden atmosphere in which American POWs are being processed and being shipped back to the U.S. . . . All interviews with repatriates are conducted in the presence of a censor and a Counter-Intelligence Corps agent. Unless the repatriate is an exceptional man, this is, to say the least, an inhibiting influence. . . . Often during the course of the interviews, ex-prisoners have turned to the counterintelligence men for consent before answering questions.

About a third of the prisoners—one thousand GIs—did talk with the press, but only a fraction of their stories got into print. A survey of wire services and major newspapers around the country showed a remarkable repetition of names and experiences. The same atrocity stories which had made headlines were constantly repeated and were ascribed to only a few score GIs, but the brutality of the headlines was rarely borne out in the stories. Generally the repatriated GIs who spoke of harsh treatment were the self-styled "bad boys" of the camps—those who had tried to escape or who had been punished for stealing food from their buddies or clothing from warehouses. They were described in the news stories as

clean-cut types "who can be found on any American street corner."
Even in these cases, the fear or expectation of punishment was described
—not punishment. The *New York Times*'s Robert Alden wrote about a
GI who had stolen wood for a fire and had been punished several times
for a "hostile attitude." He said he had learned in camp about Communist collectivism. "Collectivism," he said, "means that if I have a fire,
everyone else in the camp is supposed to have a fire." What was the punishment for adherence to rugged individualism? "They treated us like
children," he told Alden. "It just got on your nerves." The treatment
consisted of making the prisoner write self-criticism: "I did wrong when
I took the wood. I promise never to take the wood again."

Some American correspondents became specialists in atrocities, both
in their stories and in their conversation. One scene in Panmunjom was
described by Israel Epstein, a special correspondent of the *National
Guardian,* who had been United Press bureau manager in Tientsin and
Canton in 1937-38. Epstein wrote in a dispatch to the *National Guardian:*

> Among the fantastic U.S. press dispatches alleging maltreatment of prisoners,
> those of the UP's William Miller are the most consistently unscrupulous. When I
> met Miller three weeks ago in Panmunjom, he broke into a conversation I was
> having with Wilfred Burchett, Sam Summerlin of AP and John Rich of NBC.
> I had remarked that now the war was over, these pressmen would be among mil-
> lions asking what it had all been about, as the GIs already were wondering. Miller
> interrupted: "Our soldiers know what they were fighting for." Burchett com-
> mented: "They certainly don't seem to know when they get to Korea after cap-
> ture." Miller snapped: "I certainly wouldn't wonder after you people put red hot
> barbed wire under their fingernails." Burchett said: "What fingernails? Can you
> name me a single man who has been so maltreated?" Miller was silent. Burchett
> went on: "Can you name me a single man who said this was done to another?"
> Miller's reply was: "We have our imaginations." I would never have believed
> such a story possible if I had not heard it with my own ears.

My conclusions after weeks of study of the POW exchange news coverage was that there was no question that American POWs had suffered
during the first year of captivity, that their food was inadequate and their
medical attention could have been better—but their captors suffered the
same privations. One critical fact suppressed in all the stories is that the
worst suffering came during General MacArthur's drive to the Yalu, an
action which had been undertaken despite frequent warnings that it would
bring the Chinese into the conflict, as it did. The North Koreans suffered
the same forced marches as their captives. When conditions improved
for the North Koreans, they improved for the prisoners.

The returned United States Air Force personnel who had been charged

by the Chinese and North Koreans with dropping germ warfare cannis-
ters, repudiated their confessions upon release. (The parallel between
the germ warfare confessions and those of the crew of the *Pueblo*, the
United States spy ship captured off North Korea in late 1967, is striking.)
The glorification by American correspondents of GIs who admitted
stealing supplies from the prison stores and from their own buddies indicates a corruption of values among both the GIs and the correspondents.

The stream of atrocity stories made more difficult a political settlement
of the Korean and Far Eastern problems. As Secretary of State in the
Eisenhower Administration, Dulles went to Korea in August 1953 to
reassure Syngman Rhee that the United States would not sit down with
the Chinese to seek a settlement of differences. In the United Nations, the
United States made clear that it would not agree to a round-table conference on Korea and the Far East, despite the urging of its Allies. The
International News Service reported from Korea on August 16:

> There is every reason to believe that . . . the outcry of anger and bitterness against
> the Communists [over the atrocity stories] will speedily freeze out all possibilities
> of raising the question of seating Red China at the September [UN] General
> Assembly.

The United Press also reported a "hardening of opinion" because of
the "hardship stories told by prisoners." Whether there was a direct relationship between the press handling of Operation Big Switch and Washington's Far Eastern policy cannot of course be precisely proved. But on
September 12, 1953, the United States again succeeded in blocking the
government at Peking from being seated in the United Nations.

Certainly, with such critical issues at stake, the content and the emotional balance of the stories sent by the American correspondents during
this time raise serious questions about the role of the press in the development of national policy. If the correspondents, supported by the editors
and publishers at home, had been willing to challenge the military censorship and expose the distortions of the United Nations Command, the
truce negotiations need not have been so protracted, and many lives might
have been saved. Instead, the press corps acquiesced, on the basis of a
spurious patriotism, and the war and the killing went on. The brainwashing which had allegedly taken place in Korean POW camps seemed
to be far more effective in the American press camps.

# 9. The Eastland Succession

In the fall of 1954, after the Geneva conference on Southeast Asia and on the eve of the Senate censure of McCarthy, William L. Shirer, foreign correspondent and radio commentator, published a novel entitled *Stranger Come Home*. It is the story of Raymond Whitehead, American correspondent with 25 exciting years abroad, understandably anxious to raise his two children in America as Americans and to sink his roots again in his native land. An old colleague, Bob Fletcher, now vice president of a large network, signs Whitehead to a $1,000-a-week job as a Sunday evening commentator, and he brings his family to New York.

Shirer insists, with rather more emphasis than usual, that all the characters are imaginary. But we know that Shirer spent more than 20 years abroad as a correspondent, had two children and returned to broadcast on Sundays for the Columbia Broadcasting System. The jacket also notes that Edward R. Murrow was responsible for Shirer's job, which by the fall of 1954 he no longer had. Fletcher moves through the book like a mournful Murrow, along with a liberal lawyer, a constipated columnist, familiar publishing and advertising agency types, and an ex-Communist old girl friend who is a composite horror too decomposed for autopsy.

After a few hard-hitting broadcasts by Whitehead, the warnings and snipings begin. When Whitehead's best friend Steve Burnett, a State Department counselor in Switzerland, is attacked by Senator O'Brien, Whitehead defends Burnett on the air and finds himself abruptly unemployed and in the dock before Senator O'Brien. Miss Composite Horror fingers him as a "Soviet agent" and Whitehead is judged guilty in a majority committee report. Burnett is cleared by the State Department but resigns in the knowledge that his career is dead. Arm in arm, the two old friends go off to Connecticut to raise cows and write—Whitehead with a $2,500 advance from a publisher, and Burnett with a $6,500 pension. The finale is a combination of Grandma Moses's "Home for Christmas" and Horatio Alger's *Pluck and Luck* updated for the electronic age.

The book fails as fiction, but it is deadly accurate in examining the minds of newsmen who would not or could not look beneath the surface of the events which affected their own lives. Shirer insists throughout his book that Senator O'Brien is really on the wrong trail: Whitehead had rejected Communism long before "the international Communist conspiracy" became a standard of American journalism. It is cricket, he seems to be saying, to seek out and imprison "Communists"; but the rules of the game are violated when the victims are liberals. No matter how many times Shirer allows his liberal hero to take his lumps, or an FBI informer to be flushed out of a sewer; no matter how often he expresses his shock at the debasement of American culture, he will not acknowledge that the goal of Senator O'Brien was not to get the "Communists," but to stifle all informed opposition. The real-life source material for the novel was far more Kafka than Horatio Alger.

Questions about their conduct in the face of the McCarthy inquisition were to confront many newspapermen in the year that followed publication of Shirer's novel. One of the chickens who came home to roost was Harvey Matusow, earlier mentioned as one of McCarthy's more malodorous helpers, who had been appointed by McCarthy to conduct an investigation of Communism in the press (never carried out). Matusow, a frequent witness whose testimony from 1951 to 1954 had guaranteed large headlines, admitted in 1955 that he had lied in testimony before the McCarthy committee and had given false testimony in court. He had written a book, he said, detailing his transgressions. It was titled *False Witness* and was scheduled to be published by Cameron and Kahn. (Angus Cameron had been chief editor at Little, Brown & Co. but was forced out after his defiance of the McCarthy committee; Albert Kahn is the author of several books exposing right-wing reaction in America.)

Stewart Alsop, who had read the manuscript in advance, said in his column that the book "may cause major explosions [and] initiate a series of investigations of this new postwar profession of the informer." The Department of Justice under Attorney General Herbert Brownell seemed to agree—it immediately set about to silence Matusow. Cameron and Kahn were summoned before a grand jury and ordered to produce all records on the book. They denounced the move as an infringement of freedom of the press and said they would refuse. The Senate Internal Security Subcommittee, headed by James O. Eastland, Democrat of

Mississippi, also had a stake in preserving Matusow's lies as valid testimony and so it subpoenaed the publishers. Kahn was sentenced to six months in prison on a contempt charge for failing to turn over the requested material. Realizing that the Justice Department could seize the material and prevent publication of the book, he reluctantly produced the records, the sentence was revoked, and the book was published.

It will be recalled that Matusow went into Wisconsin during the election campaign of 1952 at the behest of McCarthy and later traveled to Utah, Montana, Idaho, and Washington under the auspices of the Republican National Committee. During this junket he made his initial allegations about the number of Communists employed by the *New York Times* and *Time* magazine. These statements, at the instigation of McCarthy, were later entered in the record of the McCarthy committee during testimony. Although he had invented the whole story, Matusow said, the purpose was clear: "Once the facts were in the record, McCarthy knew he could accuse the *Times* and *Time* of being pro-Communist."

The press conference at which Matusow made his first public recantation in February 1955 was a disorderly affair. Several hostile representatives of the press who specialized in witch-hunting and exposure of "Communists" were present. They felt personally betrayed, not because they had not known Matusow was lying at the time when he had provided them with information, but because he was admitting his lies. The Red specialists dominated the conference and at times heckled loud enough to create an uproar. Their stories reflected their pain—made greater because Matusow had also tagged as liars the most publicized of the government's informers in key cases: Elizabeth Bentley, Whittaker Chambers, Louis Budenz, and Paul Crouch, among others. The *New York Times* said in an editorial February 5:

> The shabby business of the paid professional informer, which has reached new dimensions under governmental encouragement during the past few years, has been given a body blow by one of the well-known practitioners of the art who now says he has been lying all along . . . [This] requires the Justice Department to reexamine all the cases in which this man's testimony did play a part. It is essential in the interests of elementary fairness that the effect of Matusow's worthless testimony be erased from every case in which he was seriously involved.

The righteousness of this indignation was deflated to a considerable degree by a new Matusow disclosure a few days later. About a year and a half earlier, he said, he had given to the *New York Times* an affidavit in which he swore that he had lied when he charged publicly that the *Times* employed 126 members of the Communist Party. The *Times* had suppressed this affidavit and made no effort to pursue the matter to determine whether Matusow had lied in other situations which had resulted in prison terms for persons unable to counter Matusow's testimony. Another Matusow affidavit, confessing to fabrications about Communists employed by *Time* magazine, had been given to *Time* executives in March 1954. *Time* also suppressed the affidavit and did nothing about exposing Matusow further. These disclosures were made during a hearing before Judge Edward J. Dimock in Federal District Court in New York on a motion for a new trial for Communist Party leaders convicted in 1950 under the Smith Act. The Justice Department vigorously opposed the move. The Department knew that if it prosecuted Matusow on a charge of perjury, it would be forced to reopen all the cases in which he had testified. A much simpler procedure would be to prove that Matusow was lying in his contention that he had lied previously. In this way, the earlier cases could be left untouched, the victims would remain in jail, and the "international Communist conspiracy" theory would remain undisturbed. In the case of the Communist leaders, the government did not entirely succeed; a new trial was ordered for two of the Communists. But in the case of Clinton Jencks, an organizer for the Mine Mill and Smelter Workers Union, the Justice Department fared better.

Jencks had been convicted in January 1954 on a charge of falsely signing a Taft-Hartley Act non-Communist affidavit in 1950, and had been sentenced to five years. Matusow had been the star witness at the trial before Judge R. E. Thomason in the U.S. District Court in El Paso, Texas. The prosecutor had told him, "Your testimony was absolutely essential to a successful prosecution." After Matusow recanted in 1955, Jencks's lawyers moved for a new trial and arguments were presented before the same Judge Thomason. Matusow swore on the stand that he had lied in his earlier testimony, but Judge Thomason denied a new trial for Jencks and sentenced Matusow to three years in prison for contempt. The U.S. Court of Appeals in New Orleans in October 1955 upheld the denial of a new trial for Jencks.

The Eastland Internal Security Subcommittee meanwhile had been holding lengthy hearings on Matusow's recantations. On the basis of the hearings the committee prepared a 120-page report—and then sat on it for eight months. It was released on December 30, 1955, the day Jencks's lawyers filed a petition for a Supreme Court review of his case. In a statement accompanying the release, Eastland said:

The Subcommittee has every reason to believe that Matusow had been telling the truth in his testimony all along until he fell into the hands of the Communists last

October [1954] and for thirty pieces of silver—that is, for a little money and notoriety—betrayed his own country to the Communist conspiracy.

The final chapter in the Matusow affair came in September 1956, when a Federal jury in New York found Matusow guilty of perjury in an action involving the trial of Communist Party leader Elizabeth Gurley Flynn. Matusow had charged that Assistant United States Attorney Roy Cohn, who subsequently became Senator McCarthy's chief counsel, had induced him to give false testimony in Miss Flynn's trial under the Smith Act. When the guilty verdict against Matusow was rendered, Justice Department representatives sighed with relief. They had succeeded in having Matusow convicted for contempt and perjury both; and while they would be infinitely more careful in screening their informers in the future, they could regard the Matusow demon as exorcised.

For the Eastland committee, however, there were other devils. It proceeded with an order of business that McCarthy, Cohn, and Matusow had been forced to relinquish, and once again the *New York Times* was very much involved. The Internal Security Subcommittee had been authorized by Senate resolution to investigate, among other things, "the extent and effect of subversive activities in the United States . . . including, but not limited to, espionage, sabotage, and infiltration by persons . . . seeking to overthrow the government of the United States by force and violence." Senator Eastland was chairman of both the Judiciary Committee and the subcommittee. His chief counsel was Jay C. Sourwine, who had been closely associated with the late Senator Pat McCarran, author of the Internal Security Act of 1950 (the McCarran Act) and the restrictive immigration law known as the Walter-McCarran Act. Sourwine shared Senator McCarran's distaste for the *New York Times* and other newspapers which had criticized both acts as undemocratic. He also shared Senator Eastland's resentment of the criticism voiced by newspapers, including the *Times,* of Eastland's troglodyte views on civil rights.

On June 29, 1955, the Eastland committee opened hearings on alleged subversion of the United States press and called as its first witness Winston C. Burdett, a correspondent of the Columbia Broadcasting System who had once worked for the now defunct *Brooklyn Eagle.* Burdett told a tale of what amounted to some extremely inept espionage on his part in behalf of the Soviet Union in several capitals of Europe and Asia where, according to his testimony, he spent considerable time waiting in hotel rooms and on snow-swept street corners for contacts who rarely turned up. At one point, he said, he was in Finland toward the close of the Soviet-Finnish war to sound out the Finns as to how they felt about the war. One would assume that the services of an agent would not have been required to determine that they felt very badly indeed about it, but there was Burdett feeling the pulse of the nation. He had a rendezvous in Sweden with a Mr. Miller who, he said, took him to a Swedish movie and then afterward asked him how the Finns had taken the end of the war. He relayed his findings, Burdett said, and Mr. Miller replied, "Well, Mr. Burdett, thank you very much. That's everything."

Burdett went also to Ankara where his mission was to find out whether the Turkish government was really neutral. It was, he determined—and the Russians, if they were paying him, ought to have asked for a refund, since it was discernible even in Presque Isle, Maine, that the Turkish government was beyond doubt pro-German. Significantly, however, at the time of Burdett's testimony before the Eastland committee, Turkey was being put forward by the United States government as an outpost of democracy in the North Atlantic Treaty Organization and, with Greece, one of the two pillars of the Truman Doctrine. Burdett's testimony therefore might have served also to allay any current doubts in the United States as to the constancy of Turkish adherence to "free world" principles.

There was more to Burdett's testimony, however, than third-rate Eric Ambler. In response to the first question put to him by Sourwine, Burdett acknowledged that he had been a member of the Communist Party branch at the *Brooklyn Eagle* from 1937 until he went abroad in 1940. He named 13 persons who he said were co-habitants of his cell, and also named ten others as Communists in those years. Among the 13 was Melvin L. Barnet, at the time of the testimony a copyreader in the financial department of the *New York Times*. Although I never knew Burdett, he and I had a common friendship with Barnet in the 1930s. Barnet was a classmate of mine at Harvard whom I recalled with affection as a rumpled fellow with a wry humor, fond of chess and Latin quotations. He had written a prize-winning honors thesis on "Rhetoric in Shakespeare," in the course of earning a Phi Beta Kappa key. After graduation he had gone to work as a reporter for the *Brooklyn Eagle*. While I would hardly nominate him as the classmate most likely to succeed in overthrowing the government by force and violence, he had a stubborn adherence to principle which had brought him, among other inconveniences, a morning in jail during the *Brooklyn Eagle* strike of 1937 for suggesting to a fellow worker descending the subway stairs at Brooklyn's Borough Hall station that the fellow worker was a scab for continuing to work. The *Eagle* strike had been called by the Newspaper Guild of New York and Burdett's testimony before Eastland was used to draw a dead Red herring across the

Guild's trail. Burdett recalled Barnet in his testimony as a "general assignment reporter." If pressed further as to his association with Barnet, he would also have disclosed that he was best man at Barnet's wedding in 1938.

On July 13, 1955, Barnet was called as a witness before the Eastland committee during four days of hearings at which 17 other newspapermen or former newspapermen testified; two others besides Barnet were from the *New York Times*. Barnet refused, invoking the Fifth Amendment, to answer any questions about the possible Communist Party membership of other persons. About himself, he said he had not been a member of the Communist Party since early in 1942 and asserted his privilege under the Fifth Amendment "as to the time prior to that." He said he had discussed his Eastland committee appearance with several executives of the *Times* after receiving a subpoena, and that the discussion concerned both his "demeanor" before the committee and the fact that he would "avail himself" of the privilege of the Fifth Amendment. At the hearing, this colloquy took place:

*Sourwine:* Were you told that if you took the Fifth Amendment here you would be discharged?
*Barnet:* Will you repeat the question, please, sir?
*Sourwine:* I asked if you were told that if you availed yourself of the Fifth Amendment before this committee you would be discharged.
*Barnet:* I was not so told, sir.

Barnet's testimony was brief. As he left the witness chair, he was handed a telegram from the *New York Times* informing him that he had been discharged. When the afternoon session opened Senator Eastland placed in the record a letter he had received, dated the same day, from Arthur Hays Sulzberger, publisher of the *Times,* on the letterhead of the *Times* Washington bureau. The letter said that Sulzberger had "just had a report" that Barnet had appeared before the committee and "refused to answer questions put to him." Enclosed, said Sulzberger, was a letter to Barnet, "which I have just signed, advising Mr. Barnet that his employment by the *New York Times* had ceased." The letter, addressed to Barnet's home in Brooklyn, read:

Dear Mr. Barnet:
  I have learned to my regret that at your appearance today before the Senate Internal Security Subcommittee you refused to answer questions put to you in connection with your alleged association with the Communist Party. The course of conduct which you have followed since your name was first mentioned in this connection culminating in your action today has caused the *Times* to lose confidence in you as

a member of its news staff. Accordingly, this will serve as notice of termination of your employment.

I have requested the auditor to pay any sums that may be due you.

Yours truly,

Arthur Hays Sulzberger

Two years earlier, on June 15, 1953, at a conference of high school students in the Bronx, Sulzberger made a strong denunciation of Senator McCarthy. In response to questions from the students, Sulzberger said that Communists had a right to earn a living, even on the *Times,* "though I would not knowingly employ a Communist in a sensitive spot on my editorial staff." But, he said, he would not permit "witch-hunting" among *Times* employes. "Such a thing would destroy the atmosphere of mutual confidence and respect built up over the years."

Yet in July 1955 Sulzberger acted to destroy the atmosphere of mutual confidence by firing an employe who had not been a Communist for many years, who had satisfied the *Times* management's demand for an explanation of his remote Communist Party membership, but who would never testify about other persons before a congressional committee. And, as Barnet said in his testimony, there had been no warning that he would be fired if he pursued this course.

Sulzberger's actions—particularly in the Barnet case—made clear that the *Times*'s devotion to the principles of the Cold War (firmly espoused also by the Eastland committee) took primacy over the traditional practices of justice and fair play which it supported editorially.

The same position was adopted by the union which had been established in 1933 to protect the rights of newspaper workers. Soon after the Eastland committee hearings ended, there was an exchange of telegrams between the committee chairman and Ralph B. Novak, executive vice president of the American Newspaper Guild. The exchange warrants reproduction to provide the flavor of the time and to indicate the hopelessness of Barnet's fight for a redress of grievances. The first telegram, dated July 20, 1955, was from Novak to Eastland:

Testimony submitted to your committee seems to have left the totally false impression in the minds of the public and those employed in the newspaper industry that the policies of the American Newspaper Guild today are still being influenced by Communist Party members and fellow travelers. Attempts being made by the press to tie today's policies to those prior to 1941 are malicious and do great damage. The American Newspaper Guild in 1941 eliminated all vestiges of Communist influences from its national administration, and the New York local did the same shortly thereafter. In order to clear the record and in the interest of truth, on behalf of the American Newspaper Guild, I respectfully request that its record on the Communist question be presented to the public through the submission of a statement or through direct testimony to your committee. The method of presentation I leave to you and your committee. However, I believe we must and should be heard. Your prompt consideration of this request would be appreciated not only by me but all newspapermen throughout the country.

The next day Eastland wired Novak:

Senate Internal Security Subcommittee is not investigating the press or radio-TV or the fourth estate or newspapermen or the Newspaper Guild. This has been repeatedly stated. We are investigating communism. The subcommittee has made no charges against nor cast any slurs upon the American Newspaper Guild. However, if you and your fellow officials of the Guild desire, notwithstanding the above, to testify publicly under oath respecting your anticommunism and think the Internal Security Subcommittee should provide a forum for such testimony, I believe the committee should grant your request. Am instructing committee counsel J. G. Sourwine to arrange hearing earliest mutually convenient date if you and your colleagues decide upon reflection that this is what you want. In view of your reference to "false impression in the minds of the public," am releasing full text of your telegram and this reply.

Novak took six days to reflect and then replied on July 27, 1955:

Thanks very much for your telegram of July 21, particularly gratifying and heartening were your statements. . . . In making public the text [of the telegrams] you have done everything possible to eliminate any false impressions in the minds of the public. It is evident what false impressions remain, and there should be none, are certainly not attributable to your committee and its actions, but rather to weaknesses in our mass communications system. Your telegram publicly setting the record straight makes it entirely unnecessary for us to make use of your generous offer to permit us to testify. Thanks for your assistance and consideration.

To ensure that the weakness of the communications system would not deprive future generations of newspapermen of the privilege of reading this exchange, Eastland had it inserted in the permanent record of the hearings. It is found in Part 16 of a series of committee publications under the grand title: "Strategy and Tactics of World Communism (Recruiting for Espionage)."

In the six days of reflection between the receipt of Eastland's telegram and the Novak response, some wiser heads at the Newspaper Guild may have concluded that the voluntary presence of Guild executives in the Eastland confessional chamber might have nauseated newspapermen who still believed that the right to remain silent should be cherished. They may also have reflected that this testimony could have elicited information about Guild executives who, like Winston Burdett, had been led astray in their youthful concern about the disinherited of the earth and joined the Communist Party. It is not inconceivable that Senator Eastland in the folds of his "generous offer" had just such an eventuality in mind.

There were two other casualties of the Eastland hearing: a reporter for the *Daily News,* who had also invoked the Fifth Amendment, was told that his "usefulness to the *News*" had been destroyed by his conduct and was fired; a former reporter for the *Daily Mirror* was asked to resign as publicity director of the National Municipal League. When he did not, he was dismissed.

Several executives of the *Nation* magazine were indicted about this same time on charges of conspiracy to obstruct justice. The charges were related to meetings between the executives and Harvey Matusow. They eventually were quashed, but it was more than coincidence that grand jurors were stirred into acting whenever Matusow's recantations were given journalistic credence. There was little doubt that the Justice Department was acting in reprisal for the *Nation*'s exposure of its unsavory stables for breeding informers.

The year 1955 also saw an increase in the persecution of editors of progressive foreign-language papers. Senator Eastland's Republican counterpart on the Internal Security Subcommitte, William Jenner, Republican of Indiana, conducted one-man hearings in June 1955 involving several such editors. At one point, when reporters asked Jenner whether he planned further investigations of the foreign-language press, Jenner called over to committee counsel: "Say, how many of these birds do we have? I mean, of this class?" "Oh, a couple of dozen," came the answer.

The Eastland hearings evoked no editorial protest although the *Nation* warned with pertinence that the committee's "real concern" was not with Communism but with the press. Sooner or later, it said, the press would have to stand its ground. But for the moment Eastland was pleased with the compliance of the newspaper industry. He said, "We have gotten more cooperation from newspapermen than from any other groups in the country, and we've had witnesses from most of the professions." This cooperation was applauded by many newspaper commentators. David Lawrence said that Winston Burdett, "former Communist but now true American," had "performed a great service to the crusade against communism." Lawrence made a fervent plea to other newspapermen to emulate Burdett's "heroic action."

The grievance committees of the Guild units at the *Times* and the *News* voted in September 1955 not to contest the dismissals of Barnet and the *News* reporter. The *Times* committee said Barnet was indefensible because he had used the Fifth Amendment not to protect himself but to protect others; that the *Times* management had declared there would be no witch-hunt on the paper and had proved its integrity by keeping two men who had been willing to inform. The committee felt "every loyal American should cooperate with authorized government agencies investigating communism."

Barnet replied with a protest against his colleagues' "apparent compulsion not only to kick me in the pants but to belabor me elsewhere below the belt." He charged the grievance committee, which was headed by A. H. Raskin, then the paper's chief labor correspondent and now assistant editor of the editorial page, with "attempting to build a more extensive case against the union member it was supposed to defend than the management itself had succeeded in constructing." He said the decision smacked of company unionism: "The hand is the hand of Raskin but the voice is the voice of Sulzberger."

Barnet won the support of the *Times* Guild unit, which voted 49 to 24 at a meeting in October to overrule the grievance committee decision and seek arbitration. The unit officers then decided on a referendum of the entire 1,385 Guild members at the *Times*. The grievance committee was upheld by 337 to 235. At the *News*, the vote went the same way against the fired staff member.

The executive board of the New York Guild felt obliged to make a show of seeking arbitration under existing national Guild policy, which required the defense of employes who were not admitted or convicted Communists in the six months preceding their dismissal. At the same time, however, the board set in motion the machinery that would enable it to ignore that policy. It sponsored a citywide referendum in mid-December 1955 on whether the local Guild would be required to enforce contracts in cases involving members who invoked the Fifth Amendment. The membership voted by 3 to 2 (3,185 to 2,064) that the Guild need not act. This meant that a witness before a Congressional committee could not depend upon his union to fight for him; if he did not wish to risk his job, he had to become an informer. The Cold War philosophy, abetted by the union leadership, had penetrated deeply into the union of newspapermen and women.

Meanwhile, the *Times* management got an injunction against the arbitration proceeding on the ground that the action of the *Times* unit prevailed. The New York Guild maintained that the *Times* contract was with the citywide Guild, not with the *Times* unit. This thornless side issue, providing a convenient diversion for both newspaper and union, was litigated inconclusively for more than a year. Ultimately, while the

*Times* was carrying to the New York Court of Appeals an adverse ruling by the Appellate Division of the Supreme Court, an amicable settlement was reached: the Guild dropped Barnet, and the *Times* dropped the appeal.

The executive board of the New York Guild abandoned the case both of Barnet and of the *News* reporter at the first meeting of the year 1957. The chief reasons given were that previous cases had been lost in arbitration proceedings, and that the membership referendum relieved the New York local of defending all Fifth Amendment firings. The union's surrender to the needs of the Cold War was now complete.

# 10. The Target: The Times

With elephantine grace the *Times* had kneeled to Eastland and fired an employe who took the United States Constitution seriously. Having done so, it rose again to present another vigorous defense of the First and Fifth Amendments and the right to dissent. The nation, it said, had at all costs to avoid "a tightly controlled society in which every dissenter, every man who wishes to think for himself, is enchained in a futile attempt to insure conformity in the name of security." The *Times* continued also to advocate implementation of the Supreme Court's 1954 decision on desegregation of the schools. Its espousal of the Fourteenth Amendment—and its own contradictions on freedom of expression, internal and external—were not lost on Senator Eastland, the plantation owner from Sunflower County, Mississippi, and he sent his hound dogs after the *Times* in a new hunt which made the hearings of June and July 1955 seem like a summertime frolic.

Subpoenas went out in November 1955 from the Internal Security Subcommittee to 38 newspapermen for private hearings in New York and Washington scheduled for the third week of the month. But the hearings were postponed because Counsel Sourwine discovered the third week of November was Freedom of the Press Week, and even he was sensitive to possible awkwardness. I was among those called, along with my colleague John T. McManus, general manager of the *National Guardian*. After Cedric Belfrage's departure for England in August 1955, I had succeeded to the editorship of the *National Guardian;* but McManus and I were both aware that we were not being called primarily because of the *National Guardian*. We knew that when Eastland referred to the "left-wing press" he was referring not to the *Guardian* but to the *New York Times*—and McManus and I had both worked for the *Times*. As we waited in the subterranean caverns of the United States Court House in Foley Square in New York to be summoned to the hearing room for private preliminaries, we exchanged greetings with a score of former colleagues. In fact, of the 38 persons called for the private hearings, 30 were present or past employes of the *Times*.

Before the public hearings were held in Washington (from January 3 to 5, 1956), *Times* executives had been busy advising subpoenaed employes. Those who had scruples about informing were urged to tell all in private to the Federal Bureau of Investigation. Then they could go before the Eastland committee, testify fully about themselves, but decline to talk about associates on the ground that they had already reported them to the FBI. When the *Times* fired Barnet some months earlier, it had implied that one major reason was lack of candor—subsequently clarified as candor-too-late. This time the axe fell more swiftly: Two staff members informed the management in November that they intended to invoke the Fifth Amendment and were immediately suspended, well in advance of testimony. Apparently their sin was candor-too-early. When the hearings were postponed, and it appeared the suspensions might continue indefinitely, the two were offered the opportunity to resign. One did. The other refused and was fired, solely on the basis of having confided to the *Times* that he planned to invoke his constitutional rights. By the time the public hearings were called to order, the list had been pared down to 18 witnesses—14 of whom were working for, or had worked for, the *Times*. The target was clear despite Eastland's bland declaration that "we are not investigating any one newspaper." The investigation, he said, was in no way an attempt to restrict the freedom of the press or to imply that Communists had influenced editorial policy on newspapers where they may have been employed.

Press coverage of the preliminaries of the hearings was wary. It seemed almost as though the newspapers which had helped to create Joe McCarthy—and then turned against him—were wondering whether the inquisition was not finally boomeranging right at them. John O'Donnell commented in the *New York Daily News* December 27, 1955:

> This investigation has as its background frequent charges (some soundly justified, in this reporter's opinion) that news reports of the early hearings held by the late Senator Pat McCarran of Nevada, and the later hearings of Senator McCarthy were given a false emphasis and twisted interpretation, in print and on the air, when they finally reached the eyes and ears of great segments of the republic.

In New York, only the *Post* sounded editorial alarm. "If the United States press is prepared to have its news columns policed by Senator Eastland and John O'Donnell," it said, "it is headed for total servitude. It is time for publishers and editors to stand up and be counted. The silence has already been disgracefully long." The *Post* called the committee's tactics "crude political blackmail" and said that the *Times* was being told that "its public shame can be reduced if it privately persuades its subpoenaed employes to 'cooperate.' " It would be tragic, the *Post* said, if the "pressures of this inquisition convinced the *Times* that men who invoke the historic protection of the Bill of Rights are disqualified from future service in our profession." The admonition was a bit late: The *Times* had already been convinced to the point of making the process servers comfortable in a conference room where the *Times* personnel department served up staff members to them. There were pressures elsewhere, too. The hearings had been timed to coincide with the New York Newspaper Guild referendum which put the question whether to "resist the dismissal of all members discharged after invoking a constitutional privilege when asked by an authorized agency about Communist Party affiliation." The lack of resistance by Guild members, reflected in the 3 to 2 vote against resistance, may well have been influenced by the committee hearings and the determined opposition of the *Times* to the use of a constitutional provision (the Fifth Amendment) by its editorial employes.

The hearings themselves provided no sensational headlines, even though witnesses had been selected for large type. With their own personnel as news items, the newspapers were less inclined to flamboyance than during the McCarthy free-for-all days. Of the *Times* employes called, only two—education editor Benjamin Fine and by-line writer Clayton Knowles—were cooperative. Fine testified to Communist Party membership while a student at Columbia University in the 1930s and named one associate there as a Communist.

Knowles had been a *Times* reporter since 1937 and earlier a participant in one of the Newspaper Guild's bitterest strikes against the Newhouse-owned *Long Island Press*. He was a leading Washington correspondent and well known to many senators when the Eastland committee began making inquiries about him the summer before. After discussion with his superiors, he went to the FBI and to the Eastland committee, which heard him in closed session. According to his public testimony, Knowles gave to both the FBI and the Eastland committee names of fellow Guild members who allegedly were Communists with him during the *Long Island Press* strike. In his public testimony he named several New York Newspaper Guild leaders of the early period who had built the local from a small editorial craft union to an industrial organization of more than 8,000 members, and had helped to increase minimum wages for Knowles's job category from about $50 weekly to $135 or more at the time of the hearings.

The committee also sought to claim James Glaser of the *New York*

*Post* as a cooperative witness, after his testimony on the inner workings of the *Daily Worker* of 20 years before. Glaser, however, characterized his questioning "an act of unwarranted and inexcusable harassment." Despite two decades of public anti-Communism in Newspaper Guild affairs after quitting the editorship of the *Daily Worker* (he had resigned from the *Times* to become editor of the *Worker*), Glaser denounced Congressional investigations which made national celebrities of renegade Communists, whom he termed degenerate intellectuals, journalistic prostitutes, and racketeers. Glaser had been succeeded as editor of the *Worker* by Louis Budenz, a paid informer since 1945. On the *Worker* staff before his time had been one of the current investigators for the Eastland committee, Benjamin Mandell, who sat beside the senators as Glaser testified.

Three other editorial employes of the *Times* refused to answer many of the committee's questions and invoked the First Amendment, among others, but not the Fifth Amendment. Two non-editorial employes of the *Times* invoked the Fifth Amendment, as did the two editorial employes who had already been forced out of their jobs by the *Times* management. The non-editorial employes retained their jobs, presumably on the ground that they were engaged in non-sensitive work. So did the three editorial employes who had invoked the First Amendment. All three subsequently were cited for contempt of Congress, tried, convicted, and sentenced. After years of litigation, the convictions were upset by higher courts, but on technicalities and not on the basic issue of freedom of the press. Two of the three subsequently became well-known *Times* by-line writers. As for Clayton Knowles, his by-line disappeared and he was put to work compiling the *Times*'s daily news index. Presumably the nature of the transfer was more purgatorial than punitive, because after about a year his by-line reappeared on New York area stories.

Two persons not connected with the *Times* also lost their jobs within hours of their testimony. They were Dan Mahoney, a rewrite man for the Hearst *Daily Mirror,* and William A. Price, a reporter for the *New York Daily News.* Mahoney invoked the Fifth Amendment, and Price the First. Price added to his defiance by refusing to respond on the ground that the questioning could serve no legislative purpose. His stand preempted the headlines and brought him commendation by telephone, telegram, and letter from all over the country. He also was indicted on a contempt charge, convicted and given a suspended sentence. But he refused to let the matter rest, and eventually, on appeal, his conviction was reversed— again on a narrow technical ground.

Although McManus and I were obviously called because of our former employment by the *Times,* most questions asked of us in public session indicated that the committee considered the *National Guardian* a special bonus target. Great emphasis was laid on publication by the *National Guardian* in 1951 of the names of American POWs in Korea at a time when these names were being withheld by the Defense Department (see chapter 8). McManus and I informed the committee, as we had told *National Guardian* readers five years earlier, that our POW names had been obtained from the *China Monthly Review* which circulated freely in the United States, and by special correspondence with its editor, John W. Powell, Jr. Considerable effort was made by the questioners to cast doubt on the authenticity of the names, although Defense Department lists of POWs issued months after the *National Guardian* articles had confirmed their authenticity. McManus particularly was badgered about the letters written by POWs from the camps: Had he made any effort to check the authenticity of the letters? Had it made any difference to him that they were critical of the United States? Had the letters been selected because they were critical of the United States?

Questions directed to me turned, as they had before with McCarthy, on my work as a press control officer in Germany. I was questioned about my association with William Hinton, with whom I had been in training at Fort Benning, Georgia, before we went off on our overseas government assignments in 1945. Hinton was sent to China. He returned to the United States after the war and then went back to China for the United Nations Relief and Rehabilitation Administration. He remained in China on his own, as an agricultural expert, and worked also on the improvement of milk cows.

(Senator Jenner and counsel Sourwine were very interested in my friendship with Hinton, but though I testified freely about it, I did not disclose that my wife, who had been born in China, had prepared a Szechwan duck for Hinton when he had dined with us a few weeks earlier. Not only would that have violated the privacy of the kitchen, but it would clearly have marked my wife as an agent of Peking, despite the fact that her hard-shell Baptist missionary grandfather had done his utmost to convert the heathen Chinese to Senator Eastland's particular form of Christianity.)

When Hinton had returned finally to the United States from China in 1953, 78 pounds of research papers, photographs, and notes from a book he was writing on China were taken from him at customs as "foreign propaganda."* He was subpoenaed by the Eastland committee in 1954 for lengthy questioning. When he made it known he planned to sue the

---

* It was eventually published as *Fanshen,* A Documentary of Revolution in a Chinese Village, by Monthly Review Press in 1966.

committee for the return of his property, the committee subpoenaed him again on March 6, 1956, for three days of hearings with full radio, press and TV coverage. Hinton, a lanky, outspoken Vermonter, immediately took the offensive and demanded the return of his papers and the punishment of those who had taken them (customs had meanwhile turned the material over to the Eastland committee). Senator Herman Welker, Republican of Idaho, replied that it was an internal security matter, whereupon Hinton demanded to know when the committee was going to investigate the defiance of the Supreme Court decisions on desegregation of the schools—defiance, he said, which Senator Eastland was organizing in the South. Eastland stalked out of the hearing room. Senator William Jenner of Indiana then took up the questioning, and Hinton's responses drove him out after Eastland. Finally Welker fell silent after this thrust from Hinton:

> Do you really think you are getting yourself reelected with this kind of show?
> . . . What will the people of Idaho say when they learn that you have been wasting your time here during the entire week when the farm bill was being debated on the Senate floor?

At this point, with the show going in Hinton's favor, the press gave up too. A man who makes a monkey of an investigating committee apparently is not good copy. When Hinton filed a $500,000 suit against the committee for the return of his property, the suit received only a few lines in the press. When Hinton got his papers back in 1957, the event was ignored in the newspapers.

There had been a latent motive in the questions directed to McManus and myself about John Powell also, as was made plain a few months later. When Powell returned to the United States from China in 1953 (he had closed his magazine because of "insurmountable financial difficulties"), he was questioned by Central Intelligence agents and, in September 1954, appeared with his wife, Sylvia Campbell Powell, before the Eastland committee as an uncooperative witness. Senator Jenner said after the hearing that Powell had come home to "soften up the American people"; he asked the Justice Department to press a treason charge, but nothing happened. The cry of treason was raised again by Welker in 1955 and, in April 1956, a grand jury returned an indictment charging sedition against Powell and Julian Schuman, an associate editor of the *China Monthly Review,* who had also returned to the United States. Powell declared that the government was trying to shut him up and said, "This is a freedom of the press case from start to finish." After the expenditure of thousands of dollars in legal fees, and reams of adverse publicity in the press, the sedition charge was dismissed. Once again, as in Hinton's recovery of his papers, the fact was not news: it received a bare notice in the general press. But the flood of publicity before and during the court proceedings served as an effective damper on anyone who sought to publish news about revolutionary China.

The Eastland hearings on the *Times,* in January 1956, generated little public controversy or interest. There were more newspapermen than spectators present during the three days of hearings in the Old Senate Caucus Room where Joe McCarthy had reigned in triumph. But the hearings did stir up a lively debate in the world of journalism about the two main issues involved: Was the *Times* being singled out for attack? Was the Eastland committee violating the guarantee of the freedom of the press? On the last day of the hearings, having disposed of its employes as it saw fit, the *Times* published a towering editorial entitled "The Voice of a Free Press." Referring back to the hearings of the previous June, the editorial said the *Times* did not question the propriety of an investigation of the press by an agency of government: the press was not sacrosanct and was as subject to inquiry as any other American institution, under the condition, of course, that Congress "make certain that any such inquiry be conducted in good faith and not motivated by ulterior purpose." Noting that not one present member of the Communist Party, "so far as we are aware," had been found among the 4,000 employes of the *Times,* the editorial then stated *Times* policy on the employment of Communists:

We would not knowingly employ a Communist party member in the news or editorial departments . . . because we would not trust his ability to report the news objectively or to comment on it honestly, and the discovery of present Communist party membership on the part of such an employe would lead to his immediate dismissal.

The *Times* would judge the cases of employes who testified to past Communist Party membership or who invoked the Fifth Amendment "for reasons of their own" on their individual merits, the editorial said, "in the light of each individual's responsibilities in our organization and of the degree to which his relations with this newspaper entitle him to possess our confidence." The *Times* did not believe in the "doctrine of irredeemable sin," and it thought it possible for an employe to atone "through good performance for past error":

We have judged these men, and we shall continue to judge them, by the quality of their work and by our confidence in their ability to perform that work satisfactorily. It is our own business to decide whom we shall employ and not employ. We do not propose to hand over that function to the Eastland subcommittee.

The tone of the editorial was firm, but the policy was not what the *Times* had followed in firing the three editorial workers. Each of the three had come to the *Times* from other jobs; each was known to be a competent craftsman; each had given information about his past to the management, but had refused on principle to become an informer. Yet the *Times,* without hearing, and rejecting the machinery provided in its contract with the Newspaper Guild, had judged all three men guilty of irredeemable sin, apparently without hope of atoning for "past error," and unable to perform their work in a manner to instill confidence. Thus the great newspaper was proclaiming that it would not yield to Eastland on its employment practices, while it was actually doing just what Eastland wanted.

After its preliminary remarks on employment practices, the editorial got into the heart of the matter. The *Times* said it would not permit the Eastland committee, or any other agency outside its office, "to determine in any way the policies of this newspaper":

It seems to us quite obvious that the Eastland investigation has been aimed with particular emphasis at the *New York Times* . . . It seems to us to be a further obvious conclusion that the *Times* has been singled out for this attack precisely because of the vigor of its opposition to many of the things for which Mr. Eastland, his colleague Mr. Jenner and the subcommittee's counsel stand . . . If this is the tactic of any member of the Eastland subcommittee, and if further evidence reveals that the real purpose of the present inquiry is to demonstrate that a free newspaper's policies can be swayed by Congressional pressure, then we say to Mr. Eastland and his counsel that they are wasting their time. This newspaper will continue to determine its own policies. It will continue to condemn discrimination, whether in the South or in the North. It will continue to defend civil liberties. It will continue to challenge the unbridled power of government authority. It will continue to enlist goodwill against prejudice and confidence against fear.

The *Times* was obviously pleased with itself. On January 7 and 9, it printed almost a full page of letters of editorial comment from newspapers around the country. Most of the comment was favorable. The *Quincy Patriot Ledger* came closest to the mark in sensing the significance of the Eastland purpose. It said:

The *Times* is probably the most respected daily newspaper in the world. It is the newspaperman's newspaper, and its editorial opinions weigh as heavily as any in the highest offices of government and business. If the moderately conservative *Times* can be discredited by a Congressional subcommittee that does not like its viewpoints and its reporting, then how many other American newspapers could become like fodder in the thinking of certain Congressmen? Any attempt to control the American press through investigation or any other kind of threat, we feel confident, would have the reverse effect. There are few papers, in our opinion, which would yield their identities as free journals without a stiff fight.

The confidence of the *Patriot Ledger* was not borne out. There was not much fight in the American press. Irving Dilliard, then editor of the editorial page of the *St. Louis Post-Dispatch,* reported the results of a survey of editorial opinion about the Eastland attack on the *Times:* Of 190 newspapers in the nation's largest cities, 112 took no editorial position; 35 were critical of some phase of the investigation, and only a "considerably smaller" number voiced strong support of the *Times*'s position; 33 papers supported the investigation and 10 took inconclusive positions. The high percentage of papers that took no editorial stand was an "impressive finding." Dilliard asked: "Did Senator Eastland's boldness in concentrating on the *Times* so impress the press that many editors found it desirable to avoid commenting?" He warned of the effect on freedom if editors "chose to keep silent . . . to accommodate themselves to the investigators."

In New York three major newspapers—the *Herald Tribune* (the *Times*'s main morning competition), the Scripps-Howard *World-Telegram & Sun* and the *News* were silent editorially; the Hearst *Mirror* and *Journal-American* approved the investigation. The *New York Post* commented:

The areas of caution, silence and doubletalk remain large. Most degrading of all has been the silence of such press bodies as the American Newspaper Publishers Association, the American Society of Newspaper Editors and the American Newspaper Guild. The Eastland committee . . . has unwittingly exposed the cowardice and submissiveness which afflicts large segments of journalism.

Drew Pearson charged the *Times* itself with taking a "weak-kneed position" until the January 5 editorial, and said it had "made no effort to defend itself or members of its staff." The *Times,* he said, had asked Democratic senators on the committee to be present at the hearings to defend it (of course, Eastland himself was a Democrat), but had no lawyer of its own available to staff members. Columnist John Crosby of the *Herald Tribune* was outraged by the Newspaper Guild referendum on mandatory support of its members. In a letter to the *Guild Reporter* he found it "incomprehensible" for newspapermen to "display such appalling ignorance of their own rights, to say nothing of their duties and responsibilities . . . Our whole charter to operate as newspapermen, our

legal right to exist at all is the First Amendment. What are we trying to do
—commit suicide?"

Crosby's indignation was not shared by William H. Slocum, president
of the ASNE, who did not comment until January 22. He agreed with the
*Times* that the press was "subject to proper inquiry," but he was concerned with "manner and motive" and fell into the rhetoric of the hunt to
give a cautious opinion: "Because it seems so apparent that the subcommittee has sent its dogs to bark up a tree where there is nothing but a
mighty lean 'coon, if any at all, there is reason to watch this committee
very closely." To Walter Lippmann, however, it seemed as though Eastland were about ready to nail the 'coonskin to the barn door. Conceding
that the investigation itself was "a dud," he said it had nonetheless raised
"a hard question about the freedom of the press and about the rights and
duties of newspapermen." He wrote in the *Herald Tribune* January 10:

> Does Congress have the power to investigate the press, and if it has, what are the
> limits of that power? There is no clear and authoritative answer to that question for
> the very good reason that it is in American experience a radically new question. Not
> for many generations, if ever before in our history, has an organ of government
> claimed the power to examine and to pass judgment on who should work on
> newspapers.

The crucial question posed by the Eastland committee, Lippmann
said, was whether Congress had the power to censor the individual employe of a newspaper. If Congress did indeed have that power in cases
where an employe was charged with being a Communist, what barrier
was there to Congress investigating newspaper employes on other grounds
—the influence of corporate interests, for example, or the financial connections of publishers, editors, and reporters? If it becomes an accepted
principle that Congress does have that power, Lippmann said, then "the
inner spirit and the practical meaning of the First Amendment will be
deeply impaired." He interpreted the Eastland committee's actions as an
attempt to effect by investigation what Congress was forbidden to effect
by law—to govern the standards of newspaper employment:

> The question, therefore, is whether the newspaper profession shall assent to or
> shall oppose the claim that Congress has the power to investigate the editorial
> management of newspapers. The hiring and firing of employes is an essential and a
> central part of the editing of a newspaper. My own view is that no part of the
> editorial management should, that no part can under the First Amendment be
> ceded legitimately to Congress. If we who are connected with newspapers
> acquiesce in the right to Congress to censor on any grounds whatever newspaper
> employment, we shall have opened the way to a grave invasion of the freedom of
> the press.

Without saying so precisely, Lippmann clearly was rebuking the *Times* for having in effect surrendered to the Eastland committee, and therefore to Congress, the right to set up standards of employment. He was entirely justified. If Eastland had not summoned the three fired employes, they might still be working for the *Times*. Nothing in their conduct had changed except their being marked by Eastland—and the mark was accepted by the *Times* as the scarlet letter.

In an editorial commending the *Times* for the libertarian sentiments of its January 5 editorial, but not for its actions, the *National Guardian* suggested to its readers that, in the spirit of the editorial, they urge the *Times* to reinstate the dismissed employes. One letter writer reported on his reply from Charles Merz, then editor of the *Times* editorial page, who, it will be recalled, collaborated with Lippmann on the brilliant exposé of the *Times*'s coverage of the Bolshevik Revolution. Merz said: "On the matter of employes who have invoked the Constitution, you are misinformed. We have never dismissed anyone solely for pleading the Fifth Amendment." Once again managerial candor was in short supply.

Lippmann also took notice of the *Times*'s view of Congress's right to investigate the press. He agreed that the press was not sacrosanct, and that newspapers, like any individual corporation, were subject to the laws of the land. What was sacrosanct, he said, was that the freedom of the press could not be abridged by Congress; and Congressional censorship of the employment of newspapermen would, if assented to and allowed to become practice, seriously threaten to abridge that freedom.

The sacrosanct principle of the First Amendment was not adopted in order to favor newspapermen and to make them privileged characters. It was adopted because a free society cannot exist without a free press. The First Amendment imposes many duties upon newspapermen who enjoy the privileges of this freedom. One of the prime duties of free journalists is that they should to the best of their abilities preserve intact for those who come after them the freedom which the First Amendment guarantees.

The *Wall Street Journal* disagreed with Lippmann. People who work for newspapers, it said in an editorial January 9, 1956, should be no more immune to questioning than other people. In fact, it said, a good case could be made "that they ought to be less immune." The keystone of a free press, it said, is honesty and truth. And honesty and truth "are not served by Communists or by those so afraid of truth as to refuse an honest answer to questions about Communism." The editorial went on:

The First Amendment safeguards a free press and thus the right of anyone to go into the business. But it does not guarantee that the man is unanswerable for what

he prints—libel laws are proof enough of that. Nor does it guarantee any newspaperman freedom from exposure about his political beliefs and associations; public
knowledge can be the best test of the value of such beliefs and associations, and
honest men need not fear exposure. Further, for newspapers to claim such a privilege when they themselves are in the daily business of exposing what other people
do and say is ludicrous, indeed.

The comment on "beliefs and associations" was in response to a statement by the American Civil Liberties Union. Concerned by the tenor of
the Eastland inquiry, the ACLU had suggested that the committee confine its questioning of newspapermen to "conspiratorial acts," and not
invade the area of "political beliefs and associations." The *Wall Street
Journal* editorial obviously found this position unsound. Propaganda, it
said, can serve Moscow as well as conspiracy:

[The ACLU] is especially unconvincing when it says the questioning of newspapermen should take that form because "the fact that they are responsible for the
gathering and presentation of news to the public makes it vitally important that
they remain free to do their job without even a hint of government pressure." We
think it is just as important that newspapers remain free to do their job without
even a suspicion of Communist pressure on the news they print.

The *Journal* editorial set forth two flagrant distortions of law and fact:
(1) It excluded from the protection of the Constitution men and women
under investigation for alleged Communist beliefs and associations;
(2) It misrepresented the manner in which a newspaper is managed and
the news is gathered.

Surely a newspaperman—or any man—is within his rights when he
invokes a constitutional amendment in his own protection if he believes
that an inquiry has no constitutional sanction in the area under inquiry,
or if he believes that the motives of the questioners are dishonest. And he
ought to be able to invoke the Constitution without inference being drawn
as to his capacity for truth or honesty. It is significant that the *Journal*
editorial set up no strictures for persons with ultra-reactionary views,
such as membership in the John Birch Society or vigilante groups. I have
worked—and I am sure many newspapermen could comment similarly—
with persons whose views would qualify them for membership in fascist
organizations, if they were not already members. Apparently such views,
in the *Journal*'s opinion, represent no threat to the people's right to know.
But in fact the right to know is concerned with news and comment about
events and policies, particularly those involving governments, and not
with the beliefs and associations of individual newspapermen. What the
*Journal* seemed to be asking for was the public posting of a non-

Communist loyalty affidavit for every person concerned with gathering or commenting on the news.

Aside from the unconstitutionality of such a procedure, the *Journal*'s fear of "Communist pressure" on the news that is printed was absurd. As the *Journal* well knew, every newspaper is structured in such a manner that the working newspaperman has very little opportunity to influence the published news. Every line of copy goes through an editor. A reporter or a rewrite man knows that if he attempts to slant a story to the radical side, it will be stopped, edited out, or handed back for rewrite—and he will be in trouble. Not one witness before the Eastland committee was in a position to influence in any significant fashion either an editorial stand or the general news content of his newspaper.

Too few newspapers are engaged in "exposure." There is ample room for exposure of the policies of government and the practices of major industry, but most newspaper publishers and editors identify themselves too closely with these enterprises to reveal their defects. Further, it is my conviction that if a committee of Congress should decide to summon a publisher of a major newspaper and question him about his private life, his political views, and his business interests and associations, it would be met with a stone wall of non-cooperation which would be supported by almost all other newspaper publishers. But working newspapermen with alleged Communist views, and with jobs subject to the political prejudices of a publisher and unprotected by a compliant union, are something else again.

Lippmann's position, on pure constitutional grounds, was in the best American tradition. But even he did not penetrate to the core of the matter. The debate on the Eastland hearings on the press was confined to the *New York Times* and the big press in general. For myself and for McManus, as representatives of a dissenting newspaper, the real concern—and it should also have been the concern of the *Times* and Lippmann and the *Wall Street Journal*—was this: Should a newspaper like the *National Guardian,* which had rejected completely the myth of the international Communist conspiracy, be subject to continuing harassment that had included three Congressional investigations and the exile of its founding editor?

There had been few editorial comments on Belfrage; fewer still on a succession of nonconformist editors brought to trial under the Smith Act and foreign-born editors under the Walter-McCarran Act. There was no comment at all on the questioning by the Eastland committee of McManus and myself—either on the obvious circumstance that we were subpoenaed to embarrass the *Times,* or the less obvious circumstance that the *National*

*Guardian* had embarrassed the government on the question of American prisoners during the Korean war. Even the most noble editorial protest against the Eastland hearings was flawed if it failed to acknowledge a fundamental fact: Any newspaper which disputed the basic McCarran Act thesis of the international Communist conspiracy (the Eastland subcommittee was a creature of this act) was fair game for harassment. Freedom of the press to support the Cold War and the mythology on which it was based was never in jeopardy. What was endangered was freedom to *dissent* from the Cold War.

If this freedom was not defended, there would be a threat to the freedom of those newspapers which supported basic Cold War policy but dissented in details, as the *Times* was discovering. This threat was implicit in a little publicized incident that occurred late in 1956.

In Onondaga County, near Syracuse, New York, the students of the senior class of Solvay High School undertook to enter a class subscription to the *New York Times*. But the Solvay board of education early in March forbade the use of the *Times* in social studies classes on the ground that the *Times* had a "Communist slant" in its news stories. There would be no benefit for the students in the subscription, the board said, since the paper was "too intellectual" and would take "too much time from other studies." The instigator of the action was school board member John Martino. Martino also was the auditor of the *Syracuse Post-Standard* which, at the time, was serializing a 100-page handbook on Communism issued by the Eastland committee.

Even with financial copyreader Melvin Barnet removed from his desk, the *Times* was still suspect.

# 11. The Bay of Pigs

At Thanksgiving time, 1960, President Dwight D. Eisenhower had settled in at the Burning Tree Club at Augusta, Georgia, for twelve days of golf. News came that the state government of Louisiana had encouraged mob action against a handful of first-grade children seeking to enter a New Orleans white public school for the first time. The President's response, if any, was not recorded. It is known that he made no public statement about this attempt to subvert the Constitution of the United States.

Soon thereafter he left the links for a round of quail shooting. Word reached him that President Ydígoras of Guatemala was calling for U.S. protection after an aborted uprising November 14 by Guatemalan army officers. The uprising, Ydígoras said, had been instigated by Cuba, where the revolutionary forces led by Fidel Castro had succeeded in overthrowing the Batista dictatorship on January 1, 1959.

This time the President acted immediately. He sent to the Caribbean the 70-plane aircraft carrier Shangri-La, five destroyers, and two Navy reconnaissance planes to police the area. The Navy's Squadron 10, with a complement of 2,000 Marines aboard the assault-helicopter carrier *Boxer,* was assigned along with other ships. It was an obvious show of force aimed at hemispheric dissenters. The Guatemalan request (joined in by Nicaragua, which had had a little rebellion of its own November 11 against President Luis Somoza Debayle) and the Eisenhower response produced fat headlines all over the hemisphere, editorial applause in the American press, and stern warnings from desk-bound warriors in the United States Congress.

Inquisitive reporters soon learned that the United States fleet had been

patrolling Guatemala's coast for five days prior to the White House announcement of the President's action. The patrol, the reporters were told,
had been undertaken by the United States Navy in response to an "oral"
request from Guatemala and Nicaragua. No correspondent was curious
enough to ask about the odd procedure by which a foreign country makes
an oral request to the United States Navy and gets action without the approval of the Commander-in-Chief. A week before the Eisenhower action,
there had also been unpublished reports of a concentration of naval vessels without markings in the area of Puerto Barrios, Guatemala's port on
the Caribbean. The vessels were presumed by Cuban reconnaissance to be
United States craft and were linked with earlier reports circulating in
Cuba of a buildup in Guatemala for an invasion of Cuba.

An editorial in the November 19 issue of the *Nation* magazine gave
substance to the Cuban reports. It was a comment on an article in the
*Hispanic American Report* by Dr. Ronald Hilton, director of the Stanford University Institute of Hispanic American and Luso-Brazilian
Studies, who had just returned from a trip to Guatemala. The *Nation*
editorial said:

The U.S. Central Intelligence Agency has acquired a large tract of land, at an
outlay in excess of $1,000,000, which is stoutly fenced and heavily guarded. Dr.
Hilton was informed that it was "common knowledge" in Guatemala that the tract
is being used as a training ground for Cuban counterrevolutionaries who are preparing for an eventual landing in Cuba. It was also said that U.S. personnel and
equipment are being used at the base. The camp is said to be located in Retalhuleu,
between Guatemala City and the coast. Fidel Castro may have a sounder basis for
his expressed fears of a U.S.-financed "Guatemala-type" invasion than most of us
realize.

The "Guatemala-type invasion" was a reference to the overthrow of
the Arbenz government in Guatemala in 1954—an action which it is now
freely admitted was directed by the CIA from Honduras. The editorial
concluded:

If Washington is ignorant of the existence of the base, or, knowing that it exists,
is nevertheless innocent of any involvement in it, then surely the appropriate authorities will want to scotch all invidious rumors . . . On the other hand, if the
reports as heard by Dr. Hilton are true, then public pressure should be brought to
bear upon the Administration to abandon this dangerous and hare-brained project.
There is a second reason why we believe the reports merit publication; they can,
and should, be checked immediately by all U.S. news media with correspondents in
Guatemala.

How did the press react to this call? In the Fall 1967 issue of the
*Columbia University Forum,* a quarterly which circulated to 120,000

graduates of Columbia, there appeared an article by Victor Bernstein and Jesse Gordon titled "The Press and the Bay of Pigs." Bernstein, a veteran newspaperman and foreign correspondent, was managing editor of the *Nation* from 1952 to 1963. Gordon, who has been a correspondent in Cuba, is an editorial consultant to the *Nation.* This is their story:

On Friday, November 11, 1960, the day the *Nation* editorial went to press, Jesse Gordon distributed 75 proofs, along with a release based on the editorial, to all the major news media, including the foreign bureaus in New York. Messengers carried copies to the key offices, and Gordon followed up with telephone calls. Three calls went to the Associated Press. Each time a different desk man said he had never seen the proof or the release and asked that they be sent out again. Three duplicates were sent in three hours, but their contents never made the AP teletype. In fact, neither the AP nor the United Press International (the United Press merged with the International News Service in 1958) used the story. Neither wire service asked its correspondents in Guatemala that weekend to check on the story.

On Monday, November 14, Gordon was on the phone again to Francis L. McCarthy, chief of the UPI's Latin American desk. Gordon reported McCarthy as saying: "Yes, there's a big base in operation in Guatemala and United States planes are flying in and out. But the Pentagon denies any knowledge and the State Department says 'no comment.' One story we hear is that the base is being built by the United States as a replacement for Guantanamo." Despite McCarthy's knowledge—or educated suspicion—the UPI carried nothing on the story.

At this point, apparently the only persons in the United States who knew about the base at Retalhuleu were readers of the *Hispanic American Report,* the *Nation,* the UPI's Francis McCarthy, who seemed unwilling to share his knowledge with UPI's clients, and the readers of the *Gazette & Daily* of York, the only daily newspaper in the country to print a story based on the *Nation* release. (In Guatemala, Clemente Marroquin Rojas, director of the newspaper *La Hora,* had defied a government order, and published the story of the base in considerable detail on October 30.)

The *New York Times* had received four copies of the release, directed to the city editor, the national news editor, Herbert L. Matthews, a member of the editorial board, and a reporter covering domestic aspects of the Cuban situation. In addition, the story was sent out by Gordon over the PR Newswire, a private teletype service. Phone calls to the *Times* elicited interest and a request for Dr. Hilton's phone number. But nothing appeared in print.

The *Gazette & Daily,* in a revealing editorial November 24, picked up the chronological story of the reluctant press. After getting the *Nation*'s release, it said:

> The *Gazette & Daily* asked the AP . . . to check [the *Nation*'s] report. The AP said the *Nation*'s article seemed "thin." . . . But when we explained that we were not requesting a rewrite of the *Nation* article, but rather a check in Guatemala, the AP went to work. Within a few days, the AP sent a story which was printed on page two of the *Gazette & Daily* on November 17, headlined: "Guatemala President Denies Reports of Anti-Castro Force." The headline reasonably sums up the story; the AP had interviewed President Ydígoras of Guatemala and he had "branded as false" the things the *Nation* had published.
>
> Now for the windup. In a letter from Stanford dated November 19, Dr. Ronald Hilton writes as follows: "On Friday, November 18, Mr. [Lyman B.] Kirkpatrick [Jr.], the Inspector General (i.e., second in command) of the CIA, spoke in San Francisco at the Commonwealth Club on the general subject of Latin America. In the question period he was asked, 'Professor Hilton of Stanford says there is a CIA-financed base in Guatemala where plans are being made for an attack on Cuba. Professor Hilton says it will be a black day for Latin America and the U.S. if this takes place. Is this true?' After a long silence, Mr. Kirkpatrick replied: 'It will be a black day if we are found out.' "

On November 20, nine days after the first *Nation* release, the *New York Times* printed a dispatch from Guatemala which helped temporarily to avert that black day. It was an unsigned dispatch, on page 32, and was based on a correspondent's interview with President Ydígoras. It said:

> The President branded the reports as a "lot of lies." He said the base . . . was one of several on which Guatemalan Army personnel was being trained in guerrilla warfare. The object of the training, he said, was to combat invasions of the type that had occurred recently in Honduras, Nicaragua and Panama.

In their *Columbia Forum* report, Bernstein and Gordon comment:

> In lying to both the *Times* man and the AP reporter, President Ydígoras displayed the virtue of consistency, at least. But there is another, more significant, observation to be made about these two dispatches. Neither reporter took the elementary journalistic step (or, if they took it, failed to report that they did so) of interviewing anyone on the staff of *La Hora,* which had published the story the previous October 30. At the very least, they should have seen—or reported an attempt to see—the newspaper's publisher, Clemente Marroquin Rojas, who was then a member of the Ydígoras cabinet (and is today Vice President of Guatemala). Moreover, according to Dr. Hilton, the base and its purposes were "common knowledge" in the country; should not the reporters have been instructed, at the very minimum, to test this "common knowledge"? . . . But both correspondents chose to go to the one man who would be sure to deny the story—the President.

In a letter to Bernstein dated April 27, 1967 (written in response to a request for elaboration of the *Times*'s actions after the *Nation*'s press release), Clifton Daniel, the managing editor, made these points:

The *Times* had talked to Dr. Hilton to determine whether he had "anything more than the hearsay evidence attributed to him." He said he had not. They asked their Washington bureau to follow up, but the bureau "drew a blank." Questions to a stringer in Guatemala brought the reply that there had been "rumors" of a United States-organized base, but it had been "impossible to get any confirmation." The November 20 interview with Ydígoras had been written by Paul Kennedy, a *Times* expert on Latin America, who had been asked to go from Nicaragua to Guatemala to check. He had also "drawn a blank" and had filed his Ydígoras interview on the nineteenth.

If the *Times* and the AP felt they had gone far enough, another newspaper decided to take Ydígoras at his word when he told the AP man: "Let them come and see for themselves." Shortly after the *Times* story appeared, the *St. Louis Post-Dispatch* sent its correspondent Richard Dudman on a fact-finding mission to Nicaragua and Guatemala. He didn't bother with Ydígoras but went elsewhere with some pertinent questions and a wandering eye. In short order he determined that there did exist a secret 1,200-foot airstrip cut out of the Guatemalan jungle 15 miles from the nearest paved road. He described the airstrip and a barracks for 500 men as a "remarkable engineering job" and quoted a Guatemalan as saying that many of the soldiers at the base spoke with a Cuban accent. He could not file his story from Guatemala and went to El Salvador to cable. The *Post-Dispatch* printed his findings and asked in an editorial:

> What is going on in Guatemala? Who is trying to conceal what, and for what purpose? Why should Richard Dudman . . . have to go to neighboring El Salvador to send a dispatch to this newspaper about what he found in Guatemala? And why should it be necessary for him to write from El Salvador that he could relate only "some" of the truth?

These questions obviously were addressed to the American government and the American press, but one was as unresponsive as the other. On December 10, the *Nation* was moved to ask: "Is it really beyond the power of the U.S. press to discover who is fomenting the Cuban crisis—Castro, or the United States?"

In mid-December, another newspaper sought an answer. The *Los Angeles Mirror* sent its aviation editor, Don Dwiggins, to Guatemala. His stories in the *Mirror* declared that United States funds were involved in the building of the airstrip and the base. The AP carried three paragraphs based on Dwiggins' long article. The *Nation* published another Dwiggins article on January 7, 1961, which noted the construction of a jet airstrip in a country whose air force did not have a single jet plane. Dwiggins reported also that pilots were being recruited in the United States at $25,000 a head, to fly planes "in a fantastic air-raid operation scheduled for some time early in 1961."

Thus, with Dr. Hilton's story no longer "hearsay," the *Times* (according to Daniel's letter to Bernstein of April 27, 1967) sent Paul Kennedy back to Guatemala to do some more digging. On January 10 it published a front-page dispatch from Kennedy which confirmed the *Nation*'s original editorial article. The Kennedy story was somewhat muffled, in the customary *Times* style of "balancing of the news." It spoke of "Guatemala's military preparations for what Guatemalans consider will be an almost inevitable clash with Cuba." But the facts in Kennedy's story made it clear that the preparations were by the United States forces and Cuban exiles, and had nothing to do with Guatemala. "Commando-like forces," Kennedy said, "are being drilled in guerrilla warfare tactics by foreign personnel, mostly from the United States," and the Americans were helping also with "materiel and ground and air facilities."

Although Kennedy's story was far more circumspect than those of Dwiggins and Dudman, the fact that it was published in the *Times* made it news. The day after the Kennedy article appeared, the *Miami Herald* published its first story on an airlift operation from Miami to Retalhuleu. An explanatory note with the article carried this significant statement:

Publication of the accompanying story on the Miami-Guatemala airlift was withheld for more than two months by the *Herald*. Its release was decided upon only after U.S. aid to anti-Castro fighters in Guatemala was first revealed elsewhere.

Thus the *Herald* acknowledged that it had had the facts on Retalhuleu even when the *Nation* was breaking the Hilton story in November. Whether it sat on the story at the request of the government or on its own decision it did not say. In any case the story was withheld until after the *Times,* pressured by journalistic competition, had decided that the "secret" had become public enough to print.

*Time* magazine which, in its January 13 issue, had sneered at Castro's "continued tawdry little melodrama of invasion" (Cuba had broken relations with Washington on January 3, 1961), on January 20 reported that the combined anti-Castro groups in the United States known as the

*Frente* were getting $500,000 from the United States. It said the whole operation was directed by the CIA.

The *New York Times* itself did little more with the story—its subsequent treatment of the Cuban crisis could have been based on State Department handouts. For example, on April 5, barely two weeks before the invasion attempt, James Reston wrote, "The Administration has reason to believe that there are now between 100 and 200 Cuban airmen in Czechoslovakia being trained to fly Soviet MIG fighters." The Administration had changed its tactics. Aware now that it could no longer conceal its plans, it was attempting to justify its planned aggression by leaks and planted stories.

The sporadic articles which appeared in the press from February to April were mixtures of fact, exaggeration, and fancy. For the most part, they were designed not to alert the American public to the potentially disastrous course of its own government, but to advance the universally accepted propaganda line that Cuba under Castro was courting disaster. A study of newspapers for a year before the Bay of Pigs invasion—April 17, 1961—by Professor Neal D. Houghton of the University of Arizona revealed "an increasing hostility of our press and our leadership." (Houghton's article was written in 1962 and appeared in the Summer 1965 *Journalism Quarterly*.) The pattern which Houghton found in the press was:

(1) Castro has perverted his revolution, (2) he has abandoned his concern for his people, (3) he has talked nastily to and about our political personalities, (4) he has taken American property, (5) our government has shown remarkable "patience" and "forbearance" in it all, (6) the time is approaching for drastic action and (7) Communism must not be allowed to get a foothold in this hemisphere—"only 90 miles from our shore."

Only a mere trickle of stories on the invasion plans seeped into the press. After it had taken place, White House correspondent David Wise wrote in the *New York Herald Tribune* on May 2, 1961:

Actually, only a handful of stories appeared, in widely scattered publications. The invasion, and United States involvement, came as a surprise to the vast majority of the American public.

It was clear, however, that it came as no surprise to the working press and their editors. The reporters had shown remarkable restraint in not pressing for publication of the facts on the preparations—facts easily available in New York, Washington, Miami, and any number of Central

American and Caribbean capitals. This was evident in the interminable now-it-can-be-told stories which appeared in the week following the collapse of the Bay of Pigs invasion. Professor Houghton wrote:

> Certainly, one of the most remarkable of all the unfortunately confused aspects of the whole tragic business was the almost total lack of seriously critical public discussion of official Washington responsibility and support for it, during the early post-invasion weeks. So little public questioning of the propriety of that support. So much of editorial and columnist indoctrination for the urgent *need* to get on with the job of overthrowing the Cuban government. Typical of much of the columnist sentiment was Stewart Alsop's April 24th declamation that "the prestige and even the honor of the United States are now obviously wholly committed to Castro's ultimate downfall."
>
> Almost the only implications of official or press regret were expressions of sadness that the job was "bungled," that it did not "succeed"—and that a well-meaning young President *got caught* and got a "bloody nose." Such words as "failure," "fiasco" and "disastrous attempt" were used, connoting open or implied disappointment and assumption that it might all have to be done over again. Even James Reston reminded folks, a week after the episode, that the American people "may yet have to redeem the promise to chase the bearded bully boy into the Caribbean," which he had said a week before the invasion "the self-interest of this nation undoubtedly requires."

The first post-mortems in the press were easy on the President and rough on the new university intellectuals who were being taken on by the Kennedy Administration. They were tough also on the CIA. That was safe because nobody could do anything about the CIA anyway. But if the press was shielding the President from the basic responsibility for the debacle, Kennedy himself knew where the blame lay and his embarrassment was great. He sought to cover it with bluster in a speech before the American Society of Newspaper Editors on April 20 in which he delivered a virtual ultimatum to the Latin American nations to help Washington overthrow Castro or face the consequences—direct intervention by Washington in their countries to safeguard the "security of our own nation."

The speech and the invasion itself were widely endorsed in the press. A straw vote poll of the editors the morning after the speech, asking the question, "Do you consider that President Kennedy is doing a good job?" got a Yes vote by a margin of 120 to 10.

Kennedy's frustration over his failure and his embarrassment increased as the post-invasion week wore on. An astute politician, he knew that public discussion of the Cuban affair was bound to uncover aspects of his policy that he would prefer to keep covered; further, the policy itself could become endangered through such public discussion—however sympathetic the discussion might be to his own personal predicament.

THE BAY OF PIGS

The strength of Kennedy's feelings about Cuba had been demonstrated before his election to the Presidency. In October 1960, he had advocated the encouragement of counterrevolution in Cuba. This forthrightness had brought him some fatherly but firm advice from Walter Lippmann, a supporter, in a column written October 25, 1960. Lippmann said:

What Mr. Kennedy advocated looks toward doing in Cuba what the [Eisenhower] Administration, as all the world knows, did do in Guatemala. The difference is that Mr. Kennedy very unwisely said what he would do about Cuba in the future, whereas the Eisenhower Administration has been boasting about what it did in Guatemala. What this shows is that neither side [the reference was to the contrasting political parties] seems to have learned the lesson so flagrantly illustrated in the U-2 affair, that when a government goes into a political black market it must keep its mouth shut.

James Reston, that same day, was blunter: "Senator Kennedy would have done better to keep quiet . . . for we are now probably in for another big splashy debate involving not only Cuba, but Guatemala and the activities of the CIA, and a lot of other things that could well be left unsaid."

These two quotations were perhaps as revealing of the basic orientation of the two commentators as they were of John F. Kennedy. What Lippmann and Reston were saying was: If you don't want to be criticized in public, for God's sake keep your mouth shut. We can protect your silence but not your public pronouncements, particularly when they are so revealing of your intentions.

Six months later, however, Kennedy had not learned the lesson; or, being President, he believed he had no further lessons to learn. On April 27, 1961, a week after his intemperate speech to the newspaper editors, he came to New York to address the Bureau of Advertising of the American Newspaper Publishers Association. The blood of the Bay of Pigs was still in his eye and he was angry over the journalistic postmortems. He made an extremely significant statement, and extensive quotation is warranted. He said:

I do ask every publisher, every editor, and every newsman in the nation to reexamine his own standards, and to recognize the nature of our country's peril. In time of war, the Government and the press have customarily joined in an effort, based largely on self-discipline, to prevent unauthorized disclosure to the enemy. In times of clear and present danger, the courts have held that even the privileged rights of the First Amendment must yield to the public's need for national security.

Today no war has been declared—and however fierce the struggle may be, it may never be declared in the traditional fashion. Our way of life is under attack. Those who make themselves our enemy are advancing around the globe. The survival of our friends is in danger. And yet no war has been declared, no borders have been crossed by marching troops, no missiles have been fired.

If the press is awaiting a declaration of war before it imposes the self-discipline of combat conditions, then I can only say that no war has ever imposed a greater threat to our security. If you are awaiting a finding of "clear and present danger," then I can only say that the danger has never been more clear and its presence has never been more imminent.

It requires a change in outlook, a change in tactics, a change in mission by the Government, by the people, by every businessman and labor leader, and by every newspaper. For we are opposed around the world by a monolithic and ruthless conspiracy that relies primarily on covert means for expanding its sphere of influence—on infiltration instead of invasion, on subversion instead of elections, on intimidation instead of free choice, on guerrillas by night instead of armies by day . . .

Its preparations are concealed, not published. Its mistakes are buried, not head-lined. Its dissenters are silenced, not praised. No expenditure is questioned, no rumor is printed, no secret is revealed. It conducts the Cold War, in short, with a wartime discipline no democracy would ever hope or wish to match.

Then Kennedy, who had graphically attributed to the "enemy" the very characteristics the United States had demonstrated in the Bay of Pigs situation, got down to what was really on his mind.

The facts of the matter are that this nation's foes have openly boasted of acquiring through our newspapers information they would otherwise hire agents to acquire through theft, bribery or espionage; that details of this nation's covert preparations to counter the enemy's covert operations have been available to every newspaper reader, friend and foe alike; that the size, the strength, the location, and the nature of our forces and weapons, and our plans and strategy for their use, have all been pinpointed in the press and other news media to a degree sufficient to satisfy any foreign power . . .

The newspapers which printed these stories were loyal, patriotic, responsible and well-meaning. Had we been engaged in open warfare, they undoubtedly would not have published such items. But in the absence of open warfare, they recognized only the tests of journalism and not the tests of national security. And my question tonight is whether additional tests should not now be adopted . . .

I am asking the members of the newspaper profession and the industry in this country to reexamine their own responsibilities—to consider the degree and nature of the present danger—and to heed the duty of self-restraint which that danger imposes upon all of us.

Every newspaper now asks itself with respect to every story: "Is it news?" All I suggest is that you add the question: "Is it in the interest of national security?"

Rarely has a government official in the United States—and in this case the nation's highest official—expressed more clearly the concept that the press should voluntarily become an arm of government. Despite all the pious words about the First Amendment which larded the President's speech, it was a call for abdication by the press of the guarantees—and the responsibilities—of the First Amendment.

The press might have risen with the righteousness of the founding fathers to denounce such a proposal. It did not. The reaction was feeble. The *New York Post* said on April 29 in a meaningless editorial that "a free society cannot function half free and half scared, half lawful and half lawless." The *Capital Times* of Madison, Wisconsin, said May 11, two weeks after the speech: "The President can survive the [invasion] blunder if he does not now make worse mistakes, one of which would be chipping away at the First Amendment."

As "the clear and present danger" from Cuba subsided, so did the public controversy over the public's right to know. Publishers dislike talking about these things in their own papers: they prefer to confine their remarks on the freedom of the press and relations between press and government to commemorative lectures honoring John Peter Zenger, who would have scorned the platitudes they utter in his name. Early in May, a committee of prominent editors was appointed to meet with the President. He rocked through a cordial session with them at the White House and nothing came of it. The editors decided that since there was no declared national emergency, they would look foolish if they discussed publicly any plan for voluntary censorship.

On May 10, the *New York Times,* uncomfortable about its own role in the Bay of Pigs saga, sought to blunt the President's criticism in an editorial entitled "The Right Not To Be Lied To." It said:

The Cuban tragedy has raised a domestic question that is likely to come up again and again until it is solved. The cause may be in something that is happening in Laos, in Central Africa or in Latin America, but the question remains the same: is a democratic government in an open society such as ours ever justified in deceiving its own people?

The existence of the cold war implies secret operations on our side in self-defense against the normal subversive operations of the other side that cannot be revealed, nor would the responsible American press want to reveal them. But the Government has a duty also. Neither prudence nor ethics can justify any administration in telling the public things that are not so.

As has been reported in this and other newspapers, there is no doubt that men were recruited in this country for the projected attack on Cuba. The fact was well known in and around Miami prior to the attack and could not be kept secret from Castro's own spies.

What some leaders of our Government stated in this regard did not square with the facts. If they could not reveal the facts, they would have done better to remain silent. A democracy—our democracy—cannot be lied to . . . The basic principle involved is that of confidence. A dictatorship can get along without an informed public opinion. A democracy cannot. Not only is it unethical to deceive one's own public as part of a system of deceiving an adversary government; it is also foolish . . .

For all its Jeffersonian phrases, there was—as with Lippmann and Reston quoted earlier—a realistic piece of advice contained in the May 10 editorial. It was this: If you cannot tell us the truth, then don't say anything. The responsibility of a newspaper to ferret out the truth—or even to print facts "well known in and around Miami"—is not discussed. Blame must be laid for an unpleasant mess and the *Times* lays it on the government.

The role of the *Times* in the Bay of Pigs fiasco is important. As the most influential newspaper in the country, it supposedly sets a standard for journalistic responsibility and ethics, although it does not often disclose its internal decision-making processes. It was therefore both significant and surprising that the role of the *Times* in April 1961 was later laid bare not by a journalistic muckraker but by the managing editor of the *Times* itself. It may have been the flood of reminiscences about the Kennedy Administration then being published (many of them involving the *Times*) that moved Clifton Daniel to the confession box—and prompted the *Times* to devote 700 words to a news story and 4,000 words to the text of Daniel's confession on June 2, 1966. The text came from an address given June 1 by Daniel to the World Press Institute in St. Paul, Minnesota.

The speech was a seemingly candid report of an agonized drama in the *Times* newsroom in the first days of April—whether to print the news (which the editors believed to be accurate) that a United States sponsored invasion of Cuba was about to be carried out. In fact, the speech revealed how the *Times* evaded its responsibility. This comes through in the tense, emotional script which must have fascinated the young reporters and journalism students at MacAlester College.

Daniel's narrative opens with the *Nation*'s editorial report of November 19, 1960, on Dr. Hilton, which the *Times* had then ignored. Daniel quoted the conclusion of the *Nation*'s article: "We believe the reports merit publication: they can, and should, be checked immediately by all U.S. news media with correspondents in Guatemala."

"With this last paragraph," said Daniel, "the *New York Times* readily agreed. Paul Kennedy, our correspondent in Central America, was soon on his way to Guatemala." This was a reference, apparently, to Kennedy's trip which produced the unsigned story in the *Times* of November 20.

At this point Daniel referred to an account of events by Arthur Schlesinger, Jr., at the time of the invasion an assistant to President Kennedy, as related in Schlesinger's book *A Thousand Days* (Houghton Mifflin, 1965). Early in April 1961, according to Schlesinger, Gilbert Harrison, publisher of the *New Republic,* sent to him galley proofs of an article slated for publication. It was a "careful, accurate and devastating account of CIA activities among the [Cuban] refugees [in Florida]." Schlesinger showed the article to the President, and, at the President's request, it was suppressed by the *New Republic.* This, said Schlesinger, was a "patriotic act which left me oddly uncomfortable." Despite his odd discomfort, Schlesinger went right on assisting the President.

About the same time, Schlesinger wrote, a story was filed to the *New York Times* by its own correspondent, Tad Szulc, telling of CIA recruitment in Florida among the refugees and reporting that a landing in Cuba was imminent. Here the drama begins. Turner Catledge, then managing editor, called James Reston, chief of the Washington bureau, for guidance.

Don't print it, Reston advised—the *Times* will bear the burden for dead invaders—or the expedition will be canceled outright. "Another patriotic act," wrote Schlesinger, still a mite uncomfortable, "but in retrospect I have wondered whether if the press had behaved irresponsibly, it would not have spared the country a disaster." It seems not to have occurred to Schlesinger that the lack of responsibility lay in the first instance with an Administration which had planned and launched this enterprise; that if the press had raised its voice against such governmental irresponsibility, it would have been acting responsibly in the genuine national interest.

Daniel himself then picked up the drama again. Schlesinger was wrong about the Szulc story, he said. The facts are that an odd thing happened to Szulc on his way from Rio de Janeiro to Washington for reassignment. He stopped in Miami to visit friends, discovered the news of the invasion force, and rushed a story. It was scheduled for a multiple-column play on page one, April 7. Then the fun began. Orvil Dryfoos, the publisher (now dead), told Catledge he was sorely troubled by the security implications of the story. Reston was called. Don't run the stuff about the imminent invasion, he advised. But since everyone knows about the recruitment in Florida, that stuff is all right. Daniel said a few words in the Szulc story were eliminated. Szulc himself says the story was drastically censored.

A change then was made in the placement of the story, from a four-column headline leading the paper to a one-column headline below the fold on page one. News editor Lewis Jordan and assistant managing editor Theodore Bernstein bitterly protested the downgrading of the story.

The scene in Daniel's drama shifts to the White House. Among those present at the gathering of the editors after Kennedy's address to the American Newspaper Publishers Association on April 27, 1961, was Catledge. Daniel said:

> That day in the White House, President Kennedy ran down a list of what he called premature disclosures of security information. His examples were mainly drawn from *The New York Times*.
>
> He mentioned, for example, Paul Kennedy's story about the training of anti-Castro forces in Guatemala. Mr. Catledge pointed out that this information had been published in *La Hora* in Guatemala and in *The Nation* in this country before it was ever published in *The New York Times*.
>
> "But it was not news until it appeared in *The Times*," the President replied.
>
> While he scolded *The New York Times,* the President said in an aside to Mr. Catledge, "If you had printed more about the operation you would have saved us from a colossal mistake."
>
> More than a year later, President Kennedy was still talking the same way. In a conversation with Orvil Dryfoos in the White House on September 13, 1962, he said, "I wish you had run everything on Cuba . . . I am just sorry you didn't tell it at the time."

Daniel did some musing of his own. "It is not so easy," he said, "it seems, even for Presidents [and] their most intimate advisors . . . to know always what really is in the national interest. One is tempted to say that sometimes—sometimes—even a mere newspaperman knows better."

His own view, Daniel said, "is that the Bay of Pigs operation might well have been canceled and the country would have been saved an enormous embarrassment if the *New York Times* and other newspapers had been more diligent in the performance of their duty—their duty to keep the public informed on matters vitally affecting our national honor and prestige, not to mention our national security."

Daniel then brought up James Reston again—the same Reston who had advised against printing the fact of the imminence of the invasion. Daniel said:

> Perhaps, as Mr. Reston believes, it was too late to stop the operation by the time we printed Tad Szulc's story on April 7.
>
> "If I had it to do over, I would do exactly what we did at the time," Mr. Reston says. "It is ridiculous to think that publishing the fact that the invasion was imminent would have avoided this disaster. I am quite sure the operation would have gone forward."

Daniel entitled his talk "A Footnote to History." There is good reason to believe, given the rivalries among the princes and the heirs apparent of the *New York Times,* that he was also writing a footnote to the history of James Reston. Neither Daniel nor Reston, it is plain, could overlook or forget the article written by Reston in the *Times* of May 10, 1961, the same day as the famous "The Right Not To Be Lied To" editorial.

In that article Reston wrote that the press "knew what was going on ahead of the landing. It knew that the United States government (1) was breaking its treaty commitments and placing the reputation of the United States in the hands of a poorly trained and squabbling band of refugees; (2) officials not only encouraged the publication of false information but (3) resented publication later of the fact that the CIA actually imprisoned Cuban refugees because the latter didn't like the way the CIA was running the show . . ."

"The same press," Reston wrote, "roared with indignation when Britain and France broke their treaty commitments to invade Suez, but it had very little to say about the morality, legality, or practicality of the Cuban adventure, when there was still time to stop it.

"If the press had used its freedom during this period to protest, it might have been influential even in the White House, where instead it was being encouraged to put out false information and was actually putting it out."

Thus Reston on May 10, 1961, and, according to Clifton Daniel, Reston on June 1, 1966. The man who right after the Bay of Pigs scolded the press (and, by inference, himself, since he had advised against the press exercising its freedom), five years later says he would do the same thing all over again. "Jack Kennedy was in no mood" to alter the invasion plans, Daniel quotes Reston. And when the President is in such a mood, a distinguished Washington commentator who has a pipeline to the White House is not going to antagonize the President and clog his pipeline—even if the reputation of the United States and the cherished principle of freedom of the press are at stake.

A different view was taken by the *Times*'s assistant managing editor, Theodore Bernstein, who had been at work in the newsroom of the *Times* on the night the Szulc story was "revised." In a letter to the *Columbia Forum* dated December 5, 1967, and published in the Spring 1968 issue, Bernstein confirmed the facts in the *Forum*'s Bay of Pigs article. He noted that Schlesinger, in his *A Thousand Days,* had quoted President Kennedy as saying, "You know, I've reserved the right to stop this thing up to 24 hours before landing time." Bernstein continued:

It does not seem impossible that had the *Times* printed the Szulc story as planned, the prestigious exposure of what was supposed to be a secret operation and the public outcry and pressure that probably would have followed might well have given Kennedy exactly the excuse he needed to call the whole thing off.

Bernstein said that the intervention by publisher Dryfoos was "the only instance of any importance that I could recall in which a publisher of the *Times* had interfered with a decision by the editors responsible for the presentation and display of the news." Then he reported what happened to him the morning after—April 7, 1961:

> Mr. Dryfoos, aware of our distress, asked me to come to his office so that he could explain his thinking. He said the matter had been put to him on the basis of the national interest. His motives, of course, were of the highest and he had acted on that basis. I argued that there was a distinction between the national interest and the national security and that he had confused the two. I pointed out, to underscore the absence of a national security consideration, that not a single American life would have been imperiled by our original plan for presenting the news.

Bernstein elaborated on the theme of "interest" and "security" for his *Columbia Forum* audience:

> When matters of national security arise in a war situation or a near-war situation, there is not the slightest question about what course the press should follow. Editors cannot have the information or specialized knowledge that would allow them to dispute an official determination that the country's safety might be jeopardized. But matters of national interest are different. They may well be political issues and one man's opinion of what is in the nation's interest may be as good as another's . . . In matters of national interest the press has not only a proper option but indeed a bounden duty to speak up. The press must keep in mind that even the President himself plays different roles on different occasions: sometimes he is the constitutional commander-in-chief; sometimes he is the country's political leader. The organs of public information have to draw the line between the national security and the national interest and then act appropriately.

Bernstein held a justifiable reputation at the *Times* for his expertise on the use of the English language. But on politics and military affairs he had himself confused the issues of *security* and *interest*. It is of course true that the President plays many roles. But his political and military roles fundamentally are indivisible. It was precisely because the architects of the American system of government wanted a political supervision of the armed forces that they insisted on a civilian commander-in-chief. Further, even in Bernstein's framework, it could be argued that, in the Bay of Pigs situation, the President was acting in the national security because of a possible threat from a Communist Cuba; and many uninformed Americans and informed newspapers would have accepted—in fact, did accept

—that interpretation on the ground of the President's "information and specialized knowledge." The *Times* itself says that it altered its news presentation for reasons of national security—reasons which Bernstein could not accept.

The Bay of Pigs indeed might have involved the nation's security if it had not been such a swift failure—but not in the sense that the *Times* argued. The recklessness of the planned and unprovoked aggression by the United States against a small, newly established socialist state might have drawn in an ally of Cuba—say, the Soviet Union—to protect Cuba against such aggression, and thereby sparked a wider conflict involving the United States and directly endangering the security of its people for no valid reason. Thus the Bay of Pigs adventure must be judged neither in the public interest nor in the public security.

While Bernstein's lecture to his publisher was as commendable as his indignation in the newsroom the night before, in the conclusion of his letter to the *Columbia Forum* he still accepts government policy as the determining factor in the newspapers' relations with government.

It is my view that at no time should newspapers draw the line if they believe that the government is on a course that endangers either the national interest or the national security, or both at the same time. That is the essence of journalistic responsibility.

# 12. The Missile Crisis

United Nations Week in October 1962 saw the United States go to the brink of World War III in what came to be known as the Cuban Missile Crisis. In violation of the United Nations Charter, President Kennedy imposed a blockade around Cuba to intercept any ship of any flag carrying cargo to Cuba. The reason was the presence of Soviet missiles in bases on Cuban soil. Washington demanded their removal—despite the fact that the United States openly maintained in Turkey, on the Soviet border, bases with nuclear weapons. Soviet Premier Khrushchev diverted Soviet ships from an encounter with United States vessels, agreed to the removal of the missiles in return for what amounted to a United States pledge not to invade Cuba, and war was averted.

The timing, the staging, and the content of the United States moves during the week were a combination of gunboat diplomacy and Madison Avenue techniques, and it brought into the open a process that has come to be known as "management of the news."

Kennedy's actions came only two weeks after a frank but conciliatory address by President Osvaldo Dorticós of Cuba at the United Nations. The Cubans had offered once again to discuss with the United States all outstanding differences, although the Cubans believed, with overwhelming evidence at hand, that they were the aggrieved party.

The blockade and the warnings to the Soviet Union of the possibility of nuclear attack on the USSR itself followed months of overtures by Moscow for a meeting between Khrushchev and Kennedy looking toward peaceful negotiations to end the stalemate over Berlin and a treaty to end the testing of nuclear weapons. It was not the alleged threat of Soviet nuclear weapons in Cuba that motivated Kennedy. It was a test of strength with the Soviet Union and the desire to maintain conditions in Cuba which might allow for a much more sophisticated Bay of Pigs adventure. There was also another factor, something entirely immediate and practical: national politics.

The crisis came on the eve of the 1962 Congressional elections. On October 26, 1962, columnist Drew Pearson wrote:

> In the end what really tipped the scales were political factors, including a report from Vice-President Johnson that Cuba was causing great damage to the Democrats in the election campaign and that the public was getting the impression that Kennedy was indecisive. The President himself had detected this and was gloomy about the prospect of losing the governorship battles in the big key states of New York, Michigan, Ohio and California, which could start a disastrous trend for 1964. This, plus the decision to keep Russia on the defensive, were the real reasons for the historic decision on Cuba. Military fear of Cuba actually had very little at all to do with it.

This kind of honest appraisal was notable for its rarity. The President's action came after an unprecedented propaganda buildup with the full cooperation of the communications media. It had all the ingredients of the Big Washington Novel except for the love-on-the-couch-in-Georgetown scenes. Officials were at their desks on Sunday; lights were burning late in the State Department; the President was closeted with his war chiefs; planes were dispatched to the far corners of the country to bring legislators of both parties back to Washington.

The President's moves were conveyed in language designed to smother still further a public already gasping under a journalistic blanket of fabrications and distortions about Cuba and the intentions of the Soviet Union concerning Cuba. The press was whipping up a war frenzy. The worst aspect of the crisis week was the almost total immobilization of American public opinion. A paralyzed nation seemed to be waiting for the doom boom to be lowered.

Security restrictions were more severe that week than they had been in World War II and the Korean war. Not a single newspaperman was permitted on any ship of the United States fleet patrolling the waters off the Cuban coast, nor was any permitted inside the United States base at Guantánamo. The correspondents in Washington professed to be as much in the dark as the public about what was in the wind (although it became evident later that this was not entirely the case). There was much grumbling over the drying up of news from government sources and the unavailability of government officials.

On October 30, 1962, toward the end of the crisis week, Arthur Sylvester, Assistant Secretary of Defense for Public Affairs (and a former

Washington correspondent of the *Newark News*), called a press conference. It was a tense session. The newspapermen were charging the government with withholding the facts regarding the Cuban crisis and giving out misleading and even untruthful information. Sylvester responded:

> I can't think of a comparable situation, but in the kind of world we live in, the generation of news by actions taken by the government becomes one weapon in a strained situation. The results, in my opinion, justify the methods we use . . . News generated by actions of the government as to content and timing are part of the arsenal of weaponry that a President has in application of military force and related forces to the solution of political problems, or to the applications of international political pressure.

A Defense Department spokesman, enlarging on Sylvester's remarks, told *Editor & Publisher* (November 3, 1962):

> The point is not concerning the manufacturing or withholding of news. When the government is acting, these actions result in the making of news. How the announcements of these actions are made is the "weaponry." Such things come into play as timing, and whether the statement is made by the President, which is the highest impact level, or is treated with a little less impact and is attributed to an informal source.

The same issue of *Editor & Publisher* said that Richard Fryklund, the *Washington Star*'s Pentagon correspondent, quoted Defense Department officials as saying that the press had been a successful weapon in the blockade. Fryklund wrote: "By careful timing and wording of announcements about blockade activities, the Administration attempted to control the image of the action shown to the world and the information reaching the Russians and the Cubans."

Sylvester and his State Department counterpart, Robert Manning (now editor of the *Atlantic Monthly*), signed orders requiring that military officers and civilian officials talking to the press report to whom they talked and what was discussed. (The State Department order was rescinded a month later; the Defense Department order continued until the fall of 1967.) The memorandum for Defense personnel read:

> SUBJECT: *Procedures for handling media representatives.*
>
> The substance of each interview and telephone conversation with a media representative will be reported to the appropriate public information office before the close of business that day. A report need not be made if a representative of the public information office is present at the interview.

A directive was issued listing 12 categories of information which publishers and editors were asked, in the national interest, to keep unreported.

Several reporters and editorial pages reacted sharply. In the November 11 *New York Herald Tribune*, Warren Rogers of the Washington staff wrote: "For more than three weeks, the United States government has been operating under a clampdown on news that has no parallel in modern history." Of a comment of Sylvester's on the need to "speak in one voice to your adversary," the *New York Times* said in an October 31 editorial: "To attempt to manage the news so that a free press should speak . . . 'in one voice to your adversary' could be far more dangerous to the cause of freedom than the free play of dissent, than the fullest possible publication of the facts."

David Kraslow of the Knight newspapers, discussing the deceptions and distortions resorted to by the government during the crisis buildup, told *Editor & Publisher*: "The direct lie is never justified. It happened with the U-2 affair, the Bay of Pigs, and now this time. What does this do to the credibility of our own government?"

Critical editorials appeared in papers both friendly and cool to the Administration. Many forgave the deception of the President's "cold"—the reason given for canceling his speaking engagement and his hurried return from Chicago to Washington during the crisis week—but all seemed concerned that the First Amendment's proscription against tampering with freedom of the press might acquire a fatal dose of pneumonia. Representative John E. Moss, Democrat of California, chairman of the House Subcommittee on Information of the Committee on Government Operations, scheduled a session to hear reporters' complaints against government information policies. He said:

Government pronouncements during a conflict of wills obviously have an effect upon the outcome of the conflict, but to imply that the entire government information process is part of the maneuvers in international relations is to ignore the workings of our democratic system.

For Louis M. Lyons, then curator of the Nieman Foundation for Journalism at Harvard, Sylvester's statement that the "results justify the means we use" sounded "like a pitchman using hidden persuaders to sell deodorants" (*New York Herald Tribune*, November 11, 1962). He said:

It is indefensible coming from a professional news man . . . whose job it is to guide the Administration in meeting its responsibility to communicate to the people of a democracy through the channels of a free press . . . He justly receives our condemnation for justifying as a policy the use of deception in news as a weapon. This is the philosophy of totalitarianism. It is of course self-defeating. It forfeits public confidence. If the press did not resist and denounce it, our free press would be meaningless. It too would not be believed.

As valid as the criticism was, it was misdirected. Sylvester and Manning and their associates, who became unidentified government spokesmen in many news articles, were ultimately responsible to their own superiors. In the Cuban missile crisis, they were responsible only to one man: the President. Only a few newsmen said this outright. In the *Herald Tribune,* Warren Rogers wrote (November 11, 1962), "The finger inevitably points to the White House, where sits the boss of them all." In the *New York Post,* November 4, William V. Shannon wrote:

> It is actually at the White House that this policy originated. It was not Sylvester or [White House press secretary] Salinger but Mr. Kennedy himself who ordered the ruthless closing down of all sources of information. He was determined that the Administration in this crisis would speak with but one voice—his own.

In his book *The Missile Crisis* (J. B. Lippincott Co., 1966), Elie Abel, an NBC correspondent and former Washington correspondent of the *New York Times,* supported this contention. Describing the scene in Chicago on the morning of October 19, 1962, he wrote that the President's press secretary Pierre Salinger "confronted the President in his bedroom, still half-dressed, with the unwelcome news that certain reporters were asking questions about troop movements in the direction of Florida. What could he tell them?" Abel continued:

> The President instructed Salinger to say that there was "nothing to" such reports. The portly press secretary was not himself persuaded. But, having been told nothing more, he passed the word to inquiring reporters. The Pentagon, fending off queries later in the day about a published report by [syndicated columnists] Paul Scott and Robert S. Allen about missiles in Cuba, took the occasion to issue a two-in-one denial. It said the Government has "no information indicating the presence of offensive weapons in Cuba," adding that no alert had been ordered or "any emergency measures" set in motion against Cuba. The alert, in fact, had just been ordered. Messages went out at 1:20 P.M. on Friday to the Atlantic and Caribbean commands, warning of possible air attacks on the Panama Canal, Ramey Air Force Base, and the Naval Station at Roosevelt Roads, Puerto Rico. Hawk antiaircraft missile batteries were directed to increase their readiness for possible action. Somehow the President's secret remained a secret; the Pentagon's deliberate double lie probably helped.

By October 21, Abel wrote, the troop movements were beginning to draw public attention. Continuing his description of the events of the week, he told of some Sunday telephone calls by the White House:

> Both the *Washington Post* and the *New York Times* had put together a fairly shrewd notion of what was coming. So the President telephoned Orvil Dryfoos,

then publisher of the *Times,* and Philip Graham, publisher of the *Post,* asking them not to give the game away in Monday morning's newspapers. [Secretary of Defense] McNamara made a similar appeal to John Hay Whitney, publisher of the *New York Herald Tribune.* Publishing less than it knew, the *Times* that night carried a front-page story about preparations for an unspecified major crisis.

How did the Washington newspapermen react to this acquiescence to government appeals for restraint? One indication came in a statement on the crisis coverage by John Lindsay of *Newsweek* magazine, in the March 1963 issue of *Nieman Reports* of Harvard University. He wrote:

> It is no great surprise to me that despite the red herring dragged across the trail, cover stories and other devices used, two newspapers nailed the story of the Administration's plan for the handling of the introduction of Soviet missiles into Cuba. That they sat on this at the request of the Administration may be news management, but if it was, the precedents are clear and unassailable.

The untroubled Lindsay did not cite the clear and unassailable precedents. Far from being concerned with the implications of the press-government relationship, he was overwhelmed by the "curiosity, imagination, boldness and the insight" which the two newspapers employed to get past the Administration screen. He professed himself "green with envy." Others were more concerned with the whole practice. Murrey Marder wrote in the *Washington Post,* November 22, 1962:

> While even many newspapermen may tend to pass off the present flap [over news management] as a passing phase that is only a product of the Cuban crisis, and will disappear with it, Administration officials frankly acknowledge in private that this is not true. They concede—in fact, assert—that long before the Cuban crisis many officials in the Administration were seriously rethinking the whole Government-press relationship.

If the government was doing a lot of rethinking, the men who own the newspapers and those who write for them and about them were not. An exception was Ben. H. Bagdikian, for many years a working newspaperman and a thoughtful commentator on the press. In an article on "Press Independence and the Cuban Crisis" in the Winter 1963 issue of the *Columbia Journalism Review,* he said:

> The central dilemma for a free society is that in a world of missiles and nuclear bombs, technology demands that we grant our President godlike powers of decision; yet history has convinced us that politically it is unsafe to let any mortal play God.

But the *New York Times* did. Once again the source of this revelation is the *Times*'s managing editor, Clifton Daniel. In the same "Footnote to History" speech at St. Paul, June 1, 1966, which described the inside *Times* story of the Bay of Pigs, Daniel said:

> The Bay of Pigs, as it turned out, was a prelude to an even graver crisis—the Cuban missile crisis of 1962. In Arthur Schlesinger's opinion, failure in 1961 contributed to success in 1962. President Kennedy had learned from experience, and once again *The New York Times* was involved.

Daniel told of a handwritten letter sent by the President to Mrs. Orvil Dryfoos on May 28, 1963. Dryfoos had died some months before. Mrs. Dryfoos, who has since become Mrs. Andrew Heiskell (he is chairman of the board of *Time-Life*), gave Daniel permission to make the letter public. After expressing his sympathy for her husband's death, Kennedy wrote:

> Two experiences I had with [Dryfoos] gave me a clear insight into his unusual qualities of mind and heart. One involved a matter of national security—the other his decision to refrain from printing on October 21st [1962] the news, which only the man from the *Times* possessed, on the presence of Russian missiles in Cuba, upon my informing him that we needed 24 more hours to complete our preparations.
>
> This decision of his made far more effective our later actions and thereby contributed greatly to our national safety.

According to Daniel, things at the *Times* were "handled somewhat differently" than at the time of the Bay of Pigs. This time Kennedy telephoned directly to publisher Dryfoos (a fact corroborated by Elie Abel). He had been invited to do so by Dryfoos at the White House a month before Dryfoos's death, during a conversation on security leaks and how to prevent them.

"Mr. Dryfoos had told the President," Daniel said, "that what was needed was prior information and prior consultation. He said that, when there was danger of security information getting into print, the thing to do was call in the publishers and explain matters to them. In the missile crisis, President Kennedy did exactly that."

As in the Bay of Pigs episode, James Reston also had a role. Daniel reported in St. Paul what Reston had told him of that fateful October 21, 1962. This is Daniel's report:

> "The President called me," Reston said. "He understood that I had been talking to Mac Bundy [McGeorge Bundy, Presidential assistant and the man perhaps closest to the President] and he knew from the line of questioning that we knew

the critical fact—that Russian missiles had indeed been emplaced in Cuba. The President told me that he was going on television on Monday evening to report to the American people. He said that if we published the news about the missiles Khrushchev could actually give him an ultimatum before he went on the air. Those were Kennedy's exact words. I told him I understood, but I also told him I could not do anything about it . . . I told the President I would report to my office in New York and if my advice were asked I would recommend that we not publish. It was not my duty to decide. My job was the same as that of an ambassador—to report to my superiors. I recommended to the President that he call New York. He did so."

Dryfoos, said Daniel, in turn put the issue up to Reston and his staff, "and the news that the Soviet Union had atomic missiles in Cuba only 90 miles from the coast of Florida was withheld until the President announced it."

What conclusions did Daniel reach from these facts? What moral did he draw from his story? He told the young reporters in his audience:

My conclusion is this: Information is essential to people who propose to govern themselves. It is the responsibility of serious journalists to supply that information —whether in this country or in the countries from which our foreign colleagues come.

Still, the primary responsibility for safeguarding our national interest must rest always with our Government, as it did with President Kennedy in two Cuban crises. Up until the time we are actually at war or on the verge of war, it is not only permissible—it is our duty as journalists and citizens to be constantly questioning our leaders and our policy, and to be constantly informing the people, who are the masters of us all—both the press and the politician.

On October 31, 1962, an editorial in the *New York Times* warned of the danger to the cause of freedom in speaking "in one voice to your adversary." On October 21, ten days before this grave editorial appeared, the *Times* had already agreed—from publisher on down through knowing staff—to the one-voice approach. The *Times* remained silent until the President spoke. His voice was the only one.

Why Daniel laid out the editorial hypocrisy of the *Times* in the missile crisis—just as he had exposed the individual hypocrisy of James Reston in the Bay of Pigs episode—would seem to be a mystery. The explanation may be that Daniel did not regard the *Times*'s role in 1962 as hypocrisy. He may have seen no contradiction between the October 31 editorial and the policy of his paper. This time round, Daniel had no disagreement with Reston.

The vital question of government-press relations required a much fuller airing than it received immediately after the missile crisis. The discomfort evidenced by some newspapermen was encouraging, but a nag-ging question persisted: Were the newspapermen concerned because they disliked and feared the increasingly stringent news policies—or were they concerned because they were not taken more fully into the confidence of the policy makers?

In all the welter of words, not one reporter or editor or critic of the press condemned the blockade of Cuba and the ultimatum to the Soviet Union which might have led to a nuclear war. Here a comment by Reston is as enlightening as it is cynical. On November 2, 1962, he wrote of the management-of-the-news controversy:

> What is ironical about the thing is that the whole controversy did not blow up until Arthur Sylvester admitted that the release of news was part of the Govern-ment's weaponry. As long as the officials merely didn't tell the whole truth, very few of us complained; but as soon as Sylvester told the truth, the editors fell on him like a fumble.

In other words it was Sylvester's candor—not his comment—that caused the discomfort and the ensuing uproar.

On this point, Bagdikian in his Winter 1963 *Columbia Journalism Review* article said:

> In a sense, the Sylvester statement was refreshingly candid. Any reporter or editor who does not take for granted that the government, or any experienced source of news, always tries to manage information is naive. What was bothersome, of course, was the implication that control as a principle is good.

In the issue of his *Weekly* dated November 12, 1962, I. F. Stone, the most candid reporter in Washington, had this to say:

> Devoted as I am to free enterprise in journalism, I still find it hard to bleed in unison with my colleagues over the new restrictions on press contacts with officials at the Defense and State Departments. Nor am I surprised by Mr. Sylvester's avowal of the government's use of the press as weaponry. This has been going on in Washington for years, and it has been facilitated by the readiness of the press corps to be the willing conduit of all kinds of official misinformation and mis-chief as dished out in the capital's 57 varieties of off-the-record-but-please-use-it press conferences. The so-called information officers of the government have long been engaged in brainwashing and most of the reporters here have been as eager inculcators of the U.S. Cold War party line as their opposite numbers are to dish out the official view of *Pravda* or *Izvestia*. The handling of the Cuban affair from the beginning has hardly been a model of passionate eagerness to search out the impartial truth.

When Representative Moss spoke of the danger of the "entire govern-ment information process" becoming "part of the maneuvers in international relations," he was, as Bagdikian noted, a little behind the times: It had already become just that. Bagdikian wrote:

At the heart of the matter, much depends on whether "the entire government information process" becomes identical to the entire press information process. The government has the great advantage of original possession of information. The test is whether the press can perceive the main lines of government action, and can understand them, independent of government, for short periods.

Then he asked, "Does [the press] have to choose between provoking disaster and becoming an automatic arm of foreign policy?"

The answer to the question—but not as Bagdikian posed it—is that the press does have a clear choice. It can help prevent disaster—not provoke it or advance it—by refusing to become an automatic arm of foreign policy. The choice that confronted the press became apparent in an article in the October 23, 1962, *New York Times* by Max Frankel of the Washington staff. Noting the various reasons why the secrecy in the missile crisis was not broken by the newspapermen who were in on the facts, Frankel wrote:

The basic reason was the fear that the Soviet Union if it knew the [blockade] plans in advance, would make some move to anticipate and undercut the President's course. For example, one such move might have been a resolution in the UN.

In other words, the newspapers, with the *New York Times* setting the standard, kept the secret lest the United States be forced to adhere to the Charter of the United Nations and not take unilateral action with impunity.

The conclusion one is forced to make is that the press—the responsible press, so-called—refused to exercise its responsibility to restrain a reckless government from taking an illegal action which might have brought on World War III.

# 13. Vietnam: The Making of a Miracle

The *Los Angeles Times* on October 28, 1962, published a column by Matt Weinstock describing a scene common throughout the United States during the missile crisis week of October 22. In the junior and senior high schools of Los Angeles, Weinstock wrote, youngsters broke down and cried, "I don't want to die." In some schools the situation "became so bad that principals felt obligated to go on the public address system to calm students with fact and common sense." Fact and common sense were rare during that paralyzing week, and Weinstock did not explain how the principal had discovered and used them to comfort the young who were "unaware of what's happening in this world." Lack of awareness was not confined to the schools in the second decade of the Cold War mind-freeze. It was widespread also among the adult population. Actually, the youngsters had responded with appropriate fear, however unencumbered they were by facts.

Cuba was "only 90 miles from our shores," as the hawk flies, and the missile crisis, however misrepresented, had a geographical immediacy which could not be denied. But 10,000 miles from our shores, as the B-36 flies, the Washington Administration was already deeply involved in another crisis of infinitely greater proportion—and the absence of geographical immediacy was rarely mentioned by the newspapers which guarded our shores most zealously against the threat of Communist takeover. The name of the crisis, well fermented during the past six years with the aid of several billion dollars' worth of investment by the United States, was Vietnam.

As in the missile crisis, when "it was Mr. Kennedy himself who ordered the ruthless closing down of all sources of information" (William Shannon in the *New York Post,* November 4, 1962), there was a rigid clamp-down on news about Vietnam. The Kennedy cover-up was described by his news secretary, Pierre Salinger, in his book *With Kennedy* (Double-day, 1966). When Kennedy became President, Salinger wrote, the total United States force in Vietnam was about 600, and the United States "was acting solely as an advisor to the Government of South Vietnam."

That was much less than candid. During the last four years of the French war in Vietnam the United States had supplied 70 per cent of the military budget ($2.8 billion) and was on the brink of a massive air strike to prevent the defeat of the French forces. British resistance plus French exhaustion and confusion persuaded President Eisenhower to overrule Secretary of State John Foster Dulles and Vice President Richard M. Nixon. Nixon, as spokesman for the hard-line lobby within the govern-ment (Admiral Arthur W. Radford, chairman of the Joint Chiefs of Staff, was a prominent member), chose a significant audience before which to advocate the proposed air strike—a specially convened back-ground briefing of editors at the convention of the American Society of Newspaper Editors in Washington in the spring of 1954. The proposal was being advanced within the National Security Council, and Nixon obviously was seeking to line up editorial support. The editors, according to William McGaffin and Erwin Knoll in their book *Anything But the Truth* (G. P. Putnam & Sons, 1968), had "a negative reaction." Such a reaction, it would seem, would move the alarmed editors to break the story in their newspapers to arouse public opinion and force the Admin-istration to back off from this dangerous course. But that's not the way it was. There were a few leaks which came to nothing. If Eisenhower had agreed to the air strike, there would have been no record of editorial opposition, but there almost surely would have been an editorial rally round the flag.

By 1961 the United States government had spent more than $1 billion more on Vietnam to shore up Premier Ngo Dinh Diem and to equip his army. After a tour of inspection by President Kennedy's military adviser, General Maxwell D. Taylor, there was a gradual increase in United States troop strength. The 20,000 mark had been passed at the time of Ken-nedy's death. This 1961 tactical shift was accompanied by a decision to alter Washington's policy toward the press because, according to Salinger, "with the buildup of United States troops and supplies, this government was now going to be engaged in activities which were in clear violation of the Geneva conference of 1954." This frank admission must be bal-anced constantly against the repeated insistence by four succeeding Washington administrations, two Republican and two Democratic, that the United States has always been open to a settlement of the war "based on strict adherence to the Geneva Agreements."

Having gone through the Bay of Pigs, and still concerned with the Berlin crisis and the buildup of troops in Europe, Salinger wrote, Kennedy was "not anxious to admit the existence of a real war in Southeast Asia." On September 21, 1962, as American involvement increased in ratio to the inability of the Diem government to function, the State Department dispatched a directive, which came to be known as Cable 1006, to its Information Service in Saigon restricting the movement of correspondents and their sources of information and appealing to the press for restraint in handling information affecting national security. It didn't work: Stories began appearing with increasing regularity, Salinger said, "describing heavy involvement of United States forces in Vietnamese operations, and . . . the shooting down of United States helicopters." This clearly presented the picture of a widening war in Southeast Asia—a picture "which the Administration did not want to present."

Kennedy pressed hard to restrict the news coverage, and new guidelines kept streaming out of Washington. Basic to United States policy, as Assistant Secretary of State Robert Manning said in a report after an on-the-spot survey of press relations in South Vietnam, was the need to keep the facts from the American public: "The problem is complicated by the longstanding desire of the United States government to see the American involvement minimized, even represented as something less in reality than it is."

That "something less in reality" carried over to Washington's presentation of the Diem government as an incorruptible assembly of Vietnamese patriots whose sole desire was to establish a democratic system in South Vietnam in the face of the threat posed by a predatory Communist power to the north which sought to enslave the population of all Vietnam. Unfortunately for Washington, the reality was so much at variance with this presentation that the facts could not be kept from dribbling out and, at times, exploding. The "second war" in Vietnam as it has been called—the war of the correspondents against the combined United States-Vietnamese authority in Saigon—should be viewed in this context.

After reading and analyzing dispatches from Vietnam for more than ten years, as well as a flood of books by correspondents and government officials and critical articles in publications devoted to journalism; after discussing in person with returned correspondents the coverage of the news—after all this, I have come to the conclusion that the so-called war between the foreign correspondents and the United States government was not a war at all. Rather it was a serious conflict between some correspondents and almost all official functionaries as to how to carry out American policy most efficiently—in brief, how to win the war in the shortest possible time. This is not to deny that there were first-rate examples of honest and courageous reporting both in the field and in Saigon (where the flak from the Diem government sometimes was heavier than the attacks from the National Liberation Front). But what was so glaringly apparent was the contradiction between the reporting of the correspondents and the conclusions they drew, about both United States policy and the aspirations of the Vietnamese people.

At the core of the battle of the printed word, particularly during the three crisis years 1961 to 1963, were Ngo Dinh Diem and his mandarin family; but the involvement of the press with Diem began several years before that, on another level.

Diem had come to the United States in 1950, under the sponsorship of Michigan State University, whose services in Vietnam on behalf of the United States government, and the CIA in particular, have become public knowledge. Diem's brother, a Catholic bishop, had close relations with the American Catholic hierarchy, and Diem spent much of the next three years at the Maryknoll Seminaries in New York and New Jersey. The New York Maryknoll mission was under the supervision of Cardinal Francis Spellman, who took Diem under his wing and sponsored him at important meetings in Washington and New York. In 1954, while the Geneva talks were still in progress, the outgoing French-supported Emperor Bao Dai named Diem as his premier and Diem formed a government on July 7, 1954. Spellman became the most vocal lobbyist for Diem in the United States. At the American Legion convention in August 1954, he raised a temporal bugle to sound a requiem: "If Geneva and what was agreed upon there means anything at all," he said, "it means . . . taps for the buried hopes of freedom in Southeast Asia."

The Cardinal, in a public gesture of support for Diem, delivered in person in Saigon the first check for the Catholic Relief Service. But Spellman was only one of several influential friends, as Robert Scheer noted in his able study, *How the United States Got Involved in Vietnam*, published in 1965 by the Center for the Study of Democratic Institutions at Santa Barbara. The road to Saigon was wide open in the mid-fifties, and in the Cardinal's wake went Wesley Fishel, the man who had persuaded Michigan State to foot the bill for Diem's stay in the United States in 1950; Wolf Ladejinsky, who seemed determined, as Diem's adviser on land problems, to prove that the disfavor he found in the eyes of Joe McCarthy (who had got him fired from the Agriculture Department) was an error in judgment; and Leo Cherne, founder of the Research Institute of America, whose International Rescue Committee was godfather and angel to almost any defector from Communism.

Cherne came back from Vietnam in September 1954 persuaded that an election there in 1956 (as guaranteed by the Geneva agreement) would be won by the Communists, and equally determined that "the West cannot afford to lose from now on." To shore up Diem's "bankrupt government" (Cherne's words) he went into action immediately. He dispatched to Vietnam, to set up a branch office, the IRC's No. 2 man Joseph Buttinger, a devout Austrian anti-Communist Social Democrat, whose memoirs published in 1953 were prematurely titled *In the Twilight of Socialism.* Premature or not, his views impressed Colonel Edward Lansdale, the CIA's chief agent in Vietnam, who brought Buttinger into the Diem circle where Buttinger made Diem the object of his devotion. But Diem was determined not to make it easy for any of his advocates. His autocratic and repressive manner antagonized a strong pro-French faction in the Vietnamese army. When Diem began to move against the Buddhists, he caused some uneasiness in both General Lawton Collins, who had arrived in Vietnam as President Eisenhower's special ambassador late in 1954, and Joseph Alsop, whose columnar directives often produced respectful salutes and full-dress strategy conferences in the Pentagon. But the Spellman-Lansdale-Buttinger trinity was a formidable force, and their counterattack not only won the day for Diem but pulled loyal soldiers Collins and Alsop back into line.

Harold Oram, public relations man from Cherne's IRC, drew Spellman and Buttinger together in New York, and Spellman brought Buttinger together with Joseph P. Kennedy to work out a publicity campaign for Diem. In Washington, Kennedy arranged for Buttinger to meet with Senator Mike Mansfield, Democrat of Montana, and Kenneth Young of the State Department. Senator John F. Kennedy was in California, but Buttinger had a long discussion with his chief aide. Meanwhile, generating full steam at his Powerhouse in New York, Spellman had organized meetings for Buttinger with the editors of the *New York Times,* the editorial board of the *Herald Tribune* and the chief editors of *Life* and *Time.* On January 29, 1955, two days after Buttinger's visit, the *Times* published an editorial with comments remarkably parallel to Buttinger's petition for Diem. Under his own by-line, Buttinger presented the case for Diem in the *Reporter* magazine (now defunct) of January 27, 1955, and the *New Republic* of February 28, 1955. By the spring of 1955, there was no question of Washington's full support for the Diem administration, and the course was set for abrogating the Geneva agreements (which Washington had not signed but had pledged to guarantee), particularly the stipulation for elections to unify Vietnam as one nation.

The public line was clarified in an article by Leo Cherne in *Look* magazine (January 25, 1955) depicting the journey of Vietnamese from the north to the south during the 300 days specified in the Geneva agreement for the transfer of "any civilians . . . who wish to go and live in the zone assigned to the other party." Most of the transferees were southerners, many of them Catholic, who had withdrawn with the Viet Minh to the north at the end of the war with the French,* and who had expressed a desire to return home. Although the Geneva agreement declared that the transferees should get any assistance needed, they got little from Diem's officials. Their difficulties were attributed solely to the authorities in the north who allegedly had made life for them a living hell. Cherne's article was a clever mixture of politics and pity: "Battered and shunted about by the war, they are too weary to resist the Reds without us." South Vietnam is "still free but will fall under Red control if Communists win elections set for July of 1956." Cherne posed this anguished question for the nation: "Asians are convinced that U.S. prestige and influence in Asia cannot survive another defeat . . . No more than 18 months remain for us to complete the job of winning over the Vietnamese before they vote. What can we do?"

Things were done. One was the formation of the American Friends of Vietnam "to extend more broadly a mutual understanding of Vietnamese and American history, cultural customs and democratic institutions." In practice this meant getting the American public accustomed to increased American involvement in Vietnam, and propaganda was a vital instrument here. The composition of the committee reflected this understanding. Listed on the letterhead, among others, were columnist Max Lerner and author Arthur Schlesinger, Jr. On the executive committee were two staff members of the *New Leader* magazine, Leo Cherne, the ubiquitous Joseph Buttinger, and Elliot Newcomb, a partner in the publicity firm of Newcomb-Oram which, shortly before the founding of the American Friends of Vietnam, had signed a contract ($3,000 a month plus expenses) to represent the Diem government in the United States. Scheer wrote in his study:

> Up to this point Vietnam had not been a popular subject for American scholarship or journalism. There were few "experts" on the area in the universities or the press. The vastly expanded American role in the period following the Geneva Accords produced a great demand for knowledge about the country. As a result, those

---

* The Viet Minh was the all-Vietnamese patriotic force led by Ho Chi Minh which defeated the French. Under the Geneva agreement, they withdrew north of the Seventeenth Parallel pending a general settlement for all Vietnam.

who were most intimately involved in the American program there generally blossomed as the chief sources of information and opinion. This was natural, but most of them were committed protagonists and their writing soon became propaganda for the cause.

The propaganda barrage in the press was given the overall title "The Miracle of Vietnam." It was a miracle accomplished by the stifling of all opposition—religious and political—and the institution of a system of graft, corruption, and nepotism enforced by the Vietnamese army and Diem's own special police force fashioned by experts from Michigan State University. For the American public it was a miracle of deception. In 1957, when Diem visited the United States, the *New York Times* reported (May 9) that "by establishing democratic forms, President Diem had carved a deep niche in official esteem in Washington." As a mark of this esteem, President Eisenhower had sent his personal plane, the "Columbine," to Saigon to bring Diem to Washington and met him at the airport. The only other person the President had so honored in the four preceding years, the *Times* noted with some awe, was King Ibn Saud of Saudi Arabia. The reception for Diem was altogether royal—an address to a joint session of Congress, an official New York City reception, and a banquet presided over by *Time*'s Henry R. Luce. Many of Diem's speeches were the product of Joseph Buttinger's imaginative mind. The *Times* noted, in an editorial headed "Diem on Democracy," a strongly spiritual, rather than political note in Diem's definition of democracy with which "Thomas Jefferson would have no quarrel." For *Life,* in its issue of May 13, 1957, one of Diem's great accomplishments was preventing "the famous Geneva election." According to *Life,* most Vietnamese expected the Viet Minh under Ho Chi Minh to win and therefore would have "hedged by voting on this assumption." Diem, said *Life,* saved his people from this agonizing prospect simply by refusing to permit the plebiscite and "thereby he avoided national suicide."

Diem himself attributed the miracle to the Lord, "of whose invisible hand he was but an instrument." This modest self-portrait came in an interview with Wolf Ladejinsky, by then a Diem intimate, published in the *Reporter* magazine of December 24, 1959. Democracy under Diem, Ladejinsky conceded, was not perfect, and because of the threat of Communism, Diem was "compelled to ration it." Apparently the rationing also was a divine directive. Wesley Fishel, in Vietnam as head coach of the Michigan State Project, wrote several magazine articles about the Diem miracle. The unconcern of editors and publishers about their contributors' involvement, both materialistic and subjective, with the Diem regime was miraculous in itself.

As late as November 21, 1960, he was still "doughty little Diem" to *Time* magazine, and for Ernest K. Lindley in *Newsweek* (June 29, 1960) he was "one of Asia's ablest leaders." The newsmagazines, caught in the spell of the miracle-makers, could not or would not see that the mark of doom already was upon Diem, placed by Diem's own ruthless policy. The seeming stability that prevailed in South Vietnam was made possible not so much by the introduction of American arms and money as by the forbearance of a population which still clung to the hope that the election promised at Geneva would be held. Then the citizens could elect a government of their own choice. But by early 1959 this hope had been entirely dispelled, and Diem's brutal policy of absolute control was beginning to create an active political opposition in South Vietnam where none had existed before. It was at this point that the Diem regime coined the phrase "the Viet Cong," and the Diemist newspaper *Cach Mang Quoc Gia* wrote in February 1959: "Let us mercilessly wipe out the Viet Cong, as if we were in a state of war with them, no longer considering them human beings." In effect Diem was declaring war against a whole people.

There is not and never has been an entity by the name of "Viet Cong," even though the term, because of constant repetition in the press, has become fixed in the American mind and is used—a testament to the effectiveness of press brainwashing—even by opponents of the war in Vietnam. Viet Cong, a short name for Vietnamese Communists, was used, and still is, to designate anyone who is suspected of being, or might confess under torture to be, an opponent of the Saigon regime. The requirements of the succeeding regimes, from Diem through the military juntas and the succession of puppets from Khanh and Ky to the present, were to secure dictatorial control under the American umbrella by liquidating all possible dissent. Suspects were hunted down and eliminated; hamlets and villages were raided by troops and the police; thousands were killed, detained and tortured, or sent fleeing into the jungles where they became opponents of the regime, and then armed for self-defense.

Thus the despotism of Saigon produced not a civil war but a national uprising against Diem and his marauders. It was an uprising joined by peasants, Buddhist priests, craftsmen, urban intellectuals, and even civil servants in the employ of the Diem regime.

In his book, *The Furtive War* (International Publishers, 1963), Wilfred Burchett described the practices under Diem's Law, 10/59, put in effect in 1959, a lineal descendant of the Nuremberg code. Kangaroo military tribunals traveled about the country to do "legally" what had been done crudely by the military and the police. By mid-1959, these tribunals with mobile guillotines were moving through the provinces of

South Vietnam in a manner reminiscent of the bloody assizes of England's "Hanging Judge" Jeffreys in the seventeenth century.

Finally, in mid-December, a month after a near-successful army coup against Diem, a national revolutionary force was organized against the predatory government. It was called the National Liberation Front— guided, staffed, armed, and developed by Vietnamese living in South Vietnam. Despite the popularly instilled belief that it was organized and directed "from Hanoi," Ho Chi Minh is known to have discouraged such a front for some years after Geneva, and the Soviet Union gave it no hope of survival. The NLF was formed as, and remained, a broad coalition of ethnic, political, and religious elements within South Vietnam. Its program called for democratic rule based on free elections and for neutralism in foreign policy. Reunification with North Vietnam was envisioned as a long-range goal; more immediately it advocated a "zone of peace and neutrality comprising Cambodia, Laos, and South Vietnam." The prevailing spirit of the organization was not Communism but nationalism.

These developments went almost entirely unreported in the American press, except for a few left-wing weeklies. Burchett, as the correspondent of the *National Guardian* and a contributor to newspapers abroad, set up a home base in Cambodia and traveled extensively throughout Southeast Asia. He was a frequent visitor to North Vietnam and was one of the few Western correspondents allowed into the areas of South Vietnam controlled by the National Liberation Front. His cabled and airmailed dispatches appeared regularly in the *National Guardian*. As its editor, I frequently had extra proofs of his stories run off and sent, with a covering release, to the dailies in New York and elsewhere and to the wire services. They were ignored.

Occasionally a Burchett report which had been published in the *Asahi Shimbun* in Tokyo (circulation 5,000,000) was relayed back to the United States where it appeared in abbreviated fashion in a few newspapers. Later, when the war was admittedly going badly for the United States forces, and when it became apparent that Burchett had access to authoritative information both in Hanoi and in the liberated areas of South Vietnam, the Associated Press requested articles from him which appeared with an italic precede describing him as a "Communist journalist," and warning that his dispatches should be read with that in mind. Burchett protested to the Associated Press and the description was modified to "close to Communist leaders." In the United States press, the introduction never disappeared: Burchett was a prisoner of his precede. I never asked Burchett about his affiliations. I was satisfied that his dispatches were documented and supplemented by photographic and quoted evidence to support his contentions. I accepted, with admiration, that his sympathies always lay with peoples bent on self-determination for their countries. Surely he was as qualified as the ablest of the "capitalist journalists," who were never so labeled.

The revolt of the Saigon army's paratroopers on November 21, 1960, burst the bubble of the miracle. The rebellion was put down, but not before the death of at least 400 civilians who had joined the paratroopers in their march on the presidential palace. The United States press took notice of these developments and the editorial tone changed. Diem was soon being described as "high-handed" and "authoritarian," and stories began to appear about the Ngo dynasty which ruled the country with an iron hand. Curiously, the change in the press coincided with a shift in allegiance by Joseph Buttinger, who by this time was working with Vietnamese elements in the United States which sought to replace Diem; by Leo Cherne, who went on a mission to Saigon to reason with Diem; and by Wesley Fishel, no longer a Diem intimate, whose Michigan State Project was to end a few months later.

As the rumbling and dissatisfaction over Diem increased in the next year, the State Department in December 1961 produced a contradictory white paper seeking to justify its increased intervention in the affairs of Vietnam. The title was: "A Threat to the Peace; North Vietnam's Effort to Conquer South Vietnam." It denounced what it described as a determined and ruthless campaign of propaganda, infiltration, and subversion by the Communist regime in North Vietnam to destroy the Republic of Vietnam. But it conceded that the guerrilla army was made up largely of residents of South Vietnam, and that the National Liberation Army's weapons were almost entirely captured French and American equipment, or weapons forged in jungle arsenals. The White Paper signaled the beginning of full-scale involvement by the United States in Vietnam, based on the "intervention" by a foreign power (North Vietnam), although as late as March 1963, General Paul D. Harkins, the American commander in South Vietnam, told the *Washington Post* that the guerrillas were not being reinforced or supplied systematically from North Vietnam, China, or any other place. He confirmed that they depended for their weapons on what they could capture or manufacture themselves. Tad Szulc, in the *New York Times* on June 18, 1963, quoting "top United States officials," wrote: "In fact, the Chinese and the North Vietnamese have exercised care to avoid the sending of guerrillas into South Vietnam. [The] officials said that the guerrilla units that infiltrate from the North in support of the Communist Viet Cong operations are South Vietnamese who stayed north of the armistice line at the end of the Indo-China war of 1954."

Editorial comment, however, did not reflect the reports in the news columns. The theme rather was the continuing threat from the north (with the Chinese and the Russians ominously in the background) and the sacredness of the American pledge to the government at Saigon to guarantee "freedom of choice" in South Vietnam. But there were increasing doubts that Diem, who was doing his utmost to stifle any kind of freedom, was the most attractive display in the Asian showcase of Free World democracy.

By mid-1961, the press was beginning to acknowledge that the "reds" had considerable support in the Vietnamese countryside, acquired by ruthless terror and blackmail, or by "creating a favorable image of themselves," as Robert Trumbull wrote in the *New York Times Magazine,* July 2, 1961. Trumbull suggested that what Diem needed was an improved public relations program in the countryside, along with "improvement projects" and a stepped-up war against the guerrillas (*New York Times Magazine,* January 7, 1962). But Diem, with an unwilling conscript army, a corrupt administration which was sluicing off large amounts of American dollar assistance to its own bank accounts, and a policy of utter bestiality toward his own people, was rendering useless even the most elaborate Madison Avenue public relations campaign, Asian style.

The *New York Times,* aware that something was wrong in the Vietnam picture, sent one of its ablest reporters, Homer Bigart, to Vietnam. With his successor, David Halberstam, and with Neil Sheehan of the United Press, Malcolm Browne of the Associated Press, and the correspondents of *Newsweek* and *Time,* Bigart became involved in an unusual contest with the American Mission in Vietnam and the Diem government that continued for 18 months. The degree of involvement was assessed by John Mecklin, public affairs officer of the Mission from May 1962 to July 1964, in his book *Mission in Torment* (Doubleday, 1965):

American reporters in Vietnam achieved an influence in the making of U.S. foreign policy that had been equaled in modern times only by the role of the New York newspapers in precipitating the Spanish-American war more than a half century earlier. There was a significant difference. In the earlier case it was deliberate . . . In Vietnam, a major American policy was wrecked, in part, by unadorned reporting of what was going on.

As dramatic as the situation was, Mecklin attributed to the reporters far more power than they had, or desired. By insisting on presenting to the American public the facts about the Diem government and the ineptitude of the American officials, the newspapermen in Vietnam hastened a review of Washington's *tactics,* which was inevitable, but not of its *policy.*

The policy remained unaltered from President Kennedy's decision to commit United States forces in depth in Vietnam to the negotiations in Paris seeking an end to the fighting (but not an end to the policy). That policy was threefold: (1) If victory was not possible, to achieve a stalemate situation to prevent a revolutionary government from coming to power; (2) to test the reaction of socialist governments to counterrevolutionary intervention by the United States in other countries—that is, to test the socialist "boiling point"; (3) to use the Vietnam war as a laboratory for training Americans in counter-insurgency warfare and to try out the weapons of "grass roots" warfare—the helicopters, napalm bombs, "weed killers," and pacification of the villages. Overriding all these efforts, and directed toward the main issue, was the containment of China.

The group of remarkably able and courageous newspapermen assigned to Vietnam in the years 1962-63 worked mightily to get the American public—and the government—to realize and acknowledge that the miracle of Diem was a costly myth and that a change was needed. Their goal, however, was not an end to American intervention, but the reform of that intervention to attain an American victory.

# 14. The Miracle Unmade

An unusually frank Associated Press dispatch from Saigon appeared in the *New York Times* of March 24, 1962. One battle being fought in Saigon, it said, involves finding out what is going on and reporting it to the people of the United States. Many correspondents "feel they are losing." One was quoted as saying:

> The Vietnamese government is against us. They figure we are all spies or Communist propagandists. The United States will not tell us much beyond the broad outlines of their policy and we cannot even be sure of that. After prying for weeks to get a story from unofficial sources, we may end up being blocked by the censors.

The AP dispatch said the United States government was "eager to avoid alienating the South Vietnamese government, and its official sources." For various reasons, the United States "is seeking to avoid press emphasis on the role it is playing here . . . United States officials are reluctant to show newsmen military operations in which United States servicemen are performing combat duties." Washington at that time was insisting that American servicemen were in Vietnam in a purely advisory capacity; in fact, American pilots were flying bombing missions with untrained and terrified Vietnamese carried along as window-dressing, and American officers were directing ground operations against the Liberation Front, with Saigon's officers in nominal command.

The day the AP dispatch was written (its author was correspondent Malcolm Browne), expulsion orders were issued by the Saigon government against Homer Bigart of the *Times* and François Sully of *Newsweek*.

Sully was a seventeen-year resident of Vietnam who had been wounded as a teen-ager with the French Resistance in Paris in World War II. He had volunteered to fight against the Japanese in Indo-China and had remained to cover the Indo-China war for *Newsweek* and other publications through the French disaster of Dienbienphu.

Both the United States Mission in Saigon and the CIA would have been delighted to see Bigart go, but his standing as a two-time winner of the Pulitzer Prize for reporting (let alone his association with the *Times*) would have caused an uproar and probably revealed the actual United States role in Vietnam. The State Department therefore instructed the Mission in Saigon to impress upon Diem the consequences of such a development.

The expulsion order against Bigart was withdrawn. So was the one against Sully, but only after Sully's colleagues in Saigon had forced the State Department to intervene in his behalf also. Bigart wrote in April 1962 in *Times Talk,* the house organ of the *New York Times:*

I regarded my reprieve with mixed feelings. This has not been a happy assignment. Saigon is a nice place to spend a few days in. The food and wine are good, the city is attractive, most hotels and restaurants are air-conditioned. But to work here is peculiarly depressing. Too often correspondents seem to be regarded by the American mission as tools of our foreign policy. Those who balk are apt to find it a bit lonely, for they are likely to be distrusted and shunned by American and Vietnam officials. I am sick of it. Each morning I take a pen and blot off another day on the Saigon calendar. At this writing I have 83 more days to go.

John Mecklin, in his book *Mission in Torment,* presented an apologia for the attitude of American officials in Saigon toward the "press mess," as it was called. His major responsibility upon his arrival in May 1962, shortly after the Bigart-Sully incident, was dealing with the press. The trouble, he said, was that "much of what the newsmen took to be lies was exactly what the Mission genuinely believed, and was reporting to Washington." Events, he said, were to prove that the Mission itself was unaware how badly the war was going: "Our feud with the newsmen was an angry symptom of bureaucratic sickness." This was gross oversimplification, as Mecklin himself conceded only a few pages later. The root of the ailment, he wrote, "was the fact that the U.S. had bet all its chips on Diem. There was no alternate, fall-back policy if Diem failed us." Even the "severest critics of Diem" conceded merit in the argument that dumping him would not lead to an improvement: "The Communists had long since drained off many of the ablest Vietnamese leaders. The French and/or Diem had suppressed many of the remainder, or driven them into exile." The very real danger in the collapse of Diem would be a power vacuum and the immediate threat of a Communist victory. That of course was unthinkable (even though it might place in positions of authority "many of the ablest leaders"), so the policy of supporting Diem "became an article of faith, and dissent became reprehensible."

The breakdown in communications between the Mission and the United States press was further exacerbated, Mecklin said, "by the special political considerations that enveloped our operations in Vietnam like a terminal-care oxygen tent." This was an elaborate way of saying that the American Mission was duty bound to cover up the lies that were being told by Washington about the American presence in Vietnam, and to camouflage the fact (here Mecklin confirms Salinger's comments in his book *With Kennedy*) that "the U.S. decision in 1961 to intervene massively in Vietnam amounted to outright abrogation of the Geneva Agreement of 1954." This did not appear to suggest to Mecklin or any other Mission official that Washington's course might not be the wisest or most honorable one. Communism was the enemy. The abrogation of a treaty was simply one more weapon in democracy's arsenal, and democracy was something "the other side" could not understand or accept anyway.

Since the United States was committed to Diem and had to maintain cordial relations with his regime, it responded sympathetically to the regime's complaints against the American newspapermen and rebuked the correspondents for "damaging the U.S. national interest." To put it another way, Mecklin wrote, "it became unpatriotic for a newsman to use an adjective that displeased Mme. Nhu" (the influential and vindictive sister-in-law of President Diem).

Denied information and criticized for what they wrote, the reporters became increasingly resentful. Many redoubled their efforts to get information from whatever source they could. The result was more undesirable (from an official point of view) publicity than a candid approach to the press would have produced. Another result was a new directive from Washington—the famous cable No. 1006. Under the guise of liberalizing the rules for the press, cable 1006 further restricted the channels of information.

As a newspaperman on leave for government service (he was a foreign correspondent for *Time* and its bureau chief in San Francisco), Mecklin was ambivalent about the correspondents. On the one hand, there was admiration in his picture of the intrepid young reporters snarling their way through the daily United States briefing sessions (the "Five O'Clock Follies") and banging into the offices of the United States Information Service apoplectic about the new restriction or a misleading government press release. But Mecklin did have a complaint. The young reporters had absolutely no sense of humor, he said, in a situation that cried for some fun. He provided some unconscious humor of his own when he wrote: "To the best of my knowledge, no responsible U.S. official in Saigon ever told a newsman a really big falsehood. Instead there were endless little ones. They were morally marginal and thus difficult to dispute." If the reporters were humorless, the United States officials were marked by "self-righteous witlessness," said Mecklin, and this applied to General Paul Harkins, Ambassador William E. Nolting and most of the senior officials in Saigon, and Washington itself. At one Washington meeting a "negative" story in the *Times* by Bigart was under discussion. A "senior official" said that "Mr. Bigart spells his name wrong"—it should be bigot. The room burst into laughter. A more famous story was told about Admiral Harry D. Felt, who was asked a difficult question at a press conference in Saigon. Felt asked the reporter's name, and the reply was, Malcolm Browne of AP. "So you're Browne," said Felt. "Why don't you get on the team?"

Cut off from official sources, Halberstam, Sheehan, and Browne, joined by Sully and Charles Mohr of *Time* magazine, developed their own sources of information among the second echelon Americans and Vietnamese in the field. One source was Colonel John Paul Vann, senior American adviser to the Seventh South Vietnamese Division. He was described by Roger Hilsman in *To Move A Nation* (Doubleday, 1967) as "an energetic, idealistic, dynamic officer with strong convictions about the need for a more aggressive and efficient conduct of the war and a willingness, in order to achieve it, to tread on the toes of either his Vietnamese counterparts or his own American superiors." Vann resigned his commission in frustration in 1963. He was, it might be said, a prototype of *The Ugly American,* that much misunderstood composite figure created by Eugene Burdick and William J. Lederer, who is actually the most efficient agent of American policy, if only the bureaucratic managers of the policy could understand and use him properly.

It was natural that Halberstam and Sheehan were attracted to a man like Vann. They had many qualities in common. "While we were sympathetic to the aims of the U.S. government," Halberstam is quoted in John Hohenberg's *Foreign Correspondence: The Great Reporters and Their Times* (Columbia University Press, 1964), "we had to be critical of the representatives of our government who created a policy of optimism about the war that simply was not justified. There was no choice for us. We had our duty to our newspapers, the public that reads them, and that was to tell the truth."

It is difficult to avoid a sense of exasperation and impatience as one reviews the "Yes, you dids" and "No, I didn'ts" of the government-press battle in Saigon. Much of it has the character of childish tantrums, but there is a bit of high social hilarity too. For example, Mecklin complains that not once did the "young Turks," as the press critics of Diem were called, ever invite the Mission people to lunch. Halberstam, for his part, said: "I was never invited to Nolting's house, nor were any of the other young resident correspondents. But visiting reporters got the full treatment from Nolting, and were constantly given the pitch that they were mature and could understand the big picture. The implication was always that we were a bunch of punk kids." It was true that the visiting reporters were older and far more attuned to the acceptance of high-brass handouts as gospel. They represented the bureaucracy of the journalistic establishment. But it was also true that Homer Bigart was 55 when he was working in Vietnam.

The battle came to a head when *Newsweek* published an article (August 22, 1962) by Sully titled: "Vietnam: The Unpleasant Truth." Sully quoted the historian Bernard Fall (who was killed in Vietnam in 1967) as saying that the Americans were inept in their teaching of military tactics against the guerrillas, and that the Saigon government was woefully inadequate. The article termed the war "a losing proposition." The Diem regime was outraged. The Saigon press attacked Sully as a Communist, a French spy, a participant in sex orgies, an opium smuggler, and even a promoter of the bombing attack on the presidential palace in February 1962. On September 3, Sully was ordered to leave Vietnam. *Newsweek* protested, and the resident correspondents asked the Mission to intervene, but to no avail. There was a bizarre prelude to Sully's departure, as described by Mecklin in *Mission in Torment:*

> The Sully affair provoked some equally painful agonizing among the newsmen. A dozen of them argued until 3 A.M. in a room at the Hotel Caravelle. They were torn between those who wanted to fight back with a strongly worded protest, and those who feared that they too might be expelled if the protest angered the palace. There were numerous epithets, e.g. "coward." The dispute reached a McCarthyesque moment when Sully was formally required to say whether he was (1) a French spy, or (2) a Communist. He replied no to both questions.

Sully's private thoughts about this inquisition were not recorded. The meeting broke up with no agreement, but six correspondents (*New York Times, Time,* AP, UPI, CBS, and NBC) sent a message of protest to Diem and to President Kennedy. The palace rejected the protest as "iniquitous blackmail." Kennedy responded with "appreciation" of the newsmen's concern about their colleagues and a promise that "our officials will continue to assist you in every way feasible to carry out your all-important task." The correspondents, said Mecklin, "appeared to be pleased. In fact it was a brush-off."

The extent of the brush-off became evident a few weeks later when James Robinson, NBC's Southeast Asia correspondent, an American citizen, was ordered to leave South Vietnam for an alleged violation of a visa regulation. Robinson, at the suggestion of the United States Mission, wrote a letter of apology but the order was not rescinded. His "crime," as it turned out, was not a visa violation, but a remark. It had been reported to Diem that Robinson had said an interview with the president was a waste of time. Nine fellow correspondents signed a protest to Diem this time, but Robinson was forced to leave for Hong Kong November 5, 1962. There was nothing the Mission could do, Mecklin said, "short of provoking a crisis that would surely help the Viet Cong more than NBC."

President Kennedy's promise to the newsmen of "every feasible support" was strangely kept in Washington—with a club and a whip. After the Sully affair, *Newsweek* was bombarded with official complaints about his dispatches, particularly one written after he had left Saigon. The magazine decided to get on the team by sending to Vietnam for a "new look" columnist Kenneth Crawford, a cautious liberal turned cautiously conservative. The December 10 issue of *Newsweek* featured a flattering cover story about Diem and the progress of his reforms, the enthusiastic response of the peasants, and Diem's application of "the right strategy." Mme. Nhu, who had been a "detested" figure in Sully's stories, was transformed into a "beautiful and strong-willed" woman. The Crawford view was all the more remarkable because the *Times*'s Halberstam, the wire service reporters, and *Newsweek*'s competitor, *Time* magazine, were simultaneously reporting increasing deterioration of the Diem administration and setbacks in the war. There was a concomitant deterioration in the relations between the press corps in Saigon and the United States Mission.

Tormented almost beyond endurance by the ambivalence of his position as newsman-bureaucrat, Mecklin determined on a new tack with the reporters: He would take them into his confidence, tell them everything that was going on—even if on a no-publication basis. After all, he reasoned, there was nothing reprehensible in what the Mission was doing: "On the contrary, we could justly be proud of our effort to help this small and tortured country stave off Communist envelopment. Our present policy, under Cable No. 1006, made it look as though we, not the Viet

Cong, had something to hide." But the torment only became worse because, as Mecklin must have realized, his job was precisely to hide as much as he could. "It was a frustrating position," he said. Mecklin was unable to maintain this masterly restraint, however, when he was asked to submit a background memorandum on the press problem in Vietnam for a visiting dignitary from Washington. He worked on it through most of one night in February 1963, and since it was classified, he was candid. But the candor was not sufficient for General Harkins and Ambassador Nolting, who sent it back to him for a tougher critique of the newspaper corps in Saigon. Mecklin complied. He characterized the American newsmen as inexperienced, unsophisticated, and malicious individuals whose "irresponsible, sensationalized, astigmatic reporting" had damaged United States interests in Vietnam. Someone in the Mission made certain that the newspapermen thus described saw a copy of the memorandum. "We said nothing about it," said Halberstam in his book *The Making of a Quagmire* (Random House, 1965), "but we were the wiser for it." Mecklin, in his own behalf, said that the bulk of the memorandum was a plea in behalf of the reporters, but he conceded that his situation had progressed from frustrating to "untenable." Later he told a member of the Saigon press corps: "That memo was the stupidest thing I ever did . . . Once I was forced to rewrite it, I should never have signed my name to it."

Mecklin and I had joined the Sunday staff of the *New York Times* about the same time in 1946. He was then a pleasant person, unhappy at a desk job, and he soon left the *Times* to work for *Time* magazine as a foreign correspondent. We did not meet again until a memorable night in Palo Alto, California, in May 1965. He was by then chief of *Time*'s San Francisco bureau, and I was on a speaking tour of several California colleges as editor of the *National Guardian*. Mecklin and I had both participated in an evening press panel at a teach-in on Vietnam at Stanford University—the first ever held at Stanford, which, unlike other California colleges, had not witnessed much protest on its campus about the war in Vietnam. I spoke first, and devoted a good part of my talk to the newspapermen in Vietnam and their problems. I noted particularly the campaign by American officials and the Diem regime to silence Bigart, and said that I was persuaded that the CIA would have been pleased to see Bigart leave the country. Mecklin spoke afterward and apparently felt constrained to refute my position. The audience was attentive (there were 1,200 students in the hall and 700 more seated on the lawn in the dark outside auditorium). As an insider in Saigon, Mecklin said, he could state with authority that not only did the CIA not want Bigart out of the country, but had "gone to bat" for him after his ouster had been ordered.

Until then the students had been demonstrative but polite in their responses. This time they howled with derision. Mecklin appeared stunned, but went bravely on.

The events of the spring and early summer of 1963 involved several American newspapermen so deeply in internal Vietnamese politics that it may fairly be said their actions helped speed the end of Ngo Dinh Diem. In May, the Saigon government forbade the display of religious flags to mark the birthday of Buddha—although Roman Catholic flags had been widely in evidence in Hue a few weeks earlier at a celebration of the twenty-fifth year of the bishopric of Diem's brother, Ngo Dinh Thuc, Archbishop of Hue. Thousands of Buddhists demonstrated in protest and were fired on by Diem's troops; nine were killed. The demonstration sparked the beginning of a nationwide Buddhist upheaval which brought on a severe governmental crisis. The Buddhists turned to the United States Mission for help but found the Mission's commitment to Diem so complete they could not even get a hearing. They turned to the American newspapermen, who, equally rebuffed by the Mission, were eager for news and information.

The correspondents were tipped in advance to demonstrations and other actions, including the advice that two monks had volunteered for death if Buddhist demands were not met. On the morning of June 9, telephone calls to American newspapermen reported that something might happen that day; but several false alarms had produced skepticism in the press corps. Only the AP's Malcolm Browne took the call seriously and he was the sole reporter watching a street procession that morning, a camera hanging from his shoulder. At the busy intersection near the Xa Loi Pagoda, a sedan pulled up and an elderly school teacher named Thich Quang Duc got out and settled cross-legged on the pavement. As 350 monks and nuns chanted and wailed and waved banners, two other monks poured gasoline over him. Quang Duc lighted a match and was enveloped instantly in flames. The police were stunned. Monks threw themselves in front of fire trucks to prevent firemen from foiling the suicide. Browne photographed the whole sequence and sent it with his story immediately to the Associated Press.

It was a picture that jolted the United States and the world into an acute awareness of the extent of the crisis in Saigon. Particularly in Asia, the photograph was used effectively for anti-American propaganda, but antiwar forces in the United States also seized on it. Full-page advertisements appeared in the *New York Times* and the *Washington Post,* sponsored by a group of clergymen, with a reproduction of the photograph captioned "We too protest." In Saigon, Diem put a question to Ambassador Nolting: Was it true that Browne had bribed the Buddhist monks to murder the old teacher by fire to get a good picture? The United States Mission reacted predictably. It clamped down even more severely on its news sources and on the newspapermen. Getting any uncensored news or photographs out of Vietnam became a major smuggling operation. Airline pilots, departing soldiers, and visiting diplomats became impromptu couriers at the Tonsonhut airport for news copy to be cabled from a neighboring country or to be delivered in the United States.

Phones of newspapermen were monitored 24 hours a day by the Saigon secret police, spies and tails were everywhere, and threats of bodily harm and even death were frequent. At all costs, the Kennedy Administration wanted to maintain the impression that its policy in Vietnam was succeeding. Otherwise—and here a distinctly domestic angle entered the picture, as Halberstam perceived it—"it could have disastrous repercussion in the [1964] presidential election." The Mission worked overtime to keep the reporters from "finding out anything which reflected badly on the government," Halberstam said, "but the city was full of dissident Americans and Vietnamese who talked freely." The Halberstam-Sheehan-Browne reports (they often had to pool their resources because of the restrictions) were shattering the illusion of progress in Vietnam that United States officials and most of the editorial comment in the United States press sought to maintain.

One of the most flagrant demonstrations of cynical distortion in the coverage of the war—involving the press corps directly—was supplied by *Time* magazine in the fall of 1963. Charles Mohr, *Time*'s chief correspondent in Southeast Asia, returned home from time to time to confer with his editors—and to complain about rewriting of his stories in New York to provide a Pentagonian bias. The editors uniformly told Mohr that he was too close to the scene and couldn't see "the big picture" as it was presented to them at briefing lunches at the Pentagon. In mid-August 1963 Mohr was asked for a detailed story on the press corps in Saigon, how it worked, the reasons for the controversy with the Saigon government and the Mission, what solutions were possible. Mohr wrote the story and soon got another request—to compose with his assistant Mert Perry, who had been in Vietnam for two years, a full roundup story on the war, with emphasis on the situation in the Mekong Delta. They worked hard on the story and filed 25 pages of copy in three days. It was a hard-hitting story with a terse lead: "The war in Vietnam is being lost." In *The Making of a Quagmire,* Halberstam wrote:

The [roundup] story left no doubt that the American mission had come to the end of one road, and that our past policy had failed. Unfortunately, this was not what the editors of *Time* wanted to hear; in New York, Mohr's file was put aside, and Greg Dunne, a young contributing editor, was told to write an optimistic piece. Dunne refused and announced that he would write no more stories about Vietnam, but others stepped in. Eventually a story was printed which bore no relation to Mohr and Perry's file; among other things, it said that "Government troops are fighting better than ever."

The article clashed so sharply with reports being sent by the wire services and the major television and radio networks that an explanation seemed required. Otto Fuerbringer, *Time*'s managing editor (he was subsequently elevated to the editorship), had already decided, without informing its author, to discard Mohr's piece on the press corps in Vietnam. In the January 1964 issue of the *Nieman Reports,* Stanley Karnow, who had preceded Mohr as *Time*'s Southeast Asia chief and had resigned for similar reasons, told how Fuerbringer proceeded to set the record crooked. Summoning a writer to his office, and with "nothing more than his own preconceptions to guide him," he dictated the gist of an article for his magazine's Press section. The article appeared September 20, 1963, under the heading: "Foreign Correspondents—The View from Saigon." It opened with a first-rate example of *Time* at its worst:

> For all the light it shed, the news that U.S. newspaper readers got from Saigon might just as well have been printed in Vietnamese. Was the war being won or lost? Was the Buddhist uprising religiously inspired or Communist inspired? . . . Uncertainty out of Washington is not exactly news, but one of the more curious aspects of the South Vietnam story is that the press corps on the scene is helping to compound the very confusion that it should be untangling for its readers at home.

The story, mingling compassion with scorn, presented a picture of lonesome, inbred correspondents herding together, relaxing in each other's company, pooling "their convictions, information, misinformation and grievances." But such companionship, Fuerbringer concluded, was not conducive to independent thought:

> The reporters have tended to reach unanimous agreement on almost everything they have seen. But such agreement is suspect because it is so obviously inbred. The newsmen have themselves become a part of Vietnam's confusion; they have covered a complex situation from only one angle, as if their own conclusions offered all the necessary illumination. Such reporting is prone to distortions. The complicated greys of a complicated country fade into oversimplified blacks and whites . . . Any other version of the Vietnam story is dismissed as the fancy of a bemused observer . . .

Richard Clurman, *Time*'s chief of correspondents, unhappy about the article, had tried to locate publisher Henry Luce to block its publication, but Luce reportedly was unreachable at a football game in Atlanta. After the story appeared, sensing that Mohr would quit, Clurman called him in Saigon and asked for a meeting in Paris. Mohr told Clurman the only thing that would keep him at *Time* was a by-line article of equal space to refute the Fuerbringer story. Luce was upset at the thought of losing a favorite reporter but was unwilling to put down a senior editor. He ordered Clurman to Saigon to write a second piece on the Saigon press corps. Clurman complied, and Mohr and Perry resigned.

The second article, again drastically rewritten in New York, was a backhanded apology. This time it presented the young reporters as imbued "with a strong sense of mission" which sometimes got them in trouble. The implication was that they were still giving an emotion-packed and "unduly pessimistic" view of the progress of the war. The article quoted favorable appraisals of the press corps, but the effect of the first article was of course dominant. *Time* readers would be skeptical about all future stories filed by the inbred huddlers at the bar of the Caravelle.

It was not a very large group of huddlers, actually. Until late 1963 Halberstam was the only full-time representative of a daily newspaper in Vietnam. Most newspapers depended on the Associated Press and the United Press International. The embattled group in Saigon earned much of its reputation (and notoriety) by default of the publishers in the United States. *Time,* in its October 11 "apology," reported that Browne of AP and Sheehan of UPI were getting into heated arguments with their home offices, and that the AP had told Browne to take a month off "to quiet down."

But the noise was kept up in Washington, where White House press secretary Pierre Salinger was telling White House correspondents that the news reports out of Vietnam were emotional and inaccurate, and other White House assistants were confiding to all who would listen that the Vietnam press corps never went out in the field to report. These confidences, however, were being exploded daily by photographs of dangerous patrol actions taken by wire service photographers and by Browne and Sheehan themselves. In fact, Halberstam dwelt so much on his experiences with troops in the field that he was criticized by some of his colleagues for paying too little attention to the political and social problems of Vietnam.

Kennedy himself, only a year away from the 1964 election, was furious about the coverage. It was therefore not surprising that a brigade of well-known journalistic personalities was dispatched to Vietnam in the summer and fall of 1963 and prominent among them was an intimate of the President—Joseph Alsop. Alsop's arrivals and departures in Vietnam were always handled by the armed forces in a manner befitting a chief of staff, and Alsop's style and content made it clear that he so regarded himself. Special planes were put at his disposal and special junkets arranged, with briefings both in Saigon and by commanders in the field. His advice, if not always sought, was always given.

The 1963 trip was no exception. But this time Alsop's war was not with the Vietnamese enemy but with the American press corps in Saigon. They were "young crusaders," he determined, akin to the misguided reporters in China who in effect had lost China for the United States by ascribing a special virtue to Mao Tse-tung and his revolutionary army. Alsop also had some comments on the reporting from Cuba, "up to and including the triumph of Fidel Castro." The deposed dictator Fulgencio Batista was every bit as awful as everyone said, Alsop wrote, "but what stands out from that episode in American newspaper history was the display of far-seeing political acumen by that far-seeing progressive, Herbert Matthews of the *New York Times*."* It was hard to determine from this free-floating statement whether Alsop was saying that Matthews was trying to warn the United States about the real Castro, or whether he had helped lose Cuba for the United States, as had been frequently charged. In any case, Alsop wrote (a gauge of the urgency of his directives is the number of "high times" that appear), "it is high time to recall these episodes of the past, which were not without influence on the course of events; for a good many newspapermen in Saigon have been carrying on another of these egregious crusades for a number of years." It is easy enough "to paint a dark, indignant picture without departing from the facts," he said, conceding that some of the "doings" of the Diem government were "remarkably misguided." Then he attributed a remarkable measure of effectiveness to a few newspapermen:

In some measure, it must be added, the crusaders have contributed to the Diem government's misguidedness. The government has asked for it, since the press relations have always been idiotic. But the constant pressure of the reportorial crusade against the government has also helped mightily to transform Diem from a courageous, quite viable national leader, into a man afflicted with a galloping persecution mania, seeing plots around every corner, and therefore misjudging everything. It is

* Matthews had interviewed Fidel Castro in the Sierra Maestra mountains of Cuba in 1957—an interview which for the first time in the general American press laid out the aims and aspirations of the revolutionary movement. He also wrote *The Cuban Story* (George Braziller, 1961).

not only high time to make the foregoing points, it is also high time to ask whether American crusades to reform foreign governments really are a good idea at any time. Was Chiang, with all his defects, so much worse for the Chinese people and, above all, for the American people than Mao Tse-tung? Has Cuba gained and, above all, have we in the United States gained by the Batista-Castro exchange? What are we in Vietnam for anyway? Surely we are here to win the war. And the most annoying feature of the whole situation is that we actually were winning the war this spring, until the Diem government went right around the bend with considerable help from the highminded crusaders.

The implication was that if the war was lost the newspapermen would be responsible—not poor persecuted Diem. Alsop's colleague, the late Marguerite Higgins, who was married to a general, was not so circumspect. After her brief tour of duty in Vietnam that summer for the *New York Herald Tribune,* she wrote: "Reporters here would like to see us lose the war to prove they are right." Among others who found that the war was going fine was Richard Tregaskis, a correspondent who had earned a splendid reputation as a battlefront reporter in World War II, and Frank Conniff of the Hearst Task Force, whose other members were publisher William Randolph Hearst, Jr. and Bob Considine. Conniff reached back to the United States to charge that "the assignment of young reporters, most of them in their twenties, to decipher an involved story reflects small credit on the prescience of American editors." Conniff, 49 at the time, later conceded that he had to excuse himself early from a dinner given by Halberstam in Saigon because he was exhausted after a day spent visiting United States military advisers by helicopter.

An episode of pressure at the highest level was recounted by Halberstam in *The Making of a Quagmire:*

On October 22 Arthur Ochs Sulzberger, the new publisher of the *Times,* went to the White House to pay a courtesy call on the President of the United States. Except for Vietnam, the Administration was riding high. Kennedy was sure that Goldwater would be his opponent in the next year's presidential election and that the Democrats would win easily. Almost the first question from the President was, "What do you think of your young man in Saigon?" Mr. Sulzberger answered that he thought I was doing fine. The President suggested to the publisher that perhaps I was too close to the story, and too involved—which is the most insidious kind of comment one can make about a reporter. No, said Sulzberger, he did not think that I was too involved. The President then asked if the publisher had been thinking of transferring me to another area. No, said the publisher, the *Times* was quite satisfied with my present assignment. (As a matter of fact, at that particular point I was supposed to go on a breather for a two-week rest, but to its everlasting credit, the *Times* immediately canceled the holiday lest it appear to have acquiesced to this pressure.)

In the midst of all this, Ambassador Nolting was replaced by Henry Cabot Lodge, whose arrival signaled a shift in relations with the newspapermen. As he got off the plane, Lodge's first words were: "Where are the gentlemen of the press?" It was the first time a high American official in Saigon had expressed such a degree of concern and interest, and the press corps seemed to dissolve in gratitude. The new ambassador set about at once cultivating the reporters. The no-lunch policy at the Mission was replaced by a tête-à-tête lunch table—one correspondent at a time, intimate and frank conversation, with a carefully planned leak for each. "The leak," said Lodge, "is one of my weapons for doing a job." There were no press conferences and no briefings for the massed press during the ten months of the Lodge ambassadorship, except for his arrival and his departure. Despite this, there were no complaints from the correspondents. He offered the reporters little, but his methods of flattery (he constantly sought the reporters' "advice") and favor paid off for him. In a troubled outpost, after months of bickering and frustrations, the new technique worked wonders: Not one uncomplimentary story about Lodge was filed by the Saigon press corps in ten months. The astute young Irish raja in Washington had sent a white Anglo-Saxon brahmin who could deal on equal terms with, and command the respect of, the oriental mandarin in the presidential palace in Saigon.

But the harmony did not endure long. As more Americans poured into Vietnam, the conflict with the regime became more acute. The war was going badly, and a decision was made in Washington that it could no longer be "Sink or Swim With Ngo Dinh Diem." The new slogan was "Diem Must Go." On November 1, 1963, the regime of Ngo Dinh Diem was overthrown, and on November 2, Diem was assassinated with his brother Ngo Dinh Nhu. A Revolutionary Military Council was set up under Generals Duong Van Minh, Ton That Dinh, and Tran Van Don, the three men who had carried out the coup with the approval of Ambassador Lodge and the President of the United States.

Twenty days later, John F. Kennedy was assassinated in Dallas, Texas.

# 15. Patriotism and Policy

The scene was a bar in Saigon frequented by the United States press corps. The time was 1967. A woman reporter on a magazine assignment was denouncing the war as genocide. She thought the United States had no business there, ought to pull its troops out, and offer some kind of reparations for the damage it had done to the people and their country. She was Martha Gellhorn, journalist and novelist. Ward Just, assigned to Vietnam by the *Washington Post,* describes the scene in his book *To What End, Report from Vietnam* (Houghton Mifflin, 1968). There was a gap of a generation between Miss Gellhorn and Ward, and she kept coming back to the war in Spain. Just asked her "if the correspondents covering the [Spanish] war regarded it as a noble one." "Nothing *but,*" she answered, "and we knew we were right. We knew, we just *knew,* that Spain was the place to stop fascism. This was it. There was no other place."

It is apparent from his book and his reportage that Just is a sensitive man, and the encounter with Miss Gellhorn gave him pause. Her approach, he said, seemed anachronistic in 1967, "where reporters of my generation prided themselves on a professional detachment. The compulsion was to tell it like it was, even if what it was was your own country at war and the way it was, if told truthfully, was not 'helpful' to the effort." Was it because of the "doubts over the legitimacy of the struggle" and the disparity of conditions of life in Saigon, where the war was being managed, and the field, where it was being fought—was it because of these things that a correspondent felt like a voyeur? Just wrote:

The correspondent of the *Washington Post* was not obliged to live in a Special Forces Camp at the Cambodian border, or to eat C rations in a jungle for a fortnight. In Spain the correspondents felt closer to the war and less like spectators at least in part because of the common privations. It seemed to me an appealing thought, and I wondered if the reporting would be different if Saigon were under siege and bombs burst nightly in Lam Son Square, if food and liquor were scarce. Would the perception of the war be altered if there were no Sunday night dances at the Brinks B.O.Q. in downtown Saigon? Would the cause of the war seem nobler if the Saigon government and the Americans were under greater pressure: But how would Hemingway and Matthews and Martha Gellhorn have reacted if it had been the loyalists who bombed Guernica?

Just's comment and questions brought to mind the hero in Graham Greene's *The Quiet American,* a man of boundless sympathy for the Vietnamese soldiers (Vietnam then was "Indo-China" and the enemy was French), saying: "With a return ticket, courage becomes an intellectual exercise, like a monk's flagellation. How much can I stick? Those poor devils can't catch a plane home."

For even the most outraged correspondent in Vietnam, there was always a plane home, but the parallel with Spain remained for the Vietnamese. Ward Just felt that for the people of Vietnam there was no ideology in the war; it was simply "the Vietnam war." But there is ideology in Vietnam, as there was, and still is, in Spain. Guernica was bombed by German and Italian fascists under the Franco flag to murder a fledgling democracy in Spain, and to test the latest weapons for quick and efficient murder anywhere. It was just because they thought the Loyalists incapable, and the Fascists more than capable, of bombing women and children and historic shrines—and events justified their belief—that nearly all the world's intellectuals favored the Loyalists.

The United States has bombed Vietnam, North and South, to prevent the people of Vietnam from determining their own future, and to test the most modern devices to suppress insurgency wherever it threatens to create conditions which will permit self-determination. The National Liberation Front and the government of North Vietnam regard it as unthinkable to bomb their own people. For Ward Just and other American reporters it may be simply "the Vietnam war," because they regard the Vietnamese not so much as people but as pawns on the chess board of American foreign policy. But to the Vietnamese it is very much an ideological war, not between two Vietnamese ideologies, but between the Vietnamese and the United States which has deployed half a million troops in Vietnam to prevent self-determination of a whole people. This is the core of the Vietnam story, and it has been neither reported nor analyzed.

The unfortunate American soldier, introduced into the situation without preparation and without genuine cause, is a tragic figure. When Just cited to Miss Gellhorn the bravery of the Americans in combat, she replied that it was a case of "just buddies." However terse and seemingly cold that may sound, it is nevertheless true. The American soldiers in Vietnam were concerned primarily with preserving themselves and their comrades, linked together in the bleakness of a mystifying war against a determined enemy who did not want to be their enemy at all. For almost all the Americans in Vietnam there was no ideology at all—and what there was had been superimposed, not self-developed.

For the American soldier, with limited education and deliberately distorted lessons in history, forced into a draft army to do the bidding of prejudiced superiors, it was one thing to be a bewildered victim. But for educated and trained correspondents who witnessed daily the brutality visited upon a whole people by the government of the United States, and who still insisted there was no alternative, there could be no explanation in innocence. It might have been wiser for some of the young correspondents in Vietnam to have withheld their long-range judgments until their experiences could be weighed in the perspective of maturity. Nonetheless, it is helpful to have their thoughts and experiences immediately, because these works do make up the material of history.

In fairness to the correspondents—that is, the permanently based reporters in Southeast Asia rather than the fly-by-nighters operating in Washington's behalf—their precise conclusions after their tours of duty will be carefully set down here. Some of the correspondents returned to Vietnam for different newspapers and wire services. Malcolm Browne, for example, went back in 1965 for the ABC television network, and Charles Mohr for the *New York Times*. Neil Sheehan went to Washington for the *Times*, while Halberstam left daily journalism, after an assignment in Poland for the *Times*, became an associate editor of *Harper's* magazine and a book writer on more nearly domestic political themes. Of major significance also is the attitude of the newspaper publishers and managers of the press services toward their men in Vietnam, and the emphasis they placed on coverage from Vietnam. Finally, there should be an assessment of the role of the journalist in the making and unmaking of government policy, with inevitable stress on the question of objectivity in the news.

The most generous governmental estimate of the journalists was given by John Mecklin in the conclusion of his *Mission in Torment,* written after he himself had left government service and returned to journalism. It was unlikely that any of the news coverage from Vietnam in the 1962-64 period "would be memorialized in journalism schools for literary excellence or brilliant analysis," he said. The newsmen assigned to Vietnam were no better or worse than those assigned elsewhere; but by their personal courage and doggedness "in refusing to be intimidated . . . they performed a distinct public service."

Overriding the issue of the quality of reporting, Mecklin wrote, was the institution of the American information media itself: "Whether the reporting was good or bad the American people got just about what they were willing to pay for, or anyway what the media editors believed the people wanted." But these are two distinctly different things—payment and selection—which cannot be lumped together. The readers pay a fixed price for their paper, and they have no voice in the assignment of personnel. For the most part, the assignments are made by the publishers and editors, according to their budgets and preferences, and they have in mind not so much what they think the people want as what they want the people to think.

In the critical years of Diem's decline, only the Associated Press, the United Press International and the *New York Times* had full-time correspondents in Vietnam. When a major story broke, a stream of special correspondents poured in from Hong Kong, Bangkok, and Tokyo. But the day-to-day coverage—and the unexpected news breaks—were left to the permanent correspondents who, as Mecklin said in a rather poor analogy, compared in pay, age, and experience with "junior officers in the armed services." Middle-aged men (meaning mature reporters) were hard to come by, according to Mecklin, because they were "getting ahead" in the profession and did not want to move their families to Saigon. Besides, "it was the judgment of the editors back home that Vietnam was a good story but that it did not generate enough reader interest to justify ordering a high-priced man to move to Vietnam." It was more likely that the editors, in keeping with Washington's desire, did not want to generate greater reader interest in what the United States was doing in Vietnam. As for the high-priced men, there were always funds available to send them out when the "young Turks" needed some taking down. If the publishers couldn't pay, the trips could be financed, as Assistant Secretary of Defense Arthur Sylvester testified before the Senate Foreign Relations Committee in 1966, by the United States government. Government transportation was provided not only for American newsmen but for foreign ones as well.

Malcolm Browne addressed himself to the reader-as-consumer question in an article entitled "Vietnam Reporting: Three Years of Crisis" in the Fall 1964 issue of the *Columbia Journalism Review:*

The flow of news from the event to the reader, listener, or viewer is essentially a two-way street. It depends not only on the news itself but on the demands of the news consumer. The news consumer in America is a busy man or woman. He or she is leading a life of his own or her own in which news may be consumed as entertainment, as information, or a combination of the two. There is little time for detailed study of issues and complicated situations like those that pertained, for example, in South Vietnam in 1963. Readers and editors demand their news in the simplest capsule available, sometimes limiting their consumption to mere head-lines . . .

Vietnam does not lend itself well to numerical reporting, or even to the kind of simple narrative statement required of the average newspaper lead. There are too many uncertainties, too many shades of gray, too many dangers of applying English-language clichés to a situation that cannot be described by clichés . . . In short, I believe one of the deficiencies of reporting is in the news consumer himself. He gets exactly as much substantial information as he asks for—neither more, nor less.

Browne pursued this theme in an interview in *Variety* (November 2, 1966), commenting mainly on television's coverage of the war. He said he left the television industry because of his inability to communicate the subtler aspects of the war to the American people. Whenever he would deal with an economic or political problem, he said, either "people turn off their sets" or "the producer switches you off and cuts in the footage that he deems most illustrative of what you're talking about." While there is ample evidence to validate the criticism of the producers, the comments about the public would seem to be less valid. The public has never had the opportunity to "turn off" the political and economic side of the situa-tion in Vietnam because it has never been presented on television in depth. What has been shown, for the most part, has been officially ap-proved propaganda about progress in the pacification program or the "strategic hamlets," for example, with only an occasional program which got down to basic factors.

By 1966, Browne seemed to have grown weary of the war. He said that South Vietnam was "a rather venal and corrupt country" and that democracy was out of the question for the foreseeable future: "We're not defending the Vietnamese people against some system that's an awful lot worse than what they've already got." The only credible basis for the United States presence in Vietnam, he said, was the containment of China. Eight months later, Browne's malaise about Vietnam seemed even more severe. In a perceptive review of Roger Hilsman's *To Move a Nation* in the June 5, 1967, *Nation,* he developed the role that Hilsman had played as a master planner of President Kennedy's counter-insur-gency policy. The review was written before President Johnson's decision not to run again in 1968, so Johnson was still the man with the spiked shoes, as Browne wrote in the idiom of baseball: "Johnson is still at bat, but we're in the ninth inning now, and the home team is still badly be-hind." He went on:

One can't resist the image of a Vietnamese *nha que* [peasant] sitting in front of his hut, reading Hilsman's new book, a wry smile on his face. Is it possible that the old *nha que* is thinking, "a pox on all their houses"? I think that's exactly how Vietnam reacts to the torture of American policy politics. When America is not politically bungling its relations with Asia, it seems to vent its spleen by bombing and destroying. Either way, Vietnam is the loser. Granting that Asian communism is a brutal force that hardly does much to make life happier for the average peasant, America has yet to demonstrate that it can do better. Putting down Hilsman's book, one wonders whether some form of isolationism with respect to Asia would really be such a bad idea after all. Would Asia really be so much worse off without us around? Would we really be any worse off without Asia? Probably we shall never have the chance to find out. Asia and America seem doomed to play out the tragic drama to the end.

The tragic drama, as I perceive it, is not so much in a misguided estimate of an Asia equally at fault with the United States in the failure to solve the "Asian-American" problem, as in Browne himself, who seemed to have absorbed so little, despite the enormous wealth and range of his experiences. The scenario of the Asian-American drama was written in the United States. The answer is not isolation, which would concede the failure of our imperialist aggression, but an honorable withdrawal by the United States and an acceptance of the nations of Asia on an equal footing. The interminable cliché about the brutality of Asian Communism is passed on once again without a flicker of conscience to a public which, according to Browne in 1964, gets only the news it asks for. I doubt whether the American public is sufficiently informed about Asian Communism to know what to ask for, because the facts have never been presented fairly.

For all the limitations of his views, Browne's progress was visible in his migration from acceptance of the "credible" American presence in Vietnam (1966) to a rather plaintive speculation about isolationism (1967). But these positions were presented to a small audience—in the *Nation,* to a predominantly anti-Administration readership; in *Variety,* mainly to professional people involved in the entertainment industry. If Browne had made these positions available to the American public at large as the correspondent of a worldwide wire service, they would have provoked a greater interest in Vietnam policy and perhaps a greater demand for the facts. If he had been prevented from expressing himself, that in itself would have been a significant story.

For Halberstam the "root of the journalistic problem in Vietnam," as he phrased it in *The Making of a Quagmire,* was "the traditional right of American journalists to report what they see was at stake here, even though the situation was a particularly sensitive one: ambiguous involvement in a wretched war with a ruthless enemy." Because the news was bad, he said, there were many people who did not want it exposed. Yet an American reporter "must believe, if he believes nothing else, that the United States has never survived in times of crisis by playing ostrich. Too much policy and too deep a commitment had already been made in Vietnam on the basis of too little factual information." In an interview in the January 1964 issue of *Esquire* magazine, Halberstam foresaw an "uneasy stalemate between our military superiority and the Communist political effectiveness." With that stalemate, the United States could not win; it could only not lose. But there was a further danger: "What worries me—and what the Vietcong is counting on—is that we may get worn down and fatigued, and go to Geneva to agree to a face-saving coalition. And then this pretty little country will be lost."

There again the identification with American policy, and the inability or unwillingness to see as the underlying question not whether "we" would lose Vietnam, as we lost China and Cuba, but whether the Vietnamese liberation forces could advance to a position where the people would be permitted to decide their own future. Halberstam acknowledged that American reporters were limited by their nationality in their coverage of Vietnam, but there was another kind of limitation to covering the news, he said, even though "we know more about Vietnam and the aspirations of the Vietnamese than most American officials." He said: "We were there, after all, to cover the war; this was our primary focus and inevitably we judged events through the war's progress or lack of it." For that reason, the American reporters never entered the Buddhist pagodas until after the Buddhist crisis; did not write of Nguyen Tuong Tam, the most honored Vietnamese writer and novelist of the time, until after his suicide—"and then only because his death had political connotations." They were aware of the aspirations of the peasants "because they were the barometer of the Government's failure and the war's progress, not because we were on the side of the population and against the rulers."

But in that "pretty little country," the Buddhists were a major force before the crisis. Nguyen Tuong Tam alive was a first-rate political story, and if he had been able to influence world opinion during his life, he would not have resorted to a dramatic death to do so. The "population" of Vietnam was the heart of the matter, and their aspirations were far more than a barometer of the war's progress: they were the handwriting on the wall of American failure from the moment the first American "adviser" arrived after the French defeat. It was impossible to "cover the war" without covering Vietnam. It was not, as Halberstam put it, "an ambiguous involvement in a wretched war with a ruthless enemy," but a deliberate if foredoomed involvement on the part of the United States in a most unambiguous war with an "enemy" that was ruthless only in its determination not to submit to foreign domination. What was required in the coverage of Vietnam were reporters with knowledge of the country who would be able to dissociate themselves from the American "commitment" in Vietnam (which was neither holy nor honorable), and who would be willing to tell not only the bad news but the reasons for the bad news. This could not be accomplished because the American reporters, with a few exceptions, were neither equipped nor willing to do it; and even if they had been willing, their reports, as the Mohr incident demonstrated, would not have been published.

What conclusions did Halberstam reach after his tour of duty in Vietnam? The alternatives in 1965 for him were basically the same as in 1961. The United States could not agree to a neutral Vietnam: that would bring about a "vacuum" for Communist "subversion" in six months. Withdraw? Impossible. It would mean suffering for those who sided with the United States, a drab life for the nation, and a lowering of Washington's prestige throughout the world. Above all, it would encourage "the enemies of the West" to attempt "insurgencies like the one in Vietnam" throughout the world. In essence, Halberstam's concluding chapter, written before the massive American commitment of troops, is a depressing repetition of the thesis repeatedly put forward by the "liberal" wing of the counter-insurgency policy-makers in Washington, as exemplified by Roger Hilsman in *To Move a Nation*.

In sum, according to Halberstam, the United States must get smart. The question was not one of withdrawing into the garrison state, but of selecting and dealing with the vital areas of major American concern and interest throughout the world. In this fashion, the methods of counter-insurgency could be applied before the crisis areas became noisy and noisome. "The lesson to be learned from Vietnam," Halberstam said, "is that we must get in earlier, be shrewder and force the other side to practice self-deception." But the United States got into Southeast Asia very early, long before the defeat of the French, and there was considerable shrewdness in some of its moves. The problem was that "the other side," the people of Vietnam who rejected colonial occupation, never practiced self-deception. Failure to perceive this caused the American policy-makers to deceive themselves from the very beginning, and they never yielded in this self-deception. Unfortunately the practice was contagious: it spread to and persisted in the press corps—among the best of the reporters.

One of the best was Neil Sheehan, who served in Vietnam as a correspondent from 1962 to 1964, returned in 1965, and finally left in 1966.

When he went in, it was for the United Press International; when he came out, it was for the *New York Times*. On October 9, 1966, as the *Times* man at the Pentagon, Sheehan wrote a four-year perspective article for the *Times Magazine* entitled "Not a Dove, But No Longer a Hawk." The article demonstrated conclusively the inadequacy and inaccuracy of such journalistic clichés as "hawk" and "dove." He arrived in Saigon, Sheehan said, in 1962, persuaded of the rightness of "what my country was doing in Vietnam . . . to help the non-Communist Vietnamese build a viable and independent nation-state and defeat a Communist guerrilla insurgency that would subject them to a dour tyranny." This was being accomplished with "military and economic aid and a few thousands pilots and Army advisers." When he left in 1966, there were 317,000 American servicemen in Vietnam. This situation, and the reasons for it, caused a molting of Sheehan's hawk feathers, but the new down was not that of a dove. Sheehan was clear about the Vietnamese whom Washington had selected to counter the Communist insurgency. He wrote:

> While there are some patriotic and decent individuals among them, most of the men who rule Saigon have, like the Bourbons, learned nothing and forgotten nothing. They seek to retain what privileges they have and to regain those they have lost. In Vietnam only the Communists represent revolution and social change, for better or worse according to a man's politics. The Communist party is the one truly national organization that permeates both North and South Vietnam. The men who lead the party today, Ho Chi Minh and the other members of the Politburo in Hanoi, directed the struggle for independence from France and in the process captured much of the deeply felt nationalism of the Vietnamese people. Perhaps because of this, the Communists, despite their brutality and deceit, remain the only Vietnamese capable of rallying millions of their countrymen to sacrifice and hardship in the name of the nation and the only group not dependent on foreign bayonets for survival.

Aside from the usual genuflection to "brutality and deceit" (the employers of this phrase have never explained how brutes and deceivers succeed in rallying a perceptive people to sacrifice and hardship), Sheehan presented an accurate picture of the opposing forces. But he dissipated much of his own credibility by ascribing the "tragedy of Vietnam" to the fact that "what began as a war of independence from France developed, as a result of its Communist leadership, into a civil conflict." The war has never been regarded by either the National Liberation Front or the North Vietnamese as a civil war. Further, it was precipitated not by Communist leadership, but by the efforts of Sheehan's Saigon Bourbons, at the behest of the United States government, to hang on to what they had and to retrieve what they had lost. Sheehan himself conceded only a few sentences later that Vietnam was not a civil conflict: "For its own strategic and political ends, the United States is thus protecting a non-Communist Vietnamese social structure that cannot defend itself and that perhaps does not deserve to be defended." Idealism and dedication, Sheehan was "continually chagrined to discover," were "largely the prerogative of the enemy."

Having made clear that the "Communists" were the sole force capable of unifying Vietnam under the banner of independent nationalism, and stressing the idealism and dedication of the "enemy"; having classed the Saigon Bourbons as not worthy of defending, and recognizing that it is the United States that is prolonging the war in Vietnam, Sheehan concluded on the basis of his unimpeachable evidence that the logical and honorable solution must at all costs be avoided. He fell back on the trapped-in-the-dilemma-of-history approach: Washington cannot withdraw its troops from Vietnam "without making certain an eventual Communist seizure of power there and negating all the efforts of the last decade to maintain a friendly government in Saigon." Hanoi's "best chance" to win was "in prolonging the blood-letting to the point where the American public will tire of a war for a small land whose name most Americans cannot even pronounce correctly." Like Halberstam, Sheehan worried that the latter might prove to be the case, but he was much encouraged by 1966 to believe that the United States would not pull out, that it would win, not as in World War II, but that "yet we may well prevail." It might take years, but Washington's military force was superior enough to destroy the Liberation Front and North Vietnamese main units and to "transform what is currently a military sound but politically weak position into one of some, if doubtful, political strength."

Sheehan, with some regret but with firm resolve, concluded that morality in Vietnam would have to yield to the amorality of great-power politics. The Vietnamese were mere pawns, and the fiction that the United States was in Vietnam to maintain the independence of the country could no longer be maintained: "The military junta in Saigon would not last a week without American bayonets to protect it." Sheehan saw no alternative but to accept the American strategy to "continue to prosecute the war," and to develop a "killing machine" to be turned on to the enemy "in the hope that over the years enough killing will be done to force the enemy's collapse through exhaustion and despair." He could not, however, exorcise a gnawing fear that in the process of raising the kill ratio "we are corrupting ourselves." He wrote:

I wonder, when I look at the bombed-out peasant hamlets, the orphans begging and stealing on the streets, and the women and children with napalm burns lying on the hospital cots, whether the United States or any nation has the right to inflict this suffering and degradation on another people for its own ends. And I hope we will not, in the name of some anti-Communist crusade, do this again.

But if this becomes necessary, as it apparently continues to be in Vietnam, and less apparently in Latin America and elsewhere, Sheehan, on the basis of his 1966 article, no doubt would suppress his misgivings and go along once again, because the hopes and the aspirations of Vietnamese or other peoples have no consideration in the final determination of what is the best interests of the United States.

"The pessimism of the Saigon press corps," Halberstam wrote in 1965, "was of the most reluctant kind: many of us came to love Vietnam, we saw our friends dying all around us, and we would have liked nothing better than to believe that the war was going well and that it would eventually be won. But it was impossible to believe these things without denying the evidences of our senses." The senses of the reporters led them to question the methods of American officialdom but not their ends, because the reporters were as much concerned with "winning the war" as were the officials. It was their political and social prejudices, and their lack of basic education in world politics and problems, that prevented the reporters from probing more deeply and from questioning the very presence of American troops in Vietnam.

If the reporters were appalled at the sight of their friends dying in a country they had come to love (how does one measure such love?), why were they not equally appalled at the death of Vietnamese, in battle and under torture, for love of a country which, after all, was their own? If they had been able to proceed thus far, would they not then, in the last analysis, have examined the fundamental question of "winning the war"? Winning the war for whom? For those who sought to stifle the reporters and keep the truth from the American people?

Here the question comes back to Ward Just and the civil war in Spain, and the matter of objectivity and the role of the reporter. The reporters in Spain brought to their work a political conviction and passion which obviously influenced their stories. So did some of the reporters in Vietnam. But in the latter case the passion for searching out the basic truth of the immediate internal situation was always tempered by the specter of the American national interest. The passion was for being an "honest reporter" within the guidelines set down by those who decreed what the national interest was. And the national interest, as all the reporters came to accept, was that the United States must remain in Vietnam until victory—or at least to prevent a victory by the Communists.

Both in passion and in reality, Spain and Vietnam were a world apart, and so were the worlds of the journalists involved in each war. When Martha Gellhorn told Ward Just that the reporters in Spain knew the Loyalists were right—"we just *knew*"—she was a partisan, of course. But she was a partisan of both truth and justice. These moral qualities, as Sheehan noted in his article in the *New York Times Magazine,* had no place in Vietnam: they had to yield to the amoral realities of the situation created by the dilemmas of history—that is, the dilemmas created by the foreign policy of the United States.

# 16. Free Rides to the Front

The violent departure of Ngo Dinh Diem and the shock over the assassination of President Kennedy were enormously helpful to Ambassador Lodge's campaign to pacify the American press corps in Saigon. But there was an echo of the press war of 1961-63 in the annual journalistic awards for 1963, which were announced in the spring of 1964. The most coveted award of all, the Pulitzer Prize for international reporting, was given jointly to David Halberstam of the *Times* and Malcolm Browne of the Associated Press. The foreign correspondence prize of Sigma Delta Chi, the honorary journalistic society, went to Browne. The Louis M. Lyons award for conscience and integrity, named for the curator of the Nieman Foundation at Harvard, went to Halberstam, Browne and Neil Sheehan of the United Press. Overseas Press Club awards and citations were given to five correspondents in Vietnam: Peter Kalischer of the Columbia Broadcasting System; Browne and photographer Horst Faas of the Associated Press; Lawrence Burrows, photographer, of *Life* magazine, and Richard Tregaskis for his book *Vietnam Diary*.

The awards, for the most part, were a rhetorical demonstration of independence and defiance, which cost the publishers nothing and enabled them to gather once again at their annual convocations in an aura of righteousness as the integritous upholders of the freedom of the press.

The Administration was embarking on an escalation of the war, and the Congress and the press (under cover of the awards) were willing and prepared to give their support. The pretext was an alleged attack by North Vietnamese gunboats on United States destroyers in the Gulf of Tonkin. This produced the famous Tonkin Gulf resolution, passed unanimously in the House on August 5, 1964, and by a vote of 88 to 2 in the Senate (Ernest Gruening, Democrat of Alaska, and Wayne Morse, Democrat of Oregon, dissenting), which authorized the President "to take all necessary measures to repel any armed attack against the forces of the United States to prevent further aggression." It was a blank check authorization to the President to declare war and, therefore, an abdication by Congress of its constitutional authority.

The blank check was made out even before the resolution was adopted, when the President ordered the bombing of North Vietnamese bases from which the allegedly attacking gunboats had come. But the full "necessary measures" were undertaken in February 1965, again supposedly in response to North Vietnamese aggression, when the President ordered bombing attacks above the Seventeenth Parallel. The bombings at first were sporadic, and in the three-week lull that followed the first attack, North Vietnam responded positively to peace moves made by United Nations Secretary General U Thant, President de Gaulle of France and Premier Kosygin of the Soviet Union. But the United States ignored all overtures, and the bombings were resumed on a systematic basis on March 2, 1965. Shortly thereafter, United States Marines landed in South Vietnam, and the escalation was fully under way.

The transcript of Secretary of Defense McNamara's news conference on August 5, 1964, disclosed that the newsmen present refrained from asking any questions that might embarrass the government, although it must have seemed inconceivable to any thoughtful reporter that a few small North Vietnamese gunboats would seek out and challenge the battleships of the United States fleet, knowing that such an action would provoke immediate and massive retaliation. Of 27 editorials in newspapers across the country, excerpted in the August 7 *New York Times,* 24 endorsed the bombings without qualification; two had slight reservations, and one was noncommittal.

With saturation coverage and saturation endorsement, it was hardly surprising that the first public opinion poll taken after the Tonkin Gulf incident and the bombings boosted the "approve" rating of the President's handling of the war from 42 to 72 per cent. A near-unanimous Congress and press are a potent force in molding public opinion.

The first bombings were described as "retaliatory." They were launched, the Pentagon said, in reprisal for North Vietnamese aggression which had caused some embarrassing and costly setbacks in the land war in South Vietnam. No justification was given for the second round of bombings, but the press was enlisted in a propaganda effort to portray "Hanoi and Peking" (they were always joined) as standing against negotiations to bring peace to South Vietnam. In fact, the National Liberation Front of South Vietnam, despite its victories, had called repeatedly for negotiations to end the bloodshed. Washington had consistently rejected such moves and, in mid-February 1965, while it made plans to resume bombing North Vietnam, was also unresponsive to peace pleas from Pope Paul and Prime Minister Shastri of India. James Reston in the *New York Times* of February 14, 1965, as part of the obfuscation team, wrote:

> The cause of the war [in South Vietnam] is plain enough. The North Vietnamese Communists, with the aid of Red China and to a lesser extent the Soviet Union, have sent their guerrillas into South Vietnam in violation of the 1954 and 1962 Geneva agreements, for the express purpose of taking over the government and the territory of South Vietnam. The Communists were steadily defeating the South Vietnamese armed forces, terrorizing a war-weary and indifferent population and taking advantage of a divided and quarrelsome South Vietnamese government.
> Very few people here [in Washington] question the necessity for a limited expansion of the war by U.S. bombers into Communist territory. The American and the South Vietnamese position was crumbling fast, and the political and strategic consequences of defeat would have been serious for the free world all over Asia. The immediate problem, therefore, is how to put enough pressure on the North Vietnamese to bring them into negotiations for a settlement of the war without provoking a mass Communist counterattack we are in no position to meet.

An anticipatory but precise response to the Reston-State Department position was given in a letter to the *New York Times* of February 12 by Robert S. Browne, a university professor who had served with the United States aid mission in South Vietnam from 1958 to 1961. He wrote: "While sophisticated Americans no longer expect the truth to emanate from Washington, we at least expect a modicum of respect for our intelligence." Supporting Browne's view, the record showed the following:

• The cause of the war in Vietnam was intervention by the United States to prevent the people of Vietnam from being governed by a regime of their own choosing in the scheduled election of 1956 (which was aborted by this intervention).
• No evidence had been offered to prove intervention in South Vietnam by the Soviet Union or China, or even by North Vietnam, although Hanoi has insisted that Vietnam is one nation, and Vietnamese north and south have the right—and duty—to join in resistance to an aggressor.
• The United States intervention, military and political, was in direct violation of the Geneva agreements of 1954 and 1962. This intervention countenanced suppression by terror of any opposition in South Vietnam, subversion and intervention in Laos, Cambodia, and Thailand, and re-

peated raids and bombings in North Vietnam, climaxed by the mass bombing of February 7, 1965.

Reston and less prominent but no less acquiescent journalists were in effect acting as propaganda agents for the State and Defense Departments in distorting and confusing the facts. They kept from the American public information it needed to weigh and form opinions on the war in Vietnam. This kind of complicity, dismaying enough, looks even worse when we examine the fate of some honest reporting on the war.

Wilfred Burchett had gone into the NLF-controlled areas of South Vietnam and had written a series of articles for the *National Guardian* (I was then its editor) on the progress of the war. Burchett's information profoundly contradicted claims of American victories. To ensure that the Burchett series would achieve the widest possible circulation, we sent pre-publication galley proofs of the first two articles, accompanied by a press release describing the entire series, to all the major wire services and leading newspapers. This was done on February 1, 1965.

As far as we were able to determine, no story appeared in any daily newspaper in the United States based on our proofs or release. But on February 8, the *Washington Post,* which had received the *National Guardian* advance package, carried a Reuters (British news agency) dispatch under a Tokyo dateline quoting Burchett's account of the battle of Bien Hoa, as contained in his first article. Reuters had picked up the story from the mass-circulation Tokyo daily *Mainichi Shimbun,* which had the Japanese rights to the Burchett series. The foreign desk of the *Washington Post* could have had the story a full week earlier if it had been willing to accept and credit the *National Guardian.*

The *New York Times,* apparently noting the story in the *Washington Post,* reacted after receiving a second *National Guardian* release on February 10. The *Times* foreign desk asked for an advance look at the entire series of ten articles in preparation for a story on Burchett's reportage and conclusions. We hastened to get the material ready, but in the midst of this effort came a second call from the *Times:* No rush, they said. They would wait until the entire series had been published—at the end of February. It was more than likely that a policy decision had been made at the *Times.* Heavy bombings of North Vietnam occurred on February 7, 8, and 11, and publication of material contradicting United States justification of the bombings would lower the government's credibility level. As February came to an end, so did the *Times*'s interest in the Burchett series. It never did use the stories.

The sharp decline in the credibility level in the following months proved embarrassing and distressing to at least part of the American press. At a news conference on July 13, 1965, President Johnson said in response to questions about possible peace negotiations: "I must say that candor compels me to tell you that there has not been the slightest indication that the other side is interested in negotiation or unconditional discussions, although the United States has made some dozen separate attempts to bring that about."

In its issue of November 30, 1965 (published November 15), *Look* magazine printed an article by Eric Sevareid based on an interview in London with United Nations Ambassador Adlai Stevenson. The interview took place on July 12, one day before the Johnson press conference, and two days before the death of Stevenson in a London street.

Sevareid said Stevenson told him that UN Secretary General U Thant had conveyed to Stevenson in August 1964 the willingness of the North Vietnamese to meet with representatives of the United States on neutral ground to talk peace. Stevenson had relayed the offer to Washington, where it had been rejected by Johnson and Secretary of Defense McNamara. Subsequently, the Administration denied there had been an offer. After the Sevareid article appeared, it conceded knowledge of the overture but said it had been rejected because Secretary of State Rusk's "sensitive antenna" had recorded "no serious intent on the other side." In his November 27 column, Reston wrote:

> In the Vietnamese war from beginning to end there has been a serious and widespread lack of trust in the government's statements about how well the war was going, what role our men were playing, and how well the South Vietnamese government was doing. The Administration's first problem, therefore, is not how to talk to the Vietnamese but how to talk candidly to the American people. If there is a crisis, it is not a crisis of diplomacy abroad but of confidence at home.

A crisis of confidence surely was shaping up, but the onus was not that of government alone. The press, with Reston in a prominent role, had made a significant contribution to that crisis by its own refusal to speak candidly to the American people—except when the lack of trust became so obvious that hypocritical indignation had to be displayed.

The government's program to enlist the press in its propaganda corps was explained at hearings before the Senate Committee on Foreign Relations in August 1966. There were two sessions—one on August 17, with Leonard H. Marks, director of the United States Information Agency; the other on August 31, with Arthur Sylvester, Assistant Secretary of Defense. The topic of the hearings was "New Policies in Vietnam." It might well have been subtitled: "How the Press Got Back Altogether on the Team After the Young Turks Left Vietnam."

Marks was questioned mainly about Washington's relations with foreign newspapermen, and the operation of the USIA in Saigon. He described how transportation was provided to correspondents from Europe and Asia "so they can see for themselves and get a firsthand acquaintance with the facts." This was not a new technique, he said, and it was no discredit to a newsman or educator or scientist to be "the guest of the United States government." After all, he said, "when a new hotel opens in the United States, it is customary to have a flight of newspapermen. . . . Baseball games take place every day and there are newsmen in the press boxes as guests of the management, so there is nothing new about this, and nothing wrong about it."

Having compared the war in Vietnam to a spectator sport, Marks told how USIA posts "worldwide" were urged to encourage visits by foreign correspondents to Vietnam. If financial aid was needed, all efforts would be made to see that it was forthcoming, and about 35 to 40 correspondents were assisted. Who were they? Marks was reluctant to say. Chairman J. William Fulbright suggested that the practice "may place the agency in a somewhat awkward position, since there will be concern among our citizens about whether this is a legitimate function of the USIA." He said: "Some of us thought that it was a rather questionable practice for a foreign agent to pay the way of an American newspaper reporter to go abroad and come back and write articles which usually were favorable to his client's state." He was referring to disclosures in a previous Foreign Relations Committee hearing of widespread lobbying in Washington by representatives of Chiang Kai-shek, Trujillo of the Dominican Republic, and others to plant favorable stories in American publications about their countries. The articles were written for pay by American newspapermen.

Marks bridled at Fulbright's implication. He said: "I don't believe that any newsman worthy of his name would slant a story because he was given a free airplane ride to the scene of an event."

Fulbright replied with heavy sarcasm: "I am sure they wouldn't. They will never do that."

Senator Gore, Democrat of Tennessee, wondered why the United States position in Vietnam was subject to "such worldwide questioning and doubt." Marks had a ready answer: "I am satisfied that there are major areas of misunderstanding which we must continue to correct. I am satisfied that there are some newspapers, there are some governments who are unalterably opposed to our policy and do not wish to have the facts." It was that simple—the only reason why there was opposition to United States policy was a prejudiced lack of desire for facts. Thus it became the duty of the United States government to force-feed these newspapers and governments with facts supplied by means of free junkets to Vietnam. But Marks still was reluctant to give out names. He said:

> I would hate to see this committee become the vehicle for publishing the names. In most countries, I imagine that a man from a prominent newspaper can't just disappear for three weeks or a month without having his absence known and, perhaps, having to say openly where he is going. I don't think this committee should become the vehicle for publishing the names. It would be too much like stripping the camouflage off a sniper. We are in a war and we have to adjust ourselves to this kind of situation.

This was a considerable departure from Marks's earlier comparison of a war correspondent with a sportswriter in the press box of a baseball stadium camouflaged only by a bright sports jacket. Senator Claiborne Pell, Democrat of Rhode Island, supported Marks's position that the Vietnam junket program had been well worth the effort, although he felt the program should be conducted by the CIA. "In my opinion," he said, "it is black propaganda. . . . The list of names should not be published." The Senator was far more direct than the director of the USIA; but then he had never been a public relations man.

Senator Karl Mundt, Republican of South Dakota, wanted to know whether the practice of "employing the part-time services of reporters and associates of American periodicals" had been stopped. Marks said this was no longer the practice—and then proceeded to demonstrate that it was:

> The type of thing we do, when there is a magazine article published, or a periodical story which we want to use, we ask for the rights, and in some cases we have to pay for those rights, or in limited instances, if we want an article on a specialty where only a few people have the ability to write it. Let's say it is a complicated space article; we may go to an experienced man in the field of space and say, "Will you write this?" and pay them for the piece. We do on occasion employ part-timers, or stringers.

In other words, to each according to his ability, but never full time. And apparently there was always an able-bodied journeyman available who might need a few extra dollars for a mortgage payment.

Arthur Sylvester had an arsenal of statistics for his appearance before the Fulbright committee two weeks later. As of August 1966, he said, the United States Military Command was giving assistance to 419 representatives of the news media from 22 countries. Of these, 179 were Americans, but dozens of foreigners worked for the American media. Beginning in 1964, he said, when there were only 40 newspapermen of all nationalities in Vietnam, there was considerable concern within the Defense Department that the people of the United States were not receiving "adequate factual information concerning our efforts in Vietnam." So a program of transporting United States correspondents to Vietnam was undertaken. From July 17, 1964, to August 1965, 82 newspaper, TV, wire service and magazine representatives were accommodated. It is noteworthy that the effort began just before the incident in the Gulf of Tonkin and coincident with the buildup of troops in South Vietnam.

Sylvester graded the operation as highly successful in "priming the pump." Prior to 1964, he said, newspapers "were not paying very much attention to Vietnam. In fact, they were not spending very much money covering it. The coverage was by young men and by low-priced help. That is why we invited major news organizations in the country to go out and look for themselves. As the conflict escalated . . . everyone devoted a tremendous amount of resources and money to their coverage of it. What we attempted to do in 1964 was to interest them in it."

A parallel interest was to discredit the low-priced help who, according to Sylvester, had been presenting a false picture through subjective reporting. Sylvester summed up the effort:

In the last two years the overall and general effect of the reporting has been good in the sense that the information is basically correct, basically sound. I think that the news profession as such, regardless of media, in the last 15 or 20 years has suffered a good deal from so-called interpretive reporting . . . Not only are our major media now represented in Vietnam, but also they are generally represented by first-rate correspondents characteristic of first-rate American news organizations. These newsmen are searching out and filing reports which contribute to broadening public appreciation and understanding of the situation in Vietnam.

Fulbright then raised the specter of management of the news, and Sylvester was prepared. He had learned some hard lessons from the Cuban missile crisis, when he had insisted on the right and duty of government to manage the news. The committee heard this gibberish:

I would suggest that the only place where news is managed, the only place where it can be managed, the only place where it should be managed and is managed is in every newspaper office. Newspapers have managing editors. That is their job. Television and radio news departments have too. That is the only place that I know of where news can be managed, is managed, and should be managed. But I think that the use of the term "managed news" on the part of the government has never really been taken apart and examined. If you ask somebody what he means, I have yet to find a definition or a case history of what is being talked about. . . . It frankly puzzles me. I do not know what "managed news" means.

Sylvester's cover-up for government was hardly newsworthy, but his shifting the responsibility to the press was. Fulbright picked him up on it and in the ensuing dialogue Sylvester once again assumed the role of frankly puzzled public servant.

*Fulbright:* It is very interesting that so many of our prominent newspapers have become almost agents or adjuncts of the government; that they do not contest or even raise questions about government policy. Isn't that true?
*Sylvester:* I do not find that so in my job.
*Fulbright:* You do not?
*Sylvester:* No sir.
*Fulbright:* I think you have a very friendly press in Washington.
*Sylvester:* I hope we do.
*Fulbright:* You do. No critical articles which have come to my attention have originated in any of the local press. . . . I think it is remarkable how far the consensus has gone in recent years. Do you not?

Sylvester offered to show some typewriter scars on his back, but Fulbright attributed them to "personal friction" which he had himself experienced. He said: "I think it is fairly obvious from the volume of criticism that there is a feeling on the part of the American people that they do not get the full truth."

He supposed—plaintively but accurately—that "that has always been more or less true," and ended up with a comforting summary of the exchange with Sylvester:

I think it is very reassuring to the American people to know how the news is managed, as you have described it, and I think you have made a good contribution. And if news management is a fact, since it is obvious that it not only is, but is always going to be, it is good to know that there is absolutely no possibility of avoiding it or preventing it. Knowing about it, we can evaluate the news more accurately. Would you agree with that?

Sylvester by this time was purring: "If I were a wiser man, I would not have gotten into this. But I do agree with it. Yes, I think that is obvious."

On this helpless note, the hearing ended. And, as so often occurs when the press is the subject of discussion, the matter more nearly ended with the committee. Newspaper accounts were scant or nonexistent. *Editor & Publisher* headlined its story of the Sylvester testimony: " 'Press Needs Help in Viet'—Sylvester." It meant help from the government. Fulbright's remarks about the press becoming "agents of government" went entirely unreported in *Editor & Publisher*.

The extent of governmental helpfulness was occasionally acknowledged by the press. "Reports from the battle area of South Vietnam," said the *Detroit News* in an editorial on March 24, 1965, "make it plain the United States government has established a news control policy more subject to manipulation than anything we have yet known. . . . Under these circumstances, the *News* is regretfully obliged to inform its readers that current Defense Department policy prevents reporters from bringing them the full truth."

The editorial was accurate as far as it went, but it had the quality of a due-to-circumstances-beyond-our-control disclaimer. While the "full truth" about the battle area might have been unobtainable, there were large areas of politics and policy-making which were open to full inquiry, but the troubled editorials were never followed by the kind of investigative reporting that might have yielded the "full truth."

The *New York Times* came closer to the mark in an editorial on April 30, 1965. "The most important problem," it said, "is in Washington, not Saigon. It stems from the President's own concept of the Vietnam conflict and his role in it. He has been behaving as if he were John F. Kennedy in the midst of the Cuban missile crisis, playing all the cards very close to the chest. But the methods that served the country well in a one-week confrontation over an offshore island are highly unsuitable for a complex politico-military conflict in Southeast Asia." (The *Times* spoke with the authority of personal experience, since it had been responsible for suppressing information in its possession during the Cuban missile crisis. In retrospect, the *Times* minimized the missile crisis as a one-week hassle over an "off-shore island," known to some as a sovereign republic, but no one who lived through the week could accept such a description.)

Contrary to the *Times*'s analysis, the most important problem was far more in the editorial offices of the daily press than in Washington or Saigon. Editors and publishers might grumble about government efforts to manage the news—hardly a new phenomenon—but they chose to do little to counter these efforts. Even when there seemed to be no clear signals from Washington, they determined on their own what was in the national interest, and, almost invariably, this proved to be the government's interest also.

A case in point occurred in the summer of 1965. It was a situation which had no military security implications but a great deal of political insecurity. Nguyen Cao Ky, the most recently installed premier in Saigon, was quoted in an article in the *London Daily Mirror* (circulation five million) as saying: "People ask me who my heroes are. I have only one —Hitler. I admire Hitler because he pulled his country together when it was in a terrible state in the early thirties. But the situation here is so desperate now that one man would not be enough. We need four or five Hitlers in Vietnam." The article appeared on page one, appropriately on July 4.

No representative of an American newspaper in England picked up the story and filed it. The American wire services missed it altogether. The *Mirror* published another story the following Sunday implying that the matter would be raised in Parliament. Still no American correspondent thought it newsworthy. The Ky-Hitler story had earlier appeared in briefer version the previous January in the *London Times,* so this was a second go-round. Although Ky had made the statement before becoming premier, the implications for the future of South Vietnam were clear. The story finally appeared in the United States press, in abbreviated form, only after inquiries from indignant readers. Editorial comment was even more sparing.

Speaking directly to the question of the "press crisis" in Vietnam was an article in the Winter 1965 issue of the *Columbia Journalism Review,* by a correspondent who had served a long tour of duty in Vietnam but who asked to remain anonymous.

> The tragedy of the "press crisis," as it came to be known, was that by and large there were good and honest men, professionally competent journalists, publicists, Army officers, and U.S. Foreign Service officers. On all sides, they were anxious and willing to see a better job done not only in reporting the war that was, but in in making a better war out of it, too.

How did one go about making "a better war" out of it? Anonymous Correspondent felt that the press bore a good deal of responsibility.

> The press has done a reasonably good job in Vietnam, with some outstanding instances of prize-winning caliber, and some others reflecting inexcusable lack of imagination and initiative. In both cases, only part of the responsibility can be laid to the Vietnamese and U.S. "press relations" policy; obviously the newsmen themselves must take as much blame as they do credit.

Castigating editors and publishers for forcing a handful of correspondents to do an impossible job of coverage in Vietnam (in the years 1961-63), the correspondent said that few real and sustained efforts had been made to "report the rock-bottom issues in this war."

> We have read again and again, for at least three years now, comments to the effect that "this is a political war, for the minds and hearts of the people." While this may not be the best way of describing it, there can be no denying that part of the counter-insurgency story in Vietnam has been left untold . . . The policy fault so

often charged to one or another ambassador, political officer, three- or four-star general, public affairs officer or embassy press attaché was almost always misplaced. If the policy were invalid, the place to have brought pressure for change was in editorial comment directed at the source of the policy, not in carping "news" stories aimed at individuals as close to the front lines—and sometimes closer— than the correspondents. Effective press relations depend not immediately upon the individuals who implement it, but on realistic policies. Good men can make the best of good policy; whether press officers or correspondents, they cannot make good policy out of bad.

Anonymous Correspondent was speaking of press policy, not the overall policy of whether the United States should or should not be in Vietnam. It was taken for granted by him, as it was by almost the entire press corps in Vietnam, that the United States had to be there. For him the answer to the problems of the press—and how to make it a "better war"—was for the editors and publishers to speak up for a more enlightened press policy, one that would enable the military and civilian officials to take the press more fully into their confidence, dispense more information, and thus enable the press to report in more informed fashion the efforts to "win the minds and the hearts of the people."

But dreadful events took place which made the implementation of such a plan impossible. In fact, the reporting of these events simply reinforced the view of most military and civilian United States officials in Vietnam that the American reporters by and large were little better than "agents of the Viet Cong." Some newspapermen felt that way too.

One was Martin Gershen, a feature-writer photographer for the *Newark Star-Ledger,* who covered the war in the summer of 1965 and then took a leave from his paper to study in Columbia University's advanced international reporting program. In the Winter 1966 issue of the *Columbia Journalism Review,* Gershen described his experiences after the burning down of the village of Cam Ne as a Viet Cong sanctuary by the United States Marines. Gershen was riding in a GI-driven vehicle with a young non-American correspondent who was working for an American publication. The young correspondent was berating the Americans for the burning incident. Gershen listened with increasing anger, then finally told him to shut up. He wrote:

I thought of the night I had spent with a Marine company surrounded in a jungle outpost by 300 Viet Cong. I remembered the next morning walking down a road with a Marine sergeant who smiled at all the villagers he met because he couldn't tell the good guys from the bad guys and he didn't want to antagonize friendly Vietnamese. I thought what a crazy, mixed up war this is, where you can't tell the front from the rear, Viet Cong from Vietnamese, civilians from soldiers. I turned to this young correspondent and very gently said: "Look, it was a Viet Cong village. How did you expect the Marines to handle that situation?" He hesitated for a moment, then said: "Why don't you Yanks get out of Vietnam?"

Gershen gave up. "If he is typical of the United States press representation in Vietnam," he wrote, knowing that he was not, "then the military people have been very kind to us."

Gershen had provided, in his description of the attitude of the Vietnamese village people and the insecurity of the American troops, an excellent supporting argument for the young correspondent's question. But when confronted with the question, he fell right in step with the military. For his correct cadence he was rewarded with a place in the *Congressional Record* of March 21, 1966. Representative George P. Miller, Democrat of California, requesting permission for publication of the article, said: "Anyone who feels confused over some of the press reports from Vietnam would do well to read this article, because it helps to explain some of the confusion—and the reason, Mr. Gershen points out, lies with a few of the members of the press themselves."

# 17. Journalism of the Absurd

The winter of '65-66 was a good winter for the hawks. The United States Air Force was bombing North Vietnam relentlessly, more and more troops were being landed in South Vietnam, and there was increasing talk of invasion of North Vietnam by land. It was a good winter also for the lecture bureaus who sought out returning reporters from Vietnam. One was Paul Dean, combat correspondent in Vietnam for four months for the *Arizona Republic,* one of the wealthiest newspapers in the country and a powerful voice in the American Southwest. In a speech before a Press Club forum in Phoenix in December 1965, Dean said that the United States was fighting in Vietnam because that country would be needed as a base of operation in a "future confrontation with Red China or Russia." *Editor & Publisher,* on December 15, 1965, quoted Dean: "The well-hammered belief that we are in Vietnam to stop the spread of Communism is only partly true. It is closer to the truth to say we are in Vietnam to foster the growth of democracy." Dean's interpretation of fostered democracy was expressed thus: "We want Vietnam as the final stepping stone across the Pacific, a chain of defense that right now goes from the United States to Honolulu, to Guam to Manila. Look ahead 10, 15, and 20 years. Sometime in the future, we are going to come eyeball to eyeball with Red China and/or Russia . . . Showdown time will come one day. And when it does, this country of ours will need Vietnam as a very sturdy springboard from which to raise a fist at whatever aggressor seems anxious to take us on."

Any non-democrat seeking a new philosophy would most likely flee in panic before Dean's brand of democracy and his mangled metaphor, but the assembled newspapermen and their guests at the Press Club did not take issue with him.

As Hanson Baldwin noted in an article in the *Reporter* magazine (February 24, 1966), the press corps in Saigon was changing. The press was "cleaning house," and it was "high time," he said, in the manner of Joseph Alsop. Until now, said Baldwin, few editors had been willing or able to allocate the space or time required for in-depth reporting on Vietnam. The escalation of the war was being accompanied by an escalation of the press corps, and the "distorted, biased and sensational reporting" was disappearing with the "younger" offenders. Baldwin wrote:

> Fortunately for the representatives of the press and the good of the country, the quality of reporting in Vietnam has improved. Mature and responsible correspondents head all the major bureaus of press associations, broadcasting companies, and major newspapers, and the worst offenders have departed. A good thing too, for the Vietnamese war is at a crisis, and what we do, how we do it, and how we report the situation will color the history of all our tomorrows. For unless the American public feels the war is worth winning and must be won, we face defeat no matter how many military victories we win.

Baldwin drew an analogy with the French in Algeria. There was no doubt, he said, that the French had won the Algerian war "in the military sense," but the French public had "wearied" of the fight and the war was lost at home. Joseph Alsop had drawn similar parallels with the French in Indo-China, and had attributed the defeat at Dienbienphu in 1954 not to the gallantry and persistence of the Vietminh army and the stupidity of the French command, but to war-weariness at home. For Baldwin and Alsop there were neither moral nor political inferences to be drawn from the presence of a colonial power in Asian countries seeking the right to determine their own future; or the presence in Southeast Asia of an imperialist power methodically building and extending a chain of bases from which to launch an offensive against China. For these journalists, the single-minded direction of the press could only be toward victory. Criticism, yes—but always with the goal of improving the war effort and hastening victory, and always with the goal of helping public opinion accept the wisdom and the virtue of the cause.

After the housecleaning, the press corps in Vietnam became much more acceptable to American officialdom. "Today there is no Halberstam group," *Time* quoted a "relieved" Pentagon official as saying (June 10, 1966). It described former *Times* correspondent David Halberstam as the man "who called the tune for the Diem baiters"—in other words, the man who paved the way for the downfall of Diem. The housecleaning so enthusiastically endorsed by Hanson Baldwin, according to *Time,* had been so thorough that it swept out in addition whatever harmony had existed. *Time* said, "Today Vietnam reporters hardly get along with each other." The temper of these hostile journalistic encampments was easily divined in comments about the Buddhists by Joe Fried, the *New York Daily News* correspondent in Vietnam. The trouble with too many reporters in Vietnam, he said, is that they insist on looking at Buddhist "politicians" as religious figures and take them at their word. To Fried, the immolations and amputations of the Buddhists to express their anguished protest against the war were "show biz," and it was a reporter's job to dig behind the "pizazz."

Another press critic of the press was the *Washington Star*'s Richard Critchfield, who felt that coverage of Vietnam in the American press had played into the hands of "Buddhism's political kingmakers." He said, "I don't think Tri Quang [a leader of the Buddhist protest against Diem and a dynamic figure in the succeeding years] would have really existed without the American press. He has fooled an awful lot of people for a long time into thinking he speaks for the Buddhists of South Vietnam. Now, I know he only pretends to speak for about one and a half million people." Critchfield failed to explain how stories about Tri Quang in the American press could influence the hundreds of thousands of non-English-speaking Buddhists into accepting him as their leader.

Richard West, correspondent of the *New Statesman* of London, commented in mid-1966 on the effectiveness of the free airlift operation for foreign journalists initiated by the Defense Department. He wrote:

> Even those [foreign reporters] who come at their newspapers' expense are likely to be overwhelmed by the help and hospitality they receive from the American propaganda machine . . . [These] journalists are bound to be grateful. Moreover, they feel a natural sympathy for the pleasant and long-suffering GIs. In consequence there is danger of their becoming simply a part of the military propaganda machine . . . Even liberal U.S. journalists cannot help but feel that their criticism is letting down the soldiers who actually run the risk. They share Kipling's dislike for "making mock of the uniforms that guard us while we sleep." Folksy or misanthropic, they find themselves sheltering under the USIS blanket.

The blanket's spread was measured more than a year later, during a visit by Vice President Humphrey with the troops in the field. Meeting with 30 United States correspondents in Chu Lai at the end of a trying day, Humphrey said: "When you speak to the American people give the benefit of the doubt to our side. I don't think that is asking too much. We're in this together." One veteran newsman, according to *Newsweek* (November 13, 1967), said: "Benefit of the doubt? What does he think we've been doing for the past six years?"

Richard West's general estimate of the press coverage by United States newsmen was not high—except for a few of the TV correspondents, the *New York Times* and "the admirable *Newsweek.*" Yet even *Newsweek,* whose coverage was far less biased than its snide competitor *Time,* had its less admirable moments. Another anonymous correspondent (the need for anonymity characterized the times) with 18 months' service in Vietnam wrote an article titled "The Life and Times of the Vietnam Press Corps" for *Ramparts* magazine (February 1967), and singled out *Newsweek*'s own correspondent Mert Perry as a case history of news management by newsmagazine.

Perry had resigned from *Time* in 1963 with Charles Mohr. After joining *Newsweek,* he had undertaken a 300-mile drive through the Mekong Delta in the summer of 1966—"an incredible feat," said the *Ramparts* article: "You can get ambushed on any three-mile stretch of road in the country." With him was John Vann, the colonel who had resigned his Army post in frustration during the Diem euphoria, then had returned to Vietnam as a civilian employee of the United States Agency for International Development (AID). Perry filed a story from Saigon comparing the journey with one he had taken a year before. His conclusion was that "the much heralded progress in the delta was arrant nonsense; that things had, rather, gone from bad to worse in almost every category." *Newsweek* gutted the story.

The main question at the time, West wrote in the *New Statesman,* was "whether America will invade North Vietnam." The war in the south was going badly, the enemy had not been "bombed to the peace table," in Washington's felicitous phrase, and United States reinforcements were proving ineffective, despite the regular rounds of "we-have-turned-the-corner" statements by a succession of United States commanders and Secretary of Defense McNamara. The invasion decision, West said, depended on CIA and other intelligence estimates. Obviously regarding such a move as insane, West wrote, "If they plan to launch this risky attack, surely the journalists should reveal the fact?" It was a desperate plea in question form, and West cited as a negative precedent the *New York Times,* "which discovered the plans for the Bay of Pigs expedition [but] was bullied by President Kennedy into keeping it quiet. The consequence was disastrous."

The word "bullied" was overly generous to the *Times.* No bullying had been required on the Bay of Pigs, and little would have been needed to obtain acquiescence if the Johnson Administration had attempted an invasion of North Vietnam. James Reston, himself a key figure in the Bay of Pigs incident, laid out the ground rules for the press on Vietnam in a *Times* column on June 29, 1966. He reported that Johnson was furious about disclosures regarding his military plans in Vietnam, "and this time he had some reason to complain." The newspapers, Reston said, had been "full of speculation" that bombing of the oil refineries and power plants around Haiphong and Hanoi was imminent, "and this goes beyond the proper bounds of public military information."

But Johnson himself was to blame for much of the speculation because of his press conference comment that "we must continue to raise the cost of aggression." In Johnsonian English, as Reston himself conceded, this meant that a decision had already been made to extend the bombing, and it was so interpreted in most newspapers. Reston wrote: "Public discussion of the wisdom or stupidity of extending the bombing to populous areas of these two cities is fair enough, but public disclosure of the timing of military plans is not." Such disclosures, said Reston, did not fall into the "need to know" category for the American public: "Some of us think it is a tragic blunder to extend the bombing to Hanoi and Haiphong, but the right of dissent does not extend to publishing of operational plans that help the enemy and increase the risk to our own fliers."

But the plan to bomb Hanoi and Haiphong was far more than "operational." It was a major policy decision with far-reaching implications. Reston seemed to be saying that newspapers had the right to oppose a plan during the discussion stage, but that once a decision had been made, it was unpatriotic and even criminal to continue to oppose it in print. The right of dissent did not extend that far. Even at the time of the speculation about the bombing of Hanoi and Haiphong, however, as Reston himself asserted, the decision to bomb had already been made. If this was accurate, then debate and dissent were rendered meaningless, and, rather than keep silent, responsible newspapers should have spoken out.

When President Kennedy told Turner Catledge, managing editor of the *Times,* that if the *Times* had printed all it had known about the Bay of Pigs invasion plan it would have prevented a tragic blunder for the United States, he may have been speaking in rueful hindsight, but that does not render his comment any less valid. Similarly, in hindsight, it has been demonstrated that the bombing of Haiphong and Hanoi not only increased the determination of the North Vietnamese to resist, but failed to alter the balance of the fighting in the South. It did, however, bring death to countless Vietnamese civilians, destruction to homes, schools, churches, and hospitals—and death or captivity for scores of American fliers. The greatest risk to the personnel of the Air Force, Reston notwithstanding, was not "the disclosure of the timing of the operational military plans" (the North Vietnamese were on a constant alert), but the execution of the plans.

If resistance was sporadic, there is no question that pressure on the press from the White House was relentless. John F. Kennedy was sensitive to the press and sought to manipulate it. Lyndon Johnson was supersensitive to criticism, and vain and insecure about his own judgment and political know-how to the point of megalomania. He had two wire service tickers in his office so that he could determine at any hour of the day or night what was being said about him anywhere in the world. The office of his press secretary was wired so that he could listen in on questions and answers at briefings. Corn and consensus were dominant in the Administration at that time; both were home-grown by the President in the White House, and they were employed to cover up an enormity of awfulness. "I'd like a Scotch and water right now," Johnson would tell a night visitor to the White House, "but I can't. I've got planes up tonight." He portrayed himself to interviewers as a lonely, troubled man who lay awake nights worrying about a letter from a mother wondering why her son had to go to Vietnam ("I wonder how I would feel if my President told me that my children had to go to South Vietnam," Johnson would tell the visitor). He'd be willing any time to trade the awesome powers invested in the Presidency for a chance to get down to the ranch on the shore of the Pedernales "to smell some bluebonnets, watch the deer and the antelope, and get some sand between my toes." Then perhaps a visit to the graves of his parents and grandparents to do "some hard prayin'."

It was not true, said the faithful columnists, that the President wanted only yes-men around him, but the *New York Daily News* could say admiringly and accurately: "Only one voice speaks publicly—for his Administration—Johnson's." In the *New York Times Magazine,* Tom Wicker wrote on May 23, 1966: "Mr. Johnson's constant overshadowing of all the men and works of his Administration results to a great extent from his real and direct involvement. Nowhere is this more true than in his conduct of foreign policy."

And the President was equally involved when his conduct was criticized. I. F. Stone, in the May 3, 1966, issue of his *Weekly,* made a significant revelation about the White House literary tastes. Stone had reviewed the books on the Vietnam war by David Halberstam and Malcolm Browne for the *New York Review of Books.* It was an eminently fair report, spiced with some pungent Stone comments about United States foreign policy. After the article had been published, the editors of the *New York Review* received a telephone call from White House assistant Richard Goodwin, a holdover from the Kennedy Administration, taking issue with Stone's review. Why not write a letter, suggested the editors. That would be impractical, Goodwin answered—it would have to be cleared by too many hands. Stone was a fine fellow, he added, but . . . next time there were books on Vietnam, why not give them out for review, say, to Joseph Alsop?

Periodically the John Wayne-Walter Mitty combination directing the world from the White House became too much for some of the Washington press corps, and periodically the yellow rose of Texas lost its bloom. The image of "the President of all the people" yielded to a more realistic portrait of a restless, irascible man pacing the White House corridors or the Rose Garden with a pack of panting reporters at his heels; whipping Congress into giving him a vote of confidence when none was needed; tongue-lashing his press secretary because a commencement speech he had delivered appeared on page two of the *Washington Post* rather than page one; barging into a television station at prime time (and at considerable cost to the network) to deliver an incredible speech on United States motives for intervening in the Dominican Republic; upsetting the United Nations commemorative ceremony (and 26 other speeches) by shifting his appearance there by 24 hours without notice; engaging in a six-hour tirade with his assistants because James Reston of the *Times* had suggested in advance the contents of his speech at the United Nations, prompting the President out of perversity to change the speech into a set of meaningless clichés.

Then there would be a dramatic move by the White House: A sharp increase in troop strength in Vietnam, extension of the bombing, a trip to Hawaii to meet with the incumbent premier of Saigon, or to Guam, or Punta del Este—and miraculously the mood of the press changed again. Once more there was re-created the all-embracing father figure presiding at the head of the national barbecue table; the tall gaunt man with a figurative shawl drawn across his shoulders against the night chill, pacing the dark recesses of the White House, tormented by a decision to make: To bomb or not to bomb.

To round out the image for the afternoon editions, Johnson would emerge in the morning light for an "emergency" session with Congressional leaders and would read aloud a lengthy excerpt from a Bruce Catton civil war history, *Never Call Retreat* (Doubleday, 1965). "The gist of the passage," said the *New York Times,* "was that Abraham Lincoln, faced with divided counsel, listened to everybody, then did what he thought best." Since Johnson was a notorious non-reader, the assumption was that the passage had been selected for him. Since he was also a notorious non-listener, the reading of the passage was as synthetic as the image of a deeply tormented President. Yet the press solemnly went through these rituals and just as solemnly prepared the script for a scenario which might well be titled: "The Loneliness of the Long-Distance Bomber."

By July 1966, there were 360 accredited newsmen in Vietnam, although fewer than one-third actually were correspondents. The rest were technicians and interpreters. In the preceding six months, 1,100 persons had been accredited by the United States command, the majority of them "the tourist trade" (as the regular correspondents called them): editors, publishers, and columnists on two-week junkets. The vast majority of the news reports filed to the United States concerned the battlefield and the troops (who were reported doing splendidly); very little coverage was given to internal politics. For the most part, the press corps was subscribing to the Secretary McNamara light-at-the-end-of-the-tunnel view of the war. But continuing progress by the National Liberation Front armies made it clear that the United States troops were doing poorly, and that the tunnel remained dark. By mid-1967 *Newsweek* was taking a more churlish view of events in Vietnam and the distorted picture being presented to the American public. In its July 10, 1967, issue it quoted Dr. Richard Mann, a University of Michigan social psychologist: "Newspapers are still playing heroes while the great bulk of soldiers on TV are just poor, dirty, muddy, tired people getting shot at from all directions." Most editors, *Newsweek* said, rely on wire service "spot news and supplement it with locally written editorials, almost always hawkish, or interpretive pieces stuffed with bland platitudes." It concluded:

> The daily, even hourly gushings forth of information in the American press are titanic, but the public is in danger of being surfeited, of walking along, like some teeny-bopper with her radio, in a constant cloud of unheard noise. Who is to blame? Not censorship, for there is less of that in Vietnam than in any other war the United States has fought in modern times. Undoubtedly the press itself is guilty of scanting stories it finds difficult to tell . . . Undoubtedly the Administration is to blame also, for repeated self-delusion, if not necessarily deliberate deceit. But most of all, perhaps, the public is to blame for seeking a refuge from complexity and for contenting itself with mass-circulation primers when advanced texts are available.

Here again all the implicated parties are charged with less culpability than the conveniently resurrected Boobus Americanus. Gentle reprimands for the press and government, but for "the public" a harsh scolding for failing to graduate from the comic-strip kindergarten. *Newsweek* offered no guideposts to lead a nation of teeny-boppers out of the maze of mass-circulation coverage, out of the complex web of deceit and duplicity, to the advanced texts where it would find clarity. To be sure, the advanced texts were available, increasingly in book form, in magazine articles by such historians of Vietnam as Bernard Fall and in the radical press. But the mass-circulation media rarely cited these sources or credited them with authority when they did. *Newsweek*'s sermon was transparent. The truly amazing phenomenon was that so many Americans did find their way out of the journalistic wilderness to the plains of truth. When they did, they almost invariably joined the active opposition to the war in Vietnam.

*Newsweek* on November 13, 1967, could quote its own correspondent, Mert Perry, as saying: "The South Vietnamese army, in short, is sick. Like the society which created it, it is riddled with factionalism, nepotism, corruption, inefficiency, incompetence and cowardice." Yet only two weeks later *Newsweek*'s foreign editor Robert Christopher agonized for three pages over the question "Why Are We in Vietnam?"—an agony derived from weeks of discussion with officials and experts most responsible for shaping United States policy for Vietnam, and with some critics of Washington's policies. The statement that had impressed him most, said Christopher, was one by Professor John K. Fairbank of Harvard, an authority on Asia: "When you make a mistake before history, you have to pay for it." Christopher concluded:

> But we *are* there. And, mistaken or not, this war, like all wars, must be paid for. The question is not how can we finish the war off without great cost; it is how we can finish it off at the least cost. And, as of now, it seems to me that the cost of fighting the war is far smaller than the long-range costs we would incur by retreat.

Christopher's essay hardly qualified for inclusion among the advanced texts on Vietnam. His conclusions belonged to the journalism of the absurd. What Fairbank was saying was that the United States ought to admit a mistake and then proceed to face up to it—at whatever cost. The alternative was to plow ahead with continuing mass murder of Americans as well as Vietnamese. The cost of maintaining a mistaken policy could not be limited, despite Christopher's tight-budget mind.

This point was made sharply in a comment (*Columbia University Forum,* Spring 1967) by Tran Van Dinh, a former Ambassador to the United States from South Vietnam and, in 1967, the Washington bureau chief of the English-language *Saigon Post.* Dinh's comment was made in response to the article by Neil Sheehan in the *New York Times Magazine* (see Chapter 15), but it applied precisely to Christopher also:

> Unfortunately [this] attitude [that the war must go on to victory] is prevalent not only among the American correspondents in Vietnam but also among the public in this country and even academics whom I happened to meet in my lectures in prac-

tically every state of the United States. In the long run, one of the greatest dangers this country will face as a product of the unnecessary and cruel war in Vietnam is a combination of cynicism and a blind acceptance of "absurdity." The Administration contributed a great deal to it by incredibly irrelevant statements.

The press sustained and reinforced the acceptance of absurdity by equating it with patriotism. It was truly a lunatic piece that was being presented to the American public; but the most lunatic fact of all was that the presentation was being stage-managed by seemingly sane men in government and journalism.

Absurdity had a tendency to spill over borders. Reports from Saigon of National Liberation Front "sanctuaries" in Cambodia increased in frequency and intensity whenever there was a serious United States setback in ground fighting near the Cambodian border. Often the sanctuary story was employed to explain a defeat: the NLF forces, using hit-and-run tactics, would strike and then slip back into camps across the border in Cambodia, while United States forces, honoring the boundaries of a neutral nation, were powerless to give pursuit.

But the United States-South Vietnamese command in fact showed far less reticence. Reports persisted of bombing attacks on Cambodian villages, occupation of towns for as long as a week at a time, strafings and napalm attacks, with the victims presented to the press by Cambodian officials. Invariably there were denials by the United States command. But in July 1969, on the eve of the resumption of diplomatic relations with Cambodia (they had been broken off in May 1965 by Cambodia's Prince Sihanouk because of the border violations), Washington conceded that the United States forces had indeed been guilty as charged.

In November 1967, the United States forces suffered a severe defeat at Loc Ninh, just across the Cambodian border in South Vietnam, and a sanctuary story blossomed anew. This time American correspondents were directly involved. The sensational discovery of a "Vietcong camp" in Cambodia by a group of American correspondents was reported on November 21 in an AP dispatch. In the group were George McArthur and Horst Faas (Pulitzer Prize photographer) of the AP, and Ray Herndon of UPI—all veterans of Vietnam—who agreed that the camp was "unmistakably Vietcong." The dispatch said:

Evidence found there included military records written in Vietnamese and North Vietnamese medical supplies. Dated scraps of paper indicated that the camp had been used over a period of several months dating back to last February.

By coincidence, the United States forces during the first two months of the dry season in the fall and winter of 1967-68 had by their own admission suffered unusually heavy casualties in engagements near the Cambodian border, and the defeats still rankled in the Pentagon. Immediately after the AP story appeared, former President Eisenhower and General Omar Bradley, a hero of World War II, issued statements in support of a House Armed Services subcommittee's call for an invasion of Cambodia.

Photographs of bamboo and thatch huts appeared in the press, and a jungle log road with a smiling Horst Faas walking toward the camera. The photographs recalled William Randolph Hearst's famous cable to Frederic Remington in Cuba, when the artist had asked to be relieved of his assignment just before the outbreak of the Spanish-American War: "Please remain. You furnish the pictures and I'll furnish the war."

McArthur elaborated on the story of the camp's discovery in the November 25, 1967, issue of *Editor & Publisher*. Entry into Cambodia by American newsmen had been severely restricted by Sihanouk because of what he considered fabrications about the sanctuaries. But when Jacqueline Kennedy, the President's widow, announced a visit to Cambodia for November, restrictions were eased and several Americans were allowed in on special visas. McArthur said he and Faas had hoped to be allowed to visit the border areas to check on the "Vietcong infiltration" reports, although similar inspections by Western newsmen over a two-year period had turned up no evidence. To their surprise, permission was granted to 50 Western newsmen and photographers to see for themselves. The trip was grueling, but cooperation on the Cambodian side was first rate. At a frontier post, a Cambodian army major told the correspondents that there had been occasional violations, but they were small and local, and the National Liberation Front forces always withdrew when asked to. "He was more concerned," McArthur wrote, "by the violations of American planes and offered to show us a big bomb crater that he had turned into a fish pond." McArthur did not say whether the offer had been accepted.

The search was fruitless, so the correspondents returned to Phnom Penh, "wondering what to do next." A search to the north where the border runs through deep jungle would be useless, McArthur said, because "all of us had been long in Vietnam and knew that the likelihood of finding anything in the jungle was remote unless you knew precisely where you were going."

But two days later precision was miraculously provided in a cable "from Saigon" pinpointing a spot just inside the border—a five-hour drive from Phnom Penh. With government permission McArthur, Faas, and Herndon set forth on a new expedition, accompanied near the precision point by a Cambodian security platoon with a "Russian-made 20-millimeter cannon on hand." McArthur wrote in *Editor & Publisher:*

> When one of the trails suddenly opened on a campsite, the Cambodians were astonished. It was our feeling that they genuinely did not know the camp was there. To all of us it was unmistakably a Vietcong campsite. Though the local officers explained it variously as a logging camp or a secret Cambodian base, such efforts were hollow. The evidence we found, Vietnamese papers, bits of equipment, medical supplies, simply clinched for us what we already knew.

The *Editor & Publisher* story raised several questions: How was it possible for Saigon to pinpoint this camp in the heart of the jungle? If Saigon had indeed discovered a Vietcong camp, why had the United States forces or the South Vietnamese not attacked it (they had shown no reluctance previously in crossing the border), or informed the Cambodian government or the International Control Commission set up by the Geneva agreement to police the settlement terms for Indo-China? Why had Saigon bypassed all these alternatives and instead sent a cable to an American newsman fortuitously in Cambodia along with several dozen additional Western newspapermen?

Seeking an answer to these questions, I sent the *Editor & Publisher* article to Wilfred Burchett in Phnom Penh (he had been on assignment in Europe during the incident) expressing my suspicions about the whole affair. He replied:

> It does not require an over-suspicious mind to suspect that one of the many "Special Forces" commando teams that [General] Westmoreland has planted along the frontier areas, and which are directly controlled by the CIA, infiltrated across the border, planted the documents, and Saigon then obligingly sent the cable to Herndon of UPI in Phnom Penh.
>
> The "camp" itself consisted of a few bamboo and thatch huts, similar to the temporary structures that timber-getters set up everywhere in the Cambodian forests. For anyone who knows the extraordinary security measures taken by the Vietnamese, the idea of "military records" and "dated scraps of paper" left behind is absolutely inconceivable. They even make sure there is not a shred of toilet paper left when they vacate a camp.
>
> That such things [the CIA infiltration] could easily happen is proven by the fact that a few months earlier, in the same general area, there had been a brush between Cambodian frontier militia and the "Special Forces" commandos dressed in the black peasant garb of "Vietcong" self-defense guerrillas. One of the commandos was killed, another wounded and captured, revealing at his trial that his band had orders to carry out sabotage and assassinations, to leave traces of "Vietcong" activity and, in the event of capture, to pretend they were "Vietcong" guerrillas. This was revealed at the time of the trial of the saboteur, published in the Cambodian press, but not published in the West.

As old hands in Vietnam, McArthur and his colleagues surely were as aware as Burchett of the practices of Vietnamese guerrillas in breaking camp. They knew also that the huts they found were common all over the frontier area where timber gatherers worked. And surely they are as skeptical of news sources as any correspondents in the world. Yet they accepted the cable from Saigon without question and, like a pack of beagles, went right to the spot.

My conclusion is that they were at best unwitting dupes of a clumsy plan to whip up sentiment in the United States for an invasion of Cambodia; at worst, they were willing accomplices in the shameful plan. It was Burchett's reasonable surmise that McArthur wrote the *Editor & Publisher* article to "quieten the doubts of a few of his colleagues." For years the border areas had been open to correspondents of the *New York Times,* the *Washington Post,* and others who sought evidence of "Ho Chi Minh" or "Sihanouk" trails, supply bases, routes, and sanctuaries, but nothing had been found. Military attachés of various embassies (including the Australians, who had troops in South Vietnam) were given similar opportunities to investigate, and the unanimous opinion, according to Burchett, was the "there are no such bases, sanctuaries, or supply routes."

What emerged most clearly from the incident was that, as the year 1968 began, the United States-Saigon forces were taking a bad beating from the National Liberation Front armies, and were desperately seeking to pin the blame for the defeats on something other than themselves. In this effort, a group of American newspapermen were used to deceive the public.

There was less deception in private correspondence. The difference between public and private writing about Vietnam was sharply apparent to anyone who had access to both. Reportage within the journalistic family often was revealing, as manifested by the report of Bernard Weinraub in the January 1968 issue of *Times Talk,* the *New York Times*'s house organ. Weinraub wrote:

> It's a bizarre war. There are too many confusions, too many half-truths and distortions and certainly too many laughs. You shouldn't laugh, you know you shouldn't, but then you sit at night in [the restaurants] and you laugh about the thieving province chief in I Corps or the blundering Vietnamese general in the delta or the American you interviewed in the morning whose sole job was merchandising and packaging and selling progress.

Weinraub told of the overlapping military and civilian functionaries in the JUSPAO (Joint United States Public Affairs Office) building, "whose duties are probably as elusive to them as they are to me":

To a number of these officers, the war is something one only reads about each Thursday, when *Time* and *Newsweek* finally arrive. Their link to—and knowledge of—the war is minimal. One lieutenant colonel in JUSPAO recently waved his copy of *Newsweek* to a visitor and asked: "What is this 'N.L.F.' that *Newsweek* is always writing about?"

In some cases there is also a rather brutal and remarkable insensitivity to death. At a Wednesday briefing a few months ago—one of those "deep background" sessions—a brigadier general said with a smile:

"Well, I'm happy to say that the Army's casualties finally caught up with the Marines last week."

There was a gasp. A civilian U.S. mission officer, sitting next to the general, turned and said incredulously: "You don't mean you're *happy*."

The general was adamant. "Well, the Army should be doing their job too," he said.

Jim Pringle, the bureau chief of Reuters, turned to me and whispered: "My God, this is straight out of *Catch-22*."

It was indeed. But neither the gasp nor the whisper was ever recorded in the pages of the *Times* or, to my knowledge, in any other daily newspaper at the time of the incident. Weinraub's story was quoted in a column by Nat Hentoff in the *Village Voice,* a New York weekly whose investigative reporting is generally far superior to that of the New York dailies.

Battle fatigue was increasingly in evidence among United States officials in both Saigon and Washington in 1968, and there were signs of shell-shock after the Tet (Vietnamese New Year) offensive by the NLF against Saigon and several other cities. The official attack on the press corps took an interesting turn. No longer were the "young Turks" to blame for the facts that seeped out of Vietnam contradicting the official versions of progress. Now it was the "old hands" who were "too close to the story" and had been "around too long." Wasn't it time, officials asked publicly in Saigon and Washington, for some new faces on the scene to replace the tired old journalistic war horses who were beginning to grumble too much? Why not put Old Faithful out to pasture—he just couldn't run with the prevailing propaganda winds any more.

In Washington battle fatigue was very much in evidence at the State Department. At a background briefing in February 1968 for newspapermen, a reporter asked an "unnamed spokesman" whether the surprise aspect of the NLF Tet offensive did not demonstrate a collapse of United States intelligence. The spokesman, who was identified a few days after the briefing by the uninvited *Wall Street Journal* as Secretary Rusk, exploded: "There gets to be a point when the question is, whose side are you on? I'm the Secretary of State, and I'm on our side." Asked if he was impugning the loyalty of journalists by this remark, Rusk became even more apoplectic:

> None of your papers or your broadcasting apparatuses are worth a damn unless the United States succeeds. They are trivial compared to that question. So I don't know why, to win a Pulitzer Prize, people have to go probing for things one can bitch about when there are 2,000 stories on the same day about things that are more constructive in character.

The question the reporter might have asked was not whether the newspapermen's loyalty was being impugned, but what constituted loyalty. Was it subservience to a group of men, for the most part appointed, who comprised the Executive branch of government and regarded themselves as "the country"; or was it a constant watchfulness to prevent men in office from making grievous mistakes for which the public would have to pay?

Not one of the newspapermen present at the briefing reported the hysterical outburst by an obviously distraught Secretary of State. It was only after the *Wall Street Journal* had published the story that some other papers followed. But there was no editorial suggestion anywhere that the Secretary of State, rather than the faithful old journalistic plugs, be put out to pasture as a casualty of war.

# 18. Two Men of the Times

James Brown was raised as a Quaker and for all his growing years regarded himself as a pacifist. For the most part, he still does. But the rise of fascism concerned him deeply, and a few days after Pearl Harbor in 1941 he enlisted in the Marines and served through World War II. After the war, he became a newspaperman—an able and conscientious one. He joined an Army reserve unit the day President Truman sent troops into Korea in June 1950. He was moved to take this step by his concern for the right of small countries to determine their own future, and it is my opinion that if his decision was not soundly based, nevertheless he was not alone in his uninformed indignation about the origins of the war in Korea.

As a newspaperman, his aim was to join the staff of the *Providence Journal,* a newspaper founded in 1829, which subsequently added to itself the *Providence Bulletin* and the *Sunday Journal.* The *Journal* has for years been validly regarded as one of the nation's better morning newspapers, and the *Journal-Bulletin* (morning and evening) combination is frequently cited as proving the desirability of one strong and prosperous journalistic enterprise in a large metropolitan area, rather than several weaker ones. Financial security and internal strength, the argument goes, permit greater independence and a bulwark against pressures which less stable papers cannot withstand.

Credit for the *Journal*'s reputation—its breadth of news coverage and generally liberal editorial policy were remarkable in parochial Rhode Island—rested with Sevellon Brown, no relation, whose family controlled the *Journal* for decades. He was succeeded as publisher in 1954 by John C. A. Watkins, a member of a military family, who nonetheless con-

246

tinued the liberal tradition. Watkins became president of the publishing company in 1961, while retaining his title as publisher. The atmosphere at the *Journal* in the early 60s seemed relaxed and cordial. "We have a tremendous freedom here," said an editorial writer. "Mr. Watkins stays away from our department almost completely."

That word, "almost," figured prominently in the saga of James Brown, who achieved his ambition and became an editorial writer for the *Journal* in 1962. He arrived fresh from Calcutta, where he had served for two years with the United States Information Agency—not out of devotion to the ideals of the USIA, but because he wanted to see some of the world. He was persuaded that most editorial writing reflected the slack backsides of its authors.

For four and a half years, Brown lived "an editorial writer's dream," as he phrased it. The *Journal*'s facilities and freedom, he said, were practically unmatched in the American press. These were the years of ever-increasing American involvement in Vietnam, and Brown's interest in Vietnam—which he had visited—kept pace with the growth of American intervention. He became convinced that the Gulf of Tonkin incident of August 1964 had been "deliberately provoked by somebody on our side," and that "blatant falsehoods had been propagated" to support the course of United States policy at home.

Through most of 1966, the editorial page of the *Providence Journal* generally reflected Brown's concern—until September 20, when an editorial written by Brown suggesting a moral and even Christian content to the Chinese cultural revolution was suppressed by the publisher. Brown felt that the reason for the action was not China but Vietnam, and his reasoning proved correct when shortly thereafter a directive came down from the publisher's office reversing the paper's stand on Vietnam: no more editorial criticism of the Saigon government or the United States involvement. Brown was forbidden to write on Vietnam, although he was free to comment on all other subjects, including foreign affairs. He let it be known immediately that if he could not express himself freely on Vietnam, he would leave the paper.

There were people in the upper echelons of the *Journal* who, if they did not agree with Brown's views, were sufficiently worried about the *Journal*'s reputation to seek a compromise, and one was worked out: Brown would continue to write editorials on foreign affairs—except on Vietnam. He was, in addition, to have a weekly column of his own, entitled "One Man's Opinion," which would be just that—a signed expression of his own views—including Vietnam—which need not agree with the *Journal*'s policy.

Brown's first column appeared on January 2, 1967, and began the new year explosively. It quoted at length from a letter from two friends of Brown, a Quaker missionary couple serving in Vietnam, which told of the "numb suffering" of the Vietnamese. Brown wrote: "I wonder if it is we Americans here at home who are numb—morally numb—to be able to go on living our soft, contented lives while American men and materiel systematically destroy a tiny nation and its people."

Publisher Watkins reacted immediately. In the same issue on the same page he sharply criticized Brown in a signed editorial as presenting a one-sided discussion of the war, avoiding "any mention of the deliberate terror campaign that has been conducted by the Vietcong against the civilian population in South Vietnam for years. . . ." To Brown's surprise, his column was allowed to continue, and he kept returning to the subject of Vietnam "because to my mind this foolish little war" had become the overriding issue and menace of the day. There were frequent hints from his immediate superior and colleagues that the publisher was becoming increasingly disturbed about "One Man's Opinion," so why not cease and desist about Vietnam for a while? Brown rejected the advice.

On April 17, 1967, his column defended Reverend Martin Luther King, Jr.'s significant statement opposing the war in Vietnam, and charged King's critics with failure "to perceive the moral threat that ties this man and these causes [the Vietnam war and civil rights] inescapably together." On April 21, Brown was told by the editor of the editorial page that his column was being dropped on orders from the publisher. Ironically, the *New York Times,* in its April 23 Sunday edition, reprinted the Brown column about King in its "Other Opinions" corner in the News of the Week Review.

Watkins had told an *Editor & Publisher* interviewer in June 1963 that none of the stockholders or directors of the *Journal-Bulletin* had ever tried to dictate policy or manage news. The owners and the professional managers had agreed that "a newspaper's first responsibility is to its readers. While sometimes the owners and directors disagree with the policies the newspapers adopt, they do not interfere." But in 1967, one man's opinion proved indigestible for Watkins. He said that he thought Brown had demonstrated "intellectual arrogance" and had expressed "shrill, dogmatic" opinions and "intolerance and contempt" for opposite views. The *Journal's* policy, Watkins said, was to present "reasoned argument" on both sides of a question.

Brown had not been consulted before his column was dropped, and he informed the editor of the editorial page that he would have to leave the *Journal.* "I'm an abrasive, 'ornery' character," he said. "I feel deeply about things. If an editorial is going to be of service, it must have passion . . . Journalism needs more material written by 'ornery' characters with a sense of deep conviction."

There was conviction, but no passion, in the comment of the newspaper's executive editor, Michael J. Ogden, after the incident; but even the conviction seemed borrowed from the publisher. Watkins, according to Ogden, could not accept the Brown column about King and his non-understanding critics because of "stylistic differences." In an interview with the Brown University *Daily Herald* on May 2, 1967, Ogden said: "It seemed like the only person who understood was Jim Brown. Brown's column was too shrill and dogmatic . . . The publisher's position is that he welcomes cogent and reasoned arguments, not arguments expressed in such a highly emotional manner." Ogden insisted that there had been no change in the *Journal*'s position on Vietnam, although he surely knew of the publisher's edict against editorial criticism of United States policy in Vietnam. And he could hardly have been unaware of the shrill and dogmatic opinions expressed by a fellow columnist of Brown in the pages of the *Journal*—William F. Buckley, Jr. But Buckley's dogma had the virtue of favoring United States policy.

In Brown's view, the difference was not at all stylistic. Speaking at a conference of Eastern college editors at Brown University in Providence on April 30, 1967, he said:

I believe the difference which has arisen between me and the publisher of the *Journal* is symptomatic of a larger problem that afflicts most—if not all—American newspapers today. This is the problem of preserving a vigorous, provocative forum of discussion, and if need be, dissent on the editorial pages of newspapers which are increasingly dominated by business-oriented corporate boards enjoying monopoly status in their local communities.

The issue that concerned him, Brown said, was the right of conscientious editorial writers to express their views, right or wrong, on the editorial pages. In the old days of free-wheeling personal journalism, he said, a man of his convictions could gather enough money to start his own newspaper and join the debate generated by a wide range of provocative editorial opinion. Technology had changed all that: "The modern newspaper is big business, run by a corporate board enjoying monopoly status in most cities. Editorial policy in most instances is laid down by a board of directors through the publisher. It is based on consensus—usually keyed to the lowest possible denominator." He continued:

I question whether the very considerable talents and drives that are required to rise to the top of the corporate heap are compatible with the qualities required to make a good editorial writer: namely, study, reflection, a passionate concern for human problems, and a disposition to question accepted values of the community. I think a free society requires such editorial writers. I believe therefore that if the American editorial page is to continue to perform effectively in its traditional role as gadfly to government and the community, ways must be found to insulate editors from the prejudices of boards of directors and their agents. To preserve freedom of the press in a meaningful sense, I believe editors must achieve a status similar to that accorded to professors in the good colleges and universities; that is, complete freedom for inquiry and expression.

Firm in its support of the government's position on Vietnam, the *Journal,* in an editorial on April 26, explained its position vis-à-vis Brown. "The test of the strength of a free society," it said, "is its capacity to undertake debate and accept dissent." Readers of the *Journal* agreed with the sense if not the hypocrisy of the editorial, and a torrent of letters poured into the *Journal*'s offices, overwhelmingly dissenting from the newspaper's position on Brown. The letters displayed a perceptive understanding of the First Amendment, of monopoly journalism, and the relationship between the corporations and corporate journalism. Scores of faculty members of Brown University also petitioned the *Journal* to restore Brown's column. The publisher in fact did offer to resume the column, but on terms which Brown found "not acceptable in light of recent experience." He resigned from the *Journal* in May 1967 and accepted an offer to join the *New York Times* as a member of the editorial board.

I had followed what I believed to be (correctly, as it turned out) Brown's editorials on Vietnam in the *Times,* and his signed special editorial page articles on the Middle East. His views were compassionate, intelligent, and clearly stated, but almost always halting at a point beyond which I had hoped he would venture. He had been generous in correspondence and in providing me with material on the *Journal* affair, but we had never met in person. I called him for an interview and went to see him in May 1969, two years after he had left the *Journal.*

The tenth floor of the *Times,* where the editorial board has its offices encircling the gothic, paneled reference library, has a cathedral quality which seems to discourage any notion of heresy. But Brown himself was warm and secular. While our conversation was wide-ranging, I was mainly curious to determine the effect of two years at the *Times* on Brown's person and politics. So that we would know where we stood, I outlined for him my strong opposition to the war from a radical point of view, my criticism of the general coverage of the news from Vietnam, and the lack of journalistic criticism of American policy on Vietnam.

The reporters in Vietnam, he said, were "bucking city hall," but that was not new. The fault of the press, he felt, was the fault of American life: "We've always had a fairly superficial approach. We are not trained to ask the basic questions. We have not equipped ourselves to challenge a changing world." There had been too much of a generalized approach to reporting, he said. Perhaps the publishers prefer it this way, I suggested. Perhaps they would rather avoid investigative and analytical reporting, so that the public would not become conscious of the basic aims of United States foreign policy. No, he said, he did not see "a conspiracy" (I had not suggested one) on the part of the publishers to maintain this generalized approach: "They are as much the victims of the American approach as the rest of the country."

Yet a few moments later, recalling his experience at the *Providence Journal,* he seemed to classify the publishers more as victimizers than victims. At the time of his last trouble in Providence in 1967, he said, publishers in general were becoming worried and losing confidence in the ability of the United States to win the war. They were becoming panicky, and that accounted for the tough approach by the *Journal*'s publisher to his writing. As though to underscore this point, he noted that earlier in the war, when he had lectured in the Providence area, he had encountered considerable hostility among general audiences (college audiences were always more receptive); but in the year before his departure from Providence, the general audiences had been more receptive to his criticism of the war.

Despite his experience in Providence, he was generous in his estimate of the *Journal* and its willingness to publish the opinion of columnists and letter-writers opposing the newspaper's position. He cited the dozens of published letters defending his position and said that newspapers in general were not credited sufficiently for publishing opposing views. I agreed that the *Journal* had been generous in publishing the letters about his case, but said that newspapers should not receive special commendation for permitting freedom of expression. As for the columnists, I said, taking the *Providence Journal* as an example, they ran a limited gamut from William Buckley on the far right to the liberal Max Lerner. He would not classify Lerner as a liberal, Brown said. I replied that this reinforced my point—although several columnists offered at least some criticism of government policy, not one opposed the basic policy. Although Buckley and the far right were represented in many newspapers, not one commercial newspaper offered a radical view. What would happen if a radical journalist of real talent offered such a column for publication? Brown agreed it would be rejected.

The conversation was easy in the large bright room, one of several occupied by individual editorial writers when they were not meeting with the editor of the editorial page to discuss assignments. After these preliminaries, I asked Brown the question most pertinent to my visit: Did he feel any restrictions in his work at the *Times*? He paused before answering that the very fact of the responsibility and power of the *Times* in itself sets restrictions. "We at the *Times* have a grave responsibility to think things through and not jump at conclusions," he said. "What we write has a tremendous influence. I know what the *Times* means abroad."

He related a visit, after he had joined the *Times,* to the United Nations press accreditation officer who told him the *Times* was the "bible" to most delegates—an opinion he was to hear repeated in the delegates' lounge. Reflecting on these comments, he said that just sitting where he was at the *Times* prompted such a sense of "awesome responsibility" that it must inevitably constrain him—and anyone in his position—to be as responsible as he could. He spoke with respect of John B. Oakes, the editor of the editorial page, who has been credited with taking the page out of the dull gray preserves in which it had glowered for decades.

What would happen, I asked, if Brown wrote an editorial demanding that the United States get out of Vietnam immediately? He said he would not be inclined to write such an editorial, but the ultimate decision on publication would be the editor's. There were people on the editorial board, he added, who disagreed vehemently with United States policy in Vietnam—but they did not write editorials on Vietnam.

We turned then to the general support, in varying degrees, of United States policy by editors and publishers. Why, I asked, did he think there was such an absence of questioning on their part? This, he said, was a product of the Stalin era which had produced a "defensive reaction." A whole generation of Americans, he said, had gone through that period and through the euphoria after World War II. Then came Korea, "which rallied us around the flag." In the light of the experience with Hitler and then with Stalin, he said, "you didn't ask questions." But now there was more searching, "and we have to confront the problems that the young people are facing."

On that note the interview ended, as cordially as it had begun, and I began to sort out my impressions. Was I disappointed in Brown's position? Not really. I accepted the fact (and Brown confirmed it) that the editors of the *Times* had put him through a long questioning period and had carefully checked his references before he was hired. Was Brown deluding himself that he had full freedom? No, he was not. He was, as he said, a product of his time and his training. In essence he was an idealist who believed in the American dream, and in the American system as the best of all possible systems, with all its faults and despite a nightmare like Vietnam. Within this framework he was free to write as he believed. With the experience of his generation—the genuine threat of fascism and the manufactured threat of Communism—a defensive position was a natural one. "My own feeling," he said, "is that no one should be sitting in his editorial office without a doctorate in a particular field, or disciplined training or background."

For truly free and responsible journalists, however, the doctoral qualifications are not decisive—there are Kissingers as well as Einsteins. The decisive factor is a willingness to move out of the restricted areas of a patriotism imposed by the needs of United States policy, and to examine publicly the effect of this policy on the future of the United States and the world.

The restrictions which Brown acknowledged are self-imposed by his acceptance of the American philosophy and superimposed by the institutional awesomeness of the *New York Times*. There was no contradiction in Brown's departure from the *Journal* and his arrival at the *Times*. On each newspaper he opposed the nature of United States involvement in Vietnam on moral and practical grounds. His concern for the people of Vietnam has remained passionate and unfeigned. He pressed his point to the limit at the *Journal,* and when that limit proved unbreachable, he moved on. The *Times* may permit greater flexibility, but it sets its limits also. While there is, in the *Times*'s editorial position, moral and practical opposition to many aspects of United States policy in Vietnam, there is agreement on the need for continuing American presence there as part of the American responsibility for the preservation of democracy. Here Brown has no conflict of conscience with the *Times*. To ask him to adopt a more radical position would be to ask him to leave the *Times*. Since he is not so inclined, there is no decision to make— either for Brown, or for the *Times*.

On the day the *Providence Journal* announced the cancellation of James Brown's column, a story appeared in the nation's newspapers about the denial of a Pulitzer Prize to Harrison Salisbury, an assistant managing editor of the *New York Times,* for international reporting— specifically for his reportage as the first correspondent of a major United States newspaper permitted into North Vietnam.

The Pulitzer jury, composed of newspaper editors, had voted 4 to 1 to give the award to Salisbury for his dispatches over a two-week period from December 23, 1966, to January 7, 1967. But the Advisory Board of the Pulitzer Prizes, made up of publishers and editors and the president of Columbia University, had, in an almost unprecedented decision, overruled the jury and given the prize to a reporter for the *Christian Science Monitor,* R. John Hughes, for his reports of the massive anti-Communist purge in Indonesia following the takeover by a right-wing government. The *St. Louis Post-Dispatch,* which first disclosed the behind-the-scenes dissension over the award to Salisbury, commented: "There was speculation, after the formal meeting of the board, that some members were influenced by ideological considerations rather than journalistic achievement, perhaps by the stand their respective papers had taken in favor of President Johnson's policy on the Vietnam war." Since Joseph Pulitzer, Jr., publisher of the *Post-Dispatch,* was a member of the board, it was clear that the use of the word "speculation" was a journalistic device to lend a measure of decorum to the proceedings.

A perceptive reader of the *Providence Journal* interpreted the *Post-Dispatch* comment thus: "In other words, it isn't safe to disagree with your publisher—James Brown's fate suggests that the fears of the newspapermen on the Pulitzer Prize Advisory Board were well founded. Of course the *Journal-Bulletin* 'welcomes columnists whose views differ from its own'; it's just that the views shouldn't be very different, apparently." The reaction of much of the nation's press in the Salisbury affair, particularly the Washington press corps and some of Salisbury's own colleagues at the *Times,* indicated a considerable sympathy with the Pulitzer board's fears. Indeed, the intemperance of the reaction was almost unparalleled.

Salisbury was a veteran correspondent, one of the first-ranking *Times* men, who had served for several years in the Soviet Union and had managed to get permission to write from Rumania, Bulgaria, and Mongolia when many others had failed. For more than a year he had sought a visa for North Vietnam without success. On December 14, 1966, a cable arrived at the *Times* office in New York informing Salisbury that a visa was awaiting him in Paris; he could fly into Hanoi on the International Control Commission plane.

The permission came at a time when Hanoi was charging that residential sections of the city had been bombed by United States planes. Washington offered ambiguous responses, saying first that there had been no change in the policy of restricting the bombing to military targets; then rejecting the charge that Hanoi had been bombed on the days alleged (December 13 and 14); and finally, five days later, saying that civilian areas may have been struck by accident. This last statement was issued the day before Salisbury arrived in Hanoi. Salisbury's first dispatch was published in the *Times* on December 25, without advance publicity. It said:

Contrary to the impression given by United States communiqués, on-the-spot inspection indicates that American bombing has been inflicting considerable civilian casualties in Hanoi and its environs for some time past. . . . It is fair to say that, based on the evidence of their own eyes, Hanoi residents do not find much credibility in United States bombing communiqués.

Reporting from Nam Dinh, two days later, Salisbury wrote:

Whatever the explanation, one can see that United States planes are dropping an enormous weight of explosives on purely civilian targets. Whatever else there may be or might have been in Nam Dinh, it is the civilians who have taken the punishment.

The cathedral tower looks out on block after block of utter desolation; the city's population of 90,000 has been reduced to less than 20,000 because of the evacuation; 13 per cent of the city's housing, including the homes of 12,464 people, have been destroyed; 89 people have been killed and 405 wounded.

The Pentagon, as Henry L. Trewhitt reported in the *Baltimore Sun* (December 20) from Washington, was pressing the White House (which had to approve bombing targets) to include "more of North Vietnam's industrial potential," although it was "in many cases surrounded by relatively dense population." Less than a week after the *Sun*'s article appeared, Salisbury confirmed that such bombings already were taking place. And so the protests against the bombings from Washington's Western allies and from the Vatican were reinforced by an American observer.

Official Washington was disturbed and angry. On a CBS television program with a panel of newspapermen, Secretary of State Rusk said sharply to a participant from the *Times*: "Why don't you tell your editors to ask Mr. Salisbury to go down and visit the North Vietnamese in *South* Vietnam." The Washington press corps was quick to interpret and enlarge on the official view of the Salisbury journey. Murrey Marder wrote in the *Washington Post* December 28: "Officials are particularly bitter that the attention to civilian casualties in the North has obscured the murder, kidnapings, arson and other acts of terrorism continually directed against civilians in South Vietnam by the Communists."

The *Times* itself two days later published on page one a long article by its military analyst Hanson Baldwin, a demonstrable hawk on the war in Vietnam, who quoted "Pentagon sources" to counter the Salisbury casualty figures as "grossly exaggerated." It was a difficult position to sustain, however, because in the same article Baldwin revealed that the United States Air Force was using 500,000 tons of bombs a year on North and South Vietnam—"somewhat more" than the tonnage used in the entire Pacific area during the four years of the war against Japan.

A record amount of verbal tonnage was dropped on Salisbury beginning on New Year's Day 1967 with a story in the *Washington Post* by George C. Wilson. The headline read: "Salisbury 'Casualties' Tally With Viet Reds." Wilson reported that he had come into possession of a "Communist propaganda pamphlet" which he had checked with "intelligence sources" in Washington to verify its authenticity. The figures in the pamphlet, Wilson noted triumphantly, tallied exactly with Salisbury's figures of the number of civilians killed at Nam Dinh. Wilson said the Johnson Administration was "furious," and hinted that "President Johnson had been told about the relationship between the casualty figures in the *Times* and the pamphlet." Although Wilson depicted himself as the most careful kind of reporter who checked his sources and his facts with every available official, the *Wall Street Journal* said without qualification on January 6 that the story had been planted by the Pentagon.

The *Times*'s managing editor, Clifton Daniel, responding to the *Washington Post* story, said: "It was apparent in Mr. Salisbury's first dispatch —and he so stated in a subsequent dispatch—that the casualty figures came from North Vietnamese officials. Where else would he get such figures in Hanoi?"

Salisbury could hardly have cabled to Washington, say, to Wilson's friends in the Pentagon, for confirmation of figures which, in any case, were being disputed in the Defense Department releases. The government was reluctant to concede even the possibility of civilian casualties. By reporting facts which the Administration wished to conceal, Salisbury and the *Times* had joined the enemy. Once, while Salisbury was in North Vietnam, two *Times* reporters came into the office of a Washington official. "Here come the men from the *Hanoi Times*," was the greeting.

The official reaction was not surprising; the press reaction was dismaying. On January 2, under the heading, "Ho Tries A New Propaganda Weapon," Chalmers Roberts wrote in the *Washington Post:*

Ho Chi Minh, master of guerrilla warfare and political propaganda, is now embarked on one of his most daring exploits . . . Having failed to subvert and militarily defeat the South Vietnamese . . . Ho tried frontal assault on U.S. forces with his own troops from the North. But that, too, failed . . . Now he is using another weapon, one as cleverly conceived as the poison-tipped bamboo spikes his men emplant underfoot for the unwary enemy. At long last, he has opened his country, or part of it, to an American journalist. . . . To force a halt in the American bombing of his country . . . Harrison Salisbury of the *New York Times* is Ho's chosen instrument . . .

If Salisbury was using poison-tipped typewriter keys in the service of Ho Chi Minh, the venom content could not have been as high as that in

Roberts's prose. William Randolph Hearst, Jr., in his column of January 1, took a similar view. With Salisbury in mind, he compared "news and opinion by war critics" to treasonable broadcasts in World War II by Lord Haw Haw in Germany and Tokyo Rose in Japan. Joseph Alsop on January 9 added a Soviet transmission belt to Salisbury's equipment. The right way to look at the mission "is very simple indeed," Alsop wrote. "Salisbury was invited to Hanoi to make propaganda for a proposal long pressed by the Soviets," a halt in the bombing. He added: "Whether a United States reporter ought to go to an enemy capital to give the authority of his by-line to enemy propaganda figures is an interesting question."

Crosby Noyes, foreign editor of the *Washington Star,* denounced the Johnson Administration on January 3 as the first United States government in history to permit "the systematic subversion" of its Vietnam commitment. He found it ominous that any reporter was permitted by Washington to visit Hanoi in the first place, and fired a final volley at "an important segment of the press" for its "utter lack of identification . . . with what the government defines as the national interest."

The segment defending Salisbury was not so large as Noyes made it out to be. In the *New York Post,* James Wechsler wondered if those who were saying that Salisbury got his trip to Hanoi as a reward for his criticism of Washington's Asian policy would dare say that to him in his presence, particularly in view of his documentation. Washington columnist Joseph Kraft on January 9 described the attacks as "the handmaidens of official policy on Vietnam," but he found Salisbury's reporting to be second rate, muddled, badly prepared and over-written. Walter Lippmann posed a question:

Mr. Salisbury's offense, we are told, is that in reporting the war as seen from Hanoi, he has made himself a tool of enemy propaganda. We must remember that in time of war what is said on the enemy's side of the front is always propaganda, and what is said on our side of the front is truth and righteousness, the cause of humanity and a crusade for peace. Is it necessary for us at the height of our power to stoop to such self-deceiving nonsense?

The answer is that from the government's point of view it was necessary. If a policy is based on falsehood and deception, the propaganda "on our side" must conform. The accomplices to the deception in this case were a large part of the Washington press corps and many other commentators and editors throughout the nation—the journalistic "handmaidens of official policy." It is not often that the nation is provided with such a classic demonstration of handmaidenry.

*Newsweek* on January 9 still held out some hope for Salisbury's rehabilitation once he left North Vietnam. It said:

> Salisbury wrote that although North Vietnamese officials read his copy and looked at his film, neither appeared to be censored. Yet, like any U.S. correspondent in a Communist country, Salisbury must walk the tricky tight-rope of self-censorship to keep from being expelled. To keep his balance on the tight-rope, Salisbury may have had to sacrifice some balance in his stories. He will, after all, have a chance to report free of restrictions when he returns to New York.

The assumption here is that nothing written from a Communist country can be factual, while anything written in the United States or any other part of the "free world" is automatically true. In light of the disclosures of deception by the Johnson Administration in Salisbury's dispatches, and the poisonous response by American newspapermen who participated in the deception, the *Newsweek* comment is fatuous. But it reflects the position of most American newspapermen and much of the American public.

Salisbury left Hanoi on January 9, 1967, in the midst of the furor, for Hong Kong. From there he filed five long articles which reasserted his main findings in North Vietnam.

A week later, two additional American journalists were ending a stay in Hanoi which had stirred far less fuss. They were Harry S. Ashmore, former editor of the *Arkansas Gazette,* traveling as a representative of the Center for the Study of Democratic Institutions at Santa Barbara, California, and William C. Baggs, editor of the *Miami News,* who died in 1969. They left Hanoi on January 13 and the Associated Press circulated a series written by Baggs (whose conclusions were confirmed by Ashmore in newspaper and television interviews). In an article for January 19 release, Baggs repeated Salisbury's report of the bomb damage in Hanoi, and praised Salisbury's initiative. The paragraph mentioning Salisbury was placed high in the story; but this paragraph, according to James Boylan in the *Columbia Journalism Review* (Winter 1966-67), did not appear in the *Washington Post,* which had been so sharply critical of Salisbury. Boylan saw the Baggs series as a turning point:

> Baggs, probably in part because of his more cautious tone, was subjected to little or none of the enfilading fire that has been directed at Salisbury. Baggs's dispatches, in fact, may have marked a tacitly observed turning point, the acceptance of the fact that stories from Hanoi could now be looked at primarily as news. Salisbury had broken (to use a phrase he employed in a television appearance) "the pattern of acceptability"; now it appeared that a new, broader pattern might take its place. The United States Information Agency found in its surveys of the world press that the United States had gathered praise for permitting Salisbury's trip.

One reason for the muted response to Baggs's articles was that attention drawn to them would have backed up Salisbury's reports. This conclusion is supported by the *Washington Post*'s deletion of the reference to Salisbury.

A turning point may indeed have been reached, but perhaps not the one that Salisbury—and apparently Boylan—discerned. The turning point more likely was a decision by Washington that it would no longer be possible to conceal what was being done in North Vietnam. Hence the propaganda line had to be shifted to justify the bombing of civilian centers. The emphasis now would be that the war was being directed "from Hanoi," and that it was Hanoi's intransigence alone that prevented peace. It was "the infiltration and direction from the North" that was keeping the National Liberation army alive, and the United States had no alternative except to "bomb Hanoi to the peace table," since "force was the only language the enemy understood." This line would enable the United States to bomb North Vietnam mercilessly behind the mask of peaceful piety.

As though to signal the new propaganda strategy, the Associated Press on January 21, 1967, sent out a dispatch (published on the inside pages of the *Washington Post* and the *New York Times*) which said: "Intelligence sources said today that aerial photographs showed considerable damage to civilian structures as well as to military targets in some places in North Vietnam." There was no criticism of the AP, either in Washington or in the editorial columns of the press.

What rankled most in Washington, within both the government and the loyalist press corps, was that the government of North Vietnam, through the Salisbury and Ashmore-Baggs missions, had presented its case to the American people in the nation's most authoritative newspaper and through the largest news-gathering agency. Although the facts of the bombing had appeared earlier in such papers as *Le Monde* in Paris and other prestigious publications abroad (and in a few small left-wing publications within the United States), virtually nothing about North Vietnam had appeared in the United States press that was not government sanctioned and government oriented.

The worldwide response to the Salisbury articles, and the boost in *Times* circulation that resulted, made Salisbury a natural entry for the Pulitzer Prize for 1966 (he had won the prize for international reporting from the Soviet Union in 1955). The *Times* submitted his North Vietnam series for consideration, but on May 2, 1967, as noted earlier, it was announced that the prize for international reporting had been given to Hughes of the *Christian Science Monitor*.

The *New York Times,* in its page-one story about the Pulitzer awards, gave the headline to Edward Albee, the recipient of the prize in drama for his play *A Delicate Balance.* Albee had been chosen by the drama jury in 1963 for his play *Who's Afraid of Virginia Woolf?,* but the selection had been overruled by the Advisory Board and the drama jury had resigned in protest. The irony of the 1966 awards therefore was even more striking. On page 40 of the same issue of the *Times,* where the page-one story carried over, there appeared a two-column story with the headline: RIFT IS DISCLOSED IN PULITZER VOTE. The disclosure was credited to the *St. Louis Post-Dispatch.*

In the selection of Pulitzer prizes, a jury of newspaper editors reads entries in the international, national, and local reporting categories, and submits its recommendations to the Advisory Board, which rarely rejects them. In the international reporting category for 1966, the jury voted 4 to 1 to give the award to Salisbury, saying that his dispatches showed "enterprise, world impact and total significance [that] outweigh some demerits in on-the-spot reporting." At a meeting at Arden House in Harriman, New York, on April 14, the *Post-Dispatch* said, the Advisory Board had argued long over the recommendation. The opposition took the position that Salisbury's failure to give the source of his casualty figures was a mark against him. One board member said: "Inasmuch as a number of reporters had made applications over a period of time for admission to Hanoi, Salisbury should not be given special credit for having been the one that was invited." He said that the opponents had "limited their decision to the quality of the report that Salisbury turned out and were not influenced by ideological considerations."

The Advisory Board voted 6 to 5 against giving the prize to Salisbury. Turner Catledge, then executive editor of the *New York Times,* disqualified himself from voting because Salisbury worked for his newspaper. Had he voted, the result would have been a tie and the award would have gone to Salisbury. The next day *Post-Dispatch* publisher Pulitzer asked for a reconsideration by secret ballot. The *Post-Dispatch* reported:

He [Pulitzer] made what those present agree was an eloquent plea for preserving the integrity of the awards on their journalistic merit. Pulitzer argued in the meeting that the issue should be decided solely on what Salisbury had done in breaking barriers to get into Hanoi and reporting from behind enemy lines. He pointed out that Salisbury's dispatches had compelled the Defense Department to revise earlier claims about precision bombing and to concede that civilian casualties were inevitable when targets to be bombed were in or near areas where civilians lived.

The chairman of the Advisory Board predicted that the decision not to give Salisbury the award would be greeted by newspapermen with incredulity, indignation and condemnation. He described Salisbury's work as the obvious, preeminent example of distinguished international reporting despite minor technical flaws.

Pulitzer's eloquence did not prevail. The vote was still against Salisbury and for Hughes. Asked for a comment on the Advisory Board's action, Salisbury said: "I put the judgment of the editors of the *Times* ahead of any other criteria." Obviously he was referring to the prominence and space the *Times* had given his dispatches.

Executive Editor Catledge's abstention from voting seems unnecessary. Whatever tradition might prevail on the Advisory Board, if an editor felt strongly enough to submit a reporter's work for a prize, he ought also to be willing to fight for a vindication of his own judgment—particularly when that judgment was subject to such strong attack.

Pulitzer's expectation of "incredulity and indignation" in the press did not materialize. But the *Nation* magazine, in an editorial published May 15, 1967, entitled "Salisbury in '68," said:

> Not that they deserve it, but the establishmentarians who control the distribution of Pulitzer Prizes may get a chance to redeem themselves for having withheld the award that the journalism jury so properly—indeed, almost inevitably—bestowed on Harrison E. Salisbury. It happens that his series was published in the *Times* from late December 1966 until well into January 1967; it is thus eligible for consideration in 1968 as it was in 1967.

The press of the country, the editorial said, should demand in advance that there be no tampering with the jury's decision: "It is absurd to submit a man's work to a jury of his peers, only to have their opinion cast out by men who know little and care less about professional criteria, but who are set trembling by every draft in this windy nation."

The *Times* did not resubmit the Salisbury series for consideration in 1968. The *Nation* did. Salisbury did not get the award.

# 19. Freedom and Responsibility

This book has dealt mainly with the press and foreign policy—how they have interacted, and how this interaction has affected the public. The history and case histories span more than a quarter century—from a time when newspapers were still the dominant source of news and information to a time when television has served up to accompany dinner a battlefield 10,000 miles distant. The impact of television and 24-hour all-news radio which large metropolitan areas have had since 1967 has been enormous. Millions of Americans get their news exclusively from television and radio, and form their opinions from airborne information. Newscasters whose faces have become familiar household objects are regarded by countless Americans with the same reverence once accorded movie stars. They have become identified with the news and special events they broadcast. Walter Cronkite of CBS, for example, shared almost equal status with the astronauts who landed on the moon.

Unlike the printed press, television networks and radio stations are subject to a measure of government regulation because they operate over airways supposedly belonging to the public, although the public in fact has extremely limited access to its own airways. Each radio and television station must obtain from the Federal Communications Commission a license to operate, subject to renewal every three years on the condition that the station has performed faithfully in the public service. Until recently the renewals have been perfunctory, except for the FM stations in New York, Berkeley, and Los Angeles operated by the Pacifica Foundation, which seeks to present a full range of opinion, including radical opinion. Growing competition for the vast profits of the television-radio market has given rise to contesting bids, and the resultant publicity has brought to light unsavory practices and broken promises by station operators which have stirred the FCC to more vigilant attitudes. But since commission members are appointed, such vigilance can always be tempered by Presidential appointments which ensure the precedence of profit-making over public service.

The "communications media" entity today takes in far more than the printed newspaper. It includes television, radio, newsmagazines, weekly and monthly magazines which devote a major portion of their space to news presentation and analysis, and the film industry, which is increasingly using the documentary method in presentation of events and in fictionalized representation of the current scene. The men who drew up the First Amendment guarantee of freedom of the press could hardly have envisioned the vast expansion of communication in the nation (and the world) in the second half of the twentieth century. Impressive argument has been presented for extending the freedom of the press guarantee to television and radio.

Newspaper and magazine publishers, however, have resisted any enlargement of their privileged sanctuary to include their competitors in the electronic media. They have at the same time rejected counsel and criticism which sought to persuade them to a greater sense of responsibility and public service.

The classic illustration of this resistance is the story of the Hutchins Commission Report, published in 1947, officially entitled *A Free and Responsible Press: A General Report on Mass Communications: Newspapers, Radio, Motion Pictures, Magazines, and Books.* The report was published in a slim volume by the University of Chicago, of which Robert M. Hutchins was then chancellor.

The prestigious commission was made up entirely of non-newspaper people* and financed by a $200,000 grant from Henry R. Luce of Time Inc., and $15,000 from the *Encyclopaedia Britannica.* Luce maintained

---

* The Commission: Robert M. Hutchins, chairman; Zechariah Chafee, Jr., professor of law, Harvard University, vice chairman; John M. Clark, professor of economics, Columbia University; John Dickinson, professor of law, University of Pennsylvania, and general counsel, Pennsylvania Railroad; William E. Hocking, professor of philosophy, emeritus, Harvard University; Harold D. Lasswell, professor of law, Yale University; Archibald MacLeish, former Assistant Secretary of State; Charles E. Merriam, professor of political science, University of Chicago; Reinhold Niebuhr, professor of ethics, Union Theological Seminary; Robert Redfield, professor of anthropology, University of Chicago; Beardsley Ruml, chairman, Federal Reserve Bank of New York; Arthur M. Schlesinger, Sr., professor of history, Harvard University; George N. Shuster, president, Hunter College.

an uncharacteristic detachment from the work of the commission, which met from early 1944 into 1946. The final report, drafted in October 1946, was, as James Boylan said in the *Columbia Journalism Review* (Summer 1967), "in a sense a postwar charter for the press."

The commission interviewed 58 practicing journalists and held 225 interviews with government agencies and private organizations concerned with the press. The main conclusion, as Zechariah Chafee, Jr. wrote in *Frontier* magazine (October 1953) in a retrospective article, was "that the press ought to be responsible as well as free. We did not mean legal responsibility. So far as there are shortcomings in the press, the remedy for them will have to come almost entirely from the profession itself, not through formal codes but through professional training and the professional spirit."

The commission found that the press was not living up to its responsibility, that it had developed enormously as an instrument of mass communication, but that the proportion of people who could express their ideas and opinions through the press had decreased. Those in control of the press not only had not provided a service adequate to the needs of the society, but had even engaged in practices which society condemns. While it did not recommend it, or look with favor on the idea, the commission said the abuse of the machinery of the press by the few who are able to use it could lead to regulation or control. Government regulation might remedy the abuses of the press, it said, but might kill the freedom of the press in the process.

The commission concluded that the presentation of news was warped by speed, novelty, and sensationalism; that much of the news was meaningless, distorted and flat, and that publishers were influenced by pressure groups, many of whom belonged, as did the publishers themselves, to the category of big business. It listed five requirements of a press in a free society:

1. A truthful, comprehensive and intelligent account of the day's events in a context which should give them meaning. . . . It is no longer enough to report *the fact* truthfully. It is now necessary to report *the truth about the fact.*
2. A forum for the exchange of comment and criticism.
3. The projection of a representative picture of the constituent groups in the society.
4. The presentation and clarification of the goals and values of society . . . clarifying the ideals toward which the community should strive.
5. Full access to the day's intelligence.

Among its recommendations were: recognition that the constitutional guarantee of freedom of the press included radio and motion pictures;

government facilitation of new ventures in the communication industry to keep the channels open; legislation by which a libeled person might obtain a retraction from the offender, or an opportunity to reply; the repeal of legislation prohibiting "expression in favor of revolutionary changes in our institutions where there is no clear and present danger that violence will result from that expression"; insistence that the government inform the public about its policies and their purpose, and if the private media fail to present this information, that the government "employ media of its own" to do so; financing by the media of new and experimental activities in their fields; vigorous mutual criticism by members of the press; the use of all means to increase the competence, independence, and effectiveness of staffs; the creation of academic-professional centers of advanced study, research, and publication in the field of communications.

"One of the most effective ways of improving the press," the commission said, "is blocked by the press itself: By a kind of unwritten law, the press ignores the errors and misrepresentations, the lies and scandals of which its members are guilty." To get around the blockade, the commission said:

> We recommend the establishment of a new and independent agency to appraise and report annually upon the performance of the press . . . In this field we cannot turn to government as representative of the people as a whole, and we would not do so if we could. Yet it seems to us clear that some agency which reflects the ambitions of the American people for its press should exist for the purpose of comparing the accomplishments of the press with the aspirations which the people have for it. Such an agency would also educate the people as to the aspirations which they ought to have for the press.

The commission recommended that the agency be independent of both government and press, privately endowed, and given a ten-year period to operate before a full review was made. It would help the press define workable standards of performance, inquire into the exclusion of minority groups from access to expression, appraise government's actions in relation to the press, investigate charges of lying and distortion, encourage establishment of centers for advanced studies and criticism in communications, and give "the widest possible publicity and public discussion to all the foregoing."

When the report was released late in March 1947, the press confirmed the commission's description of the press. Harry Ashmore, then editor of the *Arkansas Gazette,* reported in an article in the *Columbia Journalism Review* 20 years later (Summer 1967): "I was a member of the

American Society of Newspaper Editors when *A Free and Responsible Press* was published, and saw the august membership huddle rumps together, horns out, in the immemorial manner, say, of the National Association of Manufacturers faced by a threat of regulated prices."

The report did not get notice on page one of any newspaper in the United States, although similar critiques of other industries often got page-one display. Although the three wire services sent out stories, many metropolitan newspapers published nothing at all. No paper printed the full text. The *New York Times* published three and a half columns of summary on page 24, and the *Christian Science Monitor* carried a full-page summary, a signed article, and an editorial. In the *Atlantic Monthly,* Louis M. Lyons of Harvard's Nieman Foundation wrote: "No other institution could have been criticized by as distinguished a group as Chancellor Hutchins's commission without having the indictment land on the front page . . . It is, incidentally, one of the central points of the report on the freedom of the press that there's an unhealthy absence of self-criticism in our newspapers." The *Nashville Banner* buried the story deep inside the paper, then said in an editorial: "The very fact that the press gives prominent and liberal space to their indictments of it refutes at least some of the charges."

The *New York Times* said it could find no sign of conspiracy to distort or suppress facts (the commission had not even hinted at conspiracy). The *St. Louis Post-Dispatch* and the *Los Angeles Times* said they could not support the commission's conclusions because they advocated self-regulation. The commission in fact said it placed no hope in self-regulation.*

The headline in the *Chicago Tribune* read: "A Free Press (Hitler Style) Sought for U.S.; Totalitarians Tell How It Can Be Done." A common criticism was that the commission members were "a bunch of professors," outsiders who knew nothing about the workings of journalism. Hutchins responded by noting that Chafee was the nation's foremost authority on freedom of expression and asked, "Do newspaper writers believe that their business is so esoteric that intelligent laymen who have consumed their product all their lives can have nothing to tell them that is worth listening to?"

---

* An excellent summary of the commission's work and the press reaction may be found in Publication No. 69 of the Freedom of Information Center of the Missouri University School of Journalism, prepared by Judith Murrill. See also the Summer 1967 issue of the *Columbia Journalism Review* for the article, "The Hutchins Commission Report: A Twenty-Year View."

*Editor & Publisher* devoted ten pages to a summary (and refutation) of the report, noting with a measure of triumph in its lead story that the report had not charged advertiser-control of the nation's newspapers, but had leveled the charge against radio. Colonel Robert McCormick of the *Chicago Tribune,* not satisfied with a series of vitriolic attacks on the report in his own paper, commissioned a staff reporter, Frank Hughes, to write a book about it. Hughes labored until 1950 and produced a 642-page volume, entitled *Prejudice and the Press* (Devin-Adair), which concluded that the commission members were under the spell of socialists and Communists and were bent on shattering "the entire American constitutional structure" to create "a tyranny in the name of freedom." Hutchins was almost in despair over the reception of the report: "I never understood that the First Amendment said that the right of the press to be free from criticism is forever guaranteed."

But 23 years later, publishers and editors remain persuaded of the perpetual guarantee. Almost nothing of the commission's recommendations (which the commissioners themselves described as neither new nor startling) has been implemented. The newspapers have not notably concerned themselves with enlarging their horizons socially or culturally. Schools of journalism remain for the most part workshops divorced from the needs of society or even devoid of awareness that "society" exists somewhere outside. Standards of pay and working conditions have improved, thanks to the American Newspaper Guild, which itself remains blissfully free of any responsibility beyond wages, hours, and working conditions. Radio, and now television, is firmly in the control of advertisers, in many of whose firms television network board members hold shares. One major wire service and scores of newspapers have died since 1947. The government seeks constantly by means of the press to obfuscate its policies rather than present them clearly to the public, and the managers of newspapers commonly allow their property to be thus abused because they support the government. Most significantly, no agency to evaluate and watch over the press has ever been established, and the general sessions of newspaper and broadcasting executives are almost entirely devoid of mutual criticism.

Barry Bingham, publisher of the *Louisville Courier-Journal,* proposed in 1963 the creation of local press councils, composed of citizens from all areas of endeavor. The councils would meet with the local newspaper publishers to exchange views toward creating more responsible newspapers. But it was not until 1967, when the Lowell Mellett Foundation helped to finance experimental projects, that the press council idea took tentative hold. Councils were set up in Redwood City, California; Bend,

Oregon; and Cairo and Sparta, Illinois.* They were administered by experts in journalism from nearby universities.

The greatest value of the council is that it provides the community with the means to confront publishers with the needs and grievances of the community, and to insist that the newspaper respond. Basic to the success of the council is the receptivity of the publisher, and most publishers will not be receptive without considerable public pressure. Bingham had suggested regular television reports to the public on the council sessions, but this was not undertaken in any of the Mellett experiments. Redwood City and Sparta did not have television, in any case, but radio programs would have served nearly as well.

In some instances, the Mellett report said, council members were reluctant to speak up because of ignorance of journalistic practices; others were sharply critical of the newspapers, and still others were willing to accept anything the publisher offered. Despite many "valuable" suggestions, the changes were slight in the West Coast experiments. In Illinois, council members were reportedly infused with a greater feeling of confidence in the newspapers. In Redwood City, publisher Roy Spangler said the very fact of the community council induced a greater sense of publishing responsibility:

Another valuable byproduct is a sense of responsibility one enjoys when he knows a problem cannot merely be swept into a newspaper wastebasket if a press council is sitting nearby to ask questions about the ultimate disposition of a problem. Not that the editor would be less responsible without a press council—but with one he might be more certain and immediate.

Apparently with one eye on the wastebasket, Spangler decided after nine months that the Redwood City council was stillborn. When the Mellett money ran out, the council was abandoned. In the other three cities, however, the councils were continued—without university guidance and with community financing—as permanent advisory bodies.

Whether the press council idea would take in the larger cities depended to a large extent on public feeling on specific issues. In Seattle, a special panel was set up in 1968—also under Mellett auspices—to analyze the coverage of racial news. It was a free-swinging and frank survey, Henry MacLeod of the *Seattle Times* reported, with members of all points of

---

* A full report on these experiments, entitled "Community Press Councils," by Donald E. Brignolo, appeared in the Freedom of Information Center Report No. 217, March 1969.

view in the black community expressing themselves. The result, MacLeod said, was greater understanding. When the grant money was exhausted, the city's two newspapers and four television stations undertook the financing of the council for an additional six months.

William L. Rivers of Stanford University, who helped administer the West Coast experiments, said the results persuaded him that a press council was not needed in every city: "It would have its greatest utility in big cities where a significant portion of the population is at odds with the community power structure." Ben H. Bagdikian, president of the Mellett Fund, went further. He insisted that all newspapers would have to set up machinery to judge professional performance, or be called to account. Otherwise, he foresaw some kind of regulatory intervention similar to that governing trial coverage proceedings in the courts.

My own view is that the press council idea is a healthy one, and the reluctance of the overwhelming majority of publishers to encourage it indicates that they fear not so much an encroachment on freedom of the press (the councils are entirely advisory) as a watchful warning eye on their license to do whatever they please without accounting to the public they are supposed to serve. To be fully effective, however, council members must be drawn not from the "top" layer—prominent citizens who might be expected more often than not to sympathize with the publishers' point of view—but from all sections of the population, particularly the black, the poor, and the young. Yet even if the selection were broad, the work of the council would be almost meaningless if its efforts (and results) were not publicized in the newspapers they were counseling, and through television programs. Council members could seek also to institute neighborhood educational forums to educate the public about newspapers. This would be effective both in guiding the council from below, and in instilling in the publisher an awareness that Little Brother was watching.

An increasing awareness among publishers and editors of being watched has become evident in nervous discussions within the industry about press councils, both local and national. The *Bulletin* of the American Society of Newspaper Editors (November 1969) reported on an unusual meeting of the ASNE board of directors in London two months earlier. London had been selected as the meeting site to provide an opportunity to study the British Press Council, which the British publishers had been pressured by government and public into establishing in 1953. It took two Royal Commission reports and the threat of Parliamentary action to move the publishers. A third Commission report was required before the publishers revised the Council's constitution to provide for a chairman from outside the industry, to include members of the public, and to finance the work of the council from within the industry.

The British Press Council has eight "constituent members"—organizations of newspaper owners, editors, and working staffs. These organizations provide 20 voting members who in turn select five non-newspaper members. All 25 vote to elect the chairman. Terms are three years, and a $50,000 annual budget is supplied by the constituent members. Under Council procedure, any person who has sought and been refused satisfaction in a complaint to a newspaper may apply for action to the Council. An editor may make a complaint against individuals or groups who he believes are blocking access to the news. A staff member may complain against his own paper (it is rarely done), or an action may be instituted by the Council itself. H. Philip Levy, chief counsel of the giant Daily Mirror Newspaper Group, in a book *The Press Council, History, Procedure and Cases* (St. Martin's Press, 1967), said that British newspapers have improved since the Council came into being. He wrote: "More space is now devoted to the news, the treatment of current affairs is more mature, social and moral problems are discussed with more frankness, and generally there is greater seriousness and sense of responsibility."

An opposite view was taken by a writer named D. A. N. Jones in a new publication called *Open Secret,* established in London in July 1969 by the Free Communications Group, organized by working personnel of the British communications industry who believe "that newspapers, television and radio should be put under the control of the people who produce them." In the July *Open Secret,* Jones charged the Press Council with "flop-whiskered poltroonery" for rejecting numerous complaints of racism and malicious inaccuracies in reporting welfare problems.

A report on the Council's work in the year ending June 30, 1968, as published in the November 1968 ASNE *Bulletin,* would seem to support Jones's charge. In that year 384 complaints were processed, but all but 88 were either thrown out without hearing (76), withdrawn (36), or not "adjudicated" (184)—meaning that they were decreed not to have enough merit to be pursued. Of the 88 cases heard in closed session, 53 were rejected, and 35 upheld. That is less than 10 percent of the complaints submitted. Jones wrote in *Open Secret:*

The present members of the Council (sixteen representing proprietors and editors, six from the journalists' union, one lawyer for chairman) should be . . . kicked out. I would be satisfied with a state-imposed body, independent of publishing corporation interests, empowered to prosecute offending journals; but I know many left-wingers will think this proposal illiberal. We can agree, at least, that the

Press Council, no less than the newspapers it represents, needs to be in other hands; and the sooner the better.

The American editors who investigated the British Press Council seemed averse to establishing an American counterpart. Among the objections were the infinitely greater size of the United States, the differences in the British and American judicial systems and concepts of ethics, and public attitudes. There was, in addition, an acute distaste at the idea of "outsiders" passing judgment on their publications. Despite the general hostility to the plan, however, some editors were cognizant enough of a growing public distrust of newspapers in the United States to say: "We'd better do something."

A select committee was chosen in London to study a proposal put before the board to establish an ASNE Grievance Committee "to receive complaints of substance about the performance of daily newspapers." It would not, said ASNE president Norman E. Isaacs, editor of the *Louisville Courier-Journal,* "attempt to serve as an agency to examine the multitude of complaints coming from political figures, civic organizations, or the many other standard differences of opinion with editors' news judgments. Instead the committee would weigh only those major complaints relating to the ASNE's Code of Ethics. This might take in six or seven cases a year." And they would be confined to complaints by one newspaper organization against another.

Isaacs, in an article in the October 11, 1969, *Editor & Publisher,* described the plan as "the first major national self-policing step for American newspapering." *Editor & Publisher,* which has not in memory favored any thoroughgoing criticism of the press, was quick to endorse the plan—an almost certain guarantee that it would be ineffective. But the need of the visiting editors in London to act indicated that they had indeed discovered a mouse under their queenly chair—a mouse that seemed to be nibbling at the yellowed and brittle edges of the Code of Ethics,* which had been invoked only once by the ASNE against a member since its adoption in 1923. Under the new plan, the Code, like the Talmud, would

---

* The Code of Ethics, or Canons of Journalism, is a set of principles governing the "sound practices and just aspirations of American journalism." They embody responsibility, freedom of the press, independence, sincerity, truthfulness and accuracy, impartiality, fair play, and decency. The preamble says: "Journalism . . . demands of its practitioners the widest range of intelligence, or knowledge, and of experience, as well as natural and trained powers of observation and reasoning. To its opportunities as a chronicle are indissolubly linked its obligations as teacher and interpreter."

remain sanctified and inviolate, even though its content and purpose would remain a mystery.

Yet despite the industry's reluctance, sooner or later some form of national newspaper evaluation council will have to be established, with foundation and public support, to examine the performance of daily newspapers and grade them in a manner in which members of the Congress were once graded by labor organizations, and the way universities and hospitals are graded as to quality and accreditation. Among the areas to be examined would be:

1. Coverage of major domestic and international news.
2. Editorial positions on social and political issues.
3. Treatment of news about racial and political minorities.
4. Handling of letters to the editor, an important matter as more and more attention is focused on the question of access to the press by the public.
5. The professional standards of the newspapers.
6. The amount of space given to, and the quality of coverage of, cultural events—books, film, theater, music, art.
7. The amount of advertising in ratio to news content.
8. Evidence of acquiescence by editors and publishers to attempts by government to manage the news.
9. The amount of space devoted to crime, sensation, and trivia.
10. An evaluation of the newspaper's devotion to public service.

Under this plan, a careful study would be made of newspapers, perhaps on a sampling basis, during the year. There would also be spot checks of the treatment or non-treatment of sensitive news stories. The Council's evaluations could be supplemented by an informal appraisal submitted by a professional staff committee. This kind of continuing appraisal would cost money—hence the need for continuing foundation support. Financing by the newspaper industry (despite the unique experience of the Hutchins Commission) should be avoided. Foundation funds should be supplemented by community support from civic groups because the local readership will tend to become more involved if community money is represented. Such a council would undoubtedly encounter serious resistance from the organizations of publishers and editors. But public pressure could move some publishers and editors to an understanding that voluntary cooperation with an honest effort to establish a genuinely free and responsible press is the surest guarantee of the maintenance —and application—of the First Amendment.

The first major discussion in many years of the application of the First Amendment to the press was sparked by an article by Professor Jerome A. Barron of George Washington Law School in the June 1967 *Harvard Law Review* entitled, "Access to the Press: A New First Amendment Right." Barron contended that there was an anomaly in our constitutional law. While we protect expression once it has come to the fore, he said, "our law is indifferent to creating opportunities for expression. Our constitutional theory is in the grip of a romantic conception of free expression, a belief that the 'marketplace of ideas' is freely accessible."

Barron advanced a three-part thesis to explain why the mass media today influence so strongly the "content of ideas that reach the marketplace of expression": (1) The tendency of those who control the media to foreclose from access any idea that is inimical to their interests or prejudices. The decline of competition and the growth of monopoly enterprise increase the power of the owners in this respect. (2) The McLuhan thesis that the electronic media have replaced the older typographical media and engage people not through content but through form. The involvement is emotional, not intellectual, mesmerizing the public to the point of indifference as to the content of both visual-verbal and the printed media. (3) The importance of reaching the largest possible audience at all times, particularly in the electronic media, predisposes the managers and owners of the media to conform to already accepted public taste and opinion. Within this concept, there can be "approved dissent." But a subject in which people have not demonstrated interest will not be allowed expression. At bottom, Barron said, the media owners have no ideology and are antipathetic to all ideas. He wrote:

Retreat from ideology is not bereft of ideological and practical consequences . . . It is not that the mass communications industry is pushing certain ideas and rejecting others, but rather that it is using free speech and free press guarantees to avoid opinions instead of acting as a sounding board for their expression. What happens of course is that the opinion vacuum is filled with the least controversial and bland ideas. Whatever is stale and accepted in the status quo is readily discussed and thereby reinforced and revitalized.

A realistic view of the First Amendment, said Barron, "requires that a right of expression is somewhat thin if it can be exercised only at the sufferance of the managers of mass communications." The current view of the Constitution is that if the courts or the legislature were to guarantee some right of access to the media for ideas that could not otherwise be effectively presented to the public, this would constitute "state action" violating the First Amendment. But today, according to Barron, it is not the state but the media themselves which hold the power to abridge free-dom of expression: "Indeed, nongoverning minorities in control of the means of communication should perhaps be inhibited from restraining free speech (by the denial of access to their media) even more than governing majorities are restrained by the First Amendment—minorities do not have the mandate which a legislative majority enjoys in a polity operating under a theory of representative government." Barron wrote:

> What is required is an interpretation of the First Amendment which focuses on the idea that restraining the hand of government is quite useless in assuring free speech if a restraint on access is effectively secured by private groups. A constitutional prohibition against governmental restrictions on expression is effective only if the Constitution ensures an adequate opportunity for discussion. Since this opportunity exists only in the mass media, the interests of those who control the means of communication must be accommodated with the interests of those who seek a forum in which to express their point of view.

In this situation, Barron concluded, it is open to the courts to "fashion a remedy for a right of access, at least in the most arbitrary cases, independent of legislation." But if such an innovation were to be "judicially resisted," then "our constitutional law authorizes a carefully framed right-of-access statute which would forbid an arbitrary denial of space, hence securing an effective forum of expression for divergent opinions."

Even the most public-service-minded newspapers responded with alarm to this prospect. The *St. Louis Post-Dispatch* said editorially:

> The newspaper (which is in no way licensed by the government as a broadcast station) has an obligation to the community in which it is published to present fairly unpopular as well as popular sides to a question. Enforcing such a dictum by law is constitutionally impossible, and should be. As a practical matter, a newspaper which consistently refuses to give expression to viewpoints with which it differs is not likely to succeed, and doesn't deserve to.

The American Civil Liberties Union, which has traditionally upheld the inviolability of the First Amendment, invited Barron to address its biennial conference in 1968 as part of a continuing discussion within the ACLU on the right of access and the right of reply in the press. There was considerable sentiment within the organization to present a test case in line with Barron's ideas.

Barron persisted with his interpretation in an article in the March 1969 issue of the *George Washington Law Review* entitled, "An Emerging First Amendment Right of Access to the Media." He said the First Amendment must be understood to require *opportunity* for expression as well as *pro-*

*tection* for expression once secured. This affirmative approach, he said, was the responsibility of governmentally controlled as well as privately controlled means of communication. He had no illusions about government power as compared to private power, he said, and rejected as simplistic the idea that government is the ally of civil liberties or private power the enemy (or vice versa)—"particularly when the determination of what is public and what is private becomes an increasingly difficult task."

He was impressed with the "affirmative approach" in the broadcasting industry, and suggested that the "eighteenth century associations which still insulate the press" needed shaking up. "Attempts to identify procedures created to assure debate with the suppression of ideas must be understood for what they are: the unreflecting use of hallowed symbols for purposes which are antithetical to debate and discussion."

The First Amendment debate broadened in June 1969 when the Supreme Court upheld the constitutionality of the "fairness doctrine" promulgated by the Federal Communications Commission in 1967. That doctrine provides for the right of reply by an individual who has been personally attacked in a broadcast, or by a politician whose opponent has been endorsed in a radio or television political editorial. The Supreme Court case involved an attack by the right-wing agitator, the Reverend Billy James Hargis, upon Fred J. Cook, author and investigative reporter, broadcast over the Red Lion, Pennsylvania, radio station in 1964.

In a panel discussion at the 1969 convention of the American Bar Association, FCC Commissioner Kenneth Cox praised the Red Lion decision and recommended its extension to newspapers. He said: "It seems to me that the publisher owes the same moral duty as the broadcaster to use this medium to help fashion a better society." He accused the mass media of closing their columns and air time to "complex issues now facing us." It was the purpose of the First Amendment, he said, to preserve "the uninhibited marketplace of ideas in which truth will ultimately prevail."

In response, Clifton Daniel of the *New York Times* acknowledged the problem of access to the press but felt the remedies must be left to the press itself and to the reading public. He conceded that it was not easy for anyone with a cause or a grievance to get space in the papers, but he believed it should not be. Denying that new ideas are suppressed, he said most editors and publishers go out of their way to publish dissenting points of view. He couldn't guess what the framers of the Constitution would have said about television, "but I have a pretty good idea of what they meant by freedom of the printed word, and they certainly did not mean it should be controlled, restricted, regulated, or dictated by government officials, legislators or judges."

In the August 16, 1969, issue of *Editor & Publisher* which reported the Cox-Daniel debate, the lead editorial said fervently: "If we ever get to the point where they try to edit a newspaper by statute and by judicial interpretation or court order then only the Good Lord can help the electorate." "They" of course referred to not only Commissioner Cox but Professor Barron and the ACLU and any mortal wicked enough to suggest that the editors and publishers (with only an occasional deviant) were not the fairest, most open-minded, conscientious group of public-service-oriented citizens anointed by the Good Lord to help the electorate find its way to the truth.

In truth, "they" are right about the press—and all the communications media—but there are grave questions raised by Professor Barron's stimulating essays. American publishers to the contrary, the eighteenth century First Amendment must be considered in twentieth century terms—and beyond. The founding fathers might have determined on a federal communications commission if there had been radio and television in Thomas Jefferson's time, or they might have included radio and television in the protective fold of the First Amendment. In any case, it is difficult to justify a sanctified distinction for the printed press when the electronic medium competes so vigorously, supplementing it in providing information for most Americans, and even supplanting it as the major source of news and opinion for millions of others.

The FCC, in the best of circumstances, can perform a valuable regulatory service in radio and television. But the best of circumstances have not often prevailed, and the commission has for the most part appeared to be an adjunct of the radio-television industry. Appointments in the Nixon Administration—for example, the appointment of the ultra-conservative Dean Burch as commission chairman—forecast a shift in the FCC from the comfortable (for the industry) adjunct status to a more troublesome policing status. The aim will be to make the industry conform even more closely to the government's desires.

Clifton Daniel to the contrary, newspapers have not treated dissenting groups and ideas as a general practice with fairness. The range of critical material published does not cover the broad spectrum of the "marketplace of expression." Ideally, the press ought to discipline itself without intervention by the government or the courts. The essence of the First Amendment is still sound. But in default of responsible self-criticism and self-discipline, would petition to the government and the courts for a

redress of grievances be the wisest course? Such petitions would concede
to the government the right to operate and legislate in the area of the
press.

The history of government interference with the press has not been
happy—under capitalism or socialism. In dictatorships such as Spain
or Taiwan, where the government is the all-powerful censor, there is no
freedom. In democracies such as Mexico, where the government subsi-
dizes the press, there is no criticism of the government.

In socialist countries such as the Soviet Union, where there is a proclaimed freedom of the press, newspaper editors and staff are government employes and adhere strictly in their work to guidelines laid down
by government in the government's interest. The government is identified
as the people, but the identification is made by the government, and there
is no questioning of its policies except on regional managerial or production problems. While it is true that the press of the socialist countries is
largely free of the appeals to baser human instincts (so frequently found
in the press of capitalist countries), its coverage is limited in scope, often
inadequate in presentation, and lacking the dimensions to give its readers
a full picture of events, both internally and externally.

In a revolutionary situation, strictures on the press may be understandable and even reasonable, since the press is a weapon in the struggle. But
the perpetuation of strictures and limitations on freedom—on the ground
of eternal vigilance against the enemy of the revolution—is unreasonable
and even self-defeating. Rather than reassuring the people, censorship
creates anxieties and suspicion. An informed people is the surest defense
against an enemy.

The First Amendment was designed to ensure that the press would be
the watchful eye of the public against predatory government. Today the
lines between the so-called public sector (government-financed projects)
and the private sector (industry) are so blurred that Professor Barron's
warning against simplistic distinctions between public and private power
is appropriate, but perhaps for a different reason than he suggests. Government and industry today are almost interchangeable, as is demonstrated by the movement of top personnel from industry to government,
and back again, with electoral shifts every four or eight years, and often
in between.

A public concerned with the failure of the press in the public service
would get very little aid, comfort, or remedy from government in such a
situation. In fact, such delegation of new power might solidify the failures
of the press within the easy alliance of government and industry which is
almost automatically sanctioned by the courts. Further, such new power

could easily be directed first against the dissenting press, which is also protected (more in theory than in fact) by the First Amendment.

My conclusion is that there are more dangers for the public than benefits in Professor Barron's proposals. My predilection is for preserving the eighteenth century First Amendment intact, but interpreting and applying it in accordance with twentieth century conditions. Here the public has a great responsibility. It must in effect become the watchdog of the watchdog—making sure that the press lives up to the responsibility delegated to it under the protection of the First Amendment.

An illustration of the danger of government interference with free expression was provided in November 1969 by the calculated assault on televised news presentation and on the *Washington Post* and the *New York Times* by Vice President Spiro T. Agnew. In demagogic speeches prepared with White House assistance for delivery before geographically strategic audiences (Middle West and South), Agnew singled out for special criticism the allegedly liberal bias of network news and commentary, and the "diplomatic immunity" of walled-in "conglomerates" of the Eastern shore—particularly the *Washington Post* and the *New York Times*.

There followed a series of supporting ground-fire actions from Dean Burch, the new chairman of the FCC (he was a leading functionary in the 1964 Presidential campaign of Barry Goldwater); Herbert Klein, White House communications coordinator (a new post instituted by the Nixon Administration), and Frank Shakespeare, Jr., director of the United States Information Agency (who suggested a screening process in the hiring of television personnel as a counterbalance to preponderantly "liberal" staffs.

The assault was spearheaded by a nationwide television speech on November 3, 1969, by President Nixon which was in effect a call to arms of the "silent majority" of Americans to support Administration policy on the war in Vietnam. It was a period of high excitement and great tension, as the antiwar movement grew with a "Moratorium" protest in October 1969, followed by an unprecedented "Mobilization" of hundreds of thousands in Washington and San Francisco in November demanding an end to the war.

What was the purpose of the assault? In the long range, to achieve by pressure and threat of indirect control what the government could not do by legislation; in the short range, a damper on the coverage of the November Mobilization, and antiwar demonstrations in general. There was no live coverage of the Washington events by any television network. *Variety,* the newspaper of the entertainment industry, reported that the networks had decided on their own in advance against live coverage, but the Agnew attack guaranteed that the decision would not be reversed by an industry not noted for spine.

The White House attack achieved three results: (1) a flurry of indignant editorials in the nation's press—some of them of high quality—restating the constitutional guarantees of a free press, and statements by the heads of the television networks—of varying quality and courage—declaring in essence that the networks would not be intimidated; (2) a flood of telephone calls, letters, and telegrams of support for the Nixon-Agnew position, indicating that the President's November 3 call to arms had been effective; (3) evidence—in the volume and "balance" of the coverage of the Agnew speeches and the reaction to them—that the Administration had to an extent succeeded in its purpose.

In the last analysis, as Nixon knew, the forces which control the nation's press and the television networks have no fundamental quarrel with governmental policy. If they become restless, as they had become about the war in Vietnam, when called to order they tend to bend backwards to demonstrate their fairness, and thereby weight an already lopsided balance in favor of the status quo.

There is little hope of self-reform by the press. There is even less hope for constructive reform of the press by the executive or judicial branches of government today. The remedy lies not with the legislature or the halls of diminishing justice, but with the public itself and in the professional staffs of the communications media. Pressure for a national press council is healthy and sound. Public discussion of the Barron proposals and the generation of widespread debate about the press are necessary and positive activities.

But above all, it seems to me, a public determined to achieve the dissemination of honest and uninhibited information, comment, and interpretation of the news must take radical alternative action, as the black freedom movement has done, as the antiwar movement has done, when free expression has been denied them within the existing apparatus for redress of grievances. The purpose of this action would be the establishment of an alternative to the mass media as it exists today—newspapers, magazines, radio, television, and the film industry too.

The purpose of such an alternative press would be, first, to expose and discredit the misinformation and false interpretation of the news, and to fill in the omissions in the general press; second, to offer a credible substitute for the press as it exists today, prepared in a fashion that would win the confidence of an ever-widening audience.

The history of a modest and perhaps premature effort toward this goal may be instructive.

# 20. The Alternative Press

When the *National Guardian* published its first weekly issue on October 18, 1948, *Time* magazine, with its usual dexterity in the mini-sneer, described it as a "pink shoestring." In its early years the new weekly was variously characterized as a "virtual propaganda arm of the Soviet Union" (by the House Committee on Un-American Activities), and later as "the most flamboyant pro-Chinese publication in America" (by columnists Evans and Novak). In fact, the *National Guardian*\* was founded as, and remained, an independent and independently owned newsweekly which took strong issue with basic governmental policy, foreign and domestic. That is what produced for its editors and managers a series of inquisitorial subpoenas—not the idiotic allegations of adherence to the "international Communist conspiracy." It was and has remained a Cold War axiom that any fundamental critic of United States foreign policy must owe his allegiance to a foreign power or a gaggle of such powers—Moscow, Peking, Havana, or Hanoi—depending on whose flag has been hoisted to the propaganda pinnacle as the gravest current threat to our shores.

The founders of the *National Guardian*—Cedric Belfrage, John T. McManus, and I—sought to establish a radical publication dedicated not, as were the existing publications of the left, mainly to sectarian polemics and opinion, but to supplying factual news and interpretation in areas where the facts were suppressed or distorted.

As the Cold War intensified, the *National Guardian* became a cham-

---

\* The name was changed in February 1968 to the *Guardian* by a new administration which had taken over the paper's management in the spring of 1967.

pion of its domestic victims, actual and potential. On the civil rights front, the militant black freedom movement was still in the offing, and there was a desperate need for journalistic campaigns in behalf of Willie McGee, Rosa Ingram, the Martinsville Seven, and the Trenton Six, names barely recalled by a newer generation, and dozens of others barely mentioned in the press except when they were arrested and were put to death for crimes they could not have committed.

The early years set the standard and the tone. We sought to make the *National Guardian* indispensable for any citizen concerned about "the other side," in the United States and in the world. The *National Guardian* was a counterweight to the general press which accepted and propagated without question basic United States policy and the virtue of the capitalist system. The *National Guardian* regarded United States policy as the chief source of the world's problems. It did not as policy advocate socialism as an alternative, but insisted that it be discussed as a possible alternative, and not as a horrid word. It offered a sympathetic presentation of news of the socialist world, while reserving the right to be critical. It held that the peace of the world depended upon an acceptance by the people of the West that socialism was here to stay. Whether the peoples of the Western world liked it or not was irrelevant.

A fundamental policy of the paper was to maintain a flexibility of approach that enabled it to become a forum of the American left. This flexibility countenanced neither a nonpartisan stance, nor an opportunistic approach which sought to cloak radicalism in another guise. The *National Guardian* took many forthright and unpopular positions, and rejected from the outset any proposals to dilute its radical view to achieve respectability. Rather, it insisted that radicalism *was* respectable, in the clearest American tradition, and should take its proper place in the American political debate.

It was this policy of principled flexibility, I believe, that enabled the *National Guardian* to persevere through two difficult decades—when many left publications and organizations perished—and to win the hostile respect of its adversaries. This flexibility also brought it a cordial respect abroad, where its articles and editorials were frequently reprinted. If it was regarded by some as a prophet without honor in its own country, it served to demonstrate to a considerable part of the world that there was a core of sanity and clarity among the American people on the overriding issues of racism and war.

This demonstration sustained the management and staff of the *National Guardian* through a permanent financial crisis which was overcome by involving the entire readership in financing the paper. While this is hardly the most desirable situation, it was infinitely preferable to individual financing by persons who might seek to direct editorial policy.

Several conclusions may be drawn from the experience of publishing a dissenting newspaper in the United States during the first two decades after World War II, conclusions which are still valid:

1. An independent radical newspaper engenders hostility on the right and unfortunately in too great a measure on the left.

2. There is little hope in the climate that has persisted through the Cold War years that a radical newspaper can achieve a mass circulation, or even survive without subsidy by its readership.

3. The press of the nation, with rare exceptions, shows a persistent hostility to its radical counterparts, to the extent of refusing to publish even startling new material if the source is a radical newspaper.

4. Until the radical movement can resolve its internal differences and relax its tension points, its publications will reflect these divisive factors to the point where they will be largely ineffective within the radical movement and, therefore, almost totally ineffective among the general public.

The last of these conclusions was the main reason for my leaving the editorship of the *National Guardian* in 1967. As the sole owner of the paper after the deportation of Belfrage and the death of McManus, I turned over to the staff as a whole in 1966 a 50 per cent interest. The stock had no financial value, but it was important in determining control. In a statement accompanying the stock transfer, I said that ownership and direction of a radical newspaper had to be a collective responsibility. Beyond that, I said, if the time ever arrived when the staff expressed a basic disagreement with the principles on which the paper had been founded, and in which I still believed, I would withdraw altogether. I insisted that a radical newspaper must be a unifying force, not a divisive one; that it must avoid the splintering debates that had too often distracted American radicals from the main struggle—against the makers of war and racism.

My voluntary departure in April 1967 was motivated by a profound disagreement with a large part of the staff on these very questions. An increasing sense of frustration and dissatisfaction had pervaded the staff, particularly among newer members. It was said that the *National Guardian* had "failed" because its circulation had remained at 28,000 for some years, and that it was not responsive to the hopes of a young and growing radical movement. My position was that the young radicals should be supported in their searching independence, but they had not yet manifested themselves as a movement, or even a cohesive force. Ultimately they would advance to acceptance of principles governing their

THE ALTERNATIVE PRESS   **283**

own fight for basic changes in the American system—and then they would
seek unity with radicals of all ages.

Of course there was a generation gap, but it did not look like a permanent schism to me. I believed that the *National Guardian* should continue
to be the voice of the entire radical movement, not the youth segment or
any other part. And I was convinced that the young wanted from a radical
newsweekly what other radicals wanted: the most informed news and
commentary obtainable.

Success for a radical newspaper, I felt, could not be measured by
advertising and circulation. Advertising would simply not be available
from American Telephone, General Motors, Chase-Manhattan, Lord &
Taylor, or any other fat corporation. Circulation would increase only
when the public began to weary of its general news and information diet.
Such a breakthrough would come when the impact of events—as the war
in Vietnam was demonstrating—would reveal the inadequacy and hypocrisy of news presentation in the general press.

My views did not prevail. Rather than become immobilized in a seemingly insoluble division, I left the *National Guardian,* turning my 50 per
cent share over to the staff. After my departure, the paper veered errati-
cally, seeking a base of operation within the radical movement. The name
was changed to the *Guardian,* and the dropping of the word "National"
was more than symbolic, because the focus of the paper was narrowed to
the new left. Even within the new left, support went to the segment favored by the editors of the *Guardian.* That support shifted with the varying fortunes of the dominant groups within the new left. There was no
increase in circulation, and advertising content and revenue actually
diminished.

My point here is not that a newspaper like the *National Guardian*
would be guaranteed survival and success if it adhered to its founding
principles. I do not believe, in the circumstances of the 1960s (which saw
a remarkable increase in radical *activity* without the necessary concomitant of radical *organization*), that the newspaper could have advanced
much beyond its 1967 level. But the direction taken by my successors at
the *Guardian* almost guaranteed confinement to an ever-narrowing sect of
true believers who would isolate themselves from the general public and,
finally, become embittered and useless in their isolation.

I remain persuaded that any newspaper—radical or otherwise—must
be first a newspaper and second a political entity. If it seeks to influence
the public, it must maintain flexibility without yielding on principle. The
fact that the *National Guardian* did not achieve a large circulation (it
went as high as 54,000 before the McCarthy-Korean war fear set in)

284 THE PRESS AND THE COLD WAR

does not negate the validity of the experience. The paper did achieve an influence far beyond its circulation figures, as constant harassment by the government and hostility from the journalistic establishment attested. Given the support of a mature and cohesive radical movement, a national radical weekly (with a mature and cohesive staff) could have a significant influence in the 1970s.

The *National Guardian* sought to operate within the framework of the American political system. However strong its opposition to the government's policies, its approach and its appeal were self-limiting because the paper believed basic changes were still possible within the American system. That approach seemed viable for 15 years. But in the mid-1960s, as the youth rebellion deepened, as the black militants were increasingly persecuted, as resistance to the war in Vietnam spread throughout the population, a new journalistic phenomenon arrived. That phenomenon was the underground press, which was forthright in recognizing that the managers of the American system would not yield peacefully to change.

Begun as a subjective protest against the system, and advocating a life style of bizarre dress, drugs, and sexual freedom, the underground press has become a political entity of considerable appeal, with a potential that has caused grave concern in the traditional media. Robert J. Glessing, in his research for a book on the underground press, estimated in the fall of 1969 that there were 439 such newspapers in the United States. While some of them lasted only a short time, others have been publishing successfully for years. Total circulation is more than 3 million persons—of all ages. Further, as disenchantment has grown, the anti-establishment press has spread to the schools and to Army posts (at least 45 papers are produced by servicemen). Underground journalism seems headed for a permanent life above ground.

The underground press appeals to an audience which has become convinced that commercial newspapers are neither accurate, candid, nor complete. It is staffed, with varying degrees of experience and efficiency, by young people who are willing to work for little compensation, or none at all, as simply a part of their life style. The development of offset press methods permits low-cost publication, although distribution and regularity remain problems. The effectiveness of this press and the concern it has created in the established institutions are demonstrated by the withdrawal of large advertising by recording companies (mainly of rock music) from papers which have become increasingly political.

In the usual pattern of affluent seduction, some early underground papers have become plump with advertising and correspondingly lean in their quest for political and social change. A few still adhere to the diminishing psychedelic approach, with its stress on drugs and withdrawal from society, but these publications are regarded by their politically engaged contemporaries with amused tolerance.

Attending the needs of the underground newspapers are press services which operate in the manner of conventional press associations and syndicates. One is the Underground Press Service, a cooperative which permits members to reprint one another's articles. The other is Liberation News Service, which sells its output of news, photographs, and cartoons (much of it original and exclusive material of high quality) to about 200 newspapers and organizations—including the Library of Congress, CBS, *Life,* the Soviet news agency Tass, and Peking's New China News Agency.

The underground press has already influenced American journalism, and will influence it further in the next years. It has compelled the general newspapers to loosen their approach, language, and areas of coverage. The *Detroit News,* for example, in mid-1969 initiated a weekly section of articles, art, and criticism derivative of the underground press. Interest in the new papers could provide the basis for one or more national political newspapers which would extend the *National Guardian* experiment into a new era with a potentially larger and more receptive audience. This development would attract younger members of the staffs of daily newspapers who are becoming restless within the strictures of their work, as their developing radical views clash with the policies and interests of their establishment superiors.

A striking demonstration of this disaffection took place in Chicago in the weeks following the Democratic National Convention in August 1968. Reporters and photographers who were liberally clubbed by the police, along with the young demonstrators, suffered perhaps greater injuries to their integrity when they repaired to the supposed safety of their newsrooms after the street scenes. There, as one reporter said, "our own editors told us that we didn't see what we really saw under those blue helmets." Mayor Daley "openly insulted newsmen, charged they were dupes, and assailed the integrity of the Chicago media. And as he threw verbal excrement in the faces of Chicago's journalists, we took it like slaves . . ."

But there was a revolt of the slaves—not only against the Mayor and the police, but against the editors and publishers of the Chicago press, and the radio and television stations. An Association of Working Press was formed—without any link to the American Newspaper Guild, with which all Chicago newspapers have contracts—and the monthly *Chicago Jour-*

*nalism Review* was founded as the organ of the association. The stated objectives of the association, in addition to the right to cover the news without interference by the police or other governmental agencies, are "to improve professional standards of fairness and accuracy in the media; publicly condemn obvious breaches of journalistic ethics," and "contribute to the continuing education of the press corps through seminars, lectures, and publications."

In one year the *Review* reached a circulation of 6,000, a surprisingly large part of it outside Chicago. It is a neat, professionally prepared publication carrying some of the best-known by-lines in the city over accounts of suppression of stories, of censorship and unfair treatment of personnel, kindly treatment of corporate business, omissions in reporting on major events, and exposés of the operations of the police department and other city agencies. The Chicago editors reacted to it with a mixture of hostility, warning, and prudent acceptance. Clayton Kirkpatrick of the *Tribune* said he was "reluctant to concede that this venture is necessary for reporters as a way to bring their criticism to editors' attention." Roy Fisher of the *Daily News* wondered whether there might not be a conflict of interest if a staff member used information obtained during the course of his work for his bread-and-butter paper, for an article for the *Review*. James Hoge of the *Sun-Times* felt the project was "in keeping with the temper of the times."

Even before the *Review* was launched, associations of black journalists had been formed in New York, Washington, Chicago, San Francisco and other cities by staff members of leading daily newspapers and magazines to study the performance of their publications on racial questions, and to get jobs for more black writers.

The October 15, 1969, Moratorium witnessed a new development among the working press: editorial personnel taking an active position on political issues and indicating that they would seek a voice in determining the policies and personnel practices of their publications. At the *New York Times,* representatives of 308 employes asked for (and were refused) permission to use the *Times* auditorium for a meeting on Moratorium Day. Outside the building 150 staff members held a silent vigil and then marched to a publishing industry rally nearby. At *Time, Newsweek,* and the *Wall Street Journal,* management was confronted with petitions asking for an observance of Moratorium Day. The *Time* petition was signed by 462 staff members and moved management to grant the use of the auditorium for a meeting of 500 persons—including publisher Henry Luce III. At *Newsweek,* 200 employes failed to show up for work on October 15.

Movements were underway at several publications, an article in the *Wall Street Journal* reported, for discussions with management on "the role of employes in editorial policy," and in several cities there were preparatory moves for publications like the *Chicago Journalism Review.* As these campaigns were being organized, publishers and editors indicated they would meet stiff resistance. At the *Washington Post,* executive editor Benjamin Bradlee insisted that a reporter "must not only avoid emotional involvement, but the appearance of it. In other words, no armbands, no buttons." At the *Wall Street Journal,* William F. Kerby, president of Dow Jones (publisher of the *Journal*), said it was against company policy to do anything that reflected on company policy. But at the *New York Post* in December 1969, after several meetings with management, staff members won agreement on the right to meet with top executives to discuss the paper's policies.

All these efforts by the working press took place outside the jurisdiction of the American Newspaper Guild, and there was virtually no comment about their activities from Guild officials. In New York, a Guild functionary said it was not Guild policy to become involved in "politics" (meaning newspaper policy and public affairs), except where trade union issues were involved. The Guild, however, as a member of the AFL-CIO, had become deeply involved in foreign and domestic Cold War politics. It received embarrassing publicity in 1967 in a disclosure of union activities abroad under the auspices of the CIA. The Guild's silence on the activities of staff members seeking a voice in the policies of their newspapers was obviously disapproving.

Despite the negative history of Cold War journalism as narrated in this book, there was, as the 1970s opened, a hopeful ferment in almost every area of professional life. In medicine, there was a revolt against the neanderthal practices and policies of the American Medical Association. In the law, hundreds of young lawyers were looking away from Wall Street to a career of service in behalf of the poor and the dissenters. In the clergy, there was increasing application of the principles of Christianity and Judaism as living and healing doctrines, rather than as mummified mystical dogma. And in the press, there was a movement to free journalists from the archaic authoritarianism and false objectivity which have long restricted free expression.

The ferment in journalism was not organized, and it was bound to encounter hostility from the owners and editors of the press and the leadership of the unions. But it could not be discouraged. Because the press enjoys unique constitutional privilege and protection which give it a special responsibility, the rebellion in the ranks will be enormously important in forcing the owners of the newspapers to give something more than lip service to this responsibility.

It will not be easy to accomplish, but it must be undertaken if there is ever to be a fundamental change in American journalism. If the rebellion succeeds, the education of the American public as to the overriding importance of a truly free and responsible press may be achieved largely from within the industry. If the movement is blocked, it will continue outside the industry to develop an alternative press—and this time with the assistance of departing establishment journalists.

A final word must be said here about the many journalists who have been among the *dramatis personae* in this book. Some of those who for years had served dutifully in the army of Cold War journalism seem to have seen the light. For example, many who once advocated a hard line to victory in Vietnam have decided the war is hopeless. Others, seeking to expunge their silence or acquiescence in the witch-hunts of the 1940s and 1950s, are—in the face of new attacks from government against dissent in the press and the television networks—warning against a recurrence of McCarthyism.

But the Cold War was not an aberration from the norm of United States policy, and McCarthyism was not an isolated phenomenon. The one was in the service of the other. Both have been ground into the American consciousness, and it remains to be seen whether the seemingly repentant journalists have in reality understood their own role; whether they will join with the dissenters in the critical 1970s, or whether they will revert to silence and acquiescence "in the national interest" when the next crisis arises.

Despite my grave doubt that the press of the country is willing to reform itself, I remain a realistic optimist about journalism. I believe that there is in the United States a company of honest journalists of all ages, conscious of the potential power of an informed people, who will never give up the effort to establish an honorable communications network.

The press helped to lead the nation into accepting a quarter century of the Cold War, with the awfulness that ensued. An alternative press can help dismantle the Cold War and lead the nation into accepting its place in the family of man.

# 21. The Roaring Seventies

The seventies came in shooting. The war in Vietnam groaned on, as did the efforts of the Nixon administration to rally the "silent majority" in support of its determination to continue the war. The pride of a nation was at stake, they said: America had never lost a war, and it was not going to lose this one—even if it was undeclared. Several of the country's major newspapers, including the *New York Times*, the *Boston Globe*, and the *Washington Post*, had begun to express serious misgivings about continuing armed involvement in Southeast Asia. Vice-president Agnew's barnstorming tirades against the media (with alliterative excess: "nattering nabobs of nihilism," "querulous criticism," instant analysis") were effective. The media was running scared. "I think the industry as a whole has been intimidated," said Walter Cronkite, the worried father of the electronic nation. Norman E. Isaacs, then editor of the *Louisville Courier-Journal* and president of the American Society of Newspaper Editors, said he had been buried under an avalanche of "sick mail." Significantly, half of the mail from *editors* supported Agnew's criticism. John B. Oakes, the increasingly outspoken editor of the *New York Times* editorial page, conceded that the Agnew speeches had affected the *Times*. The networks on their own decided not to cover live the greatest anti-war demonstrations in the history of the nation, then taking place in Washington.

The violence in Southeast Asia was heightened with the invasion of Cambodia by American and South Vietnamese troops on April 30, 1970. This violence was matched at home almost immediately on the campus of Kent State University in Ohio with the killing of four students by Ohio National Guard troops during a demonstration against the invasion of

Cambodia. At Jackson State University in Mississippi, two black students were fatally shot. The press, particularly television, covered these events in gory detail, but editorially there was little outrage, either about the domestic slaughter or that in Cambodia.

In the mid-term elections of 1970, the Nixon administration's platform, at home and abroad, was "law and order." The government was the law and it gave the orders. Contrary to custom, Nixon was expected to make strong gains in the elections. After Cambodia, his ratings in the polls had gone up. The country seemed thoroughly confused. But the common sense of the electorate asserted itself: There was very little change in the Congressional lineup, and the media seemed to take some courage from the results.

It needed it. Throughout 1970 the Nixon administration, in an effort further to intimidate the press, was issuing subpoenas to newspapers, newsweeklies, network news producers, and to individual journalists who were covering anti-war protests and the black freedom movement. The government sought to force the subpoenaed individuals to appear before federal grand juries with their notebooks, memorandums to editors, and outtakes (video film shot but not broadcast), supposedly in pursuit of apprehending wrongdoers. Some, like *Time* and *Life* complied. Others, like *Newsweek* and NBC News, made deals with the government to limit the requests. Earl Caldwell, a reporter who had done extensive coverage of black organizations and activities for the *New York Times*, refused to appear before a federal grand jury. He had been ordered to turn over in person his notes and tape-recordings of interviews with leaders of the Black Panthers. The *Times* assigned a lawyer to assist him but did not order him not to appear. Caldwell is black, and his case stirred a strong protest among working news people, particularly among black journalists, who felt that the government's action was aimed at them and their special relationship with the black community.

After a partial victory in the Federal District Court, which ruled that Caldwell did have to appear before the jury, but did not have to disclose confidential material "unless there was a compelling national interest that cannot be served by alternate means," Caldwell insisted on taking his case higher to support his refusal to appear altogether. The *Times* was disappointed but Caldwell went ahead with his own attorney. The government issued a new subpoena to Caldwell, and this time the case went to the Ninth Circuit Court of Appeals, where a set of judges with a clear concept of the First Amendment ruled that Caldwell could not be compelled to appear before a grand jury unless the government demonstrated a pressing need for evidence *before* ordering a journalist to testify in secret. The language was sharp:

> The very concept of a free press requires that the news media be accorded a measure of autonomy, that they should be free to pursue their own investigation to their own ends without fear of government interference, and that they should be able to protect their own investigative processes. To convert newsgatherers into Department of Justice investigators is to invade the autonomy of the press by imposing a governmental function upon them.

The Nixon administration refused to yield and the Caldwell case went to the Supreme Court, linked to the cases of two other reporters. The case became known as *Branzburg* v. *Hayes*. (Paul Branzburg was a Louisville reporter who had covered a drug-related case and had refused to testify.) The media world became divided between the ''absolutists,'' who insisted that the First Amendment was clearly fundamental here, and the ''nonabsolutists,'' who argued that news personnel could not claim special exemption if compelling need were shown by the government. Among those who supported the latter position was the *New York Times*, which had always maintained this position. Caldwell had been prudent to hire his own lawyer.

More than a year after the first court actions in the case, on June 29, 1972, the Supreme Court, in a 5-to-4 decision, with Justice Byron White joining four Nixon appointees, vacated the Circuit Court decision and ruled against Caldwell and the others. Justice White wrote: ''There is no First Amendment privilege to refuse to answer the relevant and material questions asked during a good-faith grand jury investigation.'' The good faith of Attorney General John Mitchell surely might have been questioned, but Justice William O. Douglas, the court's remaining First Amendment absolutist, saw a larger issue. In a separate opinion, he wrote: ''Now that the fences of the law and the tradition that has protected the press are broken down, the people are the victims. The First Amendment, as I read it, was designed precisely to prevent this tragedy.''

Nixon and his Attorney General could have pressed contempt charges against Caldwell but decided to let the matter lie. The Supreme Court had rendered its verdict, the media world had been warned, and Nixon had other pressing matters on his mind. It was an election year and the Committee to Reelect the President, which later became appropriately known as CREEP, was worried about the black vote. Bringing Caldwell into court for trial on a charge of contempt was hardly the route to increasing Republican favor among black votes, or lessening the ever-growing tensions with the media.

A parallel event of even greater significance to both press and government took shape in the year 1971 and came to be known as the Case of the Pentagon Papers. It required a Supreme Court decision to adjudicate this case also. This is the story.

In 1967, a sorely troubled Secretary of Defense Robert F. McNamara commissioned a top-secret study of American involvement in Vietnam—to determine what had gone wrong. The study encompassed all the agencies of government involved in policy and planning and was assigned to a group of experts instructed to be "encyclopedic and objective." They were. The three months allotted to them stretched into 18 months and their final report (the body of their work filled 47 volumes) was a devastating account of misrepresentations, falsehoods, civilian bungling, military blunders and deceptions in Southeast Asia by American government officials since the end of World War II. It was submitted on January 15, 1969, to Clark M. Clifford, who had succeeded McNamara as President Johnson's Secretary of Defense in the final months of the Johnson administration. Its secrecy was paramount to those involved, but it could not be maintained.

In March 1971, the *New York Times* obtained a copy of the report. There followed three months of agonizing discussion about whether to publish or not to publish. The business and legal branches of the paper were wary; the editorial side, for the most part, felt that the story had to be told. Publisher Arthur Ochs Sulzberger, after listening to both sides, finally gave the go-ahead. A special composing room, heavily guarded, was set up. Reporters and editors were spirited out to a temporary newsroom at the Hilton Hotel. All involved were sworn to secrecy—even to their own colleagues.

On Sunday, June 13, 1971, the *New York Times* published on page one a four-column story, under a rather innocuous "feature head," detailing the background of U.S. involvement in Vietnam. The story was based on "investigative reporting" by Neil Sheehan, who had covered the war for United Press International and then for the *Times*. Inside the paper were six solid pages of excerpts from the McNamara study, which henceforth would be called the Pentagon Papers. They had been given to the *Times* by Daniel Ellsberg, a government consultant and former Rand Corporation think-tank expert, who had been involved in their composition. Ellsberg, an early hawk on Vietnam, had become so burdened by his research about the origins of the war that he had changed from hawk to dove with a mission. The *Times* promised ten installments of the papers, accompanied by interpretive news stories. On the second day of publication, President Nixon instructed Attorney General Mitchell to take action. Mitchell called the *Times* and asked them in the interest of national secu-

rity to cease publication. The *Times* refused and published a third installment. The government obtained a Federal District Court restraining order
and, on June 17, there was no further installment in the *Times*. But the
paper notified the government that it would fight to have the restraining
order removed.

On June 19, the *Washington Post* picked up where the *Times* had left
off—again after a tense 48-hour internal battle about whether to
publish—and the Attorney General went back to court and stopped the
*Post*. Then, in rapid succession, the *Boston Globe*, the *St. Louis Post-
Dispatch* and seventeen other newspapers grabbed the relay baton and
continued publication. It was the most heartening display of newspaper
unity in years. Yet there was a curious lapse in the media coverage of the
event itself. While the press-government battle received enormous coverage in the newspapers and on television, there was almost no comment on
the contents of the Pentagon Papers and their significance for United
States policy. It was not until two years later that NBC prepared and
broadcast a two-part series on the Papers that discussed this aspect.

There was of course a great and legitimate interest in the freedom of
the press issue involved. It was a government attempt to exercise prior
restraint, and not since the Alien and Sedition Act of 1798 had an American government sought in advance to prevent a newspaper from publishing a news story or commentary—and the Alien and Sedition Act had
been abrogated before a full test could be made. The lower courts were
hesitant in the Pentagon Papers case to pass final judgment and bucked
the decision from District Court to Circuit Court and finally to the Supreme Court.

On June 30, after hearing the arguments in a dramatic confrontation
that had its reverberations within the bench itself, the Supreme Court
ruled, 6-to-3, in favor of the newspapers. This particular case involved
the *Times* and the *Post*, but the entire media was watching, and the interest abroad was great. There was jubilation among the press, those who
had been involved and those who had simply watched. Almost over-
looked in the euphoria, however, was the fact that there had been nine
separate opinions, six which in varying degrees upheld the newspapers
(two on narrow grounds), and three which favored the government's position on the basis of national security.

Justice Hugo Black, in what would be his last written opinion, represented the absolute First Amendment position: "I believe that every moment's continuance of the injunctions against these newspapers amounts
to a flagrant, indefensible, and continuing violation of the First Amendment." But there were warning signs. Professor Thomas I. Emerson, the

eminent constitutional authority at Yale Law School, was cautious. In the *Columbia Journalism Review* (September/October 1971), he wrote:

> The result was certainly favorable to a free press. Put the other way, a contrary result would have been a disaster. It would have made the press subject to a very considerable extent of advance restriction. It would have changed the whole relationship between the press and government. On the other hand, the legal theory that the court adopted is, I think, cause for concern. . . . If you assume there were four who would vigorously apply the doctrine of no previous restraint, nevertheless there were five whose opinions seriously undermine the doctrine against prior restraint. Certainly the three dissenters would have made exceptions, but also [two] announced that any anticipated publication which raised an immediate danger to national security would be grounds for an injunction, and the dissenting justices would have gone at least that far.

Thus Emerson found the media to be in a vulnerable position for the future. The rapid changes in the Supreme Court, tilting the balance distinctly toward a more restrictive view of civil liberties, were self-evident. He had some advice for the media:

> I would say that one of the main things that the media can do is to educate the public to the significance of the whole system of free expression . . . The *New York Times* case has opened up the possibility of making people aware of what the role of the press is; that its role isn't simply to take handouts given by the government; it's for the people. The major problem with the system of freedom of the press today is the inability of many points of view to find an outlet. That is a very serious problem. I think that it is important for the media to be aware of that, to anticipate it, to try to take account of it.

Emerson's Jeffersonian counsel was in a sense rejected in advance by an editorial in the *New York Times* on June 16, 1971, the day after publication of the Pentagon Papers had been suspended. It said:

> A fundamental responsibility of the press in this democracy is to publish information that helps the people of the United States to understand the processes of our government, especially when these processes have been clouded over in a veil of public dissimulation and even deception. . . . Obviously the *Times* would not have made this decision [to publish the Papers] if there had been any reason to believe that publication would have endangered the life of a single American soldier or in any way threatened the security of our country or the peace of the world. These documents belong to history.

Two days later, when the *Washington Post* began publication, the *Times* again emphasized that the documents "in no way affect current plans, operations, or policy; and there seems no longer any justification for these papers . . . to bear the kind of classification that keeps them from general access." The implication here was that neither the *Times* nor perhaps any other newspaper which had joined in the fray would publish classified material relating to current or future events, no matter how salutary to the national interest public knowledge of that material might be. The conclusion was that the *Times*, in any case, had not altered its policy in regard to such information since the Bay of Pigs fiasco in 1961. At that time it withheld information which, if published, would, in the words of President Kennedy, "have saved us from a colossal mistake."

On June 17, 1775, an "irregular peasantry commanded by a physician" engaged the British troops in what has come to be known as the Battle of Bunker Hill. It was an explosion that is celebrated annually in Boston as one of the first heroic battles of the American Revolution.

One hundred and ninety-seven years later, on June 17, 1972, an irregular group of burglars, commanded by a former Central Intelligence Agency operative, attempted a break-in at the Watergate apartment and office complex in Washington, and set off an explosion which rocked the Republic that Dr. Joseph Warren and his men at Bunker Hill had fought so valiantly to establish. That event is not celebrated annually anywhere except perhaps in the newsroom of the *Washington Post* which, in the best tradition of adversary journalism, fired the opening shots which toppled a corrupt President of the Republic.

The preliminaries to Watergate, however, were not glorious. The first story about the attempted break-in was allotted a scant few inches in most newspapers around the country, even though the burglary was attempted at the headquarters of the Democratic National Committee just before the national political conventions. In the weeks that followed, the press paid little attention to the episode as it concentrated on the presidential campaigns. By contrast, the problems of Senator George McGovern's Democratic vice presidential running mate, Senator Thomas Eagleton, concerning his psychiatric history and alleged alcoholism, drew outsize headlines which ultimately forced Eagleton to withdraw and threw the Democratic campaign into disarray. It was a shockingly disgraceful performance which drew an apology from columnist Jack Anderson (about the concocted "drinking problem") after the damage had been done. Richard Nixon was reelected in November by an overwhelming margin. Nixon had the endorsement of a large majority of American newspapers which almost from the outset of the campaign had declared McGovern to be a loser.

On June 17, 1973, in the shadow of the Bunker Hill monument, after the Watergate scandal had broken wide open, the *Boston Globe* reproduced its skimpy Associated Press dispatch of June 17, 1972, with an embarrassed apology in a side story. No other newspaper had the humility to behave similarly although every newspaper by then was publishing reams of copy about the revelations and impending investigations. From that point on no holds were barred. The famous Watergate hearings on television captured the nation—except for a large pocket of embittered soap-opera regulars who felt betrayed by the networks. Finally, the articles of impeachment adopted by the House of Representatives moved Nixon to resign his presidency on August 8, 1974.

In the months that followed, the role of the press in the Watergate scandal became news in itself. Despite growls from the right that the newspapers were out to "get" Nixon because they hated him, journalists pointed (at themselves) with pride. Publishers spoke virtuously of their newspapers as watchdogs of the people, even though loud canine snores were universally in vogue during the pre-election season. Enrollment in journalism programs in the universities rose markedly. This was attributed largely to the fame of Carl Bernstein and Bob Woodward, the metropolitan staff reporters of the *Washington Post* who were credited with breaking the Watergate story and later became enshrined as "Woodstein." They wrote two best-selling books about their investigative reporting, one of which, *All the President's Men*, was turned into a first-rate newspaper-business film starring Robert Redford and Dustin Hoffman—who in turn in the public mind became Woodstein.

Generally in the media world a good feeling prevailed about the revival of the investigative reporting, a return to the muckraking tradition exemplified by such journalists as Lincoln Steffens, Ida M. Tarbell and Upton Sinclair, a sense that the press was breaking with its passive acquiescence to government policy. While right-wing criticism persisted and had some effect on public opinion, there was considerable support for the media's new-found courage. There was skepticism, however, about the post-Watergate role of the press, and much speculation on this point. The speculation was addressed by a central figure in the Watergate developments.

On October 17, 1974, Katherine Graham, chairperson of the board of the *Washington Post*, who had fully supported her editors and reporters in the Watergate process, spoke at the annual meeting of the Magazine Publishers Association. The speech was later adapted as an article in *New York* magazine, titled: "The Press After Watergate: Getting Down to New Business." Ms. Graham spoke of the painful and confusing period of "assessment and adjustment to new standards of conduct for public officials" that the nation was undergoing. There was a "new sensitivity" to wrongdoing, she said, and that was all to the good. But "there is also a new and rather indiscriminate emphasis on disclosure as *the* index of fitness for public office, and that, I think, is doing harm—harm to the nation in general, and to the nation's press in particular.''

Candor and correctness in office are vital, she conceded, but emphasis on these qualities can distort the process if it is carried to extremes and distracts the public and the press from other equally significant questions. ''This,'' she said, ''is where I see the less healthy influence of the Watergate experience.'' The press, in her view, became ''too much a party to events, too much an actor in the drama that was being played out. Some individuals became celebrities, and the whole profession was regarded in some quarters as heroic. That is an unnatural role, and to some extent a dangerous one.'' This was brought about, she said, by a default of other institutions, the failure of the opposition party, and of the agencies of justice, particularly in the early days of the scandal.

The press, she said, bore much of the same burden with regard to Vietnam: ''It adds up to an overload, I think, which is not good for us or for society.'' In Vietnam, ''it took a new group of journalists to cut through the fog of official reassurances and reveal what was happening. To lay bare the facts of Watergate, it took two young local reporters, unburdened by habits of trust and acquaintanceship. The point is that like the rest of the country, the press discovered how badly we had been taken in. The result has been to validate that cynicism which the press is always supposed to have—and to make it not a general, professional attitude but a sharp, personal, and self-serving trait. No one wants to be burdened again.'' She concluded:

The press these days should therefore be rather careful about its role. Watergate did create some problems in terms of our image and self-image. In the past two years, I fear, we may have acquired some tendencies toward over-involvement that we had better overcome . . . Nor should too much be asked of us. We are not prosecutors, judges, or legislators—or cheerleaders—and we should never be . . . How we perform will . . . determine the extent to which the press remains healthy and, if not always well regarded, at least well read. In that respect, there is a lot to one of Thomas Jefferson's lesser-known observations about the press. He wrote: ''The printers never leave us in a state of perfect rest and union of opinion. They would no longer be useful and would have to go to the plow.''

I am inclined to believe that Jefferson would join me in saying that the lady doth protest too much in a most contradictory fashion about the role of the press in both Vietnam and Watergate. The chapters in this book about Vietnam demonstrate that the handful of fresh, uncynical reporters whom Ms. Graham cites approvingly were precisely the ones who broke through the cynical mold of their more seasoned colleagues, the ones with the "general, professional attitude," particularly those based in Washington. The capital press corps was accepting, without question, the misinformation being fed to them by their intimates in government and the military. This attitude prevailed in both their regular beats in the capital and on their red-carpet junkets to Vietnam. This is a practice Ms. Graham seemed to deplore.

It was left to two metropolitan reporters on her own staff, two young men untainted by the clubhouse routine, to take up an investigation which the regulars in the Washington press corps ignored, even though the stench was right under their noses. What Ms. Graham seemed to be suggesting was that the young journalists had had their fling and now it was time to return to established order. True, they had done splendid service to the nation, but things could get out of hand. Ms. Graham, as others had before her, properly worried that the press might aspire to be a fourth branch of government if its power increased further. But it was the traditional reporters (with the support of their editors and publishers) who were already behaving like appendages of government, leaking news as requested, suppressing facts on demand, and ignoring vital information when it came from "unauthorized" sources—that is, nongovernmental persons. This was the approach that the "young Turks" in Vietnam, had rejected, as had Woodward and Bernstein in Washington.

Caution and care are sound advice to any journalist. But when this advice comes in the aftermath of an honorable demonstration of journalistic enterprise and zeal, it can have a dampening effect. Coming from the publisher of one of the nation's most influential newspapers, in the heart of the nation's capital, it can freeze the initiative of most newspapers and their staffs. Judging from post-Watergate performance of the press in the area of investigative journalism, it has had just that effect.

Paralleling the cataclysmic events that affected the press in the early 1970s, there was a ferment within the press that was rare in the history of American journalism. The "underground press"—actually it was flagrantly above ground—flourished. Begun in 1964 as a subjective protest against "the system," it advocated a lifestyle of sexual freedom, bizarre dress, rebellion against all existing moral codes, and mind expansion through experimentation with drugs and immersion in rock-'n'-roll music. Hair was the symbol, and to the "straight" world, much of the content of the underground press was hairy indeed. Revolution was the slogan but rebellion was the reality.

By 1972 there were 450 underground papers with an estimated circulation of 3 million (it was impossible to obtain exact figures). Some of the publications were fly-by-night mimeo jobs, others were expert and imaginative productions. Some evaporated in the mists of mind-blowing drugs; other succumbed to the bait dangled before them by the rock music entrepreneurs and their advertising dollars. Their social concerns diminished in almost exact ratio to their augmented exchequers.

At the turn of the 1970s, however, there was a heartening shift by many of the publications in a new direction. As the pressures of the war in Vietnam and the young black liberation movement at home became more intense, these underground papers, still in their own fashion, began to face up to the burning issues of the world above, and in effect joined forces with the existing left-wing political publications and the increasingly cohesive peace movement. Correspondingly, the rock entrepreneurs and other advertisers lost interest in the changing publications.

The impact of this rebellion on the general press was significant. At first the managers of the press looked on with tolerant amusement and some distaste—yet with an awareness that the activities and influence of the early underground press had turned young frustrated Americans away from a political solution to the problems that has sent them underground in the first place. But when the publishers began to take a look at their circulation figures, and the market analysts began to tell them they were losing young readers in droves, they took a hard look at their product, and lo! . . .

The daily press of America began to change too. Some of the changes were ludicrous. Young people's pages sprouted in Akron and Duluth telling it to the readers "like it is" and letting them know "where it's at." The undergrounders hooted in derision. But along with the fumbles came certain fundamental changes. In consonance with the liberating Supreme Court decisions on language and sex, the papers began to lose their "uptight" strictures. Naughty words appeared in print, the human body was exposed, taboo subjects came out of the closet, and the typographical face of the American newspaper began to lose its jowls. Rock and country became accepted (or at least recognized) musical forms, and regular concerts were covered along with the riotous circus events with their thousands of screaming spectators and dozens of casualties. The advertising columns of the newspapers and magazines took on the appearance of the lobby of New York's Lower East Side's famous Fillmore East, the shrine of sound.

Inside the established press, the impact of the underground press and the disenchantment with war and racism were deep-going. Newer and younger staff members of the daily press began asking themselves some fundamental questions about their own role in the production of the papers for which they worked: Why had they no voice in policy-making, in decision-making, in hiring and firing of their editors? If publishers lunched at the country club with powerful financiers who could make or break fortunes (including the fortunes of their own paper) why did the editors frown on reporters participating in an anti-Vietnam war march on their own time?

The questions led to organization, and organization led to demands for sitdowns with the owners to discuss these matters. The specter of staff participation in respected publications such as *Le Monde* in Paris (where the staff voted on the choice of an editor-in-chief) was raised to haunt American publishers. Journalism reviews, staffed by working journalists investigating the performances of newspapers, television and radio news programs, sprouted in more than a dozen cities from Providence to Honolulu. It was a time of turmoil in the ranks of the media. Even the Newspaper Guild, the union of editorial and commercial employees, was forced to break with its traditional concept that it should concern itself only with wages, hours and working conditions, and let the publishers be solely responsible for the content and conduct of their newspapers.

In other areas, publishers were being forced by pressure from the black community and their inability to cover the black community (because of justified resentment stemming from biased news stories) to hire black journalists. The number of blacks who were taken on—in relation to the general black population of the cities—was not significant. But what was significant was how the vigilance of the new staff members forced a change in the quality, and in some cases the quantity, of the reporting and commentary about news of the black community.

In Washington, New York and other major cities, women journalists, inspired by the renascent women's liberation movement, acted in concert to close the gap of inequality between themselves and their male colleagues, and to end the patronizing and often degrading manner in which news of women was being covered. Suits were filed with state and city fair employment and human rights agencies and pressure was brought to bear on the unions involved. For the first time, outside of family-owned enterprises, women became editors and discrimination in salaries and promotions was altered or halted.

When the war in Vietnam finally ended in 1975, so did much of the dissenting political activity in the United States. The journalism reviews folded one by one and the campaign for democracy in the newsrooms came to a stop. The lack of a permanent, general political opposition center in the country became painfully clear, and the need for one even clearer. The remaining underground newspapers were converted for the most part into community-oriented newspapers—significantly in university areas—and survived bravely if precariously. Their example inspired others.

A National News Council, funded initially and to a large extent continuously by the Twentieth Century Fund, came into being in 1974. Its purpose was to monitor the performance of the major news media with a view to self-criticism and self-improvement. It had enforcement provisions or possibilities. Its governing board was composed of persons inside and outside journalism, many of them professionals of great distinction. The Council's effectiveness was minor because of the hostility of a good-sized sector of the media, particularly the executive editor and publisher of the *New York Times*, A. H. Rosenthal and Arthur Ochs Sulzberger, respectively. The *Times* refused even to carry news of the Council's findings. John B. Oakes, then editor of the *Times*'s editorial page, and a member of the committee, which drafted a statement of purpose for the Council, was a vigorous proponent. The Council died for lack of funds and clear purpose in 1984.

All of this internal activity in the media bridged the first and second Nixon administrations and was accompanied by the drumbeat of the Nixon forces assaulting the media from the White House. This assault did not end with Nixon's resignation. He left as a legacy the "Nixon Court," which under Chief Justice Warren Burger pursued his war on the press particularly in the area of libel actions. In fairness it must be said that on occasion a Kennedy or Johnson appointee led the attack and, conversely, some of the Nixon appointees later rendered decisions which upheld the Constitution ably.

What then was there to be said of the post-Watergate press as the 1980s approached with the promise of Ronald Reagan? It had weathered its internal wars, heeded the advice of Katherine Graham, soft-pedaled its public service initiative, and was making more money than ever before. By 1978, newspaper industry revenues had exceeded $14 billion a year. Ownership, under vast conglomerates, was being vested in fewer and fewer hands. Lord Thomson's arrogant decree—"The job of a newspaper is to make money"—had been posted in invisible ink on the doors leading into just about every American newsroom.

Yet despite the encircling gloom, there was some heart to be taken from the quality of a new generation of journalists, many of whom had learned their lessons in the clamorous streets of the 1970s and in the excitement of the newsrooms of the time. They were free of many of the self-induced cold-war prejudices of their elders and seemed not so prone to the blandishments of their superiors. Would they hold up under tougher testing?

# 22. The Constricting Eighties

The word "corps" brings to mind a certain reporter for the *New York World-Telegram* in the days when some otherwise first-rate reporters on a beat had trouble putting a sentence together on a typewriter. They called their stories in to rewrite. Our man covered police headquarters and one night on the phone he was telling rewrite about a body full of bullet holes that had just been fished out of the East River. He spoke of the harbor police finding the "corp". The rewriteman stopped typing for a moment and said: "Don't you mean the corpse"? The reporter replied with fine scorn: "There was only *one* body."

The elite of the Washington press corps also comprises only one body, and while many people inhabit it, it behaves in a most singular fashion: Almost everyone in it thinks and writes in a similar manner and comes to pretty much the same conclusions. In an article on the Op-Ed page of the *New York Times* some years ago, I described this behavior as "journalism of the herd." For example, when a leader of the herd—say, the *Washington Post*—breaks a particular story leading to certain conclusions, the rest of the herd takes off behind the leader. Their stories will vary only in the slightest degree, and their interpretations almost not at all. Occasionally dissent will rear its head, but then only on the part of a non-elite who will be permitted space on an Op-Ed page to demonstrate the newspaper's devotion to diversity of opinion. What produces this buffalo syndrome?

In his book *The Washington Reporters*, Stephen Hess, a senior fellow at the Brookings Institute, offered some clues in a full-dress study of the Washington journalism establishment which is somewhat sociological in its approach.

There are close to 4,000 accredited correspondents in the capital, mainly white males with degrees from "good" colleges. Despite its homogeneity, the Washington press corps is most class conscious and this consciousness is perpetuated in a series of concentric circles. The inner ring, closest to the source of heat and light (that is, the government), is composed of a very few organizations: the *New York Times*, the *Washington Post*, the *Wall Street Journal*, the Associated Press and the United Press International, the major news networks, and the newsweeklies: *Time, Newsweek, U.S News* and *World Report* and *Business Week*. This is the journalistic power center, and at the center's core is the White House Correspondents Association, whose members are approved by a combination of the Association and the White House press representatives.

A middle ring comprises papers such as the *Boston Globe*, the *Los Angeles Times*, the *Chicago Tribune*, the *Baltimore Sun* and the more prominent newspapers of the Knight-Ridder and Gannett chains. After that, in the outer ring, are the rest of the media: the smaller newspapers and broadcast news people, the weekly and monthly magazines of commentary, and the itinerant reporters. The foreign press receives special treatment according to rank—and sometimes political point of view.

Television news rates lower than newspaper coverage. Partly this is because something in print survives. Television is perfect for immediate impact, but unless there is continuing exposure—such as the President commands, or the Secretary of State, or, of course, the network anchor persons—visual fame is fleeting.

What happens under this arrangement is that the inner ring has easiest access to government officials, with its representatives often acting as confidants to these government officials. The results of these contacts are the "leak" or the "trial balloon" or the sometimes exclusive story from an "unattributed source." All too often the correspondents take on the coloration and even the goals of the government in power. Never mind that it may be Republican for four or eight years, and Democratic the next round—inner ring journalists are uncommonly adaptable.

In fact, they have too often become interchangeable as government officials, and here the *New York Times* is especially a case in point. Let us say the MacNeil-Lehrer Report on public television presents a program on the Middle East. The usual pundits are there, but present also a new trim figure introduced as an Assistant Secretary of State. He is Richard L. Burt, until recently the Pentagon correspondent of the *Times*. He was subsequently named United States Ambassador to the Federal German Republic. A few days later a statement is given out by the chief spokesman of the Office of Budget and Management. His name is Edwin L. Dale Jr., a familiar former *Times* byline.

There can be no objection if journalists leave their papers for government service and stay there, or perhaps go into some other area of work or public service. But surely there is something strange in the practice of journalists going from newspapers to government service and then back to their newspapers, loaded down with restricted information which they are pledged not to reveal, and burdened by a buddy-buddy relationship with government officials with whom they have served. Leslie Gelb of the *Times* is a prime example. He has gone from his newspaper to government for at least two tours of duty and then back to his newspaper where he served as a senior news analyst in the Washington bureau, and later became deputy editorial page editor. There is also the case of William Beecher, a very good reporter, who went from the *Times* to become Assistant Secretary of Defense, and then to the *Boston Globe*, covering the Pentagon. One day these journalists are seeking to smoke out information in the State Department or the Defense Department, and the next day they are government functionaries seeking to steer reporters away from the smoke. Yet there is no objection from the publishers, no protest from editors' organizations, and not even a grunt—at least within hearing range—from the Washington herd.

This was the Washington journalism scene to which Ronald Reagan brought his entourage after his victory over Jimmy Carter in November 1980. It was a victory over a well-informed and serious President whose reserved manner had never endeared him to the press, and whose travail over the hostages held by Iran was coming to a climax in the final days of the campaign. The Reagan forces did their utmost to make things as difficult as possible for Carter. Much of this was disclosed in May 1984, in the so-called Albosta Report, named for Representative Donald Albosta, Democrat of Michigan, a two-volume, 2,413-page document prepared after an investigation of the theft of materials from the Carter campaign headquarters. William Casey, the late director of the CIA, was manager of the first Reagan campaign.

The report disclosed the existence of a Reagan campaign intelligence team whose assignment it was to manipulate the press during the last stages of the hostage negotiations with false stories of a Carter arms-for-hostages deal and an invasion of Iran. This "disinformation" (widely published) may have sabotaged Carter's negotiating efforts and prevented the release of the hostages before the November elections—precisely the goal of the Reagan campaign strategists.

Thus the mark of the new administration was clear even before Reagan took office, surrounded by his trio of White House managers—James Baker, Edwin Meese and Michael Deaver—who protected the President from any undesirable exposure with the ferocity of guard dogs. The policy for press and public was simple and undeviating: Present a well-rehearsed President to the public with a prepared speech as often as possible. Keep unrehearsed press conferences to a minimum (Reagan held fewer official press conferences by far than any President in modern history). Establish the President as a man eager to meet the people: his packaged presentation would offer the image if not the substance of public contact.

In an article in the *Village Voice* (September 18, 1984), Mark Hertsgaard, who was preparing a book about Reagan and the media, described how the White House press apparatus worked since it took over in January 1981:

> Reagan and his advisers have assembled an extensive propaganda apparatus that does most of its work out of sight—in private White House meetings each morning to set ''the line of the day'' that will later be fed to the press; in regular phone calls to the networks intended to influence Reagan's coverage on the evening news; in quiet executive orders imposing extraordinary new government secrecy measures, including granting the FBI and the CIA permission to infiltrate the press.

The underlying principles of the Reagan team strategy, Hertsgaard said, were to plan ahead; focus on specific goals; stay on the offensive, control the flow of information, limit reporters' access to the President; talk about the issues you want to talk about; speak in one voice, and repeat the same message many times. Thus was ''the Great Communicator'' put together in as skillful an operation as the nation's capital had ever seen. Television of course was the principal medium for Reagan's successful approach. Steven R. Weisman, White House correspondent, wrote in the *New York Times Magazine* (October 14, 1984), less than a month before Reagan's second-term election victory:

> The President has displayed his news media artistry at a time when television has become the dominant means by which the public gets its news. Mr. Reagan and his aides have understood and exploited what they acknowledge to be the built-in tendency of television to emphasize appearances and impressions more than information.

In an even more significant commentary, Weisman wrote:

> Most Presidents have recognized that the press in not simply a purveyor of news, but a kind of surrogate for the public, questioning Presidential performance and, to some degree, holding the President accountable for his statements and actions. Under that broad definition, even Presidents who have disliked and distrusted the press have met with reporters on

a fairly regular basis and given spirited, detailed answers to their questions. Mr. Reagan has been an exception. During his administration he has tended to operate in a kind of cocoon, sheltered from the press. . . . Even when he entertains questions from the press— at news conferences, small gatherings with reporters and in private interviews—he offers only limited access to his ideas and attitudes themselves. . . .

The phrase "limited access" is generous when the following exchange, at a Reagan press conference eight weeks before the 1984 election, is examined:

*Reagan:* No, let me just say, we'll be back and there will be more of—we'll be having more of these. So . . .
*Reporter:* Oh, when?
*Reporter:* When?
*Reagan:* What?
*Reporter:* Before the election?
*Reporter:* We'd like to make a date.
*Reporter:* What about debates?
*Reagan:* I'm just going to wait and surprise you again.
*Reporter:* Are we going to have a full-scale half-hour news conference, sir, before the election?
*Reagan:* I don't know; but I've been talking about that myself.

Given Reagan's frequent gaffes, fumblings and inaccurate statements at press conferences, it was no surprise that the official press conference virtually disappeared in 1987 after Reagan's disastrous November 1986 press conference seeking to explain away the Iran/contra revelations. After that the President was placed back in his cocoon and tucked safely away. At times the cocoon was given a transparent exterior as the President was ferried about the nation in a series of contrived public appearances to give the impression that he was still in charge. But the magic was gone, of course, and the journalists, who had regained some spine in the manifestation of disarray in the Executive branch in 1986–1987, took after Reagan in herd-like fashion. Their ranks were intact: their direction had changed.

If the magic had vanished—along with the "magicians" who had stage-managed the Great Communicator's performances—the damage for the media, and for freedom of expression generally, which had been perpetrated by the Administration, remained. Almost from the time Reagan took office, a series of executive orders and federal agency decrees had severely restricted the ability of the media to report fully and openly about government activities, and had limited access by the public to heretofore available information. These are some of the more flagrant actions that were taken:

• A pilot program was instituted to establish the trustworthiness of Defense Department employees by subjecting 3,500 of them to lie detector tests. In addition government employees were compelled to agree to prepublication scrutiny of any writing done after the employee had left government service. These two orders were rescinded in part in 1984.

• The Justice Department issued guidelines to suppress all information falling under the Freedom of Information Act exemptions regardless of the nature of this material. Similarly, the White House issued an order warning federal agencies not to grant fee waives for reporters seeking information under the Act.

• The CIA filed charges with the Federal Communications Commission against ABC News. It maintained that in a broadcast ABC had falsely alleged CIA involvement with a banker who was under indictment on a charge of fraud.

• A Canadian journalist was expelled from the United States for providing coverage for a Cuban news agency.

• The Defense Department accused the *Washington Post* of ''aiding the enemy'' by publishing a report that an upcoming space shuttle was to be a military mission—even though the government acknowledged that all of the *Post*'s information was on the public record.

• The Reagan administration consistently sought to restrict contacts between reporters and administration officials. At one point Reagan said ''I've had it up to my keister'' with leaks. When the leaks continued the Executive branch conveniently shifted the blame to the Congress. Investigation of leaks was a common practice, often involving high Administration officials. In an investigation of United States military strategy in Lebanon, Secretary of State George Shultz said he would resign before he would take a lie-detector test.

In 1983, for the first time in a major military operation, reporters were prevented from accompanying United States military forces in the first phases of an operation. This was the invasion of Grenada. The only reports about the operation came from the Defense Department. There were protests from the press—not because of an action which was clearly in violation of international law and the charter of the United Nations, but because of the press restrictions. In the months that followed, the Defense Department worked out a set of guidelines which paid lip service to freedom of the press but permitted the final decision to rest with the Department. The press went along with the agreement. Proof that the military intended to maintain its limits on press coverage was provided in 1987 when United States Navy ships accompanied Kuwaiti tankers flying the American flag through the Persian Gulf. When the action began, reporters were kept far from the scene, and a helicopter bearing reporters was the recipient of a flare warning when it ventured too close to the action. Only one news organization—Knight-Ridder—protested. The others were silent.

As though to underscore the new tough policy of the military versus the press, Secretary of State Shultz said after Grenada that American reporters were not "on our side," but "always against us." When Reagan was asked at a news conference what Shultz meant by "us," he replied: "Our side, militarily—in other words, all of America." The Vietnam syndrome had been revived.

Another example of the "us" and "them" attitude was given in 1982 after Michael Deaver, then still in charge in the White House, issued an order forbidding questions by reporters at "photo opportunities" with the President. NBC refused to take pictures and there were reports that the other networks would follow suit. Deaver called in Robert McFarland, chief of NBC's Washington bureau, and said there would be no change in the ground rules. McFarland (obviously on orders from above) caved in. At a press conference later he said: "Well, it's their White House. He is the President of the United States of America. It is our job to report what he does. It's their Rose Garden. They set the rules."

A former network reporter behaved quite differently four years later on an issue involving a "disinformation program" directed at the Libyan leader Muammar el-Qadaffi. Prepared by National Security Adviser Admiral John Poindexter and issued by the White House, it was designed to undermine the Qaddafi administration by causing him to believe that he faced greater internal opposition than was the case. It was aimed also at creating false information about Qaddafi's alleged acts of terrorism to be published and broadcast in the United States and abroad. On October 8, 1986, Bernard Kalb, who had reported on international affairs for CBS and NBC before becoming the chief spokesman for the State Department, resigned his post, saying: "Faith in the word of America is the pulsebeat of our democracy. Anything that hurts America's credibility hurts America."

It was a rare act of principle on the part of a government functionary, and it was widely applauded by others in the Washington press corps. "I've been agonizing about this thing," Kalb said after his resignation. "I knew nothing about it. I was concerned about my own integrity. My own integrity means something to me personally but in the grand scheme of things I'm a simple asterisk. What I know is I don't want my integrity to get scooped up in this controversy."

Sam Donaldson, ABC's White House correspondent, got the news about Kalb aboard a plane filled with reporters accompanying President Reagan on a trip to Spain. He shouted out the news, Donaldson said, and the reporters said: "Attaboy, Bernie!"

Then life went on as usual.

A popular pastime among the media watchers in the 1980s was to gauge the extent to which the press had fallen out of favor with the public. How accurate and fair are reporters? the pollsters asked. Do they respect the right of privacy? Do they overstep the bounds of decency in their investigative reporting? What about leaks? Do they worry, as they dig into a story, about possible harm to the nation's security? In a long cover story in *Time* magazine (December 12, 1983), William A. Henry, who watched the media for the magazine, came to a dolorous finding:

> Public respect for journalism has fallen dramatically in recent years, threatening one of the foundations of the country's democratic system. . . . Indeed, libel verdicts have become a telling measure of public eagerness to punish the press. According to Stanford University Law Professor Marc Franklin, since 1976 nearly 85% of 106 major libel verdicts by juries have been defeats for journalist defendants. . . .
>
> Apart from manner and attitude . . . reporting from Washington tends, inevitably, to be highly speculative and to rely heavily on anonymous sources and undocumented assertions. Critics also fault the capital's press corps for preoccupation with politics and frequent failure to delve into the performance of government agencies, which spend the bulk of the nation's budget.

While some of the criticisms surely were accurate, Henry's cited complaints themselves were highly speculative. If juries were handing down verdicts simply to punish the press, that said more about a fair system of jurisprudence than it did about newspapers or television stations. Leaks are not created by journalists but by government officials or their confidants. The contents of this book demonstrate that Washington correspondents are overly conscious of the "national security" factors and more often than not will voluntarily or on request withhold information which should be in the public domain. As for their failure to cover federal agencies which spend huge sums of the public's money, why did Henry not specifically target the Defense Department which spends the most without scrutiny but is generally regarded as a "sacred cow" by the Washington press corps and, apparently, by *Time*. Having gone through his litany of criticism, however, Henry ended up with a happier conclusion about the American press:

> U.S. journalism is generally good. Reporters and editors are better educated than their predecessors and are readier to take on difficult topics. Partly as a result of the influence of television, which has made the world seem smaller, many local newspapers now publish considerably more international news. . . . Social trends, which newspapers long over-

looked . . . are now covered thoughtfully. In recent years the press has learned to report about economics, education, medicine, science and the computer revolution as fully and discerningly as it follows crime and politics.

A far less charitable estimate of the American media than Henry's strained and sometimes confusing picture was being offered in profusion during the 1980s by several ultra-conservative organizations devoted primarily to observing the media (heckling might be a more exact term). Chief among these was Accuracy in Media (AIM), guided by Reed Irvine, an indefatigable participant in television programs, letters-to-the editors columns, stockholders' meetings and public convocations. Irvine published *AIM Report*, wrote a syndicated newspaper column, and prepared a five-day-a-week radio commentary, *Media Monitor*. His work was funded by several right-wing foundations (such as Scaife and Coors) and by several big corporations, including Mobil Oil.

AIM's chief targets were any newspaper or television program which expressed concern about nuclear reactors or Agent Orange or tried to present an unbiased view of Nicaragua's Sandinista government or Jane Fonda. CBS News was a special target, according to an article by Miriam and Walter Schnier in *The Nation* (March 30, 1985). They reported Irvine writing in 1975: "At least some of the blood shed by South Vietnam when Saigon fell to the Communist aggressors last April belongs on the hands of the Columbia Broadcast Corporation. CBS' biased news . . . proved influential in turning public sentiment against the war effort."

In general, encouraged by the hostility of the Reagan administration toward the press, Irving presented the American media as a breeding ground for a left-wing conspiracy to undermine basic American institutions. Liberal and radical publications such as *The Nation*, *The Progressive*, *In These Times*, *Mother Jones*, and *The Guardian* inspected and commented adversely on the work of AIM, but the major newspapers reported fully—and almost without editorial observation—on Irvine's products, and he was handled with kid gloves on the television programs where he was an invited guest, or a perennial presence in the audience, no matter how absurd his presentation. In fact, *The Nation* reported, Arthur Ochs Sulzberger, publisher of the *New York Times*, met with Irvine once a year, and Katherine Graham, chairman of the board of the *Washington Post*, a frequent recipient of Irvine's blasts, also met with him from time to time.

Other media critics fare less well in the major newspapers. A case in point is Ben Bagdikian, dean of the Graduate School of Journalism at the

University of California at Berkeley. He is the author of several books about the media and is recognized as one of the most perceptive observers of American journalism. In 1984 Beacon Press published his latest book, *Media Monopoly*, a sobering look at the structure of the American information establishment. Bagdikian maintained that in the 1980s "the majority of American media—newspapers, magazines, radio, television, books and movies—were controlled by fifty giant corporations."

These corporations, Bagdikian wrote, financially interlocked with massive industries and some international banks, constituted a private "Ministry of Information and Culture." He concluded: "Media power is political power. . . . When fifty men and women, chiefs of their corporations, control more than half the information and ideas that reach 220 million Americans, it is time for Americans to examine the institutions from which they receive their daily picture of the world."

The news media, Bagdikian said, are not monolithic, nor are they frozen into a permanent set of standards, but "they suffer from built-in biases that protect corporate power and consequently weaken the public's ability to understand forces that create the American scene." What is reported, Bagdikian said, enters the public agenda; what is not reported may not be lost forever, but it may be lost at a time when it is needed most: "More than any other single private source, and often more than any governmental source, the fifty dominant media corporations can set the national agenda."

When reviews of the book appeared, agenda-setting was apparent. The *New York Times Review of Books* review dutifully acknowledged Bagdikian's stature as a media critic and then proceeded to assault his evidence. It concluded that he had not proved his case. Other major newspapers came to the same conclusion in reviews similarly fashioned. Even the reviewer for the *Columbia Journalism Review*, which has been proving Bagdikian's thesis in smaller doses for some years, also found his evidence wanting. Reading the reviews one came away with the feeling that Bagdikian's documentation was too strong for many reviewers (the book fared much better in smaller publications and some magazines) who simply were terrified by the book's thesis. If it were true then many of the reviewers might have had to question why they continued to work for their publications—and that they were not yet prepared to do.

The *Columbia Journalism Review* redeemed itself considerably with the publication in its November-December 1986 issue of a long and perspective article titled: "Declarations of Independence." The author was James Boylan, a historian and professor at the University of Massachusetts at Amherst, and the *Review*'s first editor. Boylan offered a retrospective of the last twenty-five years of American journalism in which he reviewed with approval the heady rebellions of the 1960s and 1970s, and then noted the changes that had set in in the 1980s, which he termed "the new age of deference."

Starting with the seizure late in 1979 of the United States embassy in Teheran, he said, and the Russian occupation of Afghanistan, the press had "both reported and joined" what had been described by former State Department official George Kennan as "the greatest militarization of thought and discourse" since World War II. This shift was enormously encouraged by statements like that of Michael J. O'Neil, then editor of the New York *Daily News*, who spoke as the retiring president of the Society of American Newspaper Editors in 1982:

> We should make peace with the government. We should not be its enemy. . . . We are supposed to be the observers, not the participants—the neutral party, not the permanent opposition. . . . We should cure ourselves of the adversarial mindset. The adversarial culture is a disease attacking the nation's vital organs.

This, of course, is the perfect guidepost for journalists in the age of the corporate media, and too many of them have adopted it as the convenient route to status and security. It is evident particularly in television news coverage of events little understood by the public because they have never been properly explained to the public. Examples are the unprovoked bombing of Libya, the invasion of Grenada, the flagging of Kuwaiti ships by the United States in the Persian Gulf, and the misrepresentation of the situation in Central America to the point where it becomes accepted "fact" that the Sandinista government of Nicaragua is a menace to the security of the United States. It spills over into the "civilian" area where television helped the public declare war at Lake Placid at the 1984 Olympics in the match of the hockey teams of the United States and the Soviet Union. The hysterical cries of "U.S.A.! U.S.A.!" not only drowned any possible hope for the survival of Olympic standards, but marked the Soviet Union as the enemy not only in the political sphere but in the sporting scene as well. And the latter served the former wall: if you can lick 'em on the ice, you can lick 'em on the ground too.

James Reston, after forty-eight years with the *New York Times*, and more than fifty years in journalism, retired from his distinguished career in 1987. In a farewell column on August 2, in a nostalgic mood, he conceded that officials were no better than they ever were, but that the reporting was better. He thought we had won the cold war but didn't know it, and that the Constitution was still working on its 200th birthday.

He described himself as an up-to-date stick-in-the-mud optimist and promised some time in the future to write a long love letter to America. There was not too much about journalism in the column, except the sense that he was quite pleased with its performance.

There was much more about journalism in a set of lectures Reston gave before the Council on Foreign Relations in 1966, later published as *The Artillery of the Press*. Reston evoked Arnold Bennett's faith in America's "saving remnant," as against the "unsound majority" of the mass of the people. First Reston advocated a noncompliant press laying down a constant artillery barrage of criticism directed against government to help the "largest number of people" understand the complexities of a changing world. But in the enfolding lectures there was a seemingly contradictory plea for an alliance between government and press. The responsibility of the press in this alliance, Reston said, would be to explain the policies of government, accomplished with the collaboration of the best minds in all sectors of the intelligent "remnant" resisting the simplistic solutions of an ignorant majority. Reston's career over the years, his easy access to those in power in government, industry and the professions, would indicate his abiding faith in the principles set forth twenty years earlier.

It should of course be the role of the press to explain government policy; but if that explanation demonstrates that the policy is detrimental to the public interest, then the press has an obligation to follow through with vigorous criticism and opposition to that policy. Unfortunately, the majority of the owners of the press—that is, corporate power—do not believe in an adversarial stance to government except as rhetorical flourishes. Michael O'Neil spoke ably in their behalf.

The communications industry is a crucial agency of the power complex which sets the course for the nation and, to a great extent, the world. The media for the most part condition the people to think the thoughts that are preferred by government, the military and industry. Given the growing concentration of ownership of the media, it is not reasonable to think that these owners will separate themselves from government—and therefore from support of its policies.

The main barrier to change, for the media and for all major institutions of American society, is the basic foreign and domestic policies of the government of the United States which have been in force since the end of World War II, guided by the theology of anti-communism. The cold war continues, with an occasional truce, and it dominates the thinking and the actions of the nation.

The task for those journalists who accept this premise is to keep on fighting to get its truth published. Then, as has happened before in our history, an enlightened public will demand change, insisting that the "consent of the governed" must be the dominating factor in the making and shaping of policy.

# 23. Spooky Tales

A main concern of this book has been the working press, the link between the owners of the newspapers and their counterparts in broadcast news, and the reading and listening public. Why such concern about this group? Because the men and women involved in the daily or weekly work of publishing a newspaper or a newsmagazine surely must assume considerable responsibility for what appears in their publications. The public often perceives of news staffs as much-put-upon people battling their superiors to get their heroic material into print. That is sometimes true, sometimes not. In too many instances, reporters and sub-editors have yielded to the wishes of their superiors without a fight. It is appropriate to examine how this group has comported itself in the post-Watergate period, and a sharp case history, with global implications, concerns the Central Intelligence Agency and the press.

From December 25–27, 1977, the *New York Times* published a series of articles detailing the interplay between the CIA and the American media. Among the distinctions of the series was the introduction into the vocabulary of international communications of a new word, "blowback," to join such linguistic horrors as "destabilization" and "disinformation." Blowback, according to the CIA's semanticists, occurred when a news story or a news analysis planted by the CIA in publications abroad (usually under CIA control) floated back across oceans and mountains and was "replayed" or appeared as "domestic fallout" in publications in the United States. This occurrence, CIA officials said, was unfortunate but often inevitable. "It hits where it hits," said one, according to John M. Crewdson in the *New York Times* (December 25, 1977).

There was little in the *Times* series that had not been published earlier, but the cumulative effect of having all the detail and documentation of press collaboration with the CIA published in one package was devastating in its implications for the traditional adversarial relationship between press and government. The series particularly confirmed the investigative reporting on the subject by Carl Bernstein (of the *Washington Post*'s Watergate team) in an article in *Rolling Stone* magazine (October 27, 1977) and earlier reports in the *Columbia Journalism Review* (Stuart H. Loory, "The CIA's Use of the Press: A Mighty Wurlitzer," September–October 1974).

The *Times* articles established without possible contradiction that the CIA for thirty years had been engaged in an "unremitting" effort to shape foreign opinion in support of American foreign policy. It had at various times owned fifty newspapers, news services, radio stations, and periodicals abroad as "cover" organizations. At least twelve American publishing houses, some "witting" (with the knowledge of the employer), some not, had printed 250 books in the English language paid for by the CIA. More than one hundred journalists (American) worked as salaried CIA operatives (while employed by news organizations) and scores more worked for free. Twelve full-time CIA personnel worked as "reporters" with writing accreditation from the newsgathering organizations they "represented." Eighteen journalists had spurned lucrative offers from the CIA. All in all, the "Propaganda Assets Inventory" of the CIA, as it was known, encompassed more than eight hundred news and information organizations and individuals.

Somehow it seemed to have become accepted by publishers and participating journalists that all this activity was quite proper as long as it did not get unloaded on the American public. After all, the reasoning went, the CIA was forbidden by its franchise in 1947 from tampering with the American mind (a restriction eased by the Reagan administration), but foreign minds were something else. Some of the practices did tend to create uncomfortable situations because they demonstrated clearly that an agency of the United States government was engaged in the business of lying. But since only foreigners were involved, it seemed quite in order. Further we were at cold war with "the international communist conspiracy," and surely all patriotic journalists would want to give their support to the cause.

In the midst of the flurry caused by the revelations about the CIA and the press, a letter was published in the *New York Times* by Miles Copeland, a former CIA official. He wrote: "To my knowledge, every American correspondent serving in the Middle East or Africa from 1947 up to . . . 1975 and 1976 qualified as a 'CIA agent,' according to Carl Bernstein's definition. You see, contrary to the current trend, foreign correspondents in those good old days were on our side.''

Despite the arrogant assumption of this remark, there is little doubt that many correspondents were motivated by a myopic sense of team loyalty and by the instinct of journalism of the herd, which permitted them to discard a natural skepticism about official pronouncements. In fact, the history of modern international reporting is littered with the unreliable remains of those who accepted the official version of the American policy and practice. Guided or misguided patriotism aside, however, there is an old fashioned matter of ethics and morality involved. Most journalists know that the CIA has manufactured and continues to manufacture false and misleading information. The First Amendment, without expressing it in precise terms, would seem to impose upon these journalists an obligation to expose all false and misleading information, no matter who the purveyor—a president of the United States, or a director of the CIA who deliberately lies under oath before a committee of the Congress. A case in point was the testimony in 1973 of Richard Helms, former director of the CIA, who later conceded that he had given false information about the CIA's role in Chile in testimony at a confirmation hearing on his appointment as ambassador to Iran.

The revelations about the CIA and the press should have roused a storm of soul-searching among American journalists, but there were merely a few drops of remorse in some cases and in others none at all. Stanley Karnow, a foreign correspondent who had served long tours of duty in France and Southeast Asia, wrote on the Op-Ed page of the *New York Times* (December 18, 1977) after the Bernstein article had appeared: ''We know, of course, that the CIA recruited members of the press for various purposes. Back in the early 1950s, in fact, a senior agency official made me an offer that, happily, I was able to refuse—not out of ethical motives, but because, I recall, a double life would have confused my existence. I presume that other newsmen acted differently.''

The presumption is as accurate as Karnow's remarkable coolness about journalistic ethics and morality. The *Times* itself, having published its exposure of CIA manipulation of the press (perhaps partnership would be a more exact description), sought to mitigate the circumstances in which journalists had cooperated. In a December 27, 1977, editorial, it said that it had been a different time, a time of war in Korea and Vietnam, a time of confrontation with the Soviet Union and the People's Republic of China, and it was therefore understandable that journalists regarded such cooperation as a natural matter—as part of the ''common struggle,'' so to speak.

History has demonstrated, however, that in the intense Cold War years, the government has invoked the slogan "common struggle" as a cover for the suppression of opposition to its policies at home and the right of self-determination abroad—all in the name of freedom. Neither American policymakers nor opinion makers in the media will ever come to grips with history, or with themselves, until they examine the assumptions that underlay, and to my mind still underlie, basic American policy. There is scant evidence that journalists of the post-Watergate era have undertaken an examination of the policy—or of themselves.

What happened when one journalist acted according to his conscience—and how his colleagues reacted to his behavior—forms the subject of the next case history. Again it involves the CIA and it is revealing of who stands sentinel over the public's right to know, and who gives way to the predators of that right. The central figure here is Daniel Schorr, for many years a leading correspondent of CBS television news, which was until its emasculation by its corporate controllers, beginning in 1986, the most respected newsgathering organization in commercial broadcasting.

In 1976 Schorr was covering the "intelligence beat" for CBS, an area which included the CIA, the FBI, and other federal security agencies. Disclosures of illegal activities by the FBI and the incursion of the CIA on the domestic front had generated much news on the beat, and Schorr had been kept very busy. He was not a popular man. Gruff in appearance and behavior, he had in the line of duty incurred the hostility of government bureaucrats, particularly that of Richard Helms, former director of the CIA. Schorr had in addition offended many of his fellow journalists in Washington because of his persistent and sometimes ungentle manner in pursuing a story. He was not, so to speak, a member in good standing of the journalistic gentlemen's club, although his credentials as a reporter were impeccable. A main characteristic of club members was their reluctance to antagonize official news sources. Here Schorr rudely disagreed.

On January 23, 1976, the House of Representatives Committee on Standards and Official Conduct, having compiled in extended hearings an uncomplimentary report on the activities of the CIA, voted to make the report public. Various sections of it had already been "leaked" to the media, and Schorr in a broadcast on January 28 had disclosed some of the contents. Among the items was an allegation that William S. Paley, the dominant figure at CBS, had cooperated with the CIA in providing journalistic cover for its agents. Paley was understandably upset over this disclosure by his own correspondent, whom he had in any case never much liked.

After the House committee vote to disclose the report, considerable pressure was exerted by Executive branch whips on Capitol Hill and the full House on January 30 voted *not* to make the report public. There was some media grumbling, but it subsided. Schorr, however, did not. He managed to obtain a copy of the report and offered it to Clay Felker, then editor of New York's iconoclastic weekly *Village Voice*. The *Voice*, in its February 11 issue, published major portions of the report with a loud splash, and Schorr—when it was disclosed that he had been the intermediary—became the target of a three-pronged assault: corporate, government, and journalistic.

CBS removed Schorr from his intelligence assignment and then suspended him, with pay. For the first time in years Schorr became a reporter without an assignment and without either work or outlet. The House committee, which had rarely conducted a serious inquiry into Congressional conduct or standards, asked for and received $350,000 to investigate the leak of its report and the possibility of criminal charges against Schorr if he refused to testify about his sources in obtaining the report.

The unkindest cuts, however, in the early days came from Schorr's colleagues in the Washington press corps. Laurence Stern of the *Washington Post* was the first to name Schorr as the person who had given the report to the *Village Voice* (the *Columbia Journalism Review*, May–June 1976). The *New York Times* passed somber judgment upon Schorr, saying that he had done "responsible" journalism a disservice in making the report available for a cash sale (editorial, March 11, 1976). Schorr had conceded that Felker had offered him a sum of money for the report, but Schorr said he would turn any proceeds over to the Washington-based Committee for Freedom of the Press, an organization of journalists which provided legal assistance for colleagues under attack. The journalists' committee expressed its willingness to accept an offer from Schorr, then announced that it would "decline any gifts that may be offered." In the *Washington Post* Charles Seib, the newspaper's ombudsman—whose job it is to evaluate the contents of his own newspaper—instructed Schorr that the "dollar sign is the danger sign in journalism." An innocent observer might have suspected, after all the talk about money, that a reporter who accepted a paycheck for his work was barren of integrity.

The journalistic attack on Schorr, however, was more sinister: many in the press had taken an act of courage and conscience and turned it into a crassly commercial transaction, which of course it never was. The criticism was doubly ironic in the case of the *New York Times*. The *Times* had published the highly classified Pentagon Papers—which it had obtained from Daniel Ellsberg in 1971 in much the same manner that the *Village Voice* had obtained the House committee report from Schorr (although no money has been reported in the Ellsberg arrangement)—and then republished the Papers for profit in the form of a book. Further, the *Times*'s book publishing subsidiary had subsequently brought out books by President Nixon's chief of staff, H. R. Haldeman, and by Nixon himself, in what can only be regarded as purely cash transactions involving authors whose credibility was something less than pristine.

The outcry against Schorr was very personal. *Newsweek* magazine (February 23, 1976) published a collection of snide anecdotes about him. Other profiles, emanating mostly from Washington, described him as ascerbic, arrogant, egomaniacal, and friendless in the media. Gradually the press settled on "abrasive" as the definitive adjective. But slowly others in the world of journalism began to see the dangers in this unprincipled attack, however juicy reading it might be. The Newspaper Guild circulated a Hands-Off-Schorr petition which had gathered 5,500 signatures by September. Soberer voices, even in the Washington press corps, began to take notice that they could be next if the House committee went after Schorr.

The committee called scores of witnesses to determine whether to cite Schorr for contempt. Then, after an expenditure of $100,000, it abruptly abandoned its pursuit. There were two obvious reasons: first, the entire House was standing for election two months hence, and its members saw the lack of wisdom in tangling with an awakening press corps upon which it depended for publicity; second, Schorr's own principled stand. When he appeared before the committee, Schorr had nine times refused to disclose his sources in obtaining the secret report. He said: "To betray a confidential source would mean to dry up many future sources for many future reporters. The ultimate losers would be the American public and their free institutions. But beyond all that, to betray a source would be to betray myself, my career and my life. To say that I refuse to do so is not saying it quite right. I cannot do it."

This clear and simple affirmation of conscience (plus the public campaign) moved the media owners themselves to begin to reclaim Schorr, in the abstract, as one of their own, and this too was not lost on the election-conscious Congress. Even the management of CBS, with Schorr still under suspension, greeted his statement as a heroic act of principle. But if the media generally had invoked this principle eight months earlier, when the storm first broke, there almost certainly would have been no Congressional hearing, no public intimidation of Schorr (and of other reporters watching the proceedings), and many members of the Washington press corps would have been deprived of the opportunity of going after a heretic in their midst with ax handles. Above all, CBS might not have dared to suspend Schorr.

As it turned out, Schorr relieved CBS of further embarrassment by resigning on September 28, 1976, after twenty-three years of service. CBS agreed to pay his salary until 1979, the end of his contract. After his departure, Schorr joined the lecture circuit, taught at a university, and wrote a book, *Clearing the Air* (Houghton Mifflin, 1977). But for many years the general American public was deprived of one of the few sharp reportorial and analytical voices which truly understood the need for maintaining an adversarial relationship between press and government. In 1986 Schorr became chief political analyst for National Public Radio and once again had a deserved and receptive audience.

What these case histories demonstrate is that when the press fulfills its adversarial task, as Schorr did, and as the *New York Times* did in its series on the CIA, it forces national recognition of an issue which cannot be ignored. When the organized employees of the press and nationally known media personalities rally to the support—finally—of one of their own who is under government fire, the federal dogs can be called off.

These cases also raise an important point: why the public generally is not motivated to come to the aid of reporters and editors when they are under attack, as they certainly were in the later years of the 1970s. A seeming contradiction levels out into an apparent truth. Public hostility to the media—particularly to the newspapers—may be engendered not because people think the press has become too powerful, but because they may feel that it has not exercised its power in the public interest. Therefore, when publishers under attack wave the banner of the First Amendment, the public understandably—if not always wisely—reacts with a measure of skepticism, and sometimes cynicism.

# Index

## A

Abel, Elie, 174, 176
Acheson, Dean, 110; on Communism, 67, 71; Under Secretary of State, 33, 35, 67
Adamic, Louis, xiv
Advertising, 13, 15, 16; McCarthy charges against *Time*, 90; *New York Times*, 18; radical newspapers, 283
Agence France Presse, 19
Agency for International Development, 234
Agnew, Spiro T., 278, 279
Akers, Milburn P., 44
Albee, Edward, 260
*Albuquerque Journal*, 81
Alden, Robert, 125
Algeria, 232
Allen, Frank A., 113
Allen, Robert S., 174
Alsop, Joseph, 19 37, 44, 204, 237; and T. Dewey, 48, 49; on McCarthyism, 65; and Vietnam war, 184, 203, 232, 257
Alsop, Stewart, 37, 44; on Cuba, 160;

Alsop, Stewart (*continued*)
and T. Dewey, 48, 49; on H. Matusow, 128; on McCarthyism, 65; on H. Wallace, 41
American Broadcasting System, 99, 208
American Civil Liberties Union, 36, 150; rights of access in press, 23, 24, 274, 276
American Federation of Labor, vii , 287
American Friends of Vietnam, 185
American Labor Party, 45
American Legion, 183
American Medical Association, 287
American Mission in Vietnam, 190
American Newspaper Guild: and Communism investigations, 134-138; and Eastland hearings, 146, 147; New York Guild, xii, l37, 138, 141; and press labor, vii - xiii, 267, 287
American Newspaper Publishers Association, 16, 20, 67; address by President Kennedy; Bureau of Advertising, 15; and Eastland committee, 147

American Revolution: and press, 11
American Society of Newspaper Editors, 20, 66, 70; and British Press Council, 269, 270; Code of Ethics, 271, 272; and Eastland committee, 147, 148; and Hutchins Commission report, 266; speech by President Kennedy, 160; speech by Vice President Nixon, 181; and Wechsler-McCarthy hearing, 88, 91-94, 101
Americans for Democratic Action, 87, 102
Americans for Intellectual Freedom, 53
Anderson, Jack, 66-68, 71, 75
Andrews, Bert, 76
Arbenz, Jacobo, 154
*Arizona Republic,* 231
*Arkansas Gazette,* 258, 265
Aronson, James: biography, vii ; Eastland committee hearing, 139, 142-144, 151; interview with J. Brown, 250-253; McCarthy committee hearing, 97-99; and *National Guardian,* 8, 94, 98, 143, 198, 280, 282; and press in Germany, x, xi, 96-98, 143; and Vietnam war, 188, 242
*Asahi Shimbun* (Tokyo), 188
Ashmore, Harry S., 258, 259, 265
Asia: anti-U.S. propaganda, 199; U.S. policy in, 107, 185, 211, 220, 257; *see also* Vietnam
Associated Press, 19, 37, 44, 81, 85, 86, 125, 196, 218; charges by H. Matusow, 90; and "Chinese in Korea" photos, 110, 111; and Korean war, 105, 107, 117, 120, 121; and radicalism, 30; and U.S. base in Guatemala, 155-158; and Vietnam war, 188, 190, 192, 195, 199, 202, 209, 240, 241, 258, 259
Association of Working Press, 285, 286
*Atlanta Constitution,* 40
*Atlantic Monthly,* 172, 266
Atlantic Pact, 52

Attorney General's list of subversive organizations, 36, 46
Australia, 243

# B

Bagdikian, Ben H., 175, 178, 179, 269
Baggs, William C., 258, 259
Baldwin, Hanson, 111, 232, 255
*Baltimore Sun,* 30, 255
Bao Dai, 183
Barnet, Melvin L.: dismissed by *New York Times,* 136-138, 140, 152; Eastland committee hearing, 132-134
Barrett, Edward W., 104, 105
Barron, Jerome A., 273-279
Barth, Alan, 72, 73
Batista, Fulgencio, 153, 203, 204
Bay of Pigs invasion: *see under* Cuba
Bayley, Edwin R., 85, 86
Beach, Keyes, 124
Belfrage, Cedric: and J. Aronson, x, xi, xiv; deportation attempts, 98-100, 139, 282; congressional committee hearings, 94-99; and press, 100-102, 151; and *National Guardian,* xiv, 59, 280
Belknap, Paul, 16
Bennett, James Gordon, 12
Bentley, Elizabeth, 76, 94, 129
Berger, Victor, 30
Berlin crisis, 42, 170, 182
Bernstein, Theodore, 167-169
Bernstein, Victor, 155-158
Bigart, Homer, 190, 192, 193, 195, 196, 198
Bingham, Barry, 267, 268
*Birmingham Post,* 43
Black, Hugo, 93
Black journalism, 286
Blacklisting, 36, 107
Bloch, Emanuel, 59, 62, 63
Bohlen, Charles, 31
Book reviews, and McCarthyism, 21; books on Vietnam war, 236, 237
Boston: press in, vii
*Boston Globe,* 21

*Boston Herald,* ix, 43
Bourdet, Claude, 108, 109
Boylan, James, 258, 259, 264
Boyle, Hal, 44
Bradlee, Benjamin, 287
Bradley, Omar, 241
Brainwashing by U.S. information
    officers, 178
Brest-Litovsk Treaty (1918), 25
Bricker, John W., 79
*Bridges v. California* (1941), 92
Brignolo, Donald E., 268*n*
Brisbane, Arthur, 13
British Press Council, 269-271
*Brooklyn Eagle,* 131, 132
Brooks, Sydney, 120
Brown, James: interview by J. Aron-
    son, 250-252; and *New York
    Times,* 250, 252, 253; and *Provi-
    dence Journal,* 246-251, 253, 254
Brown, Sevellon, 246
Browne, Malcolm: awards, 218; and
    Vietnam war, 190, 192, 195, 199,
    200, 202, 208-211, 236
Browne, Robert S., 220, 221
Brownell, Herbert, 80, 82, 128
Brucker, Herbert, 92
Bryant, William Cullen, 12
Buckley, William F., Jr., 19, 249, 251
Budenz, Louis, 129, 142
Bullitt, William C., 32
Bundy, McGeorge, 176
Burch, Dean, 276, 278
Burchett, Wilfred G.: and Korean
    war, 114-116, 120-123; and Viet-
    nam war, 187, 188, 221, 242, 243
Burdett, Winston C., 131-133, 135,
    136
Burdick, Eugene, 195
Burrows, Lawrence, 218
*Business Week,* 35
Buttinger, Joseph, 184-186, 189

# C

*Cach Mang Quoc Gia,* 187
Calder-Marshall, Arthur, xiv
Cambodia, 188, 206, 220; call for
    U.S. invasion of, 241, 243; NLF-

Cambodia (*continued*)
    VC sanctuaries, 240, 241; U.S. bor-
    der violations, 240, 241
Cameron, Angus, 128
Canham, Erwin D., 111
Capitalism, 20, 65; and socialism, 52,
    281
*Capital Times* (Madison, Wis.), 163
Carr, Robert K., 74-79
*Cass Lake* (Minn.) *Times,* 45
Castro, Fidel: and Bay of Pigs inva-
    sion, 154, 157-160, 163, 166; inter-
    viewed by H. L. Matthews, 203;
    overthrew Batista, 153, 204
Cater, Douglass, 68-72, 74, 75, 85
Catholic Church: and Diem, 183;
    lobby, 67
Catledge, Turner, 165, 166, 235, 260,
    261
Catton, Bruce, 237
*Ce Soir* (Paris), 114
Censorship, 163; and Bay of Pigs in-
    vasion, 165; and Korean war, 108,
    109, 114, 122, 124, 126; and *New
    York Post,* 82; and *New York
    Times,* xii; and press employment,
    149; and press freedom, 277; and
    H. Salisbury, 258; and Vietnam
    war, 192, 238
Center for the Study of Democratic
    Institutions, 183, 258
Central Intelligence Agency (CIA):
    and Cold War, 287; and Cuba, 154,
    156, 159-161, 165, 167; and Diem,
    183, 184, 193; and NLF-VC sanc-
    tuary in Cambodia, 242; and pro-
    posal to invade North Vietnam,
    234; and U.S. press in Vietnam,
    198, 224
Chafee, Zechariah, Jr., 30, 263*n*, 264,
    266
Chambers, Whittaker, 51, 56, 58, 63,
    74, 76, 88, 129
Cherne, Leo, 183-185, 189
Chiang Kai-shek, 67, 204, 223
*Chicago Daily News,* 34, 54, 286
*Chicago Journalism Review,* 285-287
*Chicago Sun-Times,* 286

*Chicago Tribune,* 30, 34; and T. Dewey, 49; and Hutchins Commission report, 266, 267; and underground press, 286

Childs, Marquis, 33, 36, 90

China (Mainland): assistance to North Korea, 103; cultural revolution, 247; and W. Hinton, 143, 145; and Korean war, 110, 111, 118, 119, 125; and Korean war truce talks, 112-116, 120, 123, 124; and *National Guardian,* 280; and UN, 104, 126; and U.S., 123, 126, 191, 210, 212; and U.S. press, 21, 110, 111, 203; and Vietnam, 189, 190, 220, 231, 232

China (Taiwan): press, 277; in UN, 104; U.S. lobby, 67; and U.S. Seventh Fleet, 103

*China Monthly Review,* 118, 143, 144

Chinese Committee for Peace (Peking), 119

*Christian Science Monitor,* 111; and Hutchins Commission report, 266; and Pulitzer Prize, 254, 259; and Rosenbergs, 58

Christopher, Robert, 239

Churchill, Winston, ix; anti-Communism, 31-33; speech at Fulton, Mo., 33, 34

Civil liberties, 37, 275; and *National Guardian,* 281; and Vietnam war, 248

Civil War: and press, 12

Clark, John M., 263n

Clark, Tom, 36, 46

Clemenceau, Georges, 31

*Cleveland News,* 40

Clifford, Clark, 34

Clurman, Richard, 202

Cohn, Roy, 96, 97, 131

Cold War, 95, 96, 99, 100, 134, 137; beginnings, 25, 32; and Cuba, 163, 180; and freedom of press, 152; and President Kennedy, 162; and Korean war, 107, 122, 123; and McCarthyism, 65, 66; and *National Guardian,* 280; and radicalism,

Cold War (*continued*) 282; and U.S. foreign policy, xii, 51, 52, 102, 107, 122, 178; and U.S. press, 24, 37, 38, 287, 288

*Collier's:* special World War III issue, 111-113

Collins, Lawton, 184

Columbia Broadcasting System (CBS), 127, 131, 196, 218, 255, 262, 285

*Columbia Journalism Review,* 25; on Hutchins Commission report, 264-266; on press and Cuban crisis, 175, 178, 179; on Vietnam war, 209, 228, 229, 258

*Columbia Law Review,* 58

*Columbia University Forum,* 84; and Bay of Pigs invasion, 167-169; and U.S. base in Guatemala, 154, 156; and Vietnam war, 239

*Columbus Citizen,* 42, 43

Committee to Secure Justice in the Rosenberg Case, 60

Communications media: Hutchins Commission report, 263-266; need for radical reform, 279; rights of access and reply, 273-276; *see also* Press; Radio; Television

Communism: and Indonesia, 254; and International Rescue Committee, 184; and McCarthyism, 63-75, 78-99, 101, 102; and *National Guardian,* 280; and *New York Times,* 145; and press in Germany, 96; press war on "Red Peril," 17, 19, 25-30, 33, 34, 36, 37, 40-47, 52-63, 66, 71, 72, 77, 79, 81-83, 101, 102, 107, 117, 119, 149-151, 253, 258; recantation by H. Matusow, 128-131; Truman's Loyalty Oath (1947), 36; and unions, 134-138; U.S. government anti-Communist actions, 31-36, 45, 46, 53, 60, 110; and U.S. legislation, 130; and U.S. public opinion, 33, 37, 180; and Vietnam, 182, 185, 186, 188-190, 192-194, 197, 201, 212-217, 220, 231, 255; and H. Wallace, 40-47, 88; and J. Wechsler, 87-90; in Asia,

Communism (*continued*)
107, 211; and attack on Hutchins Commission report, 267; Attorney General's list, 36; and Catholic Church, 67; and Churchill's "iron curtain," 31-33; collectivism, 125; *Collier's* special issue, 111-113; and Committee on Un-American Activities, 45, 46; and Cuba, 159, 168; and Eastland committee investigation of U.S. press, 131-136, 140-143, 145, 146, 148, 152

Community Press Councils, 267-269; British Press Council, 269-271

*Concord* (N.H.) *Monitor & Patriot*, 43

Congress: and freedom of press, 10, 24, 148, 149; and Gulf of Tonkin resolution, 218, 219; and Vietnam war, 218, 237

Congress of Industrial Organizations, vii, 38, 287

Congressional committees: investigations of subversion, 72, 75, 88, 89, 93, 142; novel by W. Shirer, 127, 128; and press, 75-78, 93, 137, 148, 151; *see also* House *and* Senate committees

*Congressional Record*, 230

Conniff, Frank, 204

Considine, Bob, 204

Constitution: 1st Amendment, 15, 21, 79, 98, 102, 139; and freedom of press, 10-12, 20, 23, 24, 88, 92, 93, 100, 142, 148, 149, 173, 250, 263, 267, 272-274, 277, 278; and national security, 161, 163; and radio and television, 276; 5th Amendment, 88, 98, 133, 136-142, 145, 149; 14th Amendment, 139; Bill of Rights protection, 141

Cook, Fred J., 275

Copley, James S., 14

Cosby, William, 10

Cowles, Gardner, 16

Cox, Kenneth, 275, 276

Crawford, Kenneth, 197

Critchfield, Richard, 233

Cronkite, Walter, 262

Crosby, Alexander L., xv

Crosby, John, 147, 148

Crouch, Paul, 129

Cuba: Bay of Pigs invasion, 159-169, 173, 177, 182, 234, 235; and Guatemala, 153, 154, 156, 158, 166; missile crisis, 170-180, 225, 227; and President Kennedy, 161; and U.S., 155, 157-160, 203, 204, 212

Cultural and Scientific Conference for World Peace (New York, 1949), 52-55

Czechoslovakia: and Cuba, 159

# D

*Daily Herald* (Brown Univ.), 249

Daily Mirror Newspaper Group, 270

*Daily Worker*, 88, 142

Daley, Richard, 285

Dana, Charles Anderson, 12

Daniel, Clifton, 157, 158; on Bay of Pigs invasion, 164-167; on Cuban missile crisis, 176, 177; and right of access, 275, 276; and Vietnam war, 256

Davies, John Paton, 66

Dean, Paul, 231

Dean, William F., 121

Defense Department: and Cuban missile crisis, 172; and Korean war prisoners, 119, 143; and McCarthyism, 70; and press restrictions, 172, 178; and Vietnam war, 220, 225, 227, 233, 256, 260

De Gaulle, Charles, 219

Democratic Party: and Communism, 36, 42; and Cuban missile crisis, 171; National Convention (Chicago, 1968), 285; and President Roosevelt, 47; and President Truman, 48; and H. Wallace, 39

*Des Moines Register*, 44

Desegregation: and President Eisenhower, 153; Supreme Court decision (1954), 139, 144

*Detroit News*, 41, 227, 285

Dewey, Thomas E., 38, 47, 48

Dickinson, John, 263*n*

Diem, Ngo Dinh: anti-Diem developments, 188-190, 205, 232, 233; Buddhist protest, 199; and Cardinal Spellman, 183, 184; political repression, 187-190; attack on U.S. press in Vietnam, 196-200, 203, 204; U.S. press buildup of Diem, 183-186; U.S. commitment to, 181, 193, 194, 199; weakness of government, 182
Dies, Martin, 32, 75
Dilliard, Irving, 147
Dimock, Edward J., 130
Dinh, Ton That, 205
Dinh, Tran Van, 239
Dominican Republic, 223, 237
Don, Tran Van, 205
Donner, Frank, 76, 77
Dorsen, Norman, 83, 84
Dorticós, Osvaldo, 170
Douglas, William O., 93
Dryfoos, Orvil: and Bay of Pigs invasion, 165, 166, 168; and Cuban missile crisis, 174, 176, 177
Du Bois, W. E. B., 62
Dudman, Richard, 157, 158
Dugan, James, xiv
Duggan, Lawrence, 51
Dulles, John Foster, 26; and Communism, 33; and Korean war, 110, 126; and South Korea, 104, 106; and Vietnam war, 181
Dunne, Greg, 201
Dwiggins, Don, 157, 158

**E**

Eastland, James O.: and desegregation, 144; and press investigation, 131-136, 139-146, 148, 149, 151, 152; and Senate Internal Security Subcommittee, 128, 130
*Editor & Publisher:* and ASNE Code of Ethics, 271; and J. Brown incident, 248; and Cuban missile crisis, 172, 173; and Hutchins Commission report, 267; and Senator McCarthy, 90; on Presidential elections, 49; and press and Viet-

*Editor & Publisher (continued)*
nam, 226; on radicalism and press, 29; and Vietnam war, 231, 241-243
Edson, Peter, 43, 44
Eisenhower, Dwight D., 65; Administration, 95, 126; and Communism, 74, 82; and Diem, 186; general, 96, 97; and Latin America, 153, 154, 161; and Senator McCarthy, 74, 79, 80, 82, 83, 85; and Vietnam war, 181, 241
El Salvador, 157
*Encyclopædia Britannica,* 263
Epstein, Israel, 125
*Esquire,* 212
*Eugene* (Ore.) *Register-Guard,* 92
Europe: Eastern Europe, 52; press reports, 95, 108; socialism, 35; U.S. troops in, 182
Evans, Rowland, 280
*Evening Transcript* (Boston), vi
Evjue, William T., 71
*Examiner* (Los Angeles), 42

**F**

Faas, Horst, 218, 240, 241
Fairbank, John K., 239
Fall, Bernard, 196, 239
Far East: U.S. policy, 66, 109, 126
Farmer, Fyke, 105, 106
Federal Bureau of Investigation (FBI), 29, 43, 54, 91, 107; and L. Duggan, 51; and Eastland committee, 139, 141; and A. Hiss, 57; and Senator McCarthy, 89, 97; and *National Guardian,* 108
Federal Communications Commission: D. Burch appointment, 276, 278; and radio and television licenses, 262, 263; regulatory agency, 276; and Supreme Court fairness decision, 275
Felt, Harry D., 195
Field, Marshall, III, 22
Fine, Benjamin, 141
Finland: and Soviet Union, 132
Fishel, Wesley, 183, 186, 189

Fisher, Roy, 286
Flanders, Ralph, 84
Fleming, D. F., 28, 33, 37, 107
Flynn, Elizabeth Gurley, 131
*Forbes*, 16, 17
Foreign language press: Jenner investigation, 136
Forman, Harrison, 110
Forrestal, James V., 55
*Forum*, 29
Foster, William Z., 44
France: and Algeria, 232; in Indo-China, 78, 103, 123; Suez invasion, 167; in Vietnam, 181, 183, 185, 189, 193, 207, 213, 214, 232
Franco, Francisco, 207
Frankel, Max, 179
Free Communications Group, 270
Freedman, Emanuel R., 106
Freedom of Information Center (Mo. Univ.), 266n, 268n
Freedom of the press, 128, 173, 218, 253, 266, 288; and attack by Nixon Administration, 279; and ASNE Code of Ethics, 271, 272; and Belfrage-McCarthy hearing, 100, 101; J. Brown on, 250; and Eastland hearings, 140, 142, 144, 145, 148, 149, 152; 1st Amendment guarantee, 10-12, 20, 23, 24, 88, 92, 93, 100, 142, 148, 149, 173, 250, 263, 267, 272-274, 277, 278; and Hutchins Commission report, 266; and President Kennedy, 163, 167; and press responsibility, 264, 269; and Wechsler-McCarthy hearing, 88, 90-93; Freedom of the Press Week, 139
*Frente*, 159
Fried, Joe, 233
*Frontier*, 264
*Frontpage*, xii
Fryklund, Richard, 172
Fuerbringer, Otto, 201, 202
Fulbright, J. William, 223-226

# G

Gallup poll: and election of President

Gallup poll (*continued*)
Truman, 47; and treason, 58; on World War III, 37
*Gazette & Daily* (York, Pa.), xiv, 155, 156
Gellhorn, Martha, 206-208, 217
*George Washington Law Review*, 274
Georgetown University Foreign Service School, 65
Germany: Berlin crisis, 42, 170, 182; press in, x, xi, 96-98, 143; U.S. lobby, 67
Gershen, Martin, 229, 230
Gibbons, John, viii
Gilmore, Eddy, 37
Gitt, J. W., xiv
Glaser, James, 141, 142
Glessing, Robert J., 284
*Gloversville* (N.Y.) *Herald*, 41
Goebbels, Joseph P., 31
Goldberg, Rube, 49
Goldwater, Barry, 204, 278
Goodwin, Richard, 236
Gordon, Jesse, 155, 156
Gore, Albert, 223
Government and press: Aronson interview with J. Brown, 250-253; T. Bernstein on, 168, 169; and constitutional law, 274-277; and Cuban missile crisis, 171, 172; C. Daniel on, 166; history, 10-13, 15; and Hutchins Commission report, 265, 267; interference by Nixon and Agnew, 278; President Kennedy on, 161-163; and Korean war, 109, 115, 123, 126; "management of the news," 170-179, 225-227; and national interest, 20-24, 109; *New York Times* on, 163-165; and Palmer raids, 30; "pattern of acceptability," 258; *Providence Journal* and U. S. policy in Vietnam, 247-249; and Rosenbergs, 62; and H. Salisbury's trip to North Vietnam, 255-258; and Secretary of State Rusk, 244, 245; shaping of public opinion, 78, 126; in Soviet Union, 277; and U.S. aid to Turkey, 55, 56; and U.S. Cold War

Government and press (*continued*)
policy, 52, 123; and Vietnam war,
182, 194-196, 200, 208, 209, 219,
222-228, 238, 259; and Wechsler-
McCarthy hearing, 91-93; *see also*
House *and* Senate committees

Graham, Philip, 175

Great Britain: British Press Council,
269, 270; and Korean war, 109,
110, 116; Suez invasion, 167; and
Vietnam war, 181

Greece, 34, 101, 132

Greeley, Horace, 12

Greene, Graham, 207

Gross, Ernest A., 113

Gruening, Ernest, 219

*Guardian: see National Guardian*

Guatemala: and Cuba, 153, 154, 156,
158; U.S. base at Retalhuleu, 154-
158, 161, 164, 166

Guerrilla warfare: Guatemala and
Cuba, 158; President Kennedy on,
162; in Vietnam, 189, 196, 214,
220, 242, 243, 256

*Guild Reporter,* 147

# H

Haeju (Kaeju), 105, 106

Halberstam, David: awards, 218, 232,
236; and Vietnam war, 190, 195-
198, 200, 202, 204, 208, 211-213,
215, 216

Hamilton, Andrew G., 11

Handelman, Howard, 115, 116

Hanley, James M., 117, 118, 120

Hansen, Traynor, 77

Hargis, Billy James, 275

Harkins, Paul D., 189, 195, 198

*Harper's,* 25, 208

Harrison, Gilbert, 165

*Hartford Courant,* 92

Hartle, Barbara, 77

*Harvard Law Review,* 273

Hashmall, Frank, 42, 43

Hearst, William Randolph, Jr., 15,
204, 257

Hearst, William Randolph, Sr., 13,
14, 241

Hearst press, 16, 53, 54, 58, 59, 77,
118, 119, 142, 147, 204

Heath, S. Burton, 47

Heiskell, Mrs. Andrew, 176

Hemingway, Ernest, 207

Henderson, Dion, 85, 86

Hentoff, Nat, 244

Herndon, Ray, 240-242

Higgins, Marguerite, 204

Hilsman, Roger, 210-213

Hilton, Ronald, 154-157, 164

Hinton, William, 143-145

*Hispanic American Report,* 154, 155

Hiss, Alger, 51, 63-65, 68, 73, 74;
and press, 52, 56, 57, 76, 80, 88;
and W. Winchell, 94

Hitler, Adolf, 112, 252; and General
Ky, 227, 228

Ho Chi Minh, 185, 186, 188, 214,
256

Hocking, William E., 263n

Hoge, James, 286

Hohenberg, John, 195

Hollenbeck, Don, 49

Honduras, 154, 157

Hoover, Herbert, 67

Hoover, J. Edgar, 29, 33

Houghton, Neal D., 159, 160

House Committee on Un-American
Activities: Belfrage hearing, 94,
95; and Cultural and Scientific
Conference, 52; and L. Duggan,
51, 52; made permanent, 32; and
*National Guardian,* 280; pamphlet
on Communism, 75, 76; and press,
74-78; spies in government investigation (1948), 45-47

House Subcommittee on Information,
173

Howard, Roy W., 14

Hsinhua (Chinese news agency), 119

Huberman, Leo, xv, 109, 110

Hughes, Frank, 267

Hughes, R. John, 254, 259, 261

Humbaraci, Aslan K., 55, 56

Humphrey, Hubert, 233

Hutchins, Robert M., 263, 266, 267;
Commission report, 263-265, 272;
press response to report, 266, 267

# I

*I. F. Stone's Weekly,* 100, 108, 178, 236; *see also* Stone, I. F.

Immigration: *see* Walter-McCarran Immigration Act

*In Fact,* 36

*Indianapolis News,* 92

Indo-China: and France, 78, 103, 123; *see also* Cambodia; Laos; Vietnam; Vietnam war

Indonesia, 254

Ingersoll, Ralph, 22

Ingram, Rosa, 281

Institute of International Education, 51

Institute of Pacific Relations, 21

Internal Security Act (1950), 78, 131, 152

International Control Commission, 242, 254

International News Service, 115, 126, 155

Iran, 33

"Iron curtain": and W. Churchill, 31, 33

Isaacs, Norman E., 271

*Izvestia,* 178

# J

Jackson, Donald L., 53

Jackson, Henry M., 97

James, Edwin L., 55

Jefferson, Thomas, 11

Jencks, Clinton, 130

Jenner, William, 136, 143, 144, 146

John Birch Society, 150

Johnson, Lyndon, 34, 68; and press, 236, 237; Vice President, 171; and Vietnam war, 210, 222, 234, 235, 254, 256-258

Joint Chiefs of Staff, 104, 181

Joint U.S. Public Affairs Office (JUSPAO), 253

Jones, D. A. N., 270

Jordan, Lewis, 166

*Journal of Commerce,* 49

*Journalism Quarterly,* 159

Joy, Turner, 114

Just, Ward, 206, 207, 216, 217

Justice Department: and Communism, 29, 30, 34, 36, 144; and A. Hiss, 76; and H. Matusow, 128-131, 136

# K

Kahn, Albert E., 55, 128, 129

Kalischer, Peter, 218

Karnow, Stanley, 201

Kaufman, Samuel H., 56, 58

Kennedy, Jacqueline, 24

Kennedy, John F.: Administration, 164; assassination, 205, 218; and Bay of Pigs invasion, 160, 161, 166-169, 176, 177, 182, 234, 235; and Cuba, 161, 165; and Cuban missile crisis, 170, 171, 174, 176, 177, 180, 227; and press, 236; and press in Vietnam, 196, 197, 202-204; speech on government and press, 161-163; and Vietnam war, 181, 182, 184, 191, 200, 205, 210

Kennedy, Joseph P., 184

Kennedy, Paul, 157, 158, 164, 166

Kennedy, Robert F., 98

Kerby, William F., 287

Khanh, Nguyen, 187

Khrushchev, Nikita: and Cuban missile crisis, 170, 177

King, Martin Luther, Jr., 248, 249

King, Oliver H. P., 105-107

Kipling, Rudyard, 233

*Kiplinger's Weekly,* 48, 49

Kirkpatrick, Clayton, 286

Kirkpatrick, Lyman B., Jr., 156

Klein, Herbert, 278

Knight, John S., 14

Knight press, 173

Knoll, Erwin, 181

Knowland, William, 84

Knowles, Clayton, 141, 142

Kohlberg, Alfred M., 67

Korea (North): assistance from Soviet Union and China, 103; charged as aggressor in war, 105-107, 109; *Pueblo* incident, 126;

Korea (North) (*continued*)
U.S. intelligence plane shot down, 22
Korea (South): election (1950), 103; and outbreak of war, 105-107; and U.S., 104, 106
Korean war, 58, 65, 66, 78, 94, 101, 171, 252, 283; U.S. censorship, 108, 109, 114, 115, 122, 124, 126; Chinese intervention, 104, 105, 110, 111, 125; germ warfare, 126; outbreak, 104-109, 246; *Pueblo* incident, 126; truce, 123, 124; truce negotiations, 112-117, 120, 122, 123; UN prisoners of war, 117-121, 123-126, 143, 152; and U.S. press, 107-111, 113-126
Kosygin, Alexei, 219
Kraft, Joseph, 257
Kraslow, David, 173
Krock, Arthur, 32
Krosigk, Schwerin von, 31
Ku Klux Klan, 41
Ky, Nguyen Cao, 187; admiration for Hitler, 227, 228

# L

*La Hora* (Guatemala), 155, 156, 166
Labor: *see* American Newspaper Guild; Press: unions; Strikes; Unions
Labor Department, 30
Ladejinsky, Wolf, 183, 186
Lansdale, Edward, 184
Laos, 163, 188, 220
Lardner, John, xiv
Lasswell, Harold D., 263n
Latin America, 160, 163, 216
Lattimore, Owen, 66, 70
"Law and order," 17, 19
Lawrence, David, 136
Lawrence, W. H., 45
*Le Monde* (Paris), 259
League of Nations, 31
Lederer, William J., 195
Lerner, Max, 19, 251; on Rosenbergs, 60, 61; and Vietnam war, 185
Levine, Isaac Don, 51

Levy, H. Philip, 270
Libel, 11, 72
Liberalism, vii, 22, 23
Liberation News Service, 285
Liebling, A. J., xiii
*Life,* 22, 111, 218, 285; charges by H. Matusow, 90; and T. Dewey, 48, 49; and Diem, 184, 186; and Soviet nuclear threat, 57
Lincoln, Abraham, 12, 237
Lindley, Ernest K., 187
Lindsay, John, 175
Lippmann, Walter: on Cuba, 161; on election of President Truman, 47; on Senator McCarthy, 69, 70, 82, 83; on press and the Cold War, 25-28; on propaganda, 257; and rights of press, 148, 149, 151
Lobbies, 67, 223
*L'Observateur* (Paris), 95, 108, 112
Lodge, Henry Cabot, 205, 218
*London Daily Express,* 114
*London Daily Mirror,* 227, 228
*London Daily Worker,* 114
*London Observer,* 19
*London Times,* 31, 228
*Long Island Press,* 141
*Look,* 46, 185
*Los Angeles Mirror,* 110, 111, 157
*Los Angeles Times,* 15, 42, 266
*Los Angeles Times-Washington Post,* 19, 180
*Louisville Courier-Journal,* 267, 271
Loyalty oaths, 78, 151
Loyalty Order (1947), 36, 39
Luce, Henry R , 49, 90, 186, 202, 263
Luce, Henry, III, 286
Ludendorff, Erich, 27
Lyons, Leonard, 61
Lyons, Louis M., 92, 173, 218, 266

# M

MacArthur, Douglas, 65, 108, 125; and Korean truce talks, 114, 118
MacDougall, Curtis, 37, 41-43, 47
MacLeish, Archibald, 263n
MacLeod, Henry, 268, 269
*Madison* (Wis.) *Capital Times,* 71

Mahoney, Dan, 142
*Maine* (battleship), 13
*Mainichi Shimbun* (Tokyo), 221
"Management of the news," 170-179, 225-227; *see also* Government and press; Press
Mandell, Benjamin, 142
Mann, Richard, 238
Manning, Robert, 172, 174, 182
Manno, Vincent J., 16
Mansfield, Mike, 184
Mao Tse-tung, 203, 204
Marcantonio, Vito, 45
Marder, Murrey, 175, 255
Markel, Lester, xi
Marks, Leonard H., 222-224
Marshall, George C., 33, 79
Martino, John, 152
Martinsville Seven, 281
Matthews, Herbert L., 155, 203, 207
Matusow, Harvey, 90, 91, 128-131, 136
May, Ronald W., 66-68, 71, 75
McArthur, George, 240-243
McCarran, Pat, 131, 140; *see also* Internal Security Act; Walter-McCarran Immigration Act
McCarthy, Francis L., 155
McCarthy, Joseph, 77, 103, 145, 283; aided by press, 21, 67-74, 78-86, 94, 98; Aronson hearing, 97, 143; Belfrage hearings, 96-98; charges against news media, 87-102, 140; and Cold War, 65, 66; and "Communist conspiracy," 63-75, 78-99, 101, 102; denounced by A. Sulzberger, 134; and President Eisenhower, 74, 79, 80, 82, 83, 85; and W. Ladejinsky, 183; and lobbies, 67; and H. Matusow, 90, 91, 128, 129, 131; McCarthyism, 64, 65, 70, 74, 78, 83-85, 107, 288; Presidential ambitions, 82, 83; press questionnaire on, 99; "public trial" (1954), 82; Senate censure, 84; and Senate Subcommittee on Investigations, 75, 110, 128; Senator, 63, 69-71, 73, 85; and A. Stevenson, 81; and President Truman, 69,

McCarthy, Joseph (*continued*)
74; U.S. Army investigation, 80-84, 94; and J. Wechsler, 87-94, 102; Wheeling, W. Va., speech, 64, 68, 72; and J. R. Wiggins, 94
McClure, Robert A., 96
McConnell, David, 113
McCormick, Anne O'Hare, 44
McCormick, Robert, 267
McGaffin, William, 181
McGee, Willie, 281
McGill, Ralph, 40, 41
McKinley, William, 13
McManus, John T., 99; and Eastland hearings, 139, 142-144, 151; and *National Guardian*, 8, 59, 280, 282
McNamara, Robert: Secretary of Defense, 34, 175, 219, 222, 234, 238
Mecklin, John, 190, 193-199, 208, 209
Mekong Delta, 200, 234
Mellett (Lowell) Foundation, 267-269
Mencher, Melvin, 81
Merriam, Charles E., 263n
Merz, Charles, 60, 149; and U.S. press Cold War, 25-28
Mexico: press, 277
*Miami Herald,* 158
*Miami News,* 258
Michigan State Project in Vietnam, 186, 189
Middle East, 35, 250; Suez crisis, 167
Miller, George P., 230
Miller, Robert C., 118, 122, 123
Miller, William, 125
Minh, Duong Van, 205
*Milwaukee Journal,* 81, 85, 86
Mohr, Charles, 195, 200-202, 208, 213, 234
Molotov, Vyacheslav, 31, 42
Monthly Review Press, 109, 143
Moody, Blair, 41
Moore, Mayor, 36
Moratorium Day (Oct. 15, 1969), 278, 286
Morgan, Richard C., 42, 43
Morse, Wayne, 219

Moss, John E., 173, 178
Mundt, Karl E., 51, 52, 224
Murrill, Judith, 266*n*
Murrow, Edward R., 127

# N

Nam Il, 114
*Nashville Banner,* 266
*Nashville Tennessean,* 37, 43
*Nation,* 30, 95, 136, 210, 211; and *Collier's* World War III issue, 112; and Cuban crisis, 157; and H. Salisbury, 261; and U.S. base in Guatemala, 154-158, 164, 166
National Broadcasting Company (NBC), 125, 196, 197
National Citizens Political Action Committee (NC-PAC), 38, 39
National Council of the Arts, Sciences, and Professions, 52, 54
*National Guardian,* xiv, 48; purposes, 280, 281; and J. Aronson, 280, 282; and Congressional committee investigations, 151; and Eastland committee hearings, 139, 142, 143, 149, 152; and FBI, 108; and House Committee on Un-American Activities, 94, 95; and Korean war, 107, 108, 118-120, 125; and Korean war prisoners, 143, 152; and McCarthy committee hearings, 96-100; and radicalism, xiv, 280-283, 285; and Rosenbergs, 59, 61-63, 94, 95; and Vietnam, 188, 221; name changed to *Guardian,* 280*n,* 283
*National Gazette,* xiv
National Liberation Front, 183, 188, 189, 192, 207, 214, 215, 219-221, 238, 259; sanctuaries in Cambodia, 240-243; 1968 Tet offensive (1968), 244
National Municipal League, 136
National Opinion Research Center, 37
National Security Council, 181
National security and press, 20-24, 161-163, 166, 168, 169, 281, 288;

National security and press
(*continued*)
and Bay of Pigs invasion, 172, 176-179; and Vietnam war, 182, 190, 194, 195, 216, 227, 257
Nellor, Edward, 76
Nevada Editors Conference, 122
New China News Agency, 285
New Deal, vii , 38, 39, 48
*New Leader,* 185
New Left: and press, 23
*New Philadelphia* (Ohio) *Times,* 47
*New Republic,* 25, 27, 39, 85, 165, 184
*New Statesman* (London), 233, 234
*New York Daily Compass,* 108
*New York Daily Mirror,* 54, 59, 107, 136, 142, 147
*New York Daily News*: and Congressional hearings, 140; description, 17; dismissal of staff member, 136-138, 142; and Eastland committee, 147, 148; and NATO, 56; and President Johnson, 236; and Vietnam war, 232
*New York Herald Tribune,* 37, 76, 113, 204; and J. Aronson, viii ; book reviews on China, 21; on Communism, 30, 54, 67; and Cuba, 159; and Cuban missile crisis, 173-175; and T. Dewey, 48; and Eastland committee investigations, 147; on government suppression of news, 173; and A. Hiss, 56; and Korean war, 117; merger, 16; and Rosenbergs, 60, 62; support for Diem, 184; on Truman Doctrine, 34; on H. Wallace, 45
*New York Journal-American,* 16, 147; and Communism, 53, 54; and A. Hiss, 57
New York Newspaper Guild; *see under* American Newspaper Guild
*New York Post,* 17; and Aronson, ix , 98; and Belfrage-McCarthy hearing, 100, 101; censorship, 82; on Communism, 33, 107; and Cuban missile crisis, 174; on Eastland committee hearings, 140-142, 147;

*New York Post* (*continued*)
editorial policy, 287; and President Kennedy's speech on press, 163; and Korean war, 117; on Rosenbergs, 60, 61; and Vietnam war, 257; and Wechsler-McCarthy hearing, 87-91, 95, 100
*New York Review of Books,* 236
*New York Star,* 108
*New York Sun,* 46, 49, 54, 76
*New York Times,* ix, 14, 44, 49, 55, 111, 132, 218, 232, 275; and J. Aronson, 5-7, 98, 99; attack by Vice President Agnew, 278; and Bay of Pigs invasion, 163-169, 176, 177, 234, 235; and J. Brown, 248, 250, 252; on Communism, 25-30, 32-34, 80, 101, 102; and Cuba, 159, 203; and Cuban missile crisis, 173-177, 179, 227; and Cultural and Scientific Conference, 54; description, 17, 18; and dismissal of M. Barnet, 133, 134, 136-139; and Eastland committee investigation, 131-134, 137, 139-142, 145-147, 149, 151, 152; on Hutchins Commission report, 266; and President Johnson, 236, 237; and Korean war, 105, 106, 113, 116, 117, 125; on "management of the news," 173, 177, 179; Matusow charge of Communists on staff, 90, 129, 130; on Senator McCarthy, 21, 80, 81, 83; and J. Mecklin, 198; Moratorium Day (October 1969), 286; policy on Communist employees, 145, 146; on government and press, 163-165; press service, 19; and Pulitzer Prize (1966), 260, 261; reviews of books on China, 21; and Rosenbergs, 60, 61, 80; and H. Salisbury's visit to North Vietnam, 253-256, 259, 260; and Solvay school board, 152; on spying, 51; support for Diem, 184, 186; on Truman Doctrine, 34; on Turkey, 55, 56; and U.S. base in Guatemala, 155-158; and Vietnam war, 189, 190,

*New York Times* (*continued*)
192, 193, 195-197, 199, 204, 208, 214, 217, 219-221, 227, 234, 239, 243, 244, 259; on H. Wallace, 45; and Wechsler-McCarthy hearing, 89, 90, 100, 101
New York Times Service, 17, 18
*New York Weekly Journal,* 10
*New York World,* 25, 29, 30
*New York World Journal Tribune,* 16, 17
*New York World-Telegram,* 35, 37, 54; on Rosenbergs, 58, 60
*New York World-Telegram and Sun,* 16, 117, 147
*New Yorker,* 23, 69
*Newark News,* 172
*Newark Star-Ledger,* 229
Newcomb, Elliot, 185
Newhouse, S. I., 14, 141
Newspaper Enterprise Association, 41, 47
Newspaper Guild: *see* American Newspaper Guild
Newspapers: *see* Government and press; National security and press; Press
*Newsweek,* 175; and Diem, 187, 190; and Moratorium Day (October 1969), 286; H. Salisbury's visit to North Vietnam, 258; and Vietnam war, 192, 193, 196, 197, 233, 234, 238, 239, 244
Nguyen Tuong Tam, 212
Nhu, Ngo Dinh, 205
Nhu, Mme. Ngo Dinh, 194, 197
Nicaragua, 156, 157; and U.S., 153, 154
Niebuhr, Reinhold, 263n
Nieman Foundation at Harvard, 92, 173, 218, 266
*Nieman Reports,* 81, 175, 201
Nixon, Richard M.: Representative, 51, 52; Senator, 63; Vice President, 88, 181; and communications media, 276, 278, 279; and A. Hiss, 56; and press, 76; and Vietnam war, 181, 278, 279
Noel, "Pappy," 120, 121

Nolting, William E., 195, 196, 198, 200, 205
North Atlantic Treaty Organization (NATO), 56, 132
Novak, Ralph B., 134, 135, 280
Novak, Robert, 280
November Mobilization, 278
Noyes, Crosby, 257
Nuckols, William P., 115, 116, 122
Nuclear weapons tests, 170
Nuremberg, xi, 187

## O

Oakes, John B., 252
O'Connell, William Cardinal, viii
O'Donnell, John, 140
Ogden, Michael J., 249
*Ogdensburg* (N.Y.) *Advance-News*, 41
Oil in Middle East, 35
Olsen, Jack, 99
*Open Secret* (London), 279
Oram, Harold, 184
Overseas Press Club awards, 218

## P

Pacifica Foundation, 262
Palmer, A. Mitchell, 29, 30, 36, 57, 65
Panama, 156
Panama Canal, 174
Paul VI (Pope), 220
Pearson, Drew, 31, 55; and T. Dewey, 49; on Kennedy and Cuba, 171; and *New York Times*, 147
Pegler, Westbrook, 45, 107
Pell, Claiborne, 224
Perry, John H., 14
Perry, Mert, 200-202, 234, 239
*Philadelphia Inquirer*, 44
Philippines, 103
*Pittsburgh Press*, 43
*Pittsburgh Sun-Telegraph*, 40
Pius XII (Pope),ix, 60, 61
*PM*, 8, 22, 23, 87, 108
Polls, 37, 47, 58
Pomerantz, Abraham L., 36

Potsdam conference, 32
Powell, John W., Jr., 118, 143, 144
Powell, Sylvia Campbell, 144
PR Newswire, 155
*Pravda,* 178
Press: ASNE Code of Ethics, 271, 272; appraisal agency proposal, 265, 267; and Bay of Pigs invasion, 160, 161, 163, 165-167, 173, 177; and C. Belfrage, 100, 101; in Boston, vii.; British Press Council, 269-271; circulation statistics, 15, 18; Community Press Councils, 267-271; competition, 13, 16, 17; and Congressional investigating committees, 75-78, 93, 137, 148, 151 (*see also under* House *and* Senate); and Cuba-U.S. relations, 154, 157, 159; and Cuban missile crisis, 171-176; and Cultural and Scientific Conference, 52-55; and Eastland committee investigations, 131-136, 139-149, 151; editorial policy, 13, 15, 249, 250; and government control, 148, 149, 161-163, 264, 265, 267, 277; and Guatemala base, 155-158; and A. Hiss, 52, 56, 57; history, 10-16; and Hutchins Commission report, 263-267; hypocrisy, 21, 22; as industry, 13, 14, 16, 19-24, 249; information to consumers, 209-211; and President Johnson, 236, 237; journalistic awards, 218; and President Kennedy, 161-163, 196, 197, 202-204, 236; and Korean war, 107-111, 113-126; McCarthy aided by press, 21, 67-74, 78-86, 94, 98; and McCarthy Army investigation, 80-83; and McCarthy press investigations, 87-102, 140; mergers, 14, 16, 20; as monopoly, 16, 22, 249, 250, 273; national council proposed, 279; and national security, 20-24, 161-163, 166, 168, 169, 172, 176-179, 182, 190, 194, 195, 216, 227, 257, 281, 288; Nixon and Agnew attack on, 278, 279; and patriotism, 13, 15; press ser-

Press (continued)
vices, 18, 19, 285; privileges and obligations of newsmen, 93, 149-151, 162, 177; public opinion molder, 50, 54, 57, 58, 61, 78, 126, 209, 273; and radicalism, 23, 24, 251, 279-284, 287, 288; responsibility and public service, 262-269, 277, 288; and right of reply "fairness doctrine," 23, 24, 273-275; Rosenbergs, 58-63; in socialist countries, 277; standardization of news, 19-24; and technological advances, 18, 19, 249, 273; underground press, 284-286; unions, vii , xiii , 18, 134-138, 141, 287 (see also American Newspaper Guild); and Vietnam hearings, 222-224; and Vietnam war, 181, 182, 186-188, 190-245, 247-250, 252; war on "Red Peril," 17, 19, 25-30, 33, 34, 36, 37, 40-47, 52-63, 66, 71, 72, 77, 79, 81-83, 101, 102, 107, 117, 119, 149-151, 253, 258; see also Freedom of the press; Government and press; under individual newspapers and writers
Price, William A., 142
Priestley, J. B., 111
Pringle, Jim, 244
Prisoners of war: see under Korean war
Progressive Citizens of America (PCA), 38, 40, 41
Progressive Party: H. Wallace, 38, 41-47
Propaganda, 280; anti-Americanism in Asia, 199; W. Lippmann on, 257; and H. Salisbury's visit to North Vietnam, 255-257; and Vietnam war, 210, 219, 221, 222, 224, 233, 244, 259
Protestant, 36
Providence Bulletin, 246
Providence Journal, 246-251, 253, 254
Providence Journal-Bulletin, 246, 248, 254
Pueblo incident, 126

Puerto Rico, 174
Pulitzer, Joseph, Jr., 254, 260, 261
Pulitzer, Joseph, Sr., 13
Pulitzer Prize, 37, 240, 245; H. Bigart, 193; Halberstam and Browne, 218; and H. Salisbury, 253, 254, 259-261
Pulliam, Eugene C., Jr., 92
"Pumpkin Papers," 51

## Q

Quang Duc, Thich, 199
Quincy Patriot Ledger, 146, 147

## R

Radford, Arthur W., 181
Radicalism: FM radio, 262; and National Guardian, 8, 280-283; and press, 23, 251, 279-284, 287, 288; witch-hunt (1920), 29, 30
Radio: control of advertisers, 267; and "fairness doctrine," 275; and Hutchins Commission report, 263, 267; 1st Amendment guarantees, 264, 276; radicalism, 262
Ramparts, 234
Rankin, John E., 32
Raskin, A. H., 137
Reader's Digest, 111
Redfield, Robert, 263n
Reid, Mrs. Ogden, 48, 49
Remington, Frederic, 241
Reporter, 68, 184, 186, 232
Republican Party: and J. McCarthy, 70, 82, 83, 129
Research Institute of America, 183, 184
Reston, James, 19; on Cuba, 159-161, 165-167; and Cuban missile crisis, 176-178; on election of President Truman, 49; and President Johnson, 237; and Vietnam war, 220-222, 234, 235
Retalhuleu: see Guatemala: U.S. base at Retalhuleu
Reuben, William A., 59, 60
Reuters, 19, 120, 221, 244

Reuther, Walter, 111
Rhee, Syngman, 103, 104, 106, 107, 126
Rich, John, 125
Ridgway, Matthew, 112, 115, 121, 122
Right-of-reply: *see under* Communications media; Press
Rivers, William L., 269
Roberts, Chalmers, 256, 257
Robinson, James, 197
Rogers, Warren, 173, 174
Rojas, Clemente Marroquin, 155, 156
Roosevelt, Eleanor, viii
Roosevelt, Franklin D.,ix, 38, 49, 51; agreements with Soviet Union, 31; Democratic Party, 47; and H. Wallace, 39
Rosenberg, Julius and Ethel: and *National Guardian*, 59, 61-63, 94, 95; and press, 58-63, 80, 94, 95
Rovere, Richard H.: on Senator McCarthy, 69-74, 78-81
Ruark, Robert C., 58
Ruml, Beardsley, 263*n*
Rushmore, Howard, 77
Rusk, Dean, 222, 244, 245, 255

## S

*Saigon Post,* 239
*St. Louis Post-Dispatch,* 30, 34, 147; and Belfrage-McCarthy hearing, 100, 101; on Hutchins Commission report, 266; on press and constitutional law, 274; and Pulitzer Prize (1966), 254, 260; and U.S. base in Guatemala, 157
Salinger, Pierre, 174, 181, 182, 194, 202
Salisbury, Harrison, 25; and Pulitzer Prize, 253, 254; visit to North Vietnam, 253-259
*San Francisco Chronicle,* 124
*Saturday Evening Post,* 34, 39, 40
*Saturday Night* (Montreal), 37
Saud, Ibn (King), 186
Scheer, Robert, 183

Schine, G. David, 96
Schlesinger, Arthur, Jr., 165, 167, 176, 185
Schlesinger, Arthur, Sr., 263*n*
Schuman, Frederick L., xiv
Schuman, Julian, 144
Scott, Paul, 174
Scripps-Howard press, 14, 16, 41, 43, 58, 77, 119, 147
*Seattle Post-Intelligencer,* 77
*Seattle Times,* 268
Seldes, George, 36
Senate Foreign Relations Committee, 209, 222-224
Senate Internal Security Subcommittee: Hinton hearing, 143, 144; investigation of press, 131-136, 139-152; McManus and Aronson hearings, 139, 142-144; and H. Matusow, 128-130
Senate Permanent Subcommittee on Investigations, 75, 90; Belfrage hearing, 96-98; Wechsler hearing, 87-90
Sevareid, Eric, 222
Shakespeare, Frank, Jr., 278
Shannon, William, 174, 180, 181
Shapley, Harlow, 52-54
Sharff, Mayer, 60
Shastri, Lal Bahadur, 220
Sheehan, Neil: awards, 218; and Vietnam war, 190, 195, 200, 202, 208, 213-217, 239
Sherwood, Robert E., 111
Shirer, William L., 127, 128
Shostakovitch, Dmitri, 52, 53
Shuster, George N., 263*n*
Sihanouk, Norodom, 240, 241
Simon, John G., 84
Slocum, William H., 148
Smith, Margaret Chase, 111
Smith, Moses, vii
Smith, Walter Bedell, 42
Smith Act, 45, 46, 77, 78, 130, 131, 151
Sobell, Morton, 58, 63
Socialism, 35, 191, 267; and capitalism, 52, 281; *Collier's* article on World War III, 111; expulsion of

Socialism (*continued*)
elected Socialists, 30; and U.S. press, 20, 28
Socialist countries: press in, 24, 277
Somoza, Luis (Debayle), 153
Sourwine, Jay C., 131, 132, 135, 139, 143
Southern Conference for Human Welfare, 40, 41
Soviet Union: alternative to capitalism, 65; assistance to North Korea, 103; atomic bomb, 57, 64; and W. Burdett, 131; in *Collier's* World War III issue, 111, 112; and Cuban missile crisis, 170, 171, 175-178; and Cuba, 159, 169; and Cultural and Scientific Conference, 52; and Korean war, 104, 108, 113; and *National Guardian*, 280; and Poland, 26; press in, 277; and H. Salisbury, 254, 259; spies in U.S., 51, 58; and U.S., 25, 31, 32, 42, 52, 54, 56, 65, 111, 112, 170, 171; U.S. intervention in Soviet Union (1918–20), 26, 28, 30; and U.S. press, 25-30, 33, 34; and Vietnam, 188, 190, 220, 231, 257; and World War II, 25
Spain: civil war, viii, 206, 207, 216, 217; press in, 277, Spanish-American war, 13, 190, 241
Spangler, Roy, 268
*Speaking of Peace,* 54
Spellman, Francis Cardinal, 183, 184
Spies, 51, 58; *see also* Hiss; Rosenberg
Stalin, Joseph, ix, 32, 47, 252
Stanford University teach-in on Vietnam, 198
*Star,* 23
*Stars and Stripes,* xi, 121
State Department: Cable 1006, 182, 194, 197; and Cold war, 66; and Cuba, 159; and Cuban missile crisis, 171; and lobbies, 67; and McCarthyism, 64, 68, 70, 72, 73, 94, 96; and press restrictions, 172, 178; and South Korea, 103, 104, 106; Soviet visas, 52, 53; and U.S.

State Department (*continued*)
base in Guatemala, 155; and U.S. foreign policy, 55; and Vietnam war, 182, 189, 193, 194, 197, 220, 221, 244
Stevenson, Adlai, 81, 222
Stokes, Thomas L., 44
Stone, I. F., 100; and Korean war, 108, 109, 113; on news management, 178; on Vietnam war, 236, 237; see also *I. F. Stone's Weekly*
Strikes, 19, 28; *Brooklyn Eagle,* 132; *Long Island Press,* 141
Stripling, Robert E., 75, 76
Strong, Anna Louise, xiv
Student demonstrations, 19, 23
Subversion: *see* Communism; House Committee on Un-American Activities; Senate Internal Security Subcommittee
Suez crisis, 167
Sullivan, Ed, 107
Sullivan, Walter, 106
Sully, François, 192, 193, 195-197
Sulzberger, Arthur Hays, 133, 134, 137
Sulzberger, Arthur Ochs, 204
Sulzberger, Cyrus L., 33, 55
Summerlin, Sam, 125
Supreme Court, 91, 92, 99, 110, 130; desegregation decision, 139, 144; "fairness doctrine" decision, 275
Supreme Headquarters Allied Expeditionary Forces (SHAEF), 96
Sweezy, Paul M., 109, 110
Sylvester, Arthur: Assistant Secretary of Defense, 171-174, 178, 209, 222, 224-226
Symington, Stuart, 97
*Syracuse Post-Standard,* 152
Szulc, Tad, 165-167, 189

**T**

Taft, Robert A., ix, 41
Taft-Hartley Act, 36, 82, 130
Tass, 285
Taylor, Maxwell D., 181

Technology: and press, 18, 19, 249, 273

Teheran agreement, 31

Television: attacks by Nixon Administration, 278, 279; and Community Press Councils, 268, 269; controlled by advertisers, 267; and 1st Amendment, 275, 276; as news medium, 262; Vietnam war coverage, 210

Thailand, 220

U Thant, 219, 222

Thomason, R. E., 130

Thompson, Dorothy, 41

Thompson, Reginald, 110

Thomson, Roy, 14, 15

Thomson Newspapers, Inc., 16

Thrasher, James, 41, 42

Thuc, Ngo Dinh, 199

*Time,* 17, 111, 176, 194, 196, 263; and Cuba-U.S. relations, 158; and Diem, 184, 186, 187, 190, 232; and H. Matusow, 90, 129, 130; and J. Mecklin, 198; on Middle East, 35; and Moratorium Day (October 1969), 286; on *National Guardian,* 280; and Vietnam war, 195-197, 200-202, 232, 234, 244; on H. Wallace, 45

*Times Talk,* 193, 243

Tito, Josef Broz, 111

Tonkin Gulf, 218, 219, 225, 247

Trade Union Veterans Committee, 82

Tregaskis, Richard, 204, 218

Trenton Six, 281

Trewhitt, Henry L., 255

Tri Quang, Thich, 233

Trujillo, Hector B., 223

Trumbull, Robert, 190

Truman, Harry S, x, 38, 57, 64, 110; Administration, 25, 95; and Communism, 31-37, 74, 80; election (1948), 47-50; and Korean war, 105, 106, 246; Loyalty Order (1947), 36, 39; and Senator McCarthy, 69, 74; and spy scares, 51; Truman Doctrine, 32, 34, 35, 39, 52, 55, 65, 132; Vice President, 39; and H. Wallace, 39, 41, 46-48

Tugman, William M., 92

Turkey: and W. Burdett, 132; and Soviet Union, 33; suppression of news, 55, 56; U.S. military aid, 34, 55; U.S. military bases, 170

## U

U-2 affair, 161, 173

Underground press, 284-286

Underground Press Service, 285

USSR: *see* Soviet Union

Unions: and Communism, 30, 134-138, 151; press, xii, 6, 7, 18, 134-138, 141, 287; *see also* American Newspaper Guild

United Nations, 32, 36, 37, 78, 170, 179, 252; China in, 104, 126; and *Collier's* World War III issue, 111, 112; Cuba in, 170; and Korean truce talks, 114-116, 120-122, 126; and Korean war, 103, 104, 118, 123; proposed expulsion of Communist nations, 67; speech by President Johnson, 237

United Nations Commission on Korea, 104

United Nations Correspondents Association, 113

United Nations High Command in Korea, 114, 121, 123, 126

United Nations Relief and Rehabilitation Administration, 143

United Press, 53, 125, 126, 155, 190, 218; and Korean truce talks, 116, 118, 122; and Korean war prisoners, 121, 124

United Press International, 19, 155; and Vietnam war, 196, 209, 214, 240, 242

*United States v. Rumely,* 93

United States Army: McCarthy investigation, 80-84

United States Information Agency: and J. Brown, 247; L. Marks as director, 222-224; and H. Salisbury, 258; F. Shakespeare as director, 278

United States Information Service, 194, 233
United States Korea Military Advisory Group, 105, 106

## V

Van Fleet, James A., 118, 123
Vandenberg, Arthur, 36
Vann, John Paul, 195, 234
*Variety*, 210, 211, 278
Vatican: plea from Pope Paul VI, 220; pleas from Pope Pius XII, 60, 61; protest of U.S. bombing of North Vietnam, 255
Vaughan, Harry, 33
Velde, Harold H., 77, 94, 95
Viet Cong, 187, 189, 197, 198, 212, 229, 230, 248; Cambodian sanctuaries, 240-242
Viet Minh, 185, 186
Vietnam: Buddhist protests, 199-201, 212, 233; coalition government, 212; elections (1956), 184-187, 220; French in, 181, 183, 185, 189, 193, 207, 213, 214, 232; Geneva agreements (1954), 181-185, 187, 194, 220, 242; nationalism, 214, 215; pacification program, 210; refugees, 185; State Department Cable 1006, 182, 194, 197; U.S. Mission in Saigon, 193, 194, 196-200, 205; *see also* Diem, Ngo Dinh; Vietnam war
Vietnam war, 180, 283, 284; antiwar demonstrations in U.S., 278; Cambodian sanctuaries, 240-243; compared to Algerian war, 232; compared to Spanish civil war, 206, 207, 216, 217; as containment of China, 191, 210, 231, 232; foreign correspondents, 223, 224, 233; Gulf of Tonkin incident, 219, 247; Gulf of Tonkin resolution, 218, 219, 225; "hawk" philosophy, 214, 231, 232, 238; "management of the news," 225-227, 234; newspaper poll, 21; North Vietnam intervention in South, 220, 255, 256,

Vietnam war (*continued*)
259; Paris negotiations, 191; pleas for negotiations, 219, 220, 222; and President Eisenhower, 181, 241; and President Johnson, 210, 222, 234, 235, 254, 256-258; and President Kennedy, 181, 182, 184, 191, 196, 197, 200, 202-205, 210; and President Nixon, 181, 278, 279; press hearing before Senate Foreign Relations Committee, 222-224; pressure on U.S. to halt bombings, 255, 257; proposal to invade North Vietnam, 231, 234; "Special Forces" commando teams, 242; Tet offensive (1968), 244; U.S. bombing of North Vietnam, 219-221, 231, 235, 237, 254-256, 258-260; U.S. escalation of war, 21, 218-220, 232; and U.S. foreign policy, 207, 211-217, 222, 223, 239, 251-253; and U.S. press, 181, 182, 186-188, 190-245, 247-250, 252 (*see also under* individual writers and newspapers); U.S. propaganda, 210, 219, 221, 222, 224, 233, 244; U.S. troop buildup, 180, 181, 191, 192, 208, 213, 214, 225, 231, 237; visit of H. Salisbury to North Vietnam, 253-257; *see also* National Liberation Front; Viet Cong; Viet Minh
*Village Voice*, 244
Villard, Oswald Garrison, 30
Vinson, Fred M., 47, 99

## W

Wadleigh, Julian, 73, 74
Waldrop, Frank C., 76
*Wall Street Journal*, 12; editorial policy, 287; on Eisenhower and McCarthy, 80; and Moratorium Day (October 1969), 286; rights of the press, 149-151; and D. Rusk, 244, 245; and Vietnam war, 256; on H. Wallace, 48
Wallace, Henry A.: and Committee on Un-American Activities, 46;

Wallace, Henry A. (*continued*)
Presidential candidate, 38, 41-48; and press, 40-48, 88; Vice President, 39
Walsh, Edmund (Monsignor), 65, 66
Walter-McCarran Immigration Act, 78, 99, 131, 151
Walters, Basil, 91
Washington, George, 11
*Washington Post*, 72, 76, 92, 237; attack by Vice President Agnew, 278; and Belfrage-McCarthy hearing, 100, 101; and Communism, 82, 94; and Cuban missile crisis, 174, 175, 180; editorial policy, 287; and "management of the news," 175; news service, 19; and Senator McCarthy, 66, 83, 94; and Vietnam war, 189, 199, 206, 221, 243, 255, 256, 258, 259
*Washington Star*, 172, 233, 257
*Washington Times-Herald*, 76
Watkins, John C. A., 246-249
Wechsler, James: and Belfrage-McCarthy hearing, 100, 101; McCarthy hearing, 87-95, 101, 102; and H. Salisbury, 257
Weinfeld, Edward, 99
Weinraub, Bernard, 243, 244
Weinstock, Matt, 180
Welker, Herman, 144
Werner, Max, xiv
West, Rebecca, 45
West, Richard, 233, 234
Westmoreland, William, 242
White, Harry Dexter, 46, 69, 80
White, Leigh, 34
Whitney, John Hay, 175
Wicker, Tom, 236

Wiggins, J. R., 92, 94, 101
Williams, Harold, 26
Williams, William Appleman, 35
Wilson, George C., 256
Wilson, Jack, 45
Wilson, Lyle C., 53
Wilson, Woodrow, 25, 26
Winchell, Walter, 94, 107, 111
Winnington, Alan, 114-116, 120, 122
Wise, David, 159
Woltman, Frederick, 37
World Press Institute, 164
World War II, 171, 241, 246, 252, 255, 257; Soviet-U.S. relations, 25, 31
World War III: *Collier's* special issue, 111, 112

## X

*Xenia* (O.) *Gazette*, 43

## Y

Yalta agreement, 31
Ydígoras, Miguel, 153, 156, 157
*York* (Pa.) *Dispatch*, 43
*York* (Pa.) *Gazette & Daily*, 100, 101
Young, Kenneth, 184
Youth movement, 282-284, 287
Yu Hae Hueng, 111

## Z

*Zanesville* (O.) *Signal*, 43
Zenger, John Peter, 10, 11, 163
Zilliacus, Konni, xiv
Zwicker, Ralph W., 82